THE LETTERS OF LORD BURGHLEY, WILLIAM CECIL, TO HIS SON SIR ROBERT CECIL, 1593–1598

THE LETTERS OF LORD BURGHLEY, WILLIAM CECIL, TO HIS SON SIR ROBERT CECIL, 1593–1598

edited by
WILLIAM ACRES

CAMDEN FIFTH SERIES
Volume 53

CAMBRIDGE
UNIVERSITY PRESS

FOR THE ROYAL HISTORICAL SOCIETY
University College London, Gower Street, London WC1 6BT
2017

Published by the Press Syndicate of the University of Cambridge
University Printing House, Shaftesbury Road, Cambridge CB2 8BS, United Kingdom
1 Liberty Plaza, Floor 20, New York, NY 10006, USA
477 Williamstown Road, Port Melbourne, VIC 3207, Australia
C/Orense, 4, Planta 13, 28020 Madrid, Spain
Lower Ground Floor, Nautica Building, The Water Club,
Beach Road, Granger Bay, 8005 Cape Town, South Africa

First published 2017

A catalogue record for this book is available from the British Library

ISBN 9781108419673 hardback

SUBSCRIPTIONS. The serial publications of the Royal Historical Society, *Royal Historical Society Transactions* (ISSN 0080-4401) and Camden Fifth Series (ISSN 0960-1163) volumes, may be purchased together on annual subscription. The 2017 subscription price, which includes print and electronic access (but not VAT), is £185 (US $309 in the USA, Canada, and Mexico) and includes Camden Fifth Series, volumes 52 and 53 and Transactions Sixth Series, volume 27 (published in December). The electronic-only price available to institutional subscribes is £155 (US $259 in the USA, Canada, and Mexico). Japanese prices are available from Kinokuniya Company Ltd, P.O. Box 55, Chitose, Tokyo 156, Japan. EU subscribers (outside the UK) who are not registered for VAT should add VAT at their country's rate. VAT registered subscribers should provide their VAT registration number. Prices include delivery by air.

Subscription orders, which must be accompanied by payment, may be sent to a bookseller, subscription agent, or direct to the publisher: Cambridge University Press, University Printing House, Shaftesbury Road, Cambridge CB2 8BS, UK; or in the USA, Canada, and Mexico: Cambridge University Press, Journals Fulfillment Department, 1 Liberty Plaza, Floor 20, New York, NY 10006, USA.

SINGLE VOLUMES AND BACK VOLUMES. A list of Royal Historical Society volumes available from Cambridge University Press may be obtained from the Humanities Marketing Department at the address above.

Printed in the UK by Bell & Bain Ltd.

CONTENTS

This volume is dedicated to Professor Paul Christianson.

PREFACE

I would like to thank the many people who helped in the preparation of this volume. I must thank Dr Patrick Zutshi, Cambridge University Archivist, for his kind permission to edit the volume for publication as well as the staff in the Cambridge University Library Manuscripts Room, Rare Books Room and Official Publications Room, the Seeley History Library at Cambridge, the British Library Manuscripts Room staff, and the staffs of the old Public Record Office at Chancery Lane and the National Archives at Kew. My doctoral supervisor, the late Sir Geoffrey Elton, was a great source of encouragement in plumbing the vast Cecil archives and related state papers, and the administration of the Principal Secretariat. The late Wallace MacCaffrey, a great friend and examiner, was always willing to discuss finer points on Burghley at the tea room of the Library and I miss him very much. The late Patrick Collinson was, in a real sense, the inspiration behind this publication. He saw that the manuscript materials relating to the Cecils' transfer of power could be better worked through in an edition of these papers than by a traditional monograph. He called the volume the 'spine' of the work of father and son.

I met John Morrill by happy fortune at Paul Christianson's house after a special lecture in Kingston, Ontario, where Paul and Daniel Woolf had mentored me. John ensured my Commonwealth Scholarship would be at Cambridge and Selwyn College. John read parts of the volume in draft and encouraged the seemingly endless hours of transcribing and noting. He and David Smith provided and continue to provide a most congenial academic home at Selwyn. Dr Smith has been the recipient of many thoughts and ideas about William Cecil, and he has borne these in his extraordinarily busy life with great patience and kindness when I took up the task of editing in 2012. A great debt of gratitude is due to him.

I must also thank Paul Hammer for his cognate work on the earl of Essex for ploughing the historiographical field into the heart of the 1590s in his work on the 'polarization' of politics during that decade, and for his many learned and delightful conversations on this material. Charlotte Merton was also a source of much information and discussion on the court. Peter Cunich was a patient tutor in the mysterious ways of the Exchequer. Richard Serjeantson gave me assistance with looking at the material structure of the volume. I would be remiss in not acknowledging the scholarly work of Pauline Croft, Hiram Morgan, James D. Alsop, Alexandra Gajda and Stephen Alford all of whom were important influences; Scott Schofield kindly read drafts.

Andrew Rampton, Abdi Olat Ibrahim, and Jonathan Eeuwes were excellent assistants. Ian Archer and Andrew Spicer have been patient and diligent Literary Directors of the Royal Historical Society whose editing of complicated drafts has been invaluable. A large debt of gratitude is owed to the production team headed by Daniel Pearce and Melanie Howe at Cambridge University Press. Miranda Bethell's meticulous copy-editing and artistry with the texts was an inspiration. The Commonwealth Scholarship Commission, the Social Sciences and Humanities Research Council of Canada, the Dean's Alumni Research Award at Western University, and Huron University College, Faculty of Theology Research Fund provided financial support for many short trips to consult the manuscripts. I must thank my colleagues at Huron for their kindness and friendship especially Bishop Bill Cliff. Alison Wood and Julian Cooling have been most hospitable; Kira von Ostenfeld, Jon Webster, and the late Joan Fitzgerald Thomas have been great friends and scholarly galvanizers. Kitty Stidworthy has always been a source of love and strength in this and so many other projects.

ABBREVIATIONS

APC	*Acts of the Privy Council of England*, NS, ed. J.R. Dasent, 46 vols (London, 1890–1964)
BL	British Library, London
Cal. Border Papers	*The Border Papers: Calendar of Letters and Papers relating to the Affairs of the Borders of England and Scotland Preserved in Her Majesty's Public Record Office, London*, ed. Joseph Bain, 2 vols (Edinburgh, 1894–1896)
CPR 35 Eliz I	*Calendar of Patent Rolls, 35 Elizabeth I (C66/1395–1404)*, ed. Christine Leighton, List and Index Society, 282 (2000)
CPR 36 Eliz I	*Calendar of Patent Rolls, 36 Elizabeth I, 1593–94 (C 66/1405–1424)*, ed. Simon R. Neal, List and Index Society, 309 (2005)
CPR 37 Eliz I	*Calendar of Patent Rolls, 37 Elizabeth I, 1594–95 (C 66/1425–1442)*, ed. Simon R. Neal and Christine Leighton, List and Index Society, 310 (2006)
CPR 38 Eliz I	*Calendar of Patent Rolls, 38 Elizabeth I, 1595–96 (C 66/1443–1457)*, ed. Simon Neal and Christine Leighton, List and Index Society, 317 (2007)
CPR 39 Eliz I	*Calendar of Patent Rolls, 39 Elizabeth I, 1596–97 (C 66/1458–1476)*, ed. Simon R. Neal, List and Index Society, 322–323 (2008)
CPR 40 Eliz I	*Calendar of Patent Rolls, 40 Elizabeth I, 1597–98 (C 66/1477–1492)*, ed. Carrie Smith, Helen Watt, Simon R. Neal, and Christine Leighton, List and Index Society, 326–327 (2009)
CUL	Cambridge University Library, Cambridge
CSPD	*Calendar of State Papers, Domestic Series, of the Reigns of Edward VI, Mary, Elizabeth [and James I] 1547–1625: Preserved in Her Majesty's Public Record Office*, ed. R. Lemon and M.A.E Green, 12 vols (London, 1856–1872)
CSPI	*Calendar of the State Papers relating to Ireland, of the Reigns of Henry VIII, Edward VI, Mary, and Elizabeth: Preserved in the State Paper Department of Her Majesty's Public*

	Record Office, ed. Hans Claude Hamilton, 11 vols (London, 1860–1912)
CSPS	*Calendar of State Papers relating to Scotland and Mary Queen of Scots, 1547–1603, Preserved in the Public Record Office, and Elsewhere in England*, ed. Joseph Bain, W.K. Boyd, H.W. Meikle, A.I. Dunlop, M.S. Guiseppi, and J.D. Mackie, 13 vols (Edinburgh and Glasgow, 1898–1969)
HMCD	Historical Manuscripts Commission, *Report on the Manuscripts of Lord De L'Isle and Dudley Preserved at Penshurst Place*, 6 vols (London, 1925–1966)
HMCS	Historical Manuscripts Commission, *A Calendar of the Manuscripts of the Most Honourable the Marquis of Salisbury, KG, &c, . . . Preserved at Hatfield House, Hertfordshire*, 24 vols (London, 1883–1976)
HPT	*The History of Parliament: The House of Commons 1558–1603*, ed. P.W. Hasler, 3 vols (London, 1981)
L&A	*List and Analysis of State Papers Preserved in the Public Record Office, Foreign Series: Elizabeth I*, ed. R.B. Wernham, 7 vols (London, 1964–2000)
ODNB	*Oxford Dictionary of National Biography*
SP	State Papers
TNA	The National Archives, Kew
TRP	*Tudor Royal Proclamations*, ed. James F. Hughes and Paul Larkin, 3 vols (New Haven, CT, and London, 1964–1969)

INTRODUCTION

The 128 letters sent by William Cecil, Lord Burghley (1520–1598) to his son, Sir Robert Cecil, later 1st earl of Salisbury (1563–1612), represent the majority of their extant correspondence in what had been a nearly daily exchange of notes and papers between 1593 1598. The correspondence demonstrates how Burghley directed affairs and communicated with the Queen through his son as well as devolving responsibility for certain matters to him. In doing so, Burghley trained Cecil in the role of Principal Secretary to Queen Elizabeth, a role which he came to perform de facto before his official appointment. Burghley trained his son during a particularly difficult period which was characterized by dearth, war, Irish rebellion, and waning continental commitments, as well as domestic strain throughout the shires, towns, and cities.

There was growing tension among the political leaders during the Queen's last years with an emerging generation and an uncertain succession. These letters give an intimate view of the relations between father and son, their work with the difficult Queen, and a transition of power. They show how their work merged the financial acuity and power of Burghley with Cecil's growing control of official papers as parcelled out by his father. In July 1596 Cecil received the office of Principal Secretary fulfilling his father's wishes, although, as these letters demonstrate, he had assumed these duties and responsibilities de facto several years before.

The letters reveal the complexity of secretarial administration. Not only were the two Cecils in receipt of a vast and wide-ranging series of reports and financial estimates, but increasingly Cecil became the conduit for their dispatch through the Queen and Privy Council. Although he was housed near his father, and their archives clearly merged, the letters show the trajectory of the secretaryship gradually being transferred under Burghley's direction, so that his son was co-ordinating the high matters of state by 1598. Furthermore, these letters illustrate the remarkable workload undertaken by the aged Lord Treasurer as offices were given to him, supposedly for interim periods, following the deaths of his Privy Council colleagues, particularly Sir Francis Walsingham in 1590. Sir Christopher Hatton's death in 1591 deprived Burghley of a close friend and the last leading privy councillor of his generation.

Military concerns came to dominate business and after Hatton's death it became harder for Burghley to retain a consensus in the Privy Council. There were military commitments not only in the Low Countries after 1585 but also, fitfully, in France, as well as Essex's daring Iberian campaigns.

The drift to rebellion in Ireland after 1593, the Nine Years War, exacerbated the political tensions at court and in the Privy Council. These letters show the move away from further continental commitments towards defeating the Irish rebels at all costs.

Against this background, the Cecilian transmission of dynastic administrative power was curbed by the vaunting influence of Robert Devereux, 2nd earl of Essex (1564–1601) and his brilliant coterie of scholars, military hopefuls, and young aristocrats of the highest rank. While the breach with these erstwhile enemies of the Cecils was long-standing, it had been overshadowed by the perception that the Cecils held sway through official patronage and the Queen. While the Essexian view tended to ascribe tyranny and weak monarchy to Elizabeth and her closest advisers – the Cecils – these letters reveal a more vulnerable alliance of father and son than the impregnable stance perceived by contemporaries.

Burghley's last years were marred by illness unrelieved by rest or leisure. Although the transfer of power to his son was marked by stately and courtly manners, the letters here reveal a man marred by bodily pain, overwork and, if it can be said, despair. Cecil's responses to his father must, save for a few rare surviving letters, be inferred from these letters. His increasing work was accepted by him willingly not only for official ambition but also out of care for his father's poor health. Both men were widowed (Cecil in 1597) and the letters show a close, if often renegade, family of children and grandchildren. Furthermore, Burghley is seen here moving away from the physical splendour of court – although he attended frequently at the Queen's command – into the shared archive of state housed in the Strand at Burghley House where most of these letters were written or dictated.

The rushed daily communications between Burghley and Cecil were nearly always informal despite Burghley's repeated address to 'my verie loving son' of letters full of fatherly care. The letters give a unique vantage-point on Burghley's use of his son during his final years, while creating in the Queen a sense of Robert's indispensability. This was Burghley's final main political achievement revealed in its minutiae. The piecemeal details in this correspondence reveals what must have been an even more substantial leveraging of power through referring Privy Council and royal tasks to his son.

At the end of Burghley's long term of public service his health failed, according to his biographers, quite precipitously in the last three or four years of his life. Thus, the threnody of illness and pain illustrate his 'morosity'. In spite of the remarkable density of their correspondence, the partial survival of this correspondence prevents a day-to-day reconstruction of political affairs and an overarching narrative, complete with all aspects of this dynastic transfer. However, corroborating sources fill out what in places within the correspondence are mere vignettes of the political affairs of the final decade of the Queen's life and the ambitions of Burghley and his son.

The Cecils and the Queen: The Making of a Secretary

The correspondence reveals Elizabeth's trust in Robert Cecil and his increasing secretarial role, particularly through his reception, digestion, and reading of the letters and accompanying materials. It is unclear how these messages were relayed to the Queen. Cecil may possibly have read them aloud while on his knees during his lengthy audiences. These conferences were made longer by Burghley's judicious packaging of documents, which merged his son's secretarial role with the financial advice and judgements Burghley provided: 'I have red your letter, wherby I perceave yow have red and shewed my letter of my hand wrytyng to hir Ma[jes]ty who sayeth that she will have a battell with my fyngars and than afor hand'.[1] James Daybell's emphasis on both the material and performative function of letters and their uses sharpens Cecil's role into a necessary mixture of messenger and interpreter: 'Renaissance letters were often written with the intention of being read out aloud and performance was integral to their presentation . . . Letters were often disseminated with enclosures which include other correspondences, written text and letters and material goods'.[2] Cecil did not cut a grand figure at court: his scoliosis was mocked by detractors such as Antonio Perez who called him 'Microgibbus' – and Burghley was 'Aeolus', the wind-bag. Still others dubbed him 'Diabolus', in the belief that sinister souls inhabited crooked bodies; from the Queen he endured 'pigmy' and 'dwarf'.[3]

An important aspect of the earlier letters before Cecil formally assumed secretarial office, was Burghley's close co-ordination of his son's role. While some of the longer letters were read

---

[1] Letter No. 73.

[2] James Daybell, *The Material Letter in Early Modern England: Manuscript Letters and the Culture and Practices of Letter-Writing, 1512–1635* (Basingstoke, 2012), 18.

[3] TNA SP 78/36/fol. 181r. Printed in Gustav Ungerer, *A Spaniard in Elizabethan England: The Correspondence of Antonio Pérez's Exile*, 2 vols (1974–1976), I, 336.

privately, Burghley wanted his words repeated. These are, in part, 'ventriloquizing' letters, but nuanced. For very complex matters presented to the Queen, Cecil had to balance the demands of his father with frayed tempers at council, court and in the Privy Chamber – to which as councillor he had immediate access from August 1591. Cecil seems to have projected a generally quiet and calming effect on the Queen, but to others he was full of cares and business. Burghley's character is predominant in these letters, while Cecil's recedes often into complete opacity. Both Cecils knew well the Queen's devotion to words; Burghley intended this effect and inculcated it in his son: 'It is my comfort that hir Ma[jes]ty maketh such a comparison of my symplicite with hir pryncely wordynes [worthyness], to which in very truth, I thynk nether forayn prynce nor brytish subiect can approache'.[4] Sir Robert Cecil assured Elizabeth while on an embassy to Henry IV in April 1598

> We have therefore thought it good to set down precisely the same language which I, the Secretary, used – for that we know your Majesty to be in all languages one of the *mieulx disans* of Europe must justly think that your Majesty had cause to be very jealous whether your meaning had been delivered in the French to the same sense which our English repetition should now express. And therefore, I, the Secretary, beseech your Majesty to pardon my errors especially, who have come so short of that significance and propriety which in your pure style did always flourish.[5]

Falling short in sight of the royal radiance was something of a Cecilian pose, leavened in these letters with humour, espousing the Lord Treasurer's uniquely close standing as counsel to the Queen, but not as her final arbiter.

Queen Elizabeth is referred to in this correspondence more frequently than any other person, appearing in 94 of 124 papers. Apart from the first dozen, instructional, letters, the Queen, together with the Privy Council, was Burghley's sole focus. In his wordier earlier letters, Burghley's own words and the deliberations of the Council were factored directly into his calculations of the probable royal response.[6] He took great care in these to be precise and timely. Burghley's deep deference to the Queen's majesty is clear – a deference which is evident in Letter No. 2. The Queen was the majestic force who bound them in service to the realm: '[I] will not be hasty therein, but will preserve

---

[4] Letter No. 120.

[5] *HMCS*, viii, 119, 5 Apr. 1598.

[6] See Letters Nos 15–138: 15–28, 30–36, 38, 40, 41, 43–55, 58–67, 69, 70, 72, 73, 74, 75, 76, 78–84, 86, 87, 89, 91, 94, 96, 97, 99, 100–103, 105, 108, 109, 111–114, 116–118, 120, 121, 123, 125–127, 130–132, 134–136, 138.

[page torn] the advise of hir ma[jest]tie may have some secret [page torn] from God hir and my director to ser[page torn].' Thus, the Queen's providential rule conjoins them all, but they are all called in their varying conditions to serve God, a blatant reminder to his son to underscoring some trepidation at shouldering these matters without his father present. The secret conversations with the Queen, Burghley is saying, are the ultimate privilege.

Sir Robert's audiences must be entertaining, but his jests are choreographed: to introduce and work with the comments and jokes of his father, her most senior and over-burdened officer. Most tellingly, 'hir and my director' admits of exactly the distance a good councillor must keep so that honesty may be preserved. In December 1595, Burghley warns the Queen through his son that his handwriting is now almost indecipherable, 'she will have a battell with my fyngars', but continues with his identification with the Queen as head, ancestress of David:

> but hir Ma[jest]y is allowed to saye as kyng David sayth in the i C xliii psalme, as the same was repeated the 30 of the last month: Benedictus Dominus meus, qui docet manus meas ad prœlium et digitos meos ad bellum. And in his next vers he added that which properly belongeth to hir Ma[jes]ty: refugium meum, susceptor meus, et liberator meus, protector meus in ipso speravi, qui subdit populum meum sub me.

He concludes, 'I durst match hir with king philip and overmatch hym'.[7] It is a resoundingly absolutist sentiment, doubtless calculated to direct the royal gaze on his son, to whom he was then devoutly wishing her enduring protection, refuge and raising up.

Here was a family succession playing out against the unquiet of the Queen's own royal one. Sir Robert had to negotiate Elizabeth's powerful temperament: 'I fynd the lady some what strange to gyve care to my request, for that she useth not to gyve audience, in clowdy and fowle wether, and herof is here to great plenty, and yet betwixt showres I do attend and follow hir trayne. Thus much metaphorically I trust without offence to hir Ma[jes]ty.'[8] In March 1596, Burghley's strong disagreement with the Queen's 'hyndrance' for the relief of Calais then under threat – his most agitated handwriting in the entire volume – contrasts their mutual 'slowness' over rushing aid to Boulogne in May 1593, thus the Treasurer and Queen were not invariably moving at the same speed in responses to crisis, nor was Burghley a constant break on the 'quickness' of 'martial men', as

[7]Letter No. 73.
[8]Letter No. 10.

he put it.[9] When Cobham's intelligence network failed to detect the 1596 Spanish attack on Calais, Burghley dreaded the loss 'for that war to offend God to whom I am sworn first'. But he would follow, 'presuming that she God's cheff minister hear it shall be God's will to have hir commanndementes obeyed'. There was, therefore, a clear distinction between royal prerogative and Burghley's own deeply held conviction that France, at that juncture must not return to the Spanish fold: 'Yow se I am in a mixture of divinite and polycye preferring in polecy, hir Majesty afor all others on the erth and in dyvynitie the Kyng of heaven above all betwixt alpha and omega'.[10] A month later the Queen 'exceedeth, all hir equalls in body and Government'.[11] Despite frequent differences of opinion over the matters presented here, Burghley always conquers his physical torment and mental care with a return to the Queen as his final point of reckoning: 'I am no opinionaster but an opyner.'[12] But her reckoning he concentrated on his son's abilities. The father could be short and demanded efficiency, a workload equal to his own: 'Sir Robert Cecill', begins one letter, with the equivalent of a shout.

Burghley's holograph conclusion to Letter No. 2 shifts to one aspect of the letters: the intimate tone designed to endear the Queen with his endless labours, the unhappiness of great debility and his inferiority to her princely state. Lady Burghley had died in 1589. Bereft of his brilliant wife and her meticulous ministrations, Burghley was in his late age and illness. He lacked the one person with whom he had shared cures and remedies, an attention to health – to say nothing of the immense pleasure of their houses and gardens, their libraries and her scholarly mind. His enormous tomb for her in Westminster Abbey was eloquence enough.[13] Without her the letters often portray an old widower whose body is falling to pieces – admittedly one with dozens of servants in three great houses to care for him. Thus, given his condition, he tied the son directly and closely in this triangle of confidence and trust: 'offerers conceave to come of the quicksilver, and therfor to give me the tyncture of Gold, my nightly paynes are so grevous'.[14] Physicians and remedies for Burghley's pain and sleeplessness give a rare portrait of an aged man reporting on his ailments in the late sixteenth

[9] Letter No. 2.
[10] Letter No. 85.
[11] Letter No. 93.
[12] Letter No. 14.
[13] Pauline Croft, 'Mildred, Lady Burghley: The matriarch', in Pauline Croft (ed.), *Patronage, Culture and Power: The Early Cecils* (New Haven, CT, 2002), 283–300.
[14] Letter No. 2.

century.[15] Burghley clearly used his ailments as a conversation piece in Cecil's briefing of the Queen. For example in early 1594, 'Even now I received your l[ette]r, wherein yow report hir Ma[jes]tie's care for my helth for which I most humbly thank hir, hopyng that her good wishyngs shall help to retorn me to strength for hir service which I esteem the service of God, whose place she holdeth in erth'.[16] He continues with a joke about how he is not even a man, but at best three quarters with 'one quarter syck'.[17] Unable to walk, Burghley allows on another occasion he will attend the Queen 'but I must be carryed there very paynfully, and unmete to be in hir Ma[jesty's] presence'.[18] Such instances of Burghley's sheer inability to sleep, sit, read, write or walk are a recurring topic in the letters; some days he must be borne on a litter or in a 'litle coche',[19] as lame as his nephew Sir Edward Hoby. The 'Anonymous Life' notes especially his digestion was failing (he spares the Queen these details) – he has broth, some artichoke leaves, (inexplicably) a 'panado'.[20] A draft of red wine and sugar revives him on another occasion – a remedy to be related to the Queen.[21] The baths are considered.[22] He suffers with his eyesight. On one occasion he is nearly 'a monoculous' within a year of his death working long into the night with only a candle.[23] His son, too, would be similarly bereft in January 1597 following the death of Elizabeth Brooke in a miscarriage. There is a curious maternal-royal relation Burghley invoked in his letters.

Habits of a lifetime continued despite the possibly severe political and personal consequences for his son: servants noted Burghley always read the Bible in Latin every morning and evening on his knees, and when unable in his bed – perhaps his early years hearing the chanting in St John's College, Cambridge formed a distinct memory.[24] Perhaps it was a half-century of following the Edwardine ordinance of 1549 preserving prayer in Hebrew, Greek or Latin.[25] Certainly he and Mildred Cecil and her extended family of learnedly devout scholars

[15] For the Queen's physicians in attendance near the end, Dr George Baker and Master Goodrosse, see *HMCS*, viii, 277.
[16] Letter No. 17.
[17] Letter No. 17.
[18] Letter No. 46.
[19] Letter No. 118.
[20] Letter No. 133. A.G.R Smith, *The 'Anonymous Life' of William Cecil* (Lewiston, NY, 1990).
[21] Letter No. 17.
[22] Letter No. 19.
[23] Letter No. 130.
[24] Smith, *The 'Anonymous Life'*, 13; John Clapham, *Elizabeth of England: Certain Observations Concerning the Life and Reign of Queen Elizabeth*, ed. E.P. and C. Read (Philadelphia, 1951), 80.
[25] Act of Uniformity 1549 (Edward 2 & 3, c.1); Burghley used the 1560 Geneva Bible in the letters here.

were capable in Latin and Greek.[26] The connection with Sir John
Cheke (1514–1557), Burghley's first wife's brother was another bond
with the Queen. Burghley knew well the importance of both prayer
and the psalms to the Queen, whose public devotions often formed
directly into a proof-text of contemporary events. He would be privy
to the suppression of her Cadiz prayer in 1596 when Essex's daring
expedition failed in its objectives. Burghley read Cicero constantly,
carrying with him 'Tully's' *Offices*, which are echoed in the aphorisms
which close Hickes's biography of him. Here Burghley quotes Psalms
and Cicero in letters to Essex during the earl's brief period of grace
in the Queen's eyes in the following year, in the summer of 1597, as
the Islands expedition optimistically set sail (only to fail and blight the
earl's reputation).[27] He dictated from memory to Maynard: wishing
the earl the best on his expedition with a hasty return to his family
of which Burghley still imagined some headship.[28] The words, again,
precisely recited doubtless to remind the earl of his place, not only as
former royal ward in the Cecil household, but in the Queen's *domus*.
They have a sense of drawing Essex back into the world of the Queen,
the court, the Church and his upbringing. Burghley's immobility also
propelled Cecil into the central orbit of political life.

   Cecil family matters occupied Burghley as he relayed news to
his constantly busy son: he referred only obliquely to the debacle
involving the earl's affair with Burghley's grand-daughter Elizabeth,
the countess of Derby, then ending with Burghley's demand that
Derby make public declaration of his grand-daughter's innocence.
To his spy on her household at Knowsley, Sir Edward Fitton, he
sent four letters, one for her alone to open in private as marked, the
rest for public reading. Burghley's direction here suggests he expected
parts of his letters to be shared, even read aloud. He rejoiced that
summer in his family.[29] His grandchildren and children gathered,
fourteen of them on one occasion, and they are 'mery' – this following
the death of Cecil's wife, Elizabeth Brooke in January 1597. His
guardianship of his two Oxford grand-daughters would pass to Sir
Robert Cecil – as much else. There was no mention of his elder son Sir

---

[26] See Caroline Bowden 'The library of Mildred Cooke, Lady Burghley', *The Library*, 7th
ser., 6 (2005), 3–29.
[27] Letter No. 117. See also Letter No. 73.
[28] Jill Husselby, 'The politics of pleasure: William Cecil and Burghley House', in Croft,
Patronage, Culture and Power, 21–46, 42; M.T. Cicero, *On Duties (De Officiis)*, ed. M.T. Griffin
and E.M. Atkins, Cambridge Texts in the History of Political Thought (Cambridge, 1991),
43, 88; Letters Nos 116 and 117, July 1597. For the countess, Letters Nos 39 and 123.
[29] Helen Payne, 'The Cecil Women at court', 265–281, in Croft, *Patronage, Culture and
Power*, treats in detail the importance to the family advance of well-placed Cecil women,
particularly the countess of Derby, 266–269.

Thomas, for theirs was a chilly relationship, extended into the future solely by his succession to the barony of Burghley and its attendant real estate.

Securing the Principal Secretary's Place

From 1593, Sir Robert Cecil acted as de facto Principal Secretary for the next three years. The formation of a secretarial role and establishment was conceived and housed within his father's official remit and physical surroundings. Against the backdrop of Burghley's age and infirmity, the time allotted to gaining the instruments and mastering the complex tasks, it was not too long before Cecil was formally appointed as Principal Secretary. Cecil swore in July 1596 to 'assist and defend all Jurisdictions, Preheminences, and Athorities granted to hir Ma[jes]tie and annexed to hir Crowne against all Forreigne Princes, Persons, prelates or potentates'.[30] Cecil later reflected on the unique and ambivalent nature of the position. In his Jacobean 'Treatise' on the office, he argued for the office of sole Secretary, that of an intimate. Perhaps, Cecil was nostalgic for Elizabeth given his somewhat distant relationship with James VI:

> As longe as the any matter of what weight is handled onely between y(e) Prince and y(e) Secretary, those Councells are compared to the mutuall affection of two lovers, discouered to their friendes. When it cometh to be Disputed in Councell, it is liken to conference of Parentes, and solemnization of Marriage, The first matter, The second Order, and indeed y(e) one y(e) Acte, y(e) other y(e) Publication.[31]

His close 'mutuall affection' with the Queen is the major counterpoint in Burghley's letters, a relationship which finally can only be guessed at in the interstices of his suggestions and jokes.[32] By that measure a degree of opacity might be expected. The Secretary's associations and designs could never be fathomed entirely.

The Queen's intimate circle, like Burghley's, was already diminishing in the 1590s exactly when the brilliant challenges from Essex and his followers demanded her notice – and that of the court and her people. And, so, the more Cecil kept inward with her, and managed (as did his father) to cope with her unique view of her realms, the Cecils' influence in the machinery of office-holding, with

[30] CUL MS Ee.2.32 fol. 349r. 'The Oath of a Secretarie of State'.
[31] Sir Robert Cecil, *The State and Dignitie of a Secretarie of Estates Place, with the Care and Perill thereof*. (London, 1642) sig. 4r.
[32] CUL MS Ee.2.32 fol. 349r.

waged and well-patronized friends and family, piled up impressively in the period 1593–1598. Cecil had a relationship in which 'Order' and publication prevailed. These letters are evidence that his father scripted quotidian aspects of it. Cecil's presentation was precisely the ground for his advance with both the Queen and her council.

The princely voice, intimate with the Secretary and given as 'solemnization' to that innermost council, here a 'conference of Parentes', is a telling choice of words, given his father's motives. Burghley's Hertfordshire prodigy house Theobalds was an essential, nearly neutral place, for the transfer of royal trust to Sir Robert, 1591–1594.[33] Letters and architectural drawings show intricate links between the house, the Queen, and the Cecils. These were especially true in the royal visits 1591 and 1594. These progresses to Theobalds were marked with the two respective masques, carefully constructed allegories for Cecil's promotion and his father's retirement – a word unknown, perhaps more properly understood as *retraite* – to Theobalds.[34] No expense was spared on the first masque in May 1591 played for the Queen and visiting court at Theobalds. Robert Cecil was knighted and sworn of the Privy Council on or soon after 2 August 1591. Burghley's trope as aged hermit made a tacit agreement that his son would aid in his work with the Queen. But the second masque during the 1594 progress had the 'hermit' (Burghley) reminding the Queen of that earlier contract: 'Sonnes are not ever of their Fathers conditions', most notably in her refusal to name Robert as Secretary in the way she had done with dispatch at the outset of her reign.[35]

Burghley's afflictions drew Elizabeth to him, also, in the role of 'Parente', nurse, even as he was in a second childhood in some ways. He extolls her great superiority in heart and mind: he 'cannot conteane in the flowyng of my hart' his thankfulness for 'hir superabundant care'.[36] But at the end of his life, 'who though she will not be a mother, yet she sheweth hirself by fedyng me with hir own princely hand, as a careful Nurss and if I may be wayned to fede my self, I shall be more redy to serve hir on the erth'. Here is a parent to Cecil's parent, a

---

[33]The vast majority of the letters were written or dictated in Burghley's chamber in the Strand. For Theobalds, either coming from or going to: see Letters Nos 12–14, 19, 20, 45, 56, 59, 98, 100, 115–118, 120–123, 125, 134, and 135.

[34]Marion Colthorpe, 'The Theobalds entertainment for Queen Elizabeth I in 1591, with a transcript of the Gardener's Speech', *Records of Early English Drama* 12, 2 (1987), 2–9; Curtis C. Breight, 'Entertainments of Elizabeth at Theobalds in the early 1590s', *Records of Early English Drama* 12, 1 (1987), 1–9.

[35]James M. Sutton's revealing analysis of the two masques, *Materializing Space at an Early Modern Prodigy House: The Cecils at Theobalds, 1564–1607* (Aldershot, 2004), 95–123, with the quotation here from 1594, taken from John Nichol's *The Progresses and Public Processions of Queen Elizabeth* (London, 1789–1823), Vol. III, 244.

[36]Letter No. 93.

double role. The long-established intimacy between the Queen and Burghley was now shared by his son. The language of parent and nurse doubtless eased what had been, for Cecil, a somewhat vexed period of newly consistent front-line exposure to the Queen. This shared relationship, built out of Burghley's guiding hand, fed by the Queen's princely wisdom in return, was one which contemporaries, such as Essex and his retinue, would soon characterize as 'evil'.

By the summer of 1598, the forays of Essex and his allies in Scotland as well as the spread of continental ideas of republicanism in the Low Countries, led to criticism of the Queen, regarding her as subject to the diabolical influence of the Cecils.[37] Open conflict in 1596 over place and precedent (principally the secretaryship) were foreshadowed in wrangling over Irish appointments in 1595 and by Essex's haste in prosecuting spies in 1594 (Lopez and York).[38] Essex was not above exposing other councillors' own agents to retribution through his ego or by the manipulation of Sir Henry Unton's embassy to Henry IV in 1596. But in 1597 the earl had turned.[39] In June or July 1598, Essex had drawn his sword and turned his back on the Queen calling out terrible oaths of disobedience. Sometime earlier, Burghley had accused Essex to his face of being a man of blood who would not live out half his days, pointing to these words in verse 23 of Psalm 55.[40] The earl's incessant lust for war, and a fully equipped Iberian armada, as outlined in the *Apologie* of late 1597, was utterly beyond the furthest capacities of the Exchequer especially against the background of the Irish situation.[41] Sidney's embassy to France had warned of reduced English aid. The Cecils' attention would turn to the Queen's 'second realm'. Ireland would be the fulcrum on which negotiation, repayment, and withdrawal of military aid to France and the States General would rest. Cecil, thus, faced the stark reality that whatever the earl's shortcomings had been, by the time of his father's death there was an unbridgeable enmity rooted partly in these divergent aims.

[37] For the growing ideological hostilities to the Cecils, Alexandra Gajda, *The Earl of Essex and Late Elizabethan Political Culture* (Oxford, 2012) is invaluable; for example, see pp. 94–95, 131–135, 127–140, 147–149, 186, 233.
[38] See Stephen Alford, *The Watchers: A Secret History of the Reign of Elizabeth I* (London, 2012), 285–325; Dominic Green, *The Double Life of Dr. Lopez: Spies, Shakespeare and the Plot to Poison Elizabeth I* (London, 2003), chs 13–16; P.E.J. Hammer, *Polarisation of Elizabethan Politics: The Political Career of Robert Devereux, 2nd Earl of Essex, 1585–1597* (Cambridge, 1999), 157 ff.
[39] Ungerer, *A Spaniard in Elizabethan England*, II, 76–78.
[40] William Camden, *Annales Rerum Angliae et Hiberniae Regnante Elizabetha*, ed. Thomas Hearne, 3 vols (London, 1717), III, 608.
[41] Gajda, *The Earl of Essex*, 197–204.

Cecil's secretary noted that this was the most melancholy time anyone had known around the old Lord Treasurer. Burghley appears almost Lear-like:

> I see yow contynue yowr care for me, for which I thank yow. I took wit your howss for that it was to neare the breathyng of westm[inste]r, nor wymbleton[42] because of the discommodites in passyng the ryv[e]r byt cam hyther to my familiar place, although forced to seke a restyng place, but without rest.[43]

By August 1597 Burghley had not been able to leave his bedchamber or bed for two weeks, yet continued with writing warrants and letters and making Exchequer judgments. The following summer his old friends, Sir Edward Hoby, George Coppin, his secretaries Maynard and Hickes, Sir Walter Cope and a few others stayed close to Burghley House on the Strand where he died on 4 August 1598. He had planned to be generous, and he was indulgent to his closest friends. He would leave Cope and Maynard their houses.[44]

Operation of the Secretaryship

The Cecils' secretariats and, particularly at the house in the Strand, were driven by Henry Maynard, the Lord Treasurer's amanuensis in many of the letters published here. Burghley House in the Strand, as it was then known, later Exeter House, was built in 1585 for its proximity to court, council, and the Exchequer. It housed the Lord Treasurer's significant household with an annex for Robert Cecil; Thomas Cecil built a house at Wimbledon to a similar design but he later inherited Exeter House which was entailed to the peerage. The Strand house was fronted by a porter's lodge, 'the west and south ranges of this court are divided into moderate-sized chambers, suitable as administrative offices and services'. Here, Burghley's secretariat worked and it was from these chambers that most of the letters in this collection were written: Michael Hickes, John Clapham and Henry Maynard were in attendance. Burghley worked in a series of two chambers with a privy closet on the ground floor. As Burghley was infirm, even unable to leave his bed for long periods during the years 1594–1598, much of the materials he used in these letters were either arranged in the house and shared freely with his younger son. Papers were brought by Cecil to

---

[42] Sir Thomas Cecil's house.
[43] Letter No. 133.
[44] *HMCS*, viii, 296, 299; Maynard to Hickes, BL Lansdowne MS, 85/no. 23 at the time of the Polish ambassador's disastrous audience with the Queen in June 1597. See Letter No. 126.

his father directly, or by any number of their servants when documents were left in various palaces – both men had suitable lodgings in court, wherever the Queen travelled – but the house was a practical necessity. Burghley's will left goods 'within my bedchamber at Westminster and my two closets and any chamber thereto adjoining and extending to the lodgings of Sir Robert Cecil'. Analysis of the plans for the Strand house suggest that the living and working arrangements for father and Sir Robert were indeed close, even intimate. Theobalds, the great Hertfordshire prodigy house completed in the 1580s, had a similar arrangement of chambers and offices set out by Cecil after his father's death. In effect, one reason for Burghley's dominance beyond his son's appointment as Secretary on 5 July 1596 was his role as collator of materials.[45]

As Burghley's leading secretary, Maynard managed foreign papers.[46] His role is especially evident in the materials enclosed with many of the letters relating to France and the Low Countries throughout the volume. Before his father's death, Cecil's secretaryship meant that he possessed a very large set of papers foreign and domestic, with the control of the signet seal, the secret service stipend, and a burgeoning list of suitors, spies, and clients.[47] Yet despite the growing archive of materials and minutes of secretarial business he is known to have procured and retained, Cecil still relied until his father's death on a massive cache of official documents. However, it was Maynard, rather than Cecil, who knew the precise contents of Burghley's archive on his

[45] Jill Husselby and Paula Henderson, 'Location, location, location: Cecil House in the Strand', *Architectural History*, 45 (2002), 159–193, see esp. 181–182 and 183–188.

[46] Henry Maynard: the clerk to whom the letters were dictated. Richard C. Barnett, *Place, Profit, and Power: A Study of the Servants of William Cecil, Elizabethan Statesman* (Chapel Hill, NC, 1969), A.G.R. Smith, 'The secretariats of the Cecils', *English Historical Review*, 83 (1968), 484–485, 491–493. His frequent handling of papers and drafts of policy is noted extensively: '[Maynard] was considered the senior man in the secretariat and was sometimes addressed as "principall" or "cheyffe" secretary'. He specialized in foreign affairs.

[47] *Guide to the Contents of the Public Record Office*, 3 vols (London, 1963–68), II, 258–259 gives a concise reading of the role of the seals. The signet seal was the proper seal of the Secretary, and several letters here show Cecil was using it but not officially before July 1596. The passage of paper and parchment moved in accordance with the Henrician statute of 1535, 27 Henry VIII c. 11, 'An Act concerning the clerks of the Signet and Privy Seal'. All grants given by the king (or prince) or in his or her name would go to the Principal Secretary or one of the clerks of the signet, where a paper copy would be made to go to the privy seal; thence from the privy seal a further paper copy would be made to go to the great seal and enrolment as letters patent. Grants made by immediate warrant, royal signature given right away, did not go through the seals. When a grant or letter or warrant was received at the signet the clerks were to make a parchment (engrossed) version of the paper (unregistered) draft. This parchment version was sent for signing at the Queen's hand, usually by the Principal Secretary. For commissions and other legal documents the solicitor general or attorney general may have assisted in the original drafting.

death.[48] When he asked leave to go to his house after Burghley's death, presumably exhausted, Maynard assured Cecil that John Clapham (whose hand is found also on the later letters here) 'is acquainted with most of the books'.[49] Burghley rarely refers, except in passing, to the working of the Exchequer, although he heard suits in equity and touching the Crown in massive numbers almost until his death.[50] When he was near death, George Coppin – for whom Burghley secured the clerkship of the Crown in Chancery[51] – was with him giving Robert Cecil nearly daily reports on his father's worsening condition. Coppin presumably, also helped to field the constant stream of suitors and causes, which he relayed and dispatched as Burghley willed.[52]

Before Cecil was named to the secretaryship, several aspirants, Nicholas Faunt and Robert Beale, wrote treatises in 1592. Faunt, as clerk of the council, prescribed a rather clerk-like approach, one which can be detected in Maynard's handling of paper. The bureau of the Secretary was to have papers organized by topic, more properly *topica*, a sort of vast *copia* or combination of missives and received correspondence endorsed clearly but copied into letter books:

> In his secretarial discourse Faunt describes one of the secretary's main tasks as the compiling of 'necessary collections made into books' – alongside a bedside book, and a journal, the secreatary should have a number of 'Bookes peculiar for foraine services', such as 'A booke of Treatises', 'A booke of present negociations'; 'Bookes for home service' such as 'A survey of y(e) lands with the Commodities thereof', 'The revenues of y(e) Land', 'The Charges of the Crowne', and 'The Courtes of Justice'.[53]

Cecil made numerous procurations to the signet office for engrossing letters in parchment for the Queen's signature, and some of these are

---

[48] *HMCS*, viii, 299 where Maynard had made a list of papers after Burghley's death concerning Exchequer causes pending to be delivered immediately to the chancellor, Sir John Fortescue. Fortescue took over immediately *pro tem* as signatory for £8,000 in Irish warrants to be sent, but the warrants were with Burghley's papers (see Letters Nos 135–138).

[49] *HMCS*, viii, 296, Maynard to Cecil, 6 Aug. 1598.

[50] Letter No. 108, for example.

[51] Letter No. 80.

[52] *HMCS*, viii, 259, 276, 277, 285. See also Letter No. 52, 8 July 1595, for Coppin relaying a bill for the creation of a provost marshal in London during apprentice riots. Ian W. Archer, *The Pursuit of Stability: Social Relations in Elizabethan London* (Cambridge, 1991), 1–2.

[53] Charles Hughes (ed.), 'Nicholas Faunt's *Discourse Touching the Office of the Principal Secretary of Estate, &c.*, 1592', *English Historical Review*, 20 (1905), 499–508 at 538. Faunt was a clerk of the signet. Robert Beale, *Instructions for a Principall Secretarie, Observed by R.B. for Sir Edwarde Wotton, Anno Domini*, 1592. Beale's treatise was published in Conyers Read, *Mr Secretary Walsingham and the Policy of Queen Elizabeth*, 3 vols (London, 1925) I, 423–443. Both treatises are discussed in all the literature on the office. See Alan Stewart, *Close Readers: Humanism and Sodomy in Early Modern England* (Princeton, NJ, 1997), 173–183.

noted here as taking a great deal of the Queen's time and necessitating the lengthy conferences Cecil's critics grew to fear. Records of Cecil's gaining and retaining procured minutes of suits and letters are uneven as administrative records. Enough survive for 1591–1594 to show a rough shape of Cecil's role with the Queen, Privy Council and his father. In May 1593 alone, for example, Cecil was credited in the signet docquets with procuring a variety of letters to that seal: he kept the Queen's minutes to the duke of Montpensier; the son of the French ambassador and Henry IV's envoy of the spring of 1593, Pregent de la Fin, vidame of Chartres; letters to the lord deputy Fitzwilliam and Council of Ireland; the ambassador to Scotland, Robert Bowes; Sir John Norris; Sir Thomas Leighton, captain of the island of Jersey; the lieutenants of the town of Portsmouth; and a letter from the Queen of England to Queen Anne of Scotland presented by her ambassador Lord Zouche, an embassy in which Cecil's hand helped form secret designs round the earl of Bothwell (see below). Letters for which Cecil retained minutes at the signet are nearly all referred to in Burghley's letters in this volume. The Queen did not use the dry stamp, or prepared signature. Hence, Cecil's receiving the procuration does form a kind of record for a small percentage of his growing retention of the presentation of papers.[54]

Moreover, the 'procuration' of a letter to the signet is an imprecise term: the masters of requests did this work routinely, each of the four taking a quarter of the year. All that need be taken from these examples is that the keeping of these minutes marked Cecil's real role in state paper control. Together these procured and retained minutes represent Cecil's first large cache of secretarial documents and work. Cecil continued receiving, and ordering the perfecting (drawing up of a clean final version for enregistering) and passing of papers at the signet, and consequently kept custody of the minutes. That every one of the hundreds of papers and warrants he received subsequently is not docketed in the National Archives SO3 (docquets of the signet) suggests his 1593–1594 procurations to the seal and retentions were not yet regarded as *ex officio*. Such minutes tail off in 1596, but Cecil continued to be named on occasion. For example, in January 1594 he retained letters missive from the Queen: to the king of Scots over the shambles of the Zouche embassy (see below); to the States General of the United Provinces of the Low Countries; the Counts William and Maurice of Nassau; Monsieur de Sourdeac and the Brittany Protestants; and for the lord president of her Council in the North, the earl of Huntingdon – retention of drafts which go very far in

---

[54]Letter No. 4 is an excellent early example of Burghley outlining exactly what the lord keeper (Puckering) wanted for the proclamation about the current plague in May 1593.

explaining Burghley's inclusion of such matters to his son. These letters were only small part of the work done at the signet.[55] Some of these matters are touched upon in Burghley's instructions but it was Cecil who kept the administrative records and copies of letters sent. Against this growing official work the transfer of documents and his father's forwarding of papers must be understood.[56] On the other hand, Cecil would procure virtually all *conges d'elire* to deans and chapters as well as the nominations by *mandamus* of every single translation and elevation in nine dioceses during the years 1594–1596.[57] In the autumn of 1595 Cecil provided the content of warrants for Sir John Puckering, lord keeper of the great seal, for warrants for musters.[58]

While retaining the minutes of important business does tell of a growing level of administrative power in Cecil's official assistance to his father, it was in the creation of documents and attendant policy that their mutual advantage was attained. One example of how papers were shared for drafting and comment, other than by Sir Robert's constant receipt of his father's comments to the Queen and Council, emerges in how Burghley frames their collective authorship, not excluding other experts, the Queen or others of the Privy Council. Frequently the idea of a single-authored report or idea is challenged, even obscured, since exact authorship of materials apart from treatises or tracts was not known.

For example, in the summer of 1595 Burghley refers to 'our' letter to Edward Barton, the Queen's envoy to Constantinople (Istanbul): 'but hearewith must be remembered that theare be our letter written to Mr. Barton, which would be written with somm good Caution, least it might be miscarried and so cumm to the handes of suche as ar readie to detract anie thinge, thowghe never soe well ment by hir Majestie'. All of this touched directly on Polish negotiations and the work of Sir Christopher Parkins, a kind of man-of-all-work in eastern and central European correspondence; as well as the envoys of the Turkey Company (merged with the Levant Company in 1582), William Harborne with Barton. Parkins had been taken up by the Cecils but denied the Latin secretaryship which went to Sir John Wolley, clerk

---

[55] TNA SO 3/vol. 1/fols. 439r, 440r, 443r.

[56] For France, see Letters Nos 12–14; Ireland, Letter No. 17, for Cecil to press the Queen to send money; Scotland, Letter No. 16.

[57] See W.D. Acres, 'The early political career of Sir Robert Cecil, *c.*1582–1597: Some aspects of late Elizabethan secretarial administration', PhD thesis, University of Cambridge, 1991, 167–195.

[58] The lord keeper, Puckering, also asked Cecil for the names of the new deputy lieutenants in Wales to be inserted in the warrant, a matter which he remitted to Cecil's own clerks or to the office of the clerk of the Crown in Chancery. Hatfield, Cecil Papers, 35/17; *HMCS*, v, 382.

of the Privy Council, in 1596. Parkins's foreign education marked him as outside the general level of Burghley's comfort, despite his evident expertise on matters in Poland, the Empire and the Baltic.[59] Seniority was not necessarily the final authority, however, as Robert Beale's extreme displeasure on being replaced in the Cecils' regular expert group by Parkins by 1597 showed the latter's worth.[60] Beale's hope to be Cecil's second secretary after Walsingham's death was overshadowed by a man of better credentials without obvious connection to the previous secretarial office. Burghley's caution about those who would 'detract' from the tone of Barton's letter might refer to Parkins's personal enemies, perhaps Beale; or he may have referred to the possibility of the pilfering or alteration of royal letters or their reading in combination with those of political rivals. The intent behind the word 'our' remains ambiguous. The collective might refer to councillors and the Queen, or any number of persons, including merchants and other advisers, who had an interest in the Turkey Company. The use of the possessive word suggests only that the drafts, whoever the authors, were kept with the Cecils' own repository, and cannot signal their authorship.[61]

More telling than attributions of single drafting in documents – nearly impossible to detect in many cases – was Burghley's exasperated tone when sending wearying papers: 'At your departure yesterdaie I had noe leisure to deliver sondrie thinges unto yowe, which nowe with thes my letters in a heape I send unto yowe'. Letters in this 'heape' were diplomatic and intelligence concerns, with drafts mixed among correspondence received, nearly all of them sent for discussion with the Queen.[62] The combination of hands and subject matter blurs the

[59] Letter No. 55 to Edward Barton the Queen's agent in Constantinople who was principally concerned with mercantile causes, while also gathering intelligence. Barton corresponded with Parkins at least once (Parkins to Barton, 18 July 1593, TNA SP 81/7/fol. 144r). For the diplomatic implications of Parkins's embassy and the Turkish implications see Letter No. 34. Although the custody of these drafts is not made clear, Cecil's control of such papers may be inferred from a signet docquet entry of Dec. 1593, at a time when Cecil was beginning to have some secretarial control of these matters: 'A letter to Edward Barton Esq. her Majesty's ambassador with the Grand Seigneur in favour of the Prince of Transilvania, The m[inute] rem[aining] with Sir Robert Cecill, dated at Hampton Court, the xxiith of December', TNA SO3/1/fol. 437v.

[60] Beale's enmity toward Parkins intensified. His letter to Cecil of 28 September 1597 complained to Cecil that negotiations with the Emperor proceeded 'without taking any account of me', see HMCS, vii, 405.

[61] For Barton in particular, see Rayne Allinson, A Monarchy of Letters: Royal Correspondence and English Diplomacy in the Reign of Elizabeth I (New York, 2012), 31, 132, 134, 135, 136, 143–150 for his sometimes sly additions to royal correspondence. See 185–193 for Allinson's summation of the role of the Queen's holograph letters, as opposed to her councillors' letters, and their importance in Turkey, and to the Emperor and other monarchs in Europe.

[62] Letter No. 58.

exact provenance of materials up to July 1596, save that Burghley directed in nearly every case exactly how his son should manage the paper. When in 1595 Cecil needed a schedule for munitions for the Isle of Man to discuss with Sir George Carew, master of the Ordnance, Burghley replied somewhat off-handedly 'yowe shall finde these letters and papers I had from him in my Chamber there at Nonsuch in one of the packettes uppon the shelfe, where my other papers are'.[63] The retention of paper is harder to grasp. Letter No. 14 ends with a need to find Sir John Norris's cipher:[64] 'I send to yow from Sir John Norreis there is a clause in Ciphre, which I cannot deciphire here readely for lack of my Alphabete which is with my bookes at the Courte'.[65] When Cecil was unable to find an important letter from Sir Thomas Bodley regarding Low Countries' intelligence in 1595: 'I praie yowe cawse your man to seek yt owt, and if yowe shall misse yt emongest your papers, yowe maie looke for yt emongest mine of the Lowe Contries, least peradventure yowe might leave them with mee.'[66] The materials were spread over several offices in royal palaces, at least in December 1593:[67] 'But if my stuff be come from Windsore, yow shall fynd a Big paper Booke in folio entituled Mattars of France, in which by looking into the table yow shall fynd the Alphabet of Sir John Norreis.'[68] Peter Proby, of the Chester posts, was doubtless typical of the servants charged with guarding the skein of transport and communication throughout the ports and towns in England and abroad. It is significant that he also had access to ciphers and to members of commissions close to the Council. It is not merely a question of the creation but also the custody of materials. When Proby fired a servant on Burghley's command, the man was sent for close questioning but not

---

[63]Letter No. 59, 3 Sept. 1595.
[64]See Acres, 'The early political career of Sir Robert Cecil', 115 n. 60, re Letter No. 17 and below, p. 55. On the rising expenditure and widening rebellion under Tyrone (the O'Neill), and O'Donnell, see Letters Nos 9, 13, 17, 27, 33, 37, 40, 43, 47, 73, 75, 82, 91, 99, 100, 103, 124, 125, 127, 132, 134, 135.
[65]Letter No. 14.
[66]Letter No. 54.
[67]Letter No. 14.
[68]Sir Robert Sidney's embassy to Henry IV in 1593 was undertaken partly to assure Henry IV's protection of the Huguenots after his conversion. The book of intelligence codes is secondary to the 'Matters of France' which can be identified in the SP Various [45/vol. 20, no. 45] list of volumes of papers Burghley left at his death at the court. Queen Elizabeth changed her mind over the best course of action concerning the relief of Pempole [Paimpol]: on reading Norris's first dispatch (the one here mentioned) she was prepared to entertain support for Henry's troops, but when the hard conditions of her offer were set forth in his second letter, she informed Norris that she would revoke (redeploy) his troops. L&A, v, Analysis no. 285; TNA SP 78/32/fols. 372r–373v, draft corrected by Burghley. Burghley's secretary with responsibility for foreign matters was Henry Maynard – Cecil had open access to the alphabet or cipher codes.

allowed to carry up with him 'my books' concerning the movement of posts.[69] By such methods, informal agents, and Crown servants, the materials of the secretarial office were to be found at council, the various palaces of court, Westminster, and in the Cecils' own chambers.

Embassies and instructions are easier to follow: they were framed and drafted, Burghley usually making the first copy with later amendments often with Cecil (and the Queen and Council), with a fair draft filed and endorsed by Simon Willis. The pattern can be observed in the modern (Victorian) volumes of what were the Cecils' archives, but the originals have been re-arranged so that the reader can see what these letters illustrate: nearly constant receipt and comment of materials. Notes to some of the letters here emphasize only a few examples of dozens throughout their shared papers, sometimes obscured in R.B. Wernham's meticulous *List and Analysis* series of the papers:[70] embassies of Sir Robert Sidney to France in 1594;[71] Sir Robert Bowes in Scotland;[72] instructions military and diplomatic for the removal of Sir John Norris out of Brittany, across the Channel Islands, and into Ireland;[73] Sir Christopher Parkins's drafts, as noted above, for further places where he was the most recent envoy;[74] and Edward Barton in Turkey. Preparations of bills, supply, and commands were also moved and amended by the Cecils.[75] Thus, while Burghley's 'booke chamber', referred to by his secretaries, may have housed the bulk of his career-long working papers, the Cecils' needs had to be met by a series of signet and Privy Council clerks, and grooms of the privy chamber, postal officers, Chancery, privy seal and Exchequer servants.[76] All of this was, of course, more complex as Essex persuaded the Dutch and French envoys in particular, Sir Thomas Edmondes, Sir Henry Unton, and Sir Thomas Bodley to begin sending him first copies of Burghley's letters (always shared with Cecil) and then original missives.[77] Cecil's ally, Sir John Stanhope, was made master of the posts in 1590, but even that manner of surveillance could not always be definitive. When Burghley was outright refused access to the letters of the lord deputy, Russell, in 1595 it is likely that a

[69] *CSPD 1595–1597*, 184–185.
[70] Scholars are also fortunate in the Calendars (published nearly verbatim) to the Hatfield House collection of Cecil Papers.
[71] Letter No. 14.
[72] Letters Nos 16, 20, 21.
[73] Letters Nos 40, 49.
[74] Letters Nos 55, 58.
[75] Letters Nos 87, 89.
[76] Letter No. 107.
[77] Hammer, *Polarisation of Elizabethan Politics*, 195.

combination of agents, including Proby, opened and re-sealed the materials.[78]

The warrants for privy seals were nearly always drawn by Burghley (see discussion on expenditure below) of which there are many examples in these letters: 'I send to yow herwith a bill for a warrant for monnny for Sir Thomas layton, which as my L[ord] Admyrall can tell yow is required to be iii^C [£300] and for Jersey ii^C [£200] with monny for iiii tons of lead. I pray yow procure these to be signed, and pass to the signet and prive seal.'[79] This process was repeatedly undertaken with bills drawn by the father and passed to the son – in nearly sixty of these letters. Although, apart from exchequer classes of the audit and declared accounts of the Pipe Rolls (extant for AO1 and E 351) where privy seals were copied into accounts, the original privy seals for much of this period are lost, Burghley's notes provide a sure reckoning.

Simon Willis, of whom very little is known, provided order in Cecil's chambers, either at court but more likely in the annex at Burghley House in the Strand where the father and son's chambers adjoined. His hand is ubiquitous in Cecil's correspondence from 1591. It would appear he was taking the role of Henry Maynard in Cecil's official paperwork. His endorsements and notations abound in the state paper collections wherever Cecil is working together with his father, or alone on a multitude of drafts and minutes. Letter No. 2 is an example of Cecil's retaining papers primarily relating to France. Dated 21 May 1593, Burghley dictated about two-thirds of this three-page missive to his son through the hand of Henry Maynard from which stems a series of Cecil-controlled documents bearing Willis's handling in the archival remains.[80] The endorsement on the letter, '21 Maii 1593, The lo[r]d Thre[sure]r to my M[aste]r' is in the distinctive hand of Cecil's secretary, Simon Willis. If Willis's hand is followed, it can be seen in materials in the present volume, and earlier. Willis worked on drafts and letters beginning at the ill-fated expedition led by the earl of Essex to assist Henry IV of France in relieving Rouen from November 1591. In that month, Cecil made a list of letters to be sent concerning the French king's movement during the siege of Rouen: 'Letters to the French king, to the Prince of Anhalt and reitmasters; to the Earl; to Sir H. Unton; to the States'.[81] Of the letters sent, those to Anhalt, the Queen's letter to Essex, and the draft of the letter to Henry IV all bear either Willis's or Cecil's

---

[78] CSPD 1595–1597, 184–185; see Letters Nos 20, 76.
[79] Letter No. 54.
[80] Letter No. 2.
[81] TNA SP 78/26/fol. 225v.

handling.[82] The Queen's angry letter to Essex over the failure of the Rouen expedition was also made in Willis's hand[83] and Cecil drafted the Queen's instructions for her ambassador Sir Henry Unton.[84] Cecil alluded to his own increased standing with the Queen in late 1591.[85] At the time when Cecil began to receive dispatches from Germany in the spring of 1593,[86] Willis drafted Cecil's first letter to a German prince, Anhalt, on the Queen's behalf in that summer.[87] Cecil's early, somewhat piecemeal, activities in Spanish intelligence, employing a secret service allowance outside the intelligence network of Privy Council, the prisons and the Customs House, bear some handling by Willis.[88] In this sense, Willis was being trained at the same time as Cecil was learning the drafting and presentation of matters before the Queen and council.

Willis and Cecil worked on a wide variety of foreign and domestic causes, both of secret and princely design. Cecil began to keep a letter book of Scottish correspondence in October 1593 which survives entire;[89] the first entry is Burghley's instructions to Robert Bowes copied by Simon Willis.[90] Willis's work as filing clerk and copyist of the letters in the Scottish book matches the chronology of the Cambridge volume: Willis's last sole Scottish copy entry in this Letter Book was made on 25 September 1596. Thereafter the hand of another Cecil secretary, Richard Percival, appears. The two secretaries' hands are then found regularly in Cecil's working papers until 1599. Percival's

---

[82] To Anhalt, TNA SP 81/7/fol. 83r–v, see instructions on the dorse, *L&A*, iii, G143-5; the French drafts of the letters to the States are not so marked by Cecil handling, but a clerk of the French secretary, Sir John Wolley, may have worked from their original, no longer extant; to Essex, Cecil's draft of the Queen's letter, TNA SP 78/26/fols. 152r–155r; and to Henry IV, in Willis's hand of early Nov. 1591, TNA SP 78/26/fol. 142r.

[83] Howell A. Lloyd, *The Rouen Campaign, 1590–1592: Politics, Warfare and the Early Modern State* (New York and London, 1973), 88–89.

[84] TNA SP 78/26/fols. 104r, 142r; 27/fol. 148r.

[85] *Correspondence of Sir Henry Unton, Knt., Ambassador from Queen Elizabeth to Henry IV King of France, in the years MDXCI and MDXCII*, ed. Joseph Stevenson (London, 1847), 168, 174–175; possibly the result of Burghley's ill-health, ibid. 146, 209.

[86] From B. Combes, a Cecil agent in the German principalities, to Sir Robert Cecil, May 1593, TNA SP 81/7/fols. 124r, 128r, 131r, 133r, 138r.

[87] TNA SP 81/7/fols. 136r, and endorsed, 137v.

[88] TNA SP 94/4/fol. 168v, which was Willis's endorsement of fol. 168r, 'Advertisements delivered to ffra: Rumbold'; Cecil's letters from agents on the Gironde, pertinent to Spanish intelligence, endorsed by Willis, TNA SP 94/4/ fol. 204v on 204r.

[89] TNA SP 52/ 52.

[90] SP 52/52/p.1. The MS volume is prefaced by an index, noting the final entry as 2 June 1597, whereas the final entry is of 25 Apr. 1599, two years before Cecil's secret correspondence with James VI began. See John Bruce, *Correspondence of King James VI of Scotland with Sir Robert Cecil and Others in England, during the Reign of Queen Elizabeth*, Camden Society, old ser., 78 (1861), 1–8, showing Cecil's correspondence with James VI did not begin until after Essex's execution in 1601.

hand appears at nearly the same time in these letters.[91] It is Willis's hand which allows the tracing of Burghley's letters here to the vast repository of re-organized Victorian classes (primarily) in the National Archives and Hatfield House. He worked closely under Cecil's directions with the clerks of the Privy Council and seals in managing the presentation of materials for consideration. While many of Burghley's letters refer specifically to the intimacy of their relations with the Queen, the matters arising before the Council were of equal concern.

Yet the letters here do not describe or allude to the personal patronage Cecil began to exercise. A later secretary, probably Levinus Munck, calendared suitors to Cecil dating from his elevation to the Privy Council in August 1591. A single name in 1591 expands to 110 in 1593; most of these suits and causes are not found amongst any of the surviving Cecilian archives. In this vein, too, nothing of Cecil's private gain with Sir Michael Hickes out of the Court of Wards and elsewhere is even alluded to here. Cecil's own penumbra of influence increased with the work parcelled out by his father before July 1596.[92]

Even after Cecil was made Secretary, in July 1596, Burghley sent a packet where he had 'severed the advertisements and wrytyngs according to ther severall conditions and tyed with threds', presumably in deference to his son's official control of papers and their keeping.[93] Up to his death, Burghley would continue to retain and add materials to his son's official materials, especially foreign letters, usually when he was unable to attend court or council.

Burghley sent additional papers, enclosures or 'advertisements', examinations of prisoners or warrants for official appointments, or referred to letters known to his son, in the text of 70 of the 124 letters remaining letters.[94] The notes here are meant to convey the substance of the materials (not possible in all cases) in their modern archival placement.

We cannot know where these forwarded documents, to Queen and Council, were retained and archived for future use. Contemporary treatises on the Principal Secretary's place, written by hopeful candidates in 1592, lay emphasis on the 'bureau' of the secret papers, all foreign papers, copies of letters sent, and retention of letters

---

[91] Willis was dismissed abruptly in 1602. Cecil doubtless feared his 'proud, excitable' clerk might be disposed to tell others of the secret correspondence he had opened with James VI, following Essex's trial and execution. Willis converted to Catholicism and rapidly relocated to Paris where Cecil's agents knew of him in 1606.

[92] Hatfield, Cecil Papers, vol. 242/2; see Smith, *Servant of the Cecils*, ch. 3.

[93] Letter No. 99.

[94] Letters Nos 15, 17, 18, 20, 21, 24, 25, 27, 28, 30, 34, 36, 37, 38, 48, 49, 51, 53–56, 58, 59, 60, 62, 63, 74, 75, 78, 80, 81–83, 88, 91, 93, 96–100, 105–107, 110, 112–118, 120, 122, 123, 124, 127, 128, 131, 133.

received. Presumably these papers merged into the so-called 'Acts' of the Privy Council imagined by J.R. Dasent. Council servants, principally the clerks of the Privy Council, are mentioned in Burghley's letters as are clerks of the signet seal. They also retained minutes and copies, it would appear. For example, Burghley directed Cecil in a private cause appealed to Council by the earl of Lincoln to get the document, 'therefore I praie yowe, to speake to the Clarke of the Connsell that attendeth theare to seke for yt'.[95] By default, the onus on the Secretary was to retain some of the minutes, most of the copies of letters missive, and to co-ordinate the drafting of replies and the circulation of discussions relating to replies. The exact nature of Cecil's administrative establishment can only be surmised before he became Secretary. Presumably, given the ease with which he exchanged documents with his father, their respective offices were in good order, shared, and open to each other's needs, but with the balance of materials shifting after 1595 to Sir Robert – a fact that is not made explicitly clear in Burghley's letters. These matters, arising among many others in a Privy Council for which imperfect or scant archival evidence remains, also had to be discussed in detail. Warrants or letters arising, as has been seen, required royal consultation. Cecil's work was heavy indeed. As his father's health became frailer, new appointees to key Exchequer offices ensured continuity in their joint access to the control of financial information.

Coppin's successful patents for perfecting all Crown materials in Chancery in 1596, as Cecil became Secretary, was one notable example.[96] Francis Guston's letters patent as auditor of the prests (advance payments out of the Exchequer, usually for troops and supply), as well as foreign accounts, was made in May 1597:

> to determine all accounts, and views of accounts of clerks and surveyors of the queen's works in England and Wales and the marches thereof, the treasurer or keeper of the queen's ships, the master of her ordnances, all persons accountable for any sums of money concerning the queen's business, the clerk or keeper of the hanaper of Chancery, the keeper of the great wardrobe and the chief butler of England.[97]

These may have been appointments with oversight of money and paper, but they presented the mechanisms through which policy could be both formed and executed around the Queen from the amenable

[95] Letter No. 29.

[96] See Letters Nos 52 and 80, *CPR 39 Eliz. I*, no. 269 dated 31 Jan. 1597, to write writs of pardon for murder, treason, homicides, felonies and all writs of extent – none of which would have kept him busy for the £40 p.a. emolument.

[97] *CPR 39 Eliz. I*, no. 386, 19 July 1597.

and quieter quarters of Burghley House and Theobalds. Throughout 1593–1596 Burghley honed his son in the mastery and in obtaining the secretaryship, surrounding him with allies in crucial financial positions. The letters are replete with advice, notes on expenses in anticipation of Cecil's eventual control of records of expenditure under privy seal, and the best way to present complex and often incomplete business to the Queen and in consultation with the Privy Council with or without Burghley in attendance.[98] There is a shift in these letters after July 1596. From the date of Cecil's secretaryship both father and son sought to retain firm control of financial affairs. In July 1596 the Lord Treasurer ordered all warrants to be signed by four privy councillors always including himself. Peculation and mysterious accounting practices were endemic in late Elizabethan England. These were found notably in war accounts (which were considerable from 1585) but in office-holding generally. As Burghley noted Sir Robert Constable was 'beggard' in a Berwick office, so it was for many of the war offices mentioned in these letters.[99] Sir Thomas Sherley's infamous grand embezzlement on the two huge declared accounts in the Low Countries (1586–1597) was matched by the chaotic scramble of the vice-treasurer in Ireland, Sir Henry Wallop, for warrants to pay favours, debts to merchants and captains, and massive decay in troops and supply.[100] Together with the much better administration of the navy board, the provisioning and supply of these two principal accountants (including also the French expeditions) were weighed down in policy, arguments, weather, and personalities.

Control of the paperwork, for good or ill, and moving expenditure rested until Burghley's death with the Cecils. Sir Thomas Heneage's death in 1595 opened the place of vice-chamberlain. A strong Cecil

---

[98] But his correspondence, Lansdowne Manuscripts, for example, contains numerous letters from the Lord Treasurer's remembrancer, Peter Osborne. Vincent Skinner's 1593 promotion to auditor of the prests vacated a place for Hickes (during Chidiock Wardour's campaign to have the Auditor retain privy seals and issue new accounts instead of the more usual use of tallies as the basis for the casting and declaration of accounts at the Pipe Roll office). See G.R. Elton, 'The Elizabethan exchequer: War in the receipt', in S.T. Bindoff, J. Hurstfield, and C.H. Williams (eds), *Elizabethan Government and Society: Essays Presented to Sir John Neale* (London and Toronto, 1961), 213–248.

[99] Letter No. 2.

[100] For Sherley's accounts see TNA E 351 (Declared Accounts at the Pipe) 243 (France 1591–1594 for the Brittany forces), 244 (Normandy 1591–Nov. 1593), 245 (May–Oct. 1593 for the Channel Islands), and the two largest accounts 240 (1 Feb. 1586/7–16 Oct. 1590) and 241 (16 Oct. 1590–10 May 1597). By May 1597 (see Letters Nos 111–114) new creditors and suppliers had to be arranged for the Islands/Azores expedition as well as reforms in Ireland. Wallop as treasurer at war in Ireland, E 351, 235 (1 Oct. 1591–30 Sept. 1595), 236 (1 Oct. 1595–30 Sept. 1597) and 237 (1 Oct. 1597–14 April 1599), the last being Wallop's death – the last two accounts cast *per executor* at nearly £20,000 total indebtedness – and the beginning of Essex's army in Apr. 1599. For Wallop's difficulties with Burghley see 'War and Ireland'.

ally, Sir John Stanhope was named then treasurer of the Chamber, with the offices of the Household, upper and lower, under his watch – and Burghley's. Stanhope was named vice-chamberlain in 1597. The Household officers were sometimes holders of lucrative Crown contracts for military supply, now coming directly under Stanhope's account at court; the posts were likewise paid out of the treasurer's account, and while Stanhope did not achieve Heneage's stature in intelligence-gathering or Privy Council examination of seditious persons, Burghley made sure that he had the control of the posts from 1590.[101]

Money estimates – mostly military – Burghley obtained by running totals of privy seals (dozens are noted in these letters) or from the termly Tellers' views, or from well-placed former personal employees now holding various Exchequer offices. Access to the workings of the Exchequer and its personnel added timeliness and weight to Burghley's views. But in military matters requiring speed he was often exasperated with the Queen. Exchequer funds warranted by letters under the privy seal and the letters refer repeatedly to their form and content, and also to the need for signatures – a role taken on by his relatively able-bodied son and council and chamber servants. In May 1597 Sir Robert Sidney at Flushing wrote of great want in the garrisons with Burghley writing his son in angry agreement: 'This lack of a resolute answer from hir Ma[jes]ty dryveth to the wall . . . hir people suffre great extremities for want of releff of monny and clothes', referring to Sidney's letter enclosed.[102] Burghley had clearly conferred on these needs with an ailing and absent Sir John Fortescue, chancellor of the Exchequer – 'I dowt how to gett Mr. Chancellor to come because he complayneth of his helth'[103] – at a critical moment when a new paymaster, William Meredith, was named as the accountant to the Low Countries and warrants required his signature.[104] Even before he was made Secretary, Cecil was moved into the front line of these expenditures and estimates: when Berwick-upon-Tweed, Carlisle, and Newcastle upon Tyne required ordnance in February 1596, Burghley sent Cecil enregistered letters for engrossing at the signet; with a privy seal he instructed 'I praye yowe procure to be signed assone as nomination of my l[ord] of Essex.'[105] These were routine instructions.

[101] After the earl of Leicester's death in 1588 no Lord Steward of the Household was named. Thus, Stanhope held one of the three senior Household offices, together with Sir William Knollys, son of Sir Francis (1512–1596), a Privy Council generational successor, named comptroller of the Household in 1596. Lord North was named treasurer, also in 1596.

[102] Letter No. 112.

[103] Letter No. 112.

[104] Named 17 May 1597. *CPR 39 Eliz I*, no. 695.

[105] Letter No. 80.

A major consideration was, of course, *specie* on hand for distribution under warrants for expenditure and while Cecil had no official role in the receipt of subsidy or other form of taxation, its disbursement and existence extended his secretarial remit. Cecil was also clearly worried for his father's health in the sheer work required for the calculation and presentation of these materials. On 9 November 1596 when Burghley wrote 'you found me not disposed to mak any censur of the certificates thynkyng the borden to heavy for me alon . . . yow may shew hir this included, which I began by Candell light, but my head would not answer my desire' – the breviates for the privy seal warrants he was then completing included reckoning of the year's Cadiz expedition (further harsh criticism for Essex), current need in the borders, Low Countries, Ireland, and in various fortifications in England. On 15 November 1596, one day after the Michaelmas accounting began on these matters – ordnance, Admiralty, victuals, powder, Ireland and the Low Countries – Cecil directed Henry Maynard, who clearly had oversight in the filing of documents relating to expense 'I desire you to survey the book of Privy Seals; Her Majesty has commended me to deliver monthly a docquet of all warrants signed for money, as with these no man meddles but me'; and he asked 'for some short breviates, and I will henceforth be my own carver'.[106]

Sir Thomas Egerton made the same complaint of the Rolls noting there had been many omissions and gaps since Walsingham's death – a confluence of complaints which suggest that during the years between 1590 and 1596 Burghley had had little time and energy to enforce or give oversight to the clerks of signet, privy and great seals.[107] Cecil's patent as Principal Secretary, for example, is not to be found on the rolls.[108] Before Cecil received the office of Secretary proper he could not operate these powerful, almost invisible levers of power. Once in charge, given custody and use of the seals, his father could rest assured of his son's ability to delegate rather than take direction constantly in obtaining copies and signatures of materials. Here, it was the Queen rather than the Lord Treasurer who was responsible. The massive number of tasks piled on Burghley's increasingly frail body since April 1590 had only very slowly been parcelled out. On one occasion in 1596 he is even referred to as earl marshal, a task he was doubtless happy to be rid of when Essex was appointed in 1597.[109] Essex, for his part, was correct on his return from Cadiz in 1596 that the granting of the

[106]TNA SP 12/265/105; *CSPD 1595–1597*, 306.
[107]TNA SO3/1 fol. 603v addressed in Oct. 1596, Egerton's complaints about missing and incorrect enrolments on the Patent Rolls now under his purview as master of the rolls.
[108]Hatfield House, Uncalendared Deeds 219/20; BL Harleian MS 36/fol. 384r.
[109]BL Lansdowne MS 82/no. 108.

Secretary's place (and Stanhope's) would prove formidable obstacles to his own policies and the progress of his many clients simply because of the erratic bureaucratic handling of letters and warrants outlined in these letters.

Nonetheless, Robert Cecil's burgeoning cache of papers from foreign and domestic correspondents probably already matched his father's by July 1596, when he was in receipt of the cabinets of papers (the daily working papers of the Privy Council), as well as the secret service emolument.[110] But now the realm of expense was directly merged into the warrants passing through the Secretary's place. By this time it was obvious that Robert Cecil was very concerned with his father's overwork. Before the secretaryship Cecil could not make direction for the control of financial records relating to expenditure. While Burghley had to be as precise and clear as possible for his son's discussions with the Queen and Council in what were, doubtless, voluminous papers and inclusions, there must have been great frustrations. Before his son's appointment Burghley asked that Cecil report to him the Queen's immediate decisions on expenses: 'I doe send to heare of hir Ma[jes]ties' amendment, for by hir impediments to order hir affayres, all hir realm shall suffer detriment'.[111] By using Robert as mutual interlocutor, the impression of great closeness to the Queen, managed very quietly, was already earning the son the jealousy and libels which would eventually shape his fame. To an extent greater than any other Elizabethan Secretary, Robert Cecil's official reach was conditioned not only by the relentless disequilibrium of dearth and want in the 1590s but by the reckonings of the Lord Treasurer and the supply of treasure itself.

Intelligence was the area in which Burghley most decidedly balked at continuing the vast and expensive remnant of Sir Francis Walsingham's service whose emolument he inherited. He stopped these initiatives almost entirely in 1590: 'servyce befor wagis is orderlie', he cautioned his son.[112] Walsingham's brother-in-law Robert Beale, clerk of the Privy Council and master of requests may have wished to follow the previous pattern of a junior secretary should Cecil have been appointed, perhaps on the expectation that the old agents and informers would remain in the pay of the Crown. He described the

---

[110]It cannot be known precisely how many of his father's papers came to Cecil when he became Secretary and how much was passed between them until Burghley's death. A huge archive of Burghley's papers, often somewhat haphazard, doubtless remained with him, while correspondents would (from July 1596) write to father and son knowing of their constant contact. The shift here is that the working cabinets, the daily papers, had to go to Cecil at this stage.

[111]Letter No. 108.

[112]TNA SP 52/50/no. 67; *CSPS 1593–1595*, 98.

work in a treatise of 1592 by describing the secrecy having a physical centre:

> A Secretarie must have speciall Cabinett, whereof he is himself to keepe the Keye, for his signets, Ciphers and secrett Intelligences, distinguishing the boxes or tills rather by letters than by the names of the Countreyes or places, keeping that only unto himself, for the names my inflame a desire to come by such thinges.[113]

Burghley's refusal to build his son's career on intelligence has been well-established.[114] Cecil was kept close to London, prisons and gaols in the region of the capital, and Westminster.[115] Other initiatives (Scotland, Ireland and the western highlands and islands)[116] were worked into the interstices of trade, ports, ships, and armies which of which these letters are so full.[117] Cecil's forays reveal themselves in Burghley's correspondence organically rather than systematically, until July 1596. Nonetheless, by 1598, when Cecil had been Secretary for two years, there was an extensive supply of secret continental news through shadowy figures handled by merchants with the foreign addresses and mysterious meeting places used by Walsingham. Indeed, the Walsingham remnant formed the spine of Essex's steely resolve to counter Cecilian control. While Cecil's secretarial establishment included secret links – and these are discussed below for Scotland and Ireland – they were of a piece with his gathering of the seals and administrative control of the office. Burghley's letters on intelligence do not make specific reference after 1596 to his son's initiatives; he knew of them, of course.[118]

> Divers other there are that doe as occasione serves and as a due to my place, advertise me of occurrents. But those I cannot foreknowe but leave order that all letteres which come to mee be brought to my Lo. My Father and all ordinarye dispatches to be then red to her Maiestye. or the letters by Mr.

---

[113] Beale, *Instructions for a Principall Secretarie*, published in Read, *Walsingham*, I, 428. Beale had been a clerk of the Privy Council since 1572.

[114] See Alford, *The Watchers*, 285–325 for a thorough analysis and contrast between the Cecils' and Essex's ideas on intelligence gathering.

[115] See Letter No. 9, for example where Cecil was clearly part of the Privy Council intelligence-gathering, notably the suspected assassination of the earl of Derby (1594) by Richard Hesketh, a sort of proto-Lopez plot. See Acres, 'The early political career of Sir Robert Cecil', 27.

[116] See pp. 53–54.

[117] Intelligence is noted in each letter where an agent of the Cecils or another of the Privy Council appears to have given information. These are too lengthy to list in this introduction.

[118] Lawrence Stone, *An Elizabethan: Sir Horatio Palavicino* (Oxford, 1956), App. III, where SP 12/265/133 is printed verbatim.

Smith, Mr. Waade or Mr. Windebancke as the nature of the advertisements requireth.[119]

Burghley's instructions in these earlier letters did not, therefore, necessarily indulge in long disquisitions on intelligence or the bearers of secret information. This was the area of greatest caution for Burghley and the last piece of the secretarial office given to Cecil.

Burghley's Governance

As Burghley came to the end of his life, the former dynamism of his relentless work faltered nearly entirely. What had been devolved entirely to his son was the competence required for office, not only the secretarial control of paper, but also his father's vision of the Queen's realms. In the last weeks of Burghley's life, the close circle of secretaries, friends, and family, together with loyal servants, provided as much comfort as possible for Burghley's pain-wracked body, while his son's attainments might have provided another kind of relief. The events of the winter of 1598 had proved Cecil triumphant in his embassy to Henry IV, as the Secretary coolly read aloud from his spies' accurate transcriptions of letters treating for peace between the French king's secretaries and those of Archduke Albert. On his return, in early April he had not paused, but went to visit his 'most dear Father', then set down immediately the work which had not been done in his absence in a 'memorial', exactly as his father would have done. In the last few months Cecil was not among the people who could be constantly present with his father. He was in attendance furthering the Cecilian succession.

The final sentence of Letter No. 138, noted as 'My lord's last letter that he wrote with his own hande', conveys Burghley's *nunc dimittis* to his son, the rule above all: 'Serve God by servyng of the Quene for all other service is in dede bondage to the Devil'. What process do these letters reveal about Robert Cecil, emerging from an able control of a contentious parliament in 1593 with his rival Essex on the Privy Council from February of that year?

The irony of this sentence follows Burghley's long career and remarkable self-preservation during Edward VI's and Mary's reigns. For just as his son's conditions of service differed markedly from his own appointment in 1558, Burghley had had to manage the politics of her succession. Elizabeth's failure to marry and produce an heir was a long-standing anxiety felt sharply from the 1580s as were her

[119] Ibid.

serious illnesses. The Queen's mortality now occupied the collective mind of the ruling orders. James VI of Scotland moved into the tacit calculations of the Privy Council over the course of the 1590s. His estate, as far as Burghley could see, was torn by the pro-Spanish positions of the northern earls, and the loose management of his nobles in the lowlands and borders, with a wary eye on the Kirk. Burghley seems to have shared the Queen's view, or indeed coloured her perceptions: Scotland was unstable in religion and external alliances across England, Ireland, and his own realm. While Elizabeth expended great energy on her own royal concept of parenthood with James, not least in a steady stream of holograph letters, Burghley mulled over the intricacies of maps and plats, projects and advises; he returned to her often in these letters as the sole means for his son's promotion. Cecil seems to have inherited the precision of the father's mind, an understanding of the Queen's own anxieties over the future of her realm, and the possible future for a Europe in which peace between Spain and France could not be bought too dearly to avoid the possible loss of Ireland. Thus, the anxiety of Scotland was as much on his mind as his father's.[120]

Perhaps the most impassioned of any letter in the volume, with the most agitated hand offered his son, with cartographic precision, an immediate relief plan for Calais in April 1596 (once he was able to write, as he was then in agony after a sleepless night of 'many cogitations') deserves full quotation here:

> what he wanteth of men or munition to defend the town [;] how he is hable to receave succors [;] of what nombres the army ar that doth besege it. Wher the battery is planted. How the haven remayneth fre for such succor to coem with shypping. if the haven be possessed by the enemy with his shipping. Why may not ayd be sent by shippiyng to a place est from Callies toward Gravelienes or to willoby and if the town may be defended for xiiii days, in this space la fare will be yelded or taken, and ther it may be hoped that the Kyng will levy the sege.[121] Wharunto he had v or v[i]^M [5,000 or 6,000] Footemen, that may be had in this sort, ii^M [2,000] from London, i^M [1,000] from Essex, ii^M [2,000] from Kent, i^M [1,000] from Sussex or such lyke for England may not endure this town to be Spanish. and the Q[ueen] that also promised hym ayde.[122]

Burghley's passion was born of intense curiosity about the Queen's realms and revenues and the need for such reckonings and complex solutions. Burghley's long-term method was to preserve her Crown lands from predation; to ensure her revenues; and to parse policies and

[120] See pp. 46–47 below.
[121] See pp. 210–211 above.
[122] Letter No. 90.

requests which had a spatial aspect.[123] Burghley's estimates here were
based, doubtless, on long experience of musters and costs to localities –
a major issue in the 1590s, particularly with new forces for Ireland and
French crises – as well as local financial need, those of the counties,
and an awareness of many previous military engagements.[124] He knew
Gravelines and Calais (and saw the Queen's wish to secure this former
royal toehold in memory of very distant Plantagenet and Angevin
ancestors) – as well as all the English plats and plans in the Queen's
Works. But he saw the expense of maintenance of fabric rather than
the glory and pomp of display. Although the relief of Calais was highly
complex, Burghley may well have produced it without reference to
detailed notes, as his close servants reported he hardly ever used
them. His son would not have the luxury of this vast memory but had
doubtless spent long hours devouring the materials in his father's book
chamber.

Burghley's governance also required careful mapping. Christopher
Saxton's 1570s maps of the shires, for example, were for the use of
tax and revenue: merely one example of this is the extraordinary
reckoning of charge by mile and horse Peter Proby had to provide
in order to extend his letters patent as carrier of posts to Chester
and Holyhead and onto shipping in 1595, his pay supported from the
Household by the treasurer of the Chamber.[125] Burghley was, by this
time, working on practised templates for nearly all of it.

The alarm over Calais shows that the Queen's realms were rapidly
affected during the 1590s by the scarcity of resources, vastly increased
cost, and radically shifting ideas, especially about war and largely
from the earl of Essex. Cecil learned of the importance of precision,
cost, measurement, and finance to the preservation of the realm.
Perhaps the tutelage over the period 1593–1598 revealed in these letters
influenced Cecil's failed 'Great Contract' of 1607–1610, a microcosmic
brokerage of royal prerogative with the limitations of production and
local political will.

At the root of Burghley's intense anxieties in the years 1593–1598,
particularly latterly, was the collapse, not only of the entire Irish
system, the danger of religious civil war, but the threat to –what he

[123]See Peter Barber 'Was Elizabeth interested in maps– and did it matter?', *Transactions of the Royal Historical Society*, 6th ser., 14 (2004), 185–198, esp. 191, on Burghley noting the importance of the new information that maps provided, and 190–194.

[124]John J.N. McGurk, *The Elizabethan Conquest of Ireland: The 1590s Crisis* (Manchester, 1997), 54–66, 108–134.

[125]Proby to Burghley and posts for Chester and Holyhead, BL Lansdowne MSS vol. 78, nos 92–100 in 1595. See Burghley's detailed notes on the provisioning and accounts for the lower Household, acatry and pantry for the uses of the board of Greencloth, ibid. 86, nos 47–53.

measured, in terms of Ciceronian reciprocity of parts – the Queen's realms, even imperium. In his seminal paper on Elizabethan offices using Burghley's ubiquitous lists, Wallace T. MacCaffrey similarly divided English officialdom into seven categories: court, central administration, regional administration, judiciary, military, church, and land administration. He defined 'office' to include 'benefits' such as annuities and grants of land 'at the disposal of the Crown', mediated through a complex patronage system ascending to the Queen, and descending from her.[126] Through office, he argued, came the 'nationalization' of the Tudor polity, begun in 1529 by Henry VIII, with his Majesty as 'centripetal' focus of an array of newly (particularly under Thomas Cromwell) reconstructed offices designed to weaken all parts of the body politic but the head.[127] The system under Elizabeth I was outwardly one of 'majestic simplicity'. In practice, it was a 'curiously complex foundation, its maintenance requiring the most assiduous practice of the arts of political persuasion'; arts, it must be concluded, of writing, flattery, and style.[128] These arts were the purpose of Burghley's tutelage, as each of these areas would come to the Secretary and his clerks in the form of suits or business to be presented to the Queen for signing or to the Privy Council. Burghley was not, despite Essex's later pejorative use of the term, training a clerk. But Essex overlooked or disregarded the rhetorical placement of the collated information and the reckonings, both calculated and forecast, before the Queen. Cecil made the presentation for her to make the final reckoning. As Stephen Alford has noted elsewhere, the fashioning of an estimate such as this fell for Burghley and his contemporaries into the category of 'definite questions', of arguing *in utrumque partem*, just as Cecil wrote *pro* and *contra* delineations of all regions of France in 1584[129]

One way of reading some of Burghley's longer communications is not only the obvious display of the material by Cecil in the privy chamber but his facility in matching and explaining precisely what was being communicated during a barrage of questions – this would have held, too, in Privy Council and ambassadorial negotiations. Burghley's

[126]Wallace T. MacCaffrey, 'Place and patronage in Elizabethan England', in Bindoff, Hurstfield, and Williams *Elizabethan Government and Society*, 95–126, 106. A list here taken from Hatfield MSS, calendared, *HMCS*, v, 195; vi, 387–388; BL Lansdowne MS 68 no. 107.

[127]MacCaffrey, 'Place and patronage', 95–97. The division of seven is a contemporary classification, probably Burghley's own.

[128]MacCaffrey, 'Place and patronage', 97.

[129]Stephen Alford, *The Early Elizabethan Polity: William Cecil and British Succession Crisis, 1558–1569* (Cambridge, 1998) for an excellent discussion of the rhetorical education and grounding of Burghley's work, 14–24, a method which the letters here make clear was shared by his son.

ability to turn the academic balancing of information quickly takes form, here and in all of Burghley's communications in these letters, to the action required, from the abstract to questions and answers: to repeat the parts of the questions in April 1596 gives an idea of this razor-sharp delineations of questions, such as those revealed in Letter No. 90 on the relief of Calais. The definite questions are posed:

'of what nombres the army ar that doth besege it'
'Wher the battery is planted'
'How the haven remayneth fre for such succor to come with shipping'
'Why may not ayd be sent by shippyng to a place est from Callies toward Gravelienes or to willoby'

These 'definite questions' could be answered by various intelligencers or officers in the government's penumbra of influence assuming Willoughby was supplied well enough to carry out the tasks communicated clearly. But they argue precise points with analysis of fortifications and munitions, troops and their naval and land deployment. Only the final point is obviously an indefinite question:

and if the town may be defended for xiiii days, in this space la fare will be yelded or taken, and ther it may be hoped that the Kyng will levy the sege

The 'hope' in this analysis was, like the Queen's intentions, an indefinite question, one that sometimes gave rise to expostulations about 'dyvynitie' and other supernatural speculations where the will of anointed monarchs was in play, for Burghley would never trust Henry IV. The Queen stalled and when the fortress had fallen rebuked the king for his insolence towards her in not granting England temporary custody of a place they had not yet taken.

Burghley's obsession with mapping, weights, distances, and the financial reckonings associated with them were all ordered in this way to the rhetorical needs of definite questions or civil theses. Against these practical exercises the Queen's will was another category of information altogether. Nonetheless, as her servitor and delegate, in his responsibility for the Queen's realms, he maintained, as it were, in his head a map of revenues and expenditures populated by office-holders known to him, their causes and cares (or those of their families), from whom he was in constant receipt of information. While military concerns bulk large in these letters, their contents merge the financial and the secretarial, the merchants, the gentry, and the office-holders, and the reckoning of their indebtedness. The official list for military offices used by MacCaffrey was compiled in 1579 by Burghley:[130] a

---

[130]MacCaffrey, 'Place and patronage', 99.

settled pattern of various fortresses and fortifications with offices in the Crown's possession together with all major Crown offices worthy of place. Each of these he knew: emoluments, accounts, fortifications, works and maintenance. For the Tower, as an example, he had drawn up a detailed list of all men on watch by shift and all inhabitants (and why they were there), for an evaluation not only of the Queen's charge but of risk. Burghley's list of military offices indicated relative stability in pre-1588 conditions, but only after the sustained Scottish situation of the 1560s.

Burghley saw the Exchequer through the costly late Elizabethan wars when by his calculations, policy could no longer fend off Philip II abroad and still pay for the Irish rebellion. In the 1570s list he calculated forty-five lords and gentlemen, 'fit by experience for captaincies at sea and nearly sixty who could undertake military commands on land'. Most of these were permanent officers of the Admiralty, Berwick (which had been reduced by two-thirds after the Scottish wars in the 1560s), the Ordnance office, and coastal and other garrisons. For the late 1580s, MacCaffrey shows another of Burghley's lists giving thirty-five commanders of domestic garrisons not including Ireland.[131] The enormous scale of English war commitments in the Low Countries by treaty began to drop to a stable and feasible level from 1591; debt repayment from the Low Countries to the Queen was negotiated by Cecil in the very last weeks of Burghley's life. French commitments appear here to be similarly waning save for Boulogne, Calais, and Amiens in 1597 under Baskerville and Sir John Savage.[132] By early 1594, the worsening Irish situation, unaffected by the move to Franco-Spanish peace, saw rebellion break out into war. Furthermore, a truce which nearly expired at Burghley's death led to the disastrous defeat at the Yellow Ford soon afterwards and the vengeful atrocities committed in September 1598 resulted in one of the largest Tudor military campaigns under Essex in 1599. With the restoration of the lieutenancy system in 1585 and without large numbers of experienced captains (approximately 475 captains would be named during the Nine Years War), military needs attracted young men desiring service and advancement. This demand enormously expanded Burghley's irenic earlier model of 1579. Robert Cecil was in the first line in the creation of warrants for pay and supply of captains and officers, with his father with whom he seems to have shared a sceptical view of their probity.[133]

[131] MacCaffrey, 'Place and patronage', 108.
[132] Letters Nos 2, 3, 10, 14, 90.
[133] The importance of the seals is discussed below, p. 13.

The expense of war appears in the first fourteen letters in the volumes up to the end of 1593, relating to Norris and the growing charge in Ireland, together with ordnance for the relief of Normandy.[134] Of the remaining 124 letters, 55 urged Cecil to expedite similar expenses.[135] Of these, almost all of them, are concerned with war *materiel* or the maintenance of troops.[136] The letters are full of requests and business by persons for whom Crown revenues were implied. These included bishops, for whom nine new translations or elevations with attendant payments occurred between 1594 and 1596; the Household and the posts and the officers of maintenance of the royal fabric; and the plethora of ordinary suitors (usually, for Burghley, causes at equity in the Exchequer). The weight of these letters, however, tends towards fortifications and garrisons, especially heavy during the removal from French soil of the bulk of the Queen's extraordinary forces into the uncertain breakdown of the Queen's rule of Ireland. The Dutch and their repayments form a counterpoint to all this foreign or Irish expense after 1595. Here is precisely where the two major officers, the Secretary and the Lord Treasurer, intersected most frequently in their business as shown these letters. Here was probably the weightiest of Burghley's roles in the Privy Council and, in persuading the Queen, he was keenly aware of their shared frugality. His knowledge of the realm, its resources, and the pay and composition of forces, musters, and funding combined with an unmatched expertise, born of long service and mastery of detail.[137]

---

[134]Letters Nos 2, 3, 10, 12 and 14.

[135]Letters Nos 15, 17, 20, 27, 33, 35, 36, 37, 38, 40, 45, 47–50, 54, 58, 59, 60–64, 73, 75, 76, 77, 80–82, 89, 90, 95, 99, 100, 103, 104, 106, 107, 109, 112–115, 117–118, 120–123, 125, 127, 132, 134, 135, 137.

[136]An exception is Letter No. 126, on the Imperial edict banning English merchants from the Empire, and the jeopardy to royal revenue implied with the loss of Danish and Hanse trade.

[137]The historiography of the Elizabethan military has been significantly revised. See Neil Younger, *War and Politics in the Elizabethan Counties* (Manchester, 2012) 4–7, when discussing the achievement of overall aims, relative solvency and the orderly succession of crowns; these challenges were faced by many other early modern monarchies with less success. See Paul Hammer, *Elizabeth's Wars: War, Government and Society in Tudor England, 1544–1604* (Basingstoke, 2003) and John S. Nolan, 'The militarization of the Elizabethan state', *Journal of Military History*, 58 (1994) 391–420. They demonstrate how counties were successful in meeting levies and Council requirements, especially where the role of the deputy lieutenants and the justices of the peace seem to have been warranted to heavy workloads in commissions not known before the 1585 revival of the lieutenancies. These matters were clearly behind Burghley's calculations and, while analysis of the present letters cannot compass this large field, his mutual work with his son did involve precisely the kind of reckoning and 'definite questions' of rhetoric in which they both flourished. See Alford, *The Early Elizabethan Polity*, 14–24 on the argumentation and rhetorical arrangement of 'memorials', lists, drafts, and plats for policy.

So, too, was knowledge of the principal characters, human frailty falling into the category of the 'indefinite'. To take a French example, in Letter No. 2 Burghley sets out the complex rhythm for the paperwork needed for the relief of Boulogne; the French servants disposed towards or against Henry IV, were well-known to both Cecils. Robert Cecil knew these people, at least by reputation, for he had written treatises on France in 1584 when a guest of Sir Edward Stafford's ambassadorial household. In them, noble connections, sources of revenue, and characteristics of various regions, *pro* and *contra*, were established in long perfected notes sent to his father. The principals of Boulogne in May 1593 and their relationships – the 'Ladye' governor, Mme de Rouillac and Épernon, for their sister Anne (all born Nogaret) had married Charles of Luxembourg whose sister Marie was married to the Leaguer enemy, the duke of Mercoeur – were all in his grasp, because that is how Burghley delineated alliances, by kin, wealth, place, and stability. This complicated family professed allegiance to Henry IV through Épernon, while he himself continued his activities in pro-Spanish Catholic plots.[138] The indefinite aspect here is surely one of the complex intentions of both the king and his attempted reduction of powerful subjects, an area of speculation rather than precision. Burghley would remit these concerns, too, to Cecil for consideration by the Queen and Council.

Lengthy letters to his father in 1587 – matched again only by the official despatches he wrote in France, while attending Henry IV during the Franco-Spanish peace negotiations of 1598 – during Cobham's commission to treat for peace at Ostend only days before the arrival of the armada of the following year.[139] These long letters are full of carefully drawn portraits of the council in Brussels. His charming manner extended his father's courtesies to long-serving servants of the king of Spain, under the duke of Parma's government, to Richardot, Le Grenier, Parma himself.[140] Father and son had beautiful manners with rapier minds. In 1598 as in 1587 the question was whether Philip II had authorized persons to treat for peace rather than to carry out an elaborate ruse of negotiation. In 1598, Cecil's group of newly minted intelligencers paid out of the secretarial emolument – and much more expense not accounted – had an agent at the heart of

---

[138] Cecil's 1584 treatise on the French aristocracy made clear the connection between Mme de Rouillac and the duke of Épernon, TNA SP 78/12/fol. 245rs, for her sister Anne married Charles of Luxembourg. See also Letters Nos 2, 56.

[139] William Brooke, 10th Baron Cobham (1527–1597), lord warden of the Cinque Ports, was Cecil's future father-in-law, *ODNB*.

[140] None of the letters in the present volume are from the period Feb.–April 1598. See, e.g. *HMCS*, viii, 104–112 and 119 for his method of delivery of the Queen's instructions.

the Archduke Albert's train sending perfect copies of the already negotiated settlement directly to Burghley for use in audience with Henry IV.[141]

Burghley had been sent to the Low Countries by Queen Mary to receive Cardinal Pole as papal legate in 1555. Cecil's viewing of the vivid scenes of desolation and want brought on by incessant war in that rich country by 1587 underlined their shared horror of the consequences of Spanish army's occupation and the division of the Netherlands by religion and civil war. War and its attendant horrors appear in Burghley's calculations, but it was the threat to stability, even outright incivility in ordinary life attendant on poverty and want, which Burghley feared and thought that military culture would only escalate: 'Martial men' were often quick, choleric and hasty to spend the Queen's treasure. The violence associated with their command spilled into the peace of England, presenting in Burghley's mind – and doubtless the Queen's – a force to be contained. For example, a Captain Troughton in Essex's employ stabbed an innocent bystander for his horse in Hertfordshire, news which reached Burghley as Lord Lieutenant:

> an honest man and a trumpett of hir Majestie's that dwelleth at Totnam whose name is ffissher, comminge throwgh the towne with his wief being a sicklie womann, this Trowghton would neades unhorse ffissher and have his horse to ride past, which the other refusinge, and the Constables & post m[aste]r beinge by, and offeringe other horses, which he refused, he drewe his rapier, and hath hurt ffissher in one of his handes.[142]

While the threat of civil war on religious (but not solely religious) lines threatened Scotland and England, becoming an expensive military irritant in Ireland, out of Spanish ideas of universal monarchy, the sorry example of Henry IV's reduction of the Catholic League was one which all members of the Queen's government were desperate to avoid. Whether that was the extension of surveillance by the Privy Council commissions against recusants and 'conventicles' in 1593 or secret plots to force James VI of Scotland to impose order on his Catholic nobles, there is a sense in Burghley's letters here of the perfidies into which a lawful kingdom might have to descend in civil war.[143] Attempts to extend the branch of Protestant unity to the Low

---

[141] R.B. Wernham, *Return of the Armadas: The Last Years of the Elizabethan War Against Spain, 1595–1603* (Oxford, 1994), 221–223; TNA SP 78/41/fols. 246r, 255r, 378r; *HMCS*, viii, 538–539.

[142] Letter No. 59.

[143] See *CPR 35 Eliz. I*, nos 569–570 on the council commissions of 26 Feb. and 26 Mar. for such investigations in and around London with powers to interrogate and commit to

Countries and the Huguenots in Brittany were exhausted during the years of these letters; their greatest success in Cecil's skilful negotiation of Dutch debt payments in June 1598.[144] In the final analysis Captain Troughton's unlicensed violence was a form of rapacity Burghley and others saw as the result of giving too much virtue to the soldier and the captain;[145] an assault, as it were, on the, *vir civilis*, in the 'publike weale'.[146] One example, the Irish, was within the Queen's second realm. James's prevarication in Scotland was undoubtedly aimed at Catholic support in England for his eventual accession. But to what sort of kingship would he accede? On the ground, it was the kind of wounds, disease and vagrancy of the returning soldier which the Cecils feared would boil into another kind of disorder.[147]

Burghley's calculation of how order should be established revolved round these questions of order and disorder, definite and indefinite questions; he reckoned the particulars of what the Queen's realms could bear or not. War dominated, even deformed, Burghley's Ciceronian balance. The letters give a sampling of coastal fortifications and defence, spies, and supply for ports and customs.[148] There were the business and intelligence links in the Council of the North. After the earl of Huntingdon's death in 1595 it was Burghley who saw the need to perfect documents for an interim presidency of the council, especially in view of the intelligence connections he ran through its membership to say nothing of the stalling of legal suits and petitions.[149] The borders had to be secured for mutual, if wary, watch on the

trial. Lisa Ferraro Parmelee, *Good Newes from Fraunce: French Anti-League Propaganda in Late Elizabethan England* (Woodbridge, 1996), 76–96 on Huguenot resistance theory and the League's response. Burghley could not travel all the way with the Politique – of Sir John Hayward's *The First Part of the Life and Reigne of King Henrie III* (1599), where 'The King is the anointed of God, and even tyrants are instruments of God's providence', 115. See also Burghley's response to Person's *Conference* on the succession as discussed below on pp. 67–68, 71–72, and Letter No. 65.

[144] Wernham, *Return of the Armadas*, 238–239. No direct references to these negotiations were made in these letters by Burghley. Both Cecils, and the Queen, wanted peace with Spain and France but could not abandon the Dutch, particularly as the debt was now rescheduled satisfactorily. For Essex's incessant clamour for pro-Dutch anti-Spanish expenditure in 1597–1598, and his *Apologie*, see below, p. 73; Gajda, *The Earl of Essex*, 97–104, 186, 233. For the growing hostilities of the Essex House men against the Cecils, ibid. 75, 147–149. For Burghley's characterization as 'Aelius Sejanus', the archetypal evil favourite, ibid. 233.

[145] Rory Rapple, *Martial Power and Elizabethan Political Culture: Military Men in England and Ireland, 1558–1694* (Cambridge, 2009), 51–85. Martial men are seen to have lost virtue, becoming, as in the case of Peter Carew, a career captain, 'a horror story in the light of the civic humanist and godly ethos of an Ascham, a Smith or a Cecil', 53.

[146] Alford, *The Early Elizabethan Polity*, 22.

[147] See P.M. Handover, *The Second Cecil: The Rise to Power, 1563–1604, of Sir Robert Cecil, Later 1st Earl of Salisbury* (London, 1959), 151–163.

[148] Letters Nos 2, 14, 98, 122, 137.

[149] Letters Nos 79, 83, 100.

raiding families with their grievances and feuds as unstable agents in the amity of England and Scotland.[150] With Spanish incursion rumoured, the Channel Islands fortifications, the office of works, and the Ordnance office were integrally connected to both financial and strategic calculations.[151] The Exchequer offices, mostly for warrants for *specie*, were crucial links to the collections of subsidies, tax, and loans vital to the royal revenues.[152]

Not only were the coastal ports important for their customs revenue, they were possible points of entry for the seditious enemies of the Queen. The officers entrusted by the Crown to these places had their own networks of informers and agents reporting to the government. As the loci of vast sums of expenditure Burghley was vigilant of their news and needs: Portsmouth was a critical naval link.[153] So, too, were Plymouth and Dover (under Cecil's father-in-law Lord Cobham as lord warden of the Cinque Ports).[154] Southampton had to be secured.[155] With the shift to Irish war, Chester assumed greater importance and Burghley's agent Peter Proby acted as overseer for Irish posts onshore and to Ireland, with his agent George Beverly as commissary of victuals and transport. These were examples of dangerous entry points into the Queen's realm.[156] They were portals for pro-Spanish agents, theft, corruption, and double-dealing, but also sites for the provisioning and embarkation of fleets (such as in 1591–1592, 1596, and 1597 under Essex). They were places where ordnance and supply needed constant provisioning but fell into dangerous want during these years of dearth. Fortifications in Berwick, officers, and their wrangling for place and food supplies were causes of concern.[157] The strategic Isle of Wight had to be looked to for intelligence and as part of the outer ring of information on shipping.[158] Milford Haven under its lord lieutenant, the earl of Pembroke, was rumoured as a Spanish landing point under threat of future Spanish armadas.[159] Even the vast ordnance of the Tower of London was considered at risk after a plot was discovered to blow up the huge store of munitions kept there.[160] These places and their officers fell into the category of what

[150] Letters Nos 30, 58, 96, 97, 106, 110, 127, 134.
[151] Letters Nos 49, 94.
[152] Letter No. 41.
[153] Letter No. 117.
[154] Letters Nos 2, 6, 73, 92, 124, 127, 130.
[155] Letter No. 14.
[156] Letter No. 91.
[157] Letter No. 15.
[158] Letter No. 104.
[159] Letters Nos 54, 58, 64.
[160] Letter No. 23.

was 'definite', and 'indefinite', for shifting loyalties were all practical and political concerns where the state lacked immediate coercion.

Such a mapping of the realms in Burghley's letters bears remarkable similarities to Cecil's youthful French almanacs. He had to include for Burghley the major nobility and their sources of revenue – important during the ravages of war in determining pro- or anti-peace families. All of these English suits represent the extension beyond Westminster of concern for the security of the realm.[161] When anti-alien riots and a deeply unpopular lord mayor of London threatened the stability of the capital, Burghley, with others, advocated the appointment of Thomas Wilford as provost marshal in London, after apprentice riots in 1595.[162] Appointees to Crown offices in reversion and long-standing suits had to be balanced against competency and pressing need. Burghley saw these as a piece, the texts of the letters providing the Ciceronian aspect of definite and indefinite (usually personal) qualities of a place or problem.

His phrase 'brytish subiectes' (discussed below) suggests that Burghley saw further than he let the Queen see: to the mix of kingdoms, provinces and shires, each complex with their own difficulties, which James VI's succession would entail.[163] He cannot have foreseen the disastrous effect a small rising in Ulster in 1593 would have throughout the Queen's realms, a possession he accepted as an empire. His son's eventual Spanish pension and negotiation of the Treaty of London in 1604 would have appealed both to his irenic Ciceronian sense of virtue in the kingdom, but it is difficult to see from these letters any softening of Burghley's rhetorical anti-Catholicism, anti-papalism, disdain for the 'boglishe', and distaste for the French. He found the Dutch difficult. Perhaps these letters were part truthful and part performative, a hard, outer defence within which more secret aspects of the Queen's rule and her Council's decisions could operate.

Suitors and the Balance of Patronage

Burghley never assumed that the Queen was immune from bad counsel: where royal power was appealed to matters required a purpose. Burghley's over-arching concern was the preservation of the kingdom. There is however, an element of rumination in these letters, where the immense worldly responsibilities merged into 'dyvynite', far from the cares of the state. In a startling neo-Platonic image

[161] See p. 55.
[162] Letters Nos 52, 80.
[163] Letter No. 120; see p. 30.

he confided to Robert, 'if sowles have sence of earthly thynges, I shall be in God's sight an intercessor for the prosperite of his chyrch here, and for hir Ma[jes]ty, as his Governor thereof to his Glory'.[164] Burghley issued a rather extraordinary warning to his son during a hotly contested election of the master of St John's College, Cambridge, where both father and son had attended, and of which the Queen's great-grandmother, Lady Margaret Beaufort, was foundress:

> my request is that if ye shall fynd any intention in hir Ma[jes]ty upon any sinister sute, to prefer any on other than the voyces of the Company shall frely choose,[165] to besech hir Ma[jes]ty, that at my sute being ther Chancellor, and havyng bene wholly brought up [ther] from my age of xiii yers, and now the only person lyving of the tyme and education, the Statutes of the Colledg to which all that ar electors ar sworn, may not be now broken, as I hope hir Ma[jes]ty will not in hir honor and conscience [do].

That the Queen could or would be swayed by a 'sinister' candidate speaks of the anxiety inherent in their direct dealings with the fount of honour, perhaps the most indefinite category of all, where Burghley exclaimed 'I remitt all to God, fiat voluntas sua'.[166] Cecil was warned not to allow the mastership to drift into the realm of courtly bidding or for the Queen to name by fiat, *mandamus*, When the non-puritan candidate Dr Richard Clayton, master of Magdalene College, Cambridge, was elected in December 1595, after some fellows' objections to the other candidate Henry Alvey, the College president, Burghley was asked his opinion as chancellor and oldest living graduate. Clergy under Alvey's patronage had been inhibited in college livings in 1582 and 1589 for veering into *classis* practices. Burghley had insisted upon the free election although Clayton may have been pressed into it. True, the fellows praised him, 'te autem (Honorissimus Maecenas) tanti beneficii authorem', author of honour and goodness their great Maecenas (a word used also to describe

[164] Letter No. 5.
[165] Cecil was only to present the fellows' dissenting petition if the Queen gave weight to outside suitors. The archbishop of Canterbury, John Whitgift, used Sir William Cornwallis to inform Cecil that he supported Laurence Stanton, as did Roger Manners. Hatfield, Cecil Papers, 36/79; *HMCS*, v, 497, 498. The archbishop's support might have indicated his desire to steer the College away from radical Protestant leadership, in the event of President Henry Alvey's certain election, by introducing a moderate. 'Sinister' meant non-Statutory, which contravenes much of the Cecils' work in ecclesiastical appointments and nominations to headships of ancient foundations during the years 1594–1596; see Acres, 'The early political career of Sir Robert Cecil', 161–192. Burghley's correspondence with the heads and fellows of the College are discussed here. See Richard Clayton (d.*c*.1612), *ODNB*. He was the Cecils' preferred candidate as distinctly against the 'presbytery' group at St John's College, Cambridge.
[166] Letter No. 31.

his son in another context), but his action was not 'sinister'. As chancellor, he supported the professor of Hebrew, Peter Baro, after his sermon in early December 1595, a few days before Whitaker's death on the 4th, in Great St Mary's, Cambridge, in which he excoriated Calvinism and sent many of the heads of houses into rebellion. Despite Burghley's support for the late master of St John's, William Whitaker, a man of decidedly Puritan sympathies who had, with Burghley's full knowledge, been shrewd and forceful in his support of Alvey as president of the College, he was not going to allow the University of Cambridge to embrace a public doctrine other than that which had been set by statute.

Burghley's true religious leanings cannot be discerned from the balancing of claims on doctrine, for example. Burghley, of course, had never warmed to the anti-Puritanism of Christopher Hatton and Richard Bancroft in 1589 and after.[167] Following his support for Baro, who had been forbidden from lecturing by the college heads, Burghley, aided by Cecil, was complicit in the suppression of the Lambeth Articles. These were a national statement of the doctrine of grace, which it was argued was not freely given by God. This was altered by Archbishop John Whitgift with the assistance of Burghley and Cecil at the behest of the Queen.[168] As the fellows of St John's College appealed to Burghley in December 1595, the church was now cursed by these divisions into ranks of papist and puritan.[169] Burghley protected their statutes, and avoided directly staking his own religious claims. Whatever his own religion was, and he attended divine service at court in the presence of bishops in rochet and chimire, the crucial instruction to his son was to protect the Queen from direct meddling in the cursed theological controversies. Thus, it is nearly impossible in this conflict to place Burghley as anything other than a distant adviser whose priority was to control governance in the University.

Cambridge in 1595 would suggest a decisive Burghley. Every statute in every place would be observed. In fact, both Cecils were adept at statutory games when it suited the Queen or when her prerogative was at stake or their motives required. When Essex supported his brilliant secretary Henry Savile as a candidate for provost of Eton in 1596, both Burghley and Cecil were wholly supportive. Savile asked

[167] See Patrick Collinson, *Richard Bancroft and Elizabethan Anti-Puritanism* (Cambridge, 2013).

[168] Parmelee, *Good Newes from Fraunce*, 103–104. The Calvinist idea of grace conditional was suppressed here, but the notion that protectors of thrones fill 'providentially designated roles' was one which Burghley's other maxims in these letters appear to support.

[169] BL Lansdowne MS 79 no. 62, fols.156r–v, 'maxime 'vero' quae nunc nostrum hanc Ecclesiam Anglicanum perturbant, papismum et puritanismum, execremae'. The petition of 23 fellows for a free election, 'libera electio'.

Burghley as one 'from whom one commendation in cold blood and seeming to proceed of judgement, shall more prevail than all the affectionate speech of my lord of Essex can use'. Burghley endorsed Savile's appointment by the Queen but it greatly angered the fellows of Eton, who on receiving her letter railed 'though by our Prerogative Roiall . . . the free and liberall disposicion of the Provoste's place is in our sole and absolute gift'. They responded by stalling his appointment for over a week. Savile consulted the former provost of Winchester, William Day, now the bishop of Winchester who offered to help to remove the offensive article of the fellows' right 'whereby all the former statutes are so left at liberty, that no fellow for transgressing of anie shalbe deemed or iudged in anye sorte subiecte to the gilt of periurie'. The royal chaplain Henry Cotton, who prevailed as royal candidate as provost of Winchester College (his letters patent already written while his nomination was contested) used almost the same argument, possibly having conferred with Savile and others about this new loophole of non-perjury. The fellows of Winchester College resisted for a time, with candidates proposed with heavy references from all sides, the Queen herself changing her candidate. But while Cotton scraped in at Winchester, Eton had to contend with Savile whose noisy demolition of the fellows' objections he called slavish in following 'every little ceremonial thinge . . . (as that the Provost should say masses and diriges some festival dayes)'. It was 'an error', he continued, 'and ignorance in law to Imagin . . . that her Ma[jesty's] naming by prerogative is tyed to anye locall statute'.[170] Winchester's fellows went through an immensely complicated struggle involving bishops, the Queen, Essex and Cecil, and the fellows of New College, Oxford: each of them finally having to cavil to Cotton whose bill, procured incidentally by Robert Cecil, was, finally, by *mandamus*: 'All other exception which may be made against him by her H[ighness] by her prerogative Roiall doth supply'.[171] These machinations on behalf of the royal prerogative contrast with Burghley's insistence on St John's College, Cambridge, as a purely local resolution albeit one with national implications for doctrine.

Burghley was similarly vigilant of the Crown's interests during the dozen or so episcopal appointments between 1594 and 1596 in which, almost routinely, certain suitors got good lands at favourable rents before the candidate was consecrated and restituted, or restored, to their temporalities – lands which would have to produce first fruits

[170] TNA SP 12/251/fol. 204r–v.
[171] TNA SO3/1/fol. 585v; Acres, 'The early political career of Sir Robert Cecil', 204–205, 206–207, 212–219; *HMCS*, vi, 184, 188, 181, 208–209, 254–255, 299–300; TNA SP 12/251/fol. 204 r–v.

and tenths.[172] But there is a sense, too, in these many appointments, elevations, and translations, that both Cecils were protective of the Queen's rights, not necessarily of candidates. Although there were some notable exceptions such as Matthew Hutton as Archbishop of York and Tobie Matthew to Durham, these were also strong intelligence connections. Elizabethan bishops were notably absent from the highest political levels, Whitgift her sole exception on the council. But bishoprics possessed great lands and wealth. Burghley urged his son to be constantly vigilant in such matters, with Winchester providing an excellent example. Essex and others of the Privy Council raised no objection to the problem of 'local' rights where Crown preserve or court appointments were urged in these cases. And so their accusation of the Cecils' alleged control of prerogative as evidence of a badly counselled Queen seems hollow by this measure. Whether Burghley was Maecenas or one whose word would 'more prevail' were words alone; they were not appeals to Burghley's or Cecil's theological proclivities, but a recognition that their authority stemmed from the ability to navigate the immensely complicated terrain of the royal will across hundreds of offices, policies and, most importantly, persons.

Burghley had intended to have another great patron at court for his son – beyond himself, as stipulated in his *Precepts* to Robert – the lord chancellor Sir Christopher Hatton.[173] But Burghley's cultivation was doubtless meant to lessen the sense that Cecil would have only one patron. The choice of Hatton suggests Burghley was seeking qualities of judgement and an ability to handle the Queen. The Leicester-Walsingham group was scattered in the wake of their patrons' deaths in 1588 and 1590 – a remnant to prove so potent for Essex and in Irish office-holding. Burghley was seeking to re-fashion a consensus for his son's advance with a great friend on the Privy Council, one not allied by family as Cobham or himself. Yet, Hatton remains one of the most elusive of Elizabeth I's senior statesmen. Burghley's choice was not, thus, one of ideology or religion or faction, but that of a man who had excelled in the Queen's estimation. Hatton had legal training but fulfilled the highest office of the law with distinction without having served in any legal office; he was active in the anti-Puritanism campaign, 1589–1591, with Robert Cecil's later strong ally Richard Bancroft. That Bancroft and Cecil could stir the so-called 'Archpriest controversy', designed to flood the public with works on

[172] See Letter No. 41; Acres, 'The early political career of Sir Robert Cecil', 192–223.
[173] P.E.J. Hammer, 'Letters from Sir Robert Cecil to Sir Christopher Hatton, 1590–1' in *Religion, Politics and Society in Sixteenth-Century England*, ed. Ian W. Archer, Camden Society, 5th ser., 22 (2003), 197–267.

loyal Catholicism, was testament to the kind of control Cecil was able to assume.[174] Hatton's letters from Robert Cecil in 1591, then on the cusp of promotion to the Privy Council, reveal their mutual closeness to Burghley. Burghley and Hatton shared a strong aversion to Sir Walter Raleigh. Essex's overbearing habits were already veering close to her prerogative. Knighthoods for captains at Rouen exceeded Elizabeth's orders, 1591–1592, where Burghley showed clemency – indeed he seems to have shown the earl sympathy until very late in his life. Elizabeth forgave the earl's transgressions having denounced him vocally and harshly; and when they were repeated she renewed the cycle. More tellingly, she was to tar his supporters with perhaps an even stronger and lasting displeasure than the earl himself, as if support for his waywardness was the royal prerogative. This threat to what in 1591 was the 'common cause' of the Privy Council had begun to grow considerably by the mid 1590s. Hatton's death in 1591 removed Cecil's other potential patron but by Burghley's death the parity between Cecil and Essex was destroyed.

After Burghley's death, Cecil promoted his own generation as the Essex circle drew into itself in bitterness and open contempt. His friendship with Bancroft is an example. As bishop of London in 1598, Bancroft controlled the printing presses and was Cecil's client; he was thus in direct control of communication among people who read. Bancroft had been a senior lecturer at Cambridge in the early 1580s when Cecil was a student at St John's College. Another Cecil chaplain, Richard Neile, a close friend in Westminster, where the Cecils held serious sway for two generations in civic and church politics, had been an undergraduate with Cecil.[175] Cecil's generation, apart from Essex and his cousin Francis Bacon, would begin to find higher office after Burghley's death but only if they avoided the Queen's knowledge that they were in the earl's penumbra of patronage. Cecil would gain intimate knowledge of all of it. Cecil would also heed his father's words to follow the Queen's train without offence in cloudy and foul weather so far as can be discerned during the period 1593–1598.

These letters do not alter radically the debates on the 1590s in recent historiography. But they add to understanding the inner workings of Burghley's mind as he sought steadily to provision his son. Burghley's ability to laugh at his physical decline does not mask it. He is very conscious of time. His lack of bodily control weighs on him very heavily. Indeed, in his handwriting a kind of barometer might be detected. There is no rigorous pattern to it, no steady decline.

[174] Susan Doran, *Elizabeth and Her Circle* (Oxford, 2015) ch. 6; Collinson, *Richard Bancroft*.
[175] Julia Merritt, 'The Cecils and Westminster, 1558–1612: The development of an urban power base', in Croft, *Patronage, Culture and Power*, 231–246.

Relations with Scotland

While Elizabeth lived, discussion of her successor on the throne was an invitation to disgrace. Nonetheless, Robert Cecil, despite his sickliness and physical weakness, looked certain in his father's sight to live to see her replacement. While a view of Scotland and Ireland was consistent with the plats and maps and almanacs of materials Burghley compiled on the continental powers and English shires, it was on this debatable ground that the Stuart accession was most problematic. Spanish designs on the British archipelago in the 1590s remained unabated after wider peace in 1598 with Philip III's continued support of the rebellion against the Queen. Burghley and Sir Robert saw a possible way of discovering Spanish plans through the Hebridean clans with their complex alliances and immediate kinship connections to Ulster and elsewhere. Burghley had been the principal voice responding to the continental Catholic critics of the Queen's legitimacy and rule: the publications of Richard Verstegan, Robert Persons (or Parsons), Joseph Creswell and Thomas Stapleton named Burghley 'Machiavel'.[176] By the 1590s, the circle through the 'British' skein of approach to Spanish incursion joined in Burghley's mind the political, religious, and practical matters of sounding out the relations and alliances of both Scotland and Spain within the archipelago, the projected future Stuart kingdom.

When letters arriving from Scotland were brought to Burghley's coach on 20 May 1594 he referred the dilemma, without advice, to his son, with a weary rejoinder that without money, the annual pension specified in the 1585 Act of Abolition, 'the kyng will contynew his delayes'. Cecil had by then gained control of diplomatic relations with James VI, particularly through the Queen and her ambassador Sir Robert Bowes.[177] Cecil was now the chief recipient of Scottish materials: 'I do retorn to yow the draught of your letter to Mr. bowes havyng no lesur nor yet cawse to alter the sence but in the report of the wordes of the Q[ueen's] letter, by them remembred'.[178] After a year of plotting in and around the Scottish court the Cecils had yet to move the Scottish king into a posture of submission to the Queen – the annual calculation for the payment of the annuity was now fixed on the willingness of the Scottish king to cast his lot with the Queen and her loyal English on the matter of Spanish designs on the amity of their crowns. The background to the Queen's plan was doubtless predicated on unsure intelligence; nonetheless

[176] Joseph Creswell *ODNB* (1557–1623), Thomas Stapleton *ODNB* (1532–1598).
[177] Letters Nos 20, 21.
[178] Letter No. 21.

Elizabeth was clearly frightened by news from disparate Catholic sources and various spies that Spain was planning an invasion through Scotland.

The 'sence' in the Queen's letter in May 1594 refers to the extent she had secretly licensed her councillors' tactics during the previous six months to coerce James into public declarations of treason against those earls who subscribed to Philip II. Letters from the earls intercepted in November 1592, the so-called 'Spanish Blanks', addressed promises of aid if they should undertake to overthrow James. This danger brackets the letters: in early 1593 Cecil's maiden parliament as a privy councillor, his fifth (by his own words), announced these discoveries of Spain in Scotland as shocking and immediate. The Cecils' response was to play on 'private mens causes' in making a party. By establishing a pro-Elizabeth group James might be encouraged to act against the pro-Spanish earls as an alternative strategy to dealing with the oppressive tactics of the Kirk. Alternatively, these forays could expose a cabal of hostile nobles and adherents – the plan cut both ways in finding more Spanish designs. Allies were to be cultivated by the Queen's accredited ambassadors, Bowes and Edward, 11th Lord Zouche, in a series of complex instructions drafted by Cecil, in consultation with his father. They were meant to enter a 'labyrinth', to use Burghley's word for the shifting Scots' loyalties. Zouche's ostensible embassy was to the christening of Princess Elizabeth (when he was recalled he was replaced by the earl of Sussex). Miscommunication among the Scots caused an escalation from promoting faction to a mock attack from 'Borough Muir' on Holyroodhouse; a small military force which so enraged James that Zouche was recalled by the time Elizabeth wrote her holograph letter in May 1594 to the king. A group around Bothwell marched against the king whose hastily assembled force routed them causing the earl to flee (apparently unbeknownst to the Queen) back into English territory.[179] Thus, Elizabeth's 'sence' pled her royal ignorance of all parts of a plan ending with this flight across the border into her realm. James would not respond to the plot save to banish Bothwell (again), and to use his secret knowledge of English councillors' and spies' tactics in his kingdom against the Queen. Nonetheless the plots opened channels for Robert Cecil particularly.

At the outset of this project, a year earlier, Burghley had cautioned Robert on the gravity of mixing private causes with princely discourses:

---

[179] Patrick Fraser Tytler, *History of Scotland*, 9 vols (Edinburgh, 1828–1843), IX, 148–149; TNA SP 52/53/nos. 24, 25; *CSPS 1593–1595*, 303–304.

> The matter yow write of concerning the answar to be made by Locke is very piquant for difficulties on both sides. Wherein the Rule of Christian Philosophie consisteth in difference between Utile, and Honestum. And yett utile incertum and Honestum certum. But if Honestum were reciproche it were to be preferred to with more Constancye. In private mens causes Cretisare cum Cretensi is allowable.

The Ciceronian distinction between 'Utile' and 'Honestum', or expediency and honesty, moral good, created here for Burghley a question: in a truly honest and beneficial action for the state could a taint of deception for gain remain secret, 'private'? To deceive the deceiver – 'Cretisare cum Cretensi' – was not, in private causes detrimental to the state if it were removed entirely from the level of princely knowledge. The plot itself verged into the darker, Tacitean world where a theatrical physical threat to the king's body was the result. In a telling postscript to this passage, Burghley advises that he is wandering, but 'If my hand were free from payne I would not commytt thus much to another mans hand', implying Maynard was utterly trustworthy. The Queen knew all about it: 'yow may impart my words to hir Majesty, without offence'. The following day, 22 May, Burghley wrote to his son further that the matter of supporting Bothwell in some design against the Scottish king was so delicate as to require Cecil to be present in person to read his father's thoughts.[180] These innermost words would then, with counsel, find their way to the Queen through Cecil. Burghley was not about to let his son or himself be saddled with responsibility for the actions of the bizarre Bothwell.

Intelligence in the shadowy work of Henry Lock and the spies near Boulogne suggest Burghley's Ciceronian clemency was not a complete view of the secretarial place.[181] For example, the cultivation of Bothwell, 'Utile Incertum', as a bogeyman to frighten James VI into public condemnation of three Catholic earls – Huntly, Erroll, and Angus – was obviously for the security of the mutual realms. Bothwell, on the other hand, was the relation of a man who had possibly murdered Lord Darnley, the king's father, and was himself a deeply frightening man to the king; accused of witchcraft and acquitted, implicated in the plots of his wife's family – of the earls of Angus, the Douglases –

---

[180] Burghley wrote to Cecil that he had written his deliberations concerning the earl of Bothwell which were so delicate that he would not trust their drafting to a secretary, and insisting that Cecil see them in person before presentation to the Queen. Hatfield, Cecil Papers, 169/81; *HMCS*, iv, 319.

[181] Henry Lok (1553?–1608?), *ODNB*, was a minor poet and Cecil agent was then entrusted with covert co-ordination with others of the faction at the Scottish court. He remained in Cecil's employ until 1599.

and now, in the summer of 1593 attainted by the king for treason. In an about-face, James would restore the earl in the autumn of 1593, when the Cecils instructed Edward, Lord Zouche, the Queen's proxy at the christening of her namesake the Princess Elizabeth. Bothwell, whose religious inclinations were as unstable as his personality, was to operate as chief Protestant counterweight to his errant in-law, Angus, who with the earls of Huntly and Erroll were the earls implicated as Spanish pensioners. Months later, Bothwell was ready to frighten his cousin again.

The Cecils and the Queen combined forces, private and princely, to set the parts of Zouche's journey. The bonds of affection with James were not obvious in the documents: Elizabeth's cover letter of 22 December 1593 to Bowes called James 'a seduced king', abusing 'council and wry guided kingdom'. A year had passed since the 'blanks' without remedy or action. Burghley drew up, from his extensive papers, genealogies of all principal Scottish nobility, many of whom were among the king's 'seducers', the earls of Huntly, Erroll, and Angus. On the Borders' Scottish side, Burghley knew in detail the alliances and members of Homes and Scotts, lairds of Buccleuch, for he had good relations with their English opposites, the wardens of the West and Middle Marches, the Eures and Scropes (the East Marches being a sinecure of the Queen's Hunsdon cousins). The lowland nobles, the houses of Douglas and Hamilton, were illustrated by notes on the bitter enmities between the families of Angus, Mar, Hamilton, and Glamis. Burghley revealed the mass of royal affinities near James; by contrast the lone Elizabeth's dangerous succession loomed. Connections to the ancient kings of the Isle of Man and detailed Irish-Highland-Hebridean kinship were shown in comprehensive genealogies of the chieftains.[182] Burghley made notes, in which he rehearsed the events of 1593 for Zouche with further additions by Sir Robert Cecil.[183]

Cecil's control of Zouche's embassy after December 1593 was prepared extensively; Cecil documented how feelers at the Scottish court could be manipulated, for example, into a chain of connections going into Ireland. The secret aspect of Zouche's embassy was to find English support for a permanent noble Protestant connection not under the influence of the Kirk.[184] Zouche would be first pawn in

[182]TNA SP 52/51/no. 75; *CSPS 1593–1595*, 248; Burghley's genealogies: TNA SP 52/51 nos. 80–86.

[183]BL Cottonian MS Caligual D ii, fol. 38r–v (transcription, BL Harleian MS 4648, p. 88; *CSPS 1593–1595*, 255–256; Thomas Birch, *Memoirs of the Reign of Queen Elizabeth from the Year 1581 until Her Death . . . and the Conduct of her Favourite, Robert Earl of Essex . . .* 2 vols (London, 1754), I, 144.

[184]TNA SP 52/52/pp. 19–22, SOS/1/fol. 439v.

a very long Cecilian network of alliances. Some of these families and individuals were useful and some were not. Their tenuous relations operated on 'utile', or the degree of secret personal affection persons felt for Elizabeth as negotiated through Cecil. John Colville of Easter Wemyss of a Borders family together with Henry Lock, knew the secrets of some members of the king's council and how alliances after Maitland of Thirlestane's fall in 1592 might play with elements around the earl of Mar or Ludovick Stuart, duke of Lennox. Cecil warned that the Queen could never be implicated with the faction. But the plans were far from secret from the outset: Zouche was immediately hampered in January 1594 by accusations (correctly) from some of the king's inner circle that Bothwell had found protection in England after his threatening visit to the king in the summer of 1593.[185]

Zouche, for his part, stayed silent. Cecil had impressed upon him also to 'leave her Majestie as ignorant as before', while understanding that 'her Majestie . . . willeth you . . . not to stande upon to many doubtes or Scruples, but to followe the Substance of her Majestie's Instructions'. Burghley could have wished for no better exposition of his maxim, 'Cretiziare cum Cretensis'. Zouche's secret strategy was to recruit 'good Patriotes' from among those councillors which supporters of the Catholic cause would inhibit. Lock would be directed by Zouche. The Queen could not be 'Author, which cannot be done without toutche to the Treatye'. Cecil was clear in his interpretation of his father's precept: 'the Q[ueen] wold have hir ministers doe that she will not avowe' was his marginal note on the instruction.[186] Zouche's meeting with the newly minted Protestant confederacy at Berwick was, according to the Queen, to include no Scots, only English and only persons already known on the Scottish side to be unconnected to Bothwell, an impossible feat as he was to learn. Elizabeth denied all knowledge of the plans while James received information about what Zouche and the Cecils were doing.[187]

Cecilian machinations moved across Scottish alliances into the Hebrides and down into Ulster towards Dublin – and back to London. A sort of circular web of informants and loosely allied chieftains – Macleans of Duart, members of the Campbell family at Inverary – fed the Queen with information about the Scottish-Irish connections and their usefulness against Spanish designs. Eventually, in November 1594 this loose alliance would be soundly defeated at the battle of Glenlivet by the forces of Erroll and Huntly, who had been banished but not

[185]TNA SP 52/52/ pp. 23–25; 20.
[186]TNA SP 52/52/ pp. 27, 28, 29.
[187]TNA SP 52/52/ pp. 30–31; 53/no. 9.

forfeited the year before. The view to Ireland through the Hebrides was even more debatable ground, but by 1596 the king would follow with a proclamation forbidding any Highland and Hebridean families from offering succour to the Irish rebels, doubtless prefiguring the *True Law of Free Monarchies* (1598). The great subjects of the Scottish peripheries – in James's phrase, 'beyond doom of forfeiture' – were equally beyond the remit of his funds and armies.[188] But they could, with rewards, and other connections, be moved as needed to protect the interests of the Scottish (and English) crowns if their alliances could be strengthened in their own regions. Burghley knew this was a possibility – hence Zouche's long list of dramatis personae. Eventually the king would proceed, after long negotiations by Cecil and his agents, with a clear strategy, at least on paper, to proclaim publicly and royally against any of his subjects who were known to send their families to fight for the Irish rebels.[189]

The strange Bothwell gambit also gained what was 'Utile' for Cecil. As the Queen's ambassador Sir Robert Bowes wrote on 13 April 1594, that 'forasmuch as her Majesty has employed the services of Sir Robert Cecil in the directions for the advertisements . . . for all Scottish matters . . . I have presumed at this time to make my certificate to him'.[190] The complex plan was symptomatic of a private and public Cecilian view: James was susceptible by poverty and faction to manipulation which they used at every opportunity largely through John Colville, Henry Lock, and a cast of shadowy characters with noble connections.[191] The northern intelligence links Cecil used employed Colville and Lock to effect further policies for the Queen in Scotland which assisted the amity of the crowns in the face of more divisive problems.[192] With the well-affected Matthew Hutton as archbishop of York installed as president of the Council in the North following the earl of Huntingdon's death – to be succeeded by Sir Thomas Cecil in 1598 – the links with the borders were moderately secure. Despite conflict among the Border families, reivers, such stalwarts as Lords Eure and Scrope, the latter married to Hunsdon's daughter Philadelphia, resorted to the Cecils with frequent letters. When the Grahams escaped Carlisle castle having been discovered as renegades in the English marches, Scrope and others turned to the Cecils. Tobie Matthew, made bishop of Durham in 1595, remained

[188] *CSPS 1593–1595*, 495, 537, 542.
[189] The king's proclamation of July 1595 against Macdonnell and Gorme of Sleat, see *CSPS 1593–1595*, 595.
[190] *CSPS 1593–1595*, 308–311, quoted from p. 308; TNA SP 52/53/no. 31, 13 Apr. 1594.
[191] Letters Nos 2, 16, 20.
[192] TNA SP 52/52/pp. 119–123, esp. 120, 122.

part of Cecil's Privy Council intelligence personnel.[193] Cecil became
'Maecenas' to Colville and his adherents.[194] Cecil, with the assistance of
the Queen, played close to the king through a dense web of informants
and shadowy connections across the well-named 'debatable lands' of
the borders. The Cecils were, of course, limited in their plans and
alliances by geography, water, and mountains. James VI negotiated
across these barriers with his own subjects, granting the Highlanders
and Islanders latitude which horrified the English queen. Guarded by
the impenetrability of their lands and supported by kinship alliances,
many of the great clans were, nonetheless, strongly attractive for
English designs.

Mercenaries for the Irish rebels' arsenal could be purchased into
neutrality by good relations from London with chieftains – Cecil
pursued these men with gifts and tokens, becoming their 'Maecenas'.
Captains were intent on gaining land in Ireland, and while the
events of 1594–1603 scarcely ensured tenure, the hope of gain was
a powerful incentive for loyalties, however expedient. The Scots
chieftains were not immune from the family tribulations which had
brought the earl of Tyrone to his position as the O'Neill; nor were
they ignorant of the Spanish assistance which bought him resources
and time. From 1594 Cecil pursued secret measures to bring under
his influence the Scottish Hebridean chiefs, in Mull particularly,[195]
in order to withstand the strength of Spanish money pouring into
the old galloglass (Scottish mercenary) families in the north.[196] Cecil
was running agents from Inverary in western Scotland to Limerick;[197]
another through Irish (Protestant) bishops;[198] yet another from the
Pale (area of initial English conquest and control centred on Dublin);
and finally, he was in charge of interrogations of captured Spanish

[193]Which connection must offer an explanation for Cecil's desire to have Matthew as
bishop of Durham. TNA SP 52/53, no. 49. For Scrope, see Letters Nos 2, 28, 30, 96, 97,
104, 106, 110, 121, 127, and 128.
[194]TNA SP 52/53/no. 52.
[195]See Cecil's instructions to the Maclean of Duart Castle, Mull, sanctioning payments
and ships, TNA SP 52/52/pp. 119–123.
[196]James VI could not control his Highlanders or Islanders, see *CSPS 1593–1595*, 495, 537,
542.
[197]TNA SP 52/58/no. 25 – The earl of Argyll's cousin, Dioness Campbell, Protestant dean
of Limerick sent Cecil numerous 'plats' on the Hebridean islands, and clans, giving detailed
descriptions of current efforts on behalf of Tyrone and Spain.
[198]Cecil's principal Irish spymaster was the bishop of Limerick, John Thornborough, who
used many shady characters, principally William Udall. TNA SP 63/184/no. 41, fol. 141r–v,
giving Cecil's protection to Udall. Thornborough: TNA SP 63/183/fols. 331r–332r, no. 106.
Cecil also used John Talbot, of Dundalk. Argyll's kinsman, Dioness Campbell, regarded
Burghley as a friend, but he was a sworn enemy of Thornborough. See Letters Nos 34, 38.

agents.[199] Sir Geoffrey Fenton was an important part of much of this work.[200]

Key players for the English crown were George Thornton, an English captain who ran a pinnace along the western Scottish coast south of Glasgow, and members of the earl of Argyll's family including his cousin Dioness Campbell, dean of Limerick, as well as John Thornborough, bishop of Limerick.[201] Part of the appeal of fledgling alliance lay in the absence of a coherent, lasting military strategy where the many layers of Irish families, government and law overlapped into the Hebrides. The Cecils hardly regarded their English governors in Ireland as innocent. Burghley blamed them entirely for the massacre of many of the O'Tooles as well as the taking of the rebel Feagh McHugh, issuing the reprimand, 'I dowt of my l[ord] deputies intention to reform it'. Furthermore, he continued to use Essex's ally, Sir Thomas Lea, against the wishes of leading English governors, including Sir John Harrington.[202] Burghley's fear was always that this barbarity was born of the English policies as much as their Irish enemies; massacres under the Queen's licence were very dark sides of her princely language with rebels. The sequestration and removal of Sir Richard Bingham in Connacht, engineered in part by both Cecils, was doubtless part of an attempt (mostly futile at the time) to limit lawlessness and brutality in what had become a bloody and uncontrolled contest.

The Spanish designs Burghley sought to monitor and frustrate within the peripheries of Scotland spread from across the Irish Sea to the north. The geographical extent of these designs was rhetorical. But they were also given credence by the intelligence of toleration emanating from the king in Scotland towards the Spanish and Jesuits. When Burghley received the English translation of *The Conference on the Succession*, published in 1595 by Richard Verstegan in Antwerp and written by the Jesuit Father Robert Persons, he wrote of pulling the reins of these connections and ideas together – all through the hands of his son – to force the king further in his public anti-Spanish posture. He wrote to his son to urge the Scottish king (by his own letters and presumably the Queen's own pen) to make a direct declaration against Spain. He must end all ambivalence towards Philip II in a proclamation. James, he suggested, must embargo Spanish ships in the Orkneys, exactly where the Spanish fleets would cross north of

[199] Cecil occasionally received intercepted letters being sent to the Spanish authorities, but he usually got these from Russell, TNA SP 63/183/no. 60, fol. 200r–v, 208r–v.
[200] e.g. TNA SP 63/183/fols. 284r–v.
[201] Letters Nos 34, 38.
[202] Letter No. 61.

Scotland to Ulster and thence, it was presumed, into the English chaos.

> I have intred onto consideracion howe the k[ing] might be stirred upp ernestlye to impeache both this and other the like[203] with Municion or graine for the king of Spaine's purpose to sett a foote A title for himself and his dawghter to the present succession to the Crowne of England, which doth appear manifestlye by a seditious Booke[204] published for the said K[ing] by a Number of Englishe Rebells residinge in Spaine, by which booke is maintained that kingdoms are at the disposition of the people withowt regard of right by Blood and sucession; and to be preferred to that for their greatnes are most hable to Governe Contries. And consequentlie the Awthors of thes Bookes have manifestlie improved anie title that the k[ing] of Scottes might pretend; and in like manner disprovinge all other pretended titles onelie preferring the k[ing] of Spaine wither himself or his eldest dawghter Bretaigne.[205]

A Spanish invasion of Ireland, abetted even slightly by Scottish ambivalence, would have tilted the European balance of power strongly and ended James's claim to the succession (a claim actually strengthened in the *Conference*). The phrase 'for their greatnes are most hable to Governe Contries' has an eerie prescience in view of Essex's future designs. But it was the republican sentiment that 'the disposition of the people' was sufficiently legitimate which tells that he was thinking also of the Irish situation where the Queen's rule was under attack. This, Burghley urged, was James's situation also.

Burghley and the council were aware that the Spanish were working through priests and their patrons in Ireland – and receiving support under cover from James himself – which only fuelled the Lord Treasurer's campaign against any response but a direct supply of men and arms into the troubled realm. His servants were certainly supplying ample information to suggest the direction of danger

---

[203] Burghley refers to James VI's reluctance to prosecute his rebellious Catholic nobility. As for stirring the king, Roger Aston reported to the English ambassador Bowes on 28 November 1598 that James VI had resolved absolutely to fight the Spanish, in Scotland and in England (which might have implied sending mercenaries or others into Ireland) *CSPS 1595–1597*, xxi, 66–67. As for the reception of the book regarding the English succession, Aston further informed Bowes on 16 December that in the English translation recently arrived from Antwerp, 'the author deloudes all those in the succession save the Derbys and the Infanta of Spain by right of her title to Brittany' (ibid. 93; see also the letter to Cecil from one of his principal agents in Scotland, George Nicolson, 96). An Italian treatise of that year discussed James's inviolate claim to England, even though he was born outside that kingdom, while urging him to establish Catholicism in Scotland, ibid. 104–111. Henry VIII's Act of Succession is not mentioned.

[204] Letter No 65. John Snowden *alias* 'Cecyll' (1558–1626), *ODNB*, was one of Cecil's earliest intelligence contacts in 1591.

[205] Letters Nos 64 and 65.

was shifting out of the Low Countries and France directly into the Queen's territories. Sir John Norris was activating an intelligence group with information from Galway with reports of Jesuit priests leaving directly from Calais or St Malo.[206] These spies were infiltrating Tyrone's adherents and adding weight to the anti-Spanish arguments. Burghley's excoriation of the attempted negotiations of Henry IV and his minister Villeroy with the Pope for the return of Jesuits into France, after the king's absolution in September 1595, showed the fulcrum of Burghley's mind, the great dangers 'the french kyng[s] reconcilment with such dishonorable and servill conditions, is lyk to work in the world'.[207] These reports he related directly to the rising charges of the Irish army where Russell had intelligence that the earl of Tyrone from December 1594 was entirely controlled by Jesuits.[208] Burghley's language in 1595 saw a singular hatred of the kind Persons attributed to him, a rhetorical outrage at the Pope as well as Spain. When forwarding documents to his son about the negotiations of the nuncio in Poland at that time, Burghley weighed his attempts to Catholicize the commonwealth there as typical, 'to slawnder hir ma[jes]tie after the accustomed manner of his master the ffather of Lies'.[209] Clement VIII's nuncios, seeking distance from Spanish control, were set to form a holy alliance against the Turks. Jesuit successes in Poland and Slovenia increased the terrain against Protestant allies, an already tenuous group about to be riven by the Imperial mandates against the Merchant Adventurers' monopolies in the Empire.

Cecil was to employ an altogether different tactic in 1598 – once Spain was at peace with France – in playing the pro-Spanish Catholics against loyal English Catholics. The opportunity to implicate James VI in the *Conference* and the risings in Ulster proved irresistible to Burghley, in fact stirring James into action against the Spanish incursions despite good intelligence of his Jesuit connections in the Irish rebels' territories. Consciously drawing James VI's attention to the inevitable realities of insurrection in Ireland with designs around Bothwell continued Burghley's policy of keeping him unsettled, all the while supporting

---

[206] Letter No. 70.

[207] Letter No. 63. Sidney felt that the Queen's refusal to assist Henry IV had created a situation whereby France would have to seek peace with Spain on conditions dictated by the enemy, *HMCS*, v, 409. Anglo-French diplomatic relations reached stalemate during the embassy of Antoine de Lomenie, lord of La Ville-aux-Clerics (1560–1638). As ambassador for Henry IV, he charged the Queen with negligence in refusing to assist in the relief of Calais. The Queen refuted vigorously these claims in Oct. 1595 following the ambassador's return to France, TNA SP 78/36/fols. 52r–54r.

[208] Letter No. 37.

[209] Letter No. 58.

roundly, in speech and writing, the unclouded amity of the crowns particularly in the chaos in the Borders.[210]

Colville and his friends were eventually persuaded to the views of the earl of Essex (who did not take up the Hebridean or the Irish end of the matrix) to secure their future with James VI. The succession bid has been analysed by Alexandra Gajda and others to have been Essex's final refuge when military and domestic greatness eluded him entirely.[211] Essex was by turns, implicated, exonerated, and deeply embarrassed by Persons' dedication to him of the *Conference on the Succession*. Essex was keen, through his Italian and other ultramontane agents, to promote a clement royalist Catholicism in England sharply delineated from the Hispanophile designs of Philip II's loyal English supporters – projects he continued, fatally, beyond the deaths of Burghley and the Spanish king in August and September 1598. Allusions to the earl's cultivation of this loyal Catholicism appears here in the examination of two converted seminary priests, William Alabaster and Thomas Wright (*c*.1561–1623): 'whoe both would be streightlie examined of many things necessarie to be understood, for their combinations and Companions'.[212] Examinations of them had already been taken by the Cecil loyalist and client Matthew Hutton, archbishop of York, where the informant, Miles Dawson, revealed among much other information about rifts with the pro-Spanish party, Wright's 'cavilling to Bacon'.[213] Mining here a rich source of information about Spanish preparations for invasion in mid 1596, Hutton forwarded evidence to the Cecils.[214] Dawson had met two of Sir Robert Cecil's erstwhile spies from 1591, a Captain Burley and John Cecil *alias* Snowden,[215] both still employed by him and supplying information across the 'British' cast of the Cecilian landscape – including Ireland.[216] Wright would compose strong praise for Essex and Anthony Bacon and find employ in the earl's growing secretarial establishment, a situation verging on danger as the only Jesuit to be so employed by any English privy councillor.[217] Burghley would not relent. His rhetoric stayed absolute against the Catholic threat. Yet, his son was able to negotiate a treaty with two Catholic

---

[210] See Letter No. 69 approving the work of Roger Aston and Sir Robert Bowes.

[211] Gajda, *The Earl of Essex*, 136–140, 214.

[212] Letters Nos 100, 127.

[213] See Anthony Bacon's dispatch of intelligence to the lord deputy, Sir William Russell, and their mutual reliance on Wright's testimonies of his intelligence and religious conformity, Birch, *Memoirs of the Reign of Queen Elizabeth*, II, 308–309.

[214] *HMCS*, vi, 431–432.

[215] John Snowden, see above, p. 28 n. 114.

[216] *HMCS*, vi, 283–284.

[217] Gajda, *The Earl of Essex*, 130–140.

powers, two thrones, without negligence or presumption; his work in 1598 on the 'Archpriest' controversy, and his greater affinity to 'ceremonialism' suggest that in all things he was not of his father's condition.

Burghley's care for the security of the realms was more than obliquely 'brytysh'. Yet nothing was sure. Following the death of the earl of Huntingdon in mid 1595, Burghley extended the Council of the North's warrants to hear the cases brought before them – letters patent of early 1596 shows Hutton chairing this group together with the bishop of Durham – Tobie Matthew, a sure Cecil controller of examination and intelligence – the earl of Cumberland, Lords Scrope and Eure, wardens of the Border marches, representatives from Berwick, York, Hull, Newcastle, and Carlisle.[218] The imagined borders of the wider archipelago indicate as much as Burghley himself would avow of his views on the eventual succession:

> I wishe it weare nowe afore hand, sent to him by order of hir ma[jes]ty hearbie to move him to take hart to him against the k[ing] of Spaines tirannous practizes, and particularlye at this time to require him to geve order to the hand as in the Northe part of his Realme,

The grouping of the Spanish incursions along the peripheries and into the heartland of the Queen's two realms was inseparable from Burghley's mental map of the Queen's kingdom. Burghley's concern over Ireland and possible Jesuit intelligence in 1595–1596 was to impose order in the Isle of Man and the coastal regions of the western coasts of Wales and Cheshire as well.[219] Referring to the fortification of Milford Haven, on 10 October 1595, he asked his son to inform the earl of Pembroke: 'which being uncertain may bring danger considering all Comen reportes from Spayne mak mention of the Haven'.[220] Burghley linked negotiations on Ireland and Scotland as a piece with the kinds of campaigns he had engineered against Persons and his fellow-writers.

---

[218] Letters Nos 79, 83. See also Letter No. 59; *CPR 38 Eliz. 1*, no. 1065. Huntingdon's remit was extended for the entire council to hear 'real and personal actions in cases where the poverty of one or both the parties impedes the ordinary execution of justice' – the membership of which included Privy Council links. Robert Beale was their secretary as well as a clerk of the Privy Council. Edward Stanhope, whose brother, Sir John, was master of the posts and treasurer of the Chamber, was also a member. Both men were close to both Burghley and Sir Robert Cecil and were viewed with favour. On occasion, they acted as messengers. See Letters Nos 45. 80, 94.

[219] Letter No. 66.

[220] Letter No. 64.

War and Ireland, 1595–1598

The Cecils cannot have predicted the impetus the Irish situation would take: £2 million pounds and thousands of men creating a virtual sinkhole of reputations – primarily Essex's – and resources, ending in 1602. Spanish war policy had shifted (sparing the Low Countries); and as the rebels increased in strength over 1595–1596 the weight of Burghley's mind in the letters had moved somewhat radically to Irish affairs. As the protracted negotiation and 'reduction' of the rebels failed repeatedly and the English war administration fell further into the morass, Burghley came to see the Queen as radically isolated, abandoned by those she had aided, France and the Low Countries. He was to characterize England's sole option as a concentration on gaining hold of the Queen's 'second realm', as 'havyng no hope nor apparence to be ayded by any other'.[221] However, in 1593, Ireland had not been foremost in anyone's mind in the Privy Council. In December 1593, while Zouche was being primed for his factional work at the Scottish court, Simon Willis had made a long list of reasons why no new assistance should go into Ireland until the spring. The rebellion there was just beginning. The French king's conversion and long series of abortive embassies from him – all handled by Cecil's correspondence – were nonetheless marked by crises. The English efforts in fulfilling the Treaty of Nonsuch with the States General of the Netherlands were under strain. In 1594 the collapse of the English system in Ireland was not anticipated.[222]

If Norris's move there from France in 1595 spelled a decisive move in retrospect, his officers were dispersed into commands secondary to existing Irish place-holders. What might have been a coherent military force with a strategy disappeared into the morass of Irish confusion. Burghley's concern for this situation, however rhetorical, ran against the concerns of those such as Essex who still rallied for continental commitment. This tension dominates the letters. Burghley was in support of Norris until his death in 1597, the best English military commander of experience. In 1595 lists of officers who had held command, notably foreign, since 1585 were drawn up for consideration by the Council. The dead and retired names subtracted still left a sizeable number of able officers. Captains with foreign experience were valuable, did not by statute interfere with trained bands in the shires or militia, and could, if needed, be persuaded to

[221] Letter No. 120.
[222] Rapple, *Martial Power*, 17.

Irish service. The lists may also have been devised as a way of tracking Essex's dominance of military matters.[223]

Cecil's counsel with the Queen was, by then, the primary source for Burghley's conservative ideas about expenditure. The later letters, 1596–1598, repeat Burghley's anxieties about a kingdom disabled with foreign military aid. Rising expense in Ireland and disputes with the States General in the Low Countries caused by the rumours of an imminent Franco-Spanish peace after 1596, were punctuated by the need for immediate relief for Henry IV in the Catholic League's attacks at Calais and Amiens in May 1596 and March 1597. Burghley wanted financial matters with the Dutch put on terms of the treaty and accounts rendered without the Queen shouldering undue burdens. These monies, he balanced against the rising cost of dealing with the Irish rebels O'Neill and O'Donnell: many of these letters relay Burghley's comments on estimates, decays, shortfalls, and needs emanating from Ireland, principally relating to Sir John Norris.[224]

As Burghley characterized Ireland, 'ther is no good newes'. Low Countries military estimates and indebtedness would be tied directly to Irish needs in Burghley's calculation as the Irish news worsened by mid decade: to find money out of an existing treaty which mandated approximately £120,000 a year for the cautionary towns and garrisons there meant arguing with the Dutch over privy seals lent but not repaid. Hence, much of the negotiations with the States General by Sir Thomas Bodley and others (Noel de Caron, the States General's English agent, and Sir Edmund Uvedale, the Queen's envoy to the *Raad van Staat*) were, privately, another aspect of the Irish debacle for Burghley.[225] On 12 May 1594 his comment on the Queen's unhappiness with Bodley's progress with the States and his return 'upon ther advise' was bleak: 'hir Ma[jes]ty is now also provoked in Irland to enter into a charg not estimable, wherto she hath no hop of any help, but of hyndrance by Spayne and otherwise'.[226] Burghley's letters here join the parts not always visible in the various classes of state papers. The States General would continue to press hard in negotiations with the Queen over the relative share expended in her cautionary towns and auxiliary forces against their common Spanish enemy, as peace between Spain and France was being rumoured in late 1596.[227]

Burghley could relent in his drive to have Henry IV make good his debts: Burghley's extraordinary upset at the assault on Calais by the League in 1596 showed his financial concerns were tempered by strategic matters.[228] The capture of Amiens by Spanish and Leaguer forces in March 1597 saw him urging immediate supply, 'I wish hir Ma[jes]ty without delay whilest the fr[ench] k[ing's] Irons ar hott supply him nombres for 2 or 3 monethes'.[229] Once the money was sent, Henry IV continued his peace negotiations, knowing the Archduke Albert was without funds to continue the siege of Amiens, earning Burghley's terse comment: 'this chantyng of peace, is a song only to allure the Q[ueen's] Ma[jes]tie to yeld hym still aide of more men or monny or both'.[230] As for Bodley, Burghley may have suspected he was too close to Essex despite his usefulness as an ambassador. The disputes over the Queen's cautionary towns were augmented by criticism by the Queen's own servants: Sir Robert Sidney, governor of Flushing, had complained pointedly to Essex in these matters. His deputy, Sir William Uvedall, who returned to England in October 1595, was to be provided royal entrée and a long conversation with Cecil, 'being as I thinke unkowen to yowe, is one who hath longe served hir Ma[jes]tie both faithfullie and carefullie in his charge at Fflushing and in other services in the Lowe Contries'. Burghley's balancing of Sidney's complaint and Bodley's information included a command for a private royal audience with Cecil in attendance. For as he told his son, 'I have been more beholding to this gentleman for his often writing to mee than to anie other'.[231]

While continental matters flared occasionally in the uneasy moves towards French-Spanish peace in November 1596, the demands in Ireland were provoking dangerous conditions: 'therfor I pray yow whan tyme may serve yow, lett hir Ma[jes]ty know that I do send to heare of hir Ma[jes]ty's ammendment for by hir impediments to order hir affayres, all hir realme shall suffer detriment'.[232] This was not favouring Ireland over, for example, the Low Countries. When Sir Robert Sidney's repeated requests for assistance at Flushing in late 1597 were rebuffed by the Queen's desire to reduce her charge, Burghley expostulated, 'This lack of a resolut answer from hir Ma[jes]ty dryveth to the wall'. Elizabeth did not enjoy spending money, particularly on war. Cecil's difficult position in these many instructions from his father was to remind the Queen

[228] Letters Nos 89, 90–92.
[229] Letters Nos 115–117.
[230] Letter No. 117.
[231] Letter No. 62.
[232] Letter No. 108.

'hir people suffre great extremite for want of releff of monny and clothes'.[233]

It was only later that Norris's 'revocation' or redeployment of his forces from France through the Channel Islands into Ireland from late 1593 assumed great significance. The rising rebellion and beginning of the Nine Years War in 1594 was not yet fully in view. With hindsight and perspective Burghley's detailed projection of Norris's movement, outlined in Letter No. 14, would have far-reaching repercussions across negotiations with the Low Countries and France, and ultimately give rise to deep and irrevocable divisions on the Privy Council. Burghley referred to his son a 'barren' Irish letter as the Privy Council rift began to open.[234] He replied with pessimism to an equally unfortunate set of Irish dispatches as he returned them to his son.[235] The quarrels of the lord deputy, Sir William Russell, with Sir John Norris over precedence, policy, and jurisdiction were given over to Cecil as he had more energy and access to the Queen and Council to deal with their incessant bickering.[236] The Irish rift mirrored growing distemper in the Queen's Privy Council over deployment of limited resources.

In December 1595, once he arrived and was established, Norris was fully in enmity with Russell. Norris was receiving intelligence from spies formerly in Brittany and in Galway who sent reports of Spanish designs on Ireland, no longer strictly French matters.[237] Some of those men examined were former priests in the Low Countries who had served French Leaguers, such as the duke of Mercouer, with connections to Spaniards investigated by Cecil at the taking of the *Madre di Dios*.[238] Up to his death in 1597, Norris occupied a critical place in Burghley's calculations despite exceeding his warrant for command outside Connacht. Norris was not the Cecils' only connection: a wide variety of office-holders from the lord deputy and provincial governors and their colleagues and servants sent masses of letters which grew only larger and more complex during the year 1594. On 25 April 1594 Burghley was working closely with his son on these matters: 'I marvell that I heare not from yow concerning the letters to be sent into Irland wyther also I have in redynes some from myself'.[239] But the presenting issue was Burghley and the lord deputy, Russell, falling into open conflict, apparently over control of captains' nominations. Russell refused to let Burghley open his packets alone, implying someone

---

[233] Letter No. 112.
[234] Letter No. 61.
[235] Letters Nos 61, 75.
[236] Letter No. 76.
[237] Letters Nos 70, 76.
[238] See Letter No. 70.
[239] Letter No. 19.

(perhaps the Queen or Essex ought to be present) so, 'I have not opened . . . as upon a Caveat geven upon the last sent from thence' and they arrived sealed for Robert's reading of them to the Queen.[240] Burghley did open Russell's letters in late December 1594 but he was simply too ill to comment merely telling Robert of their import, papers 'to be nowe diligentlie perused'. In February 1595 Burghley refused personal replies to the lord deputy: 'without prescribing to him any direction until her Ma[jes]ty shall direct the same'; 'I send yow a Copy of my privat letter, which may be affirmed or controlled by a more Generall letter from the Connsell'. Burghley's particular views – mostly relating to the squandering of money – had to be heard in the context of the Queen's and Council's views when they were opened with trepidation in Dublin, presumably with his son's own increasingly large number of letters sent in the Dublin packet. On occasion, despite Burghley's regular receipt of Irish letters until his death, he was informed by his son of the Queen's wishes: in December of 1595, 'I am glad that hir Ma[jes]ty us disposed to send some monny into Irland where suerly there is great want a matter dangerous to be known to ye rebells . . . I send yow a form for a warrant wherin hir Ma[jes]ty may do well to allow some good rownd some'.[241] A month later, Burghley sent news of Ireland of 'great Dannger'.[242] Burghley and Cecil clearly supported Sir John Norris in his quarrels with the lord deputy into which they were drawn: 'I wish my Lord [Russell] had such skill or good Luck in his government as ther neded no advertisement or advise but from hym self'.[243]

Russell, Burghley's irritant, was recalled in 1597. The Cecils meanwhile cultivated Geoffrey Fenton, obtaining a crucial place for him on the Irish council. Emboldened by his new closeness to Cecil and Sir John Norris, in early 1596 Sir Geoffrey Fenton loyally attacked the lord deputy in a letter to the Cecils. He implied (as ever in Ireland) that Russell had an inflated view of his administrative powers and was acting high-handedly. Fenton's lengthy petition to the Privy Council called for a strict ordering of both the Secretary's and surveyor general's offices which may, again, have been a mirror of the Cecils' own plans for ordering the Queen's secretarial matters:

> The Queen in her special instruction dated Greenwich 26, 1585, appointed
> that her chief secretary in Ireland should have the making of all bills, warrants,
> and other writings to pass by the signature of the lord Deputy or other head

[240] Letter No. 27.
[241] Letter No. 73.
[242] Letter No. 75.
[243] Letter No. 91.

governors there; but this is usurped from him by the deputies countenancing their private secretaries.[244]

In the margin of the manuscript is Fenton's instruction to Cecil that 'The Lord treaso[re]r's or your H[onour's] letter effectuallie written to ye new L Dep[uty] will suffyse for this', asking for the specific inclusion of a clause challenging any man's pretence or challenge 'to the same'. This makes the equation between Russell's removal and opening the way for Fenton as a powerful force in the Irish administration. Fenton and Norris were appointed by the Queen with the Cecils' strong support to investigate claims against the lord president of Connacht, Sir Richard Bingham – the captains' cabal having defeated him in his home territory.[245] Essex had cultivated Bingham, governor of Connacht since 1585, a 'licensed grotesque' whose lawlessness had saved the Crown money but whose disdain for the common law had earned repeated and lengthy investigations.[246] While Bingham was resuscitated with the earl's assistance, Norris's pre-eminence and explicit Cecilian favour was coupled with Fenton's control of paper.

But it was the Queen, not merely faction, who posed impediments (as in Calais in May 1596 and the Low Countries in late 1596) to ready supply, calling forth yet again Burghley's exasperation, 'if she shall still rest uppon stryct poyntes as I have noted she hath doone in all these Irish charges'.[247] Burghley saw that money, or at least the appearance of care, was vital in suppressing the rebel support. When the Queen finally proclaimed O'Neill and O'Donnell traitors in July 1596 he continued the theme 'therefor hir Ma[jes]ty must be forced for a present farder chardg, to proceede more rowndly with force than with words'.[248] These were very strong words, moving the Queen with profound emotion where Burghley could not 'expresse the grief to thinke of the dangerous estate of hir ma[jes]ties' Armie in Ireland', with money squandered and supply vanished, 'what great danger this maie be I doe trembell to utter, consideringe theie [the army] will force the Countrie with all manner of oppressions, rather than furnishe', an accurate assessment of how the Queen's parsimony was wasting her alliances as fast as her military resources.[249] Former close allies to the Crown, especially among the Old English families in the Pale, were

[244]Modernized spelling: *Acts of the Privy Council, 1597*, ed. J.R. Dasent (London, 1890–1964), 393.
[245]See Rapple on Bingham: *Martial Power*, 250–300.
[246]Ibid. 297.
[247]Letter No. 91.
[248]Letter No. 99, 16 July 1596.
[249]Letter No. 103.

now worryingly and anxiously seen to be moving into the penumbra of the rebels themselves.[250]

Burghley's reliance on Howard and Norris obliquely reflects Burghley's pointing away from Essex as the sole military adviser par excellence; he remained consistently loyal throughout Norris's long journey through the Scillies into Ireland, and after his arrival in April 1595, continued to be so, despite obstacles from the new Lord Deputy, Russell, in Dublin. Norris was, alone, 'reasonable'. Burghley's preference for Norris as the Queen's leading land commander doubtless rankled Essex. His theme was established in Letter No. 14 which carries throughout the letters here.[251] The sampling of these letters bears out Irish causes as definitively disorganized: there were 'allredy to manny lose men' in 1593.[252] In 1595, when Norris and Russell fought over nominations, Burghley cast about for suitable military leadership, 'there are noo Capt. in bogland than ar to serve with the ii M [2,000 men] whereof regard wold be had what shall become of them'.[253] Many of the 1595 Low Countries' captains who had moved with Norris into Ireland had no connection with previous Irish conflict, office-holding, or family affiliation there. The existing Irish captains were older, of long experience, and held considerable numbers of offices, lands, and local influence, or were of great family. In the summer of 1595 these Normandy troops were broken up and assigned to separate services as designated by the Irish Council.[254] Sir John Norris's anger with the lord deputy's decision to reduce the Irish companies from 19 to 12 in early 1595 was a battle over official powers.[255]

> And so I return to yow Sir Jhon Norrices letters wherby I see a manifest disiunction betwixt the L[ord] depute and hym and in on part I note that Sir

---

[250] Ruth Canning, 'James Fitzpiers Fitzgerald, Captain Thomas Lee, and the problem of "secret traitors": Conflicted loyalties during the Nine Years War, 1594–1603', *Irish Historical Studies*, 156 (2015), 573–594.

[251] For references to Sir John Norris's progress from Brittany to the Scillies and thence into Ireland: Letters Nos 13, 14, 17, 37, 40, 43, 48, 51, 54, 70, 76, 82, 91.

[252] Letter No. 9.

[253] Letter No. 40.

[254] This was a protracted process: see Burghley's directives to his son, Letter No 14, 7 Dec. 1593, in which the proposed move is debated in the Council and by the Queen. Sir John Norris's letters to Burghley dated 31 Oct. 1593, dated from Pontrieux: TNA SP 78/32/fols. 273r–274v; *L&A*, iv, Analysis: nos 277, 283, 397.

[255] The year before Russell had already moved to stop external nominations for Irish captaincies: Russell petitioned Cecil for the swift sending of money into Ireland in the packet of 12 Sept. 1594 in which he also asked for the Queen's further instructions on how to deal with the rebels, TNA SP 63/176/no. 16, fol. 47r. Six hundred men were sent in August, and Russell asked that no new captains be appointed as so many other petitioners begged places, *CSPI 1592–1596*, 264; TNA SP 63/175/no. 62.

Jhon Norrice, was to bold to command the Companyes in the english pale for Wat[er]ford, with out assent of the deputie, for out of Monster he hath no sole authorite.

Then:

'I feare contynually evil desasters'.[256]

Yet, Norris was given the right to nominate 30 captaincies – a startling piece of patronage when the 1595–1596 lists of officers with 'foreigne service', then drawn under instructions by the Privy Council, are considered.[257] Norris's backing by the Cecils in Ireland from April 1595 had greater influence than the lacklustre Russell whose tepid Essexian connection capped an undistinguished military career. Nonetheless, the Irish situation was growing worse in particular areas, and in early January 1596 Burghley knew the forces had to be increased and improved.[258] By March, Russell had attempted to control correspondence on all matters: 'I understand that my L[ord] Depute hath gyven commandment by his french man, that no letters are to be suffred to pass owt of Irland to me, but by his L[ord's] own warrant, what his L[ord] meneth hereby I know not thogh I can probably gess, for herein yow ar also included'. Men were leaving at a higher rate than were being sent, 'so [Peter] proby [in charge of the Chester and Irish posts] wryteth to me'. Russell complained to Burghley: 'all his family ar sought out by me'; his dark reply to Sir Robert: 'I wish they did not deserve to be sought owt'. Sir Robert had already received his father's caution of 'great Dannger' in Ireland received in early January 1596: 'I leave to yow the perusal and impartyng of these Irish bad letters to hir Ma[jes]tie and the Connsell'. The draft of the Queen's scathing letter to Russell about gross financial mismanagement and the squandering of treasure by her Irish servants ended with a paragraph in Sir Robert's

---

[256]Letter No. 76. The previous Letters Nos 74 and 75 convey the terrible Irish news in January 1596. Russell's and Norris's enmity here reached a new pitch: Norris contravened the lord deputy's warrant for raising troops – particularly where his only jurisdiction for doing do was as lord president of Munster – and had also overstepped his jurisdiction in treating with the rebels.TNA SP 63/185/no 11, fol. 27r–v. Animosity between these men dated from the time of Norris's appointment (Norris to Cecil, 4 June 1595, TNA SP 63/180/no. 9, fol. 43v; *CSPI 1592–1596*, 323–326, 323). Russell bore the brunt of the Queen's displeasure over the loss of the fort at Monaghan, on top of other charges of incompetence he was concerned to deny (ibid.; TNA SP 63/185/fol. 31r, 186/no. 6, fols. 14r–16r). The earl of Essex apparently vilified Russell at every turn, *HMCD*, ii, 197–198. In Feb. 1596 Russell alluded to Sir John and Sir Thomas Norris's continued presence in Dublin, away from their respective charges in Ulster and Munster, TNA SP 63/186/fol. 196v; *CSPI 1592–1596*, 472. The two men were allied in the efforts in Armagh during that summer.

[257]TNA SP 63/179/no. 31, fol. 68r, Norris to Cecil, 14 Apr. 1595, his first mention of Russell.

[258]*CSPI 1592–1596*, 446.

own hand warning the lord deputy against Irish councillors using war treasure for private patronage.[259]

The war council in 1597 of Essex, Raleigh, and Howard was charged with bringing order to musters, army administration, supply and transportation. Financial reform had to be attempted in Ireland. In April 1597 a cognate commission under letters patent was appointed to examine the Irish and Low Countries' war accounts. Its members included the chief financial officers of the realm: significantly both Cecils, Sir Thomas Egerton (lord keeper), Sir John Fortescue (chancellor of the Exchequer), Lord North (treasurer of the Household), Sir William Periam (chief baron of the Exchequer) and Thomas, Lord Buckhurst. They were to examine Sir Henry Wallop's Irish account 'at his own charge' for 'sundry great sums'.[260] Of these, only North, a Cecil friend and privy councillor from 1596, is mentioned here, negotiating apparel with James Jolles for Ireland.[261] Burghley's Irish laments on missing or misappropriated funds sent to various officers – lord deputies, the treasurer at war, Sir Henry Wallop, Norris and other regional commanders – dovetailed with anxieties over the Low Countries' slowness in repaying their debts to the Queen and Henry IV's manifest self-interest in preserving his crown during continued Spanish occupation in Brittany and elsewhere.[262] The deep-seated problems of finance and supply of men at arms was never resolved in a systematic way – later innovations such as Irish bills of exchange and downgrading treasurers to less costly paymasters (as with William Meredith in the Low Countries from 1597) seemed stuck in an existing system of Irish official patronage and mismanaged accounts by venal captains. While Burghley deplored the captain who deliberately 'spoiled' the good soldier, righting the finances of war proved impossible so long as the various supply systems relied on contractors' profiteering and captains' wastage of the Queen's resources. A pivotal point came in 1593 with the discovery that Sir Thomas Sherley's Low Countries' accounts, then in the process of being declared at the Exchequer (where Burghley's former secretary Vincent Skinner was now an auditor in the prests) for 1585/6, and after, revealed extraordinary systemic peculation, far in excess of what might usually be expected of a treasurer – Henry Maynard was also partially implicated. Investigation for massive embezzlement had far-reaching financial repercussions for the government, captains, and

---

[259] Letter No. 75.

[260] *CPR 39 Eliz I*, no. 285.

[261] Letter No. 134.

[262] For a typical example of Burghley's excoriation of Henry IV's motives see Letter No. 63.

merchants.[263] Massive losses led to a long series of financial investigations into declared accounts lasting two decades – and included Sherley's bankruptcy once his inadequate lands were liquidated. Thence, the Low Countries' account ran under a lesser officer, William Meredith as paymaster in June 1597.[264] The Irish accounts would include bills of exchange after Wallop's death in 1599 (and final staggering indebtedness was calculated), as well as being remitted to a paymaster rather than a treasurer at war.

The war council's amity soon broke into enmity: Essex's first serious explosions seemed to occur within the military cabal of the council of war in 1597. Placing him in opposition to the Cecils, however, must be done with great care. Essex's working papers vanished or were burned at his downfall so the actual reforms he may have anticipated in Ireland and elsewhere can only be speculation. Indeed, until 1598 Essex seems curiously absent from the one arena which gave Burghley greatest anxiety: the letters here suggest that Essex's continental ventures were heavily offset by Irish rebellion by the time of Burghley's death, a position Essex could not reverse afterwards once Franco-Spanish peace was made without further large-scale relief for the Low Countries. Relief, such as that required in the catastrophic French loss of Amiens to the Spanish in 1597, was, however heavy, fitful, and crisis-driven. If Essex wished to support Henry IV in a massive campaign to rid Brittany and Normandy entirely of Spanish military he was unable to secure it before Robert Cecil went to France in February 1598. His vicious attack on the Queen in November 1597, turning his back on her, was probably the moment when she, and Burghley, realized the earl was incapable of trust.

Ireland, the Queen's 'second realm' posed intractable problems of loyalty, command, debatable alliances, and shifting borders; perhaps the dominance of Ireland in Burghley's calculation was simply that not a single European ally, no crowned head or army, would come to her aid. Events following the death of Philip II soon after Burghley's death in September 1598 bore out his instinct that, however the French, Dutch, and Spanish pursued an uneasy peace, Elizabeth, the great heretic queen, would not be spared continual Spanish aggression and Spanish cultivation of her rebels O'Neill and O'Donnell.

---

[263] Letters Nos 113 and 114. Sherley was importuning Cecil for favours into 1597 when the full extent of his wrongdoing was revealed; imprisoned with his goods and properties sold, his case implicated other suppliers such as William Beecher or Becher (see Letters Nos 113, 114), a City merchant Sherley sued on his account for nearly £19,000. *HMCS, viii*, 447–448. For Sherley, see ibid. 36, 177, 237, 313, 339, 367.

[264] *CPR 39 Eliz I*, no. 286.

The trajectory of opposition to Essex's coalescing support for the revived continental military strategies of Leicester and others in the 1580s forms a subtle but indelible counterpoint to the Lord Treasurer's private anxieties. Burghley, by contrast, saw 'no lykhood of peace' in July 1596 only the necessity of sending more money into Ireland; in August 1597 he rushed to his son the warrants for Irish apparel.[265] A day later he implored his son to send the Irish and Berwick warrants immediately 'ffor both theise hold the Quene's service in suspence untill by these warrants I may procede'.[266] Letter No. 132 is solely concerned with the form of warrants to be sent for Irish apparel as paid for out of the Exchequer by letters under Privy Seal, whereby the forces in Ireland are shown to have increased by 1,000 men over the August 27 warrants urged on Cecil by his father.[267] This last letter points to an escalation in military commitment towards the subjugation of the Irish rebellion. Moreover, Burghley stressed that the increase in payment was to be taken out of the new bands' pay, a usual procedure. A group of merchants appointed by the Crown had agreed to procure the necessary supplies for a certain price which would increase the Queen's profit by one-third of a penny.[268] Among the final letters are three strong motions by Burghley for the better ordering of Irish supply and musters.[269]

Burghley's mounting fears over the Irish systemic faults were derived from his encyclopaedic understanding of the places and offices the Tudor conquest had entailed, and his chosen military leader, John Norris, he saw as an Irish placeholder removed from direct control of the Irish council: 'For the boglish, I think if uppon the last direction Sir Jhon norrice shall be come awey, yet my opinion Contynueth for retyring the forces to the Isles, for which lyk comission wuld be gyven to Sir Jhon Norryce electu.'[270] In the Queen's 'establishment' out of the council in Dublin chaos reigned: in December 1593, Burghley sought to bring the war account into line with the sinecures and payments of offices, doubtless in the growing disorders coming to view in Sherley's accounts as well as the catastrophic shortfall in the ordinary revenue (cess) in the Pale.[271] 'And for the questions what somme of money might be reasonablie required I think 5 or 6000 £ [pounds] varie nedefull so

[265] Letters Nos 99, 124.

[266] Letter No. 125.

[267] Letter No. 132.

[268] Ibid.

[269] Letters Nos 134, 135, 137.

[270] For the threat to Sir John Norris's forces at this juncture, Wernham, *After the Armada*, 521.

[271] See Burghley's metaphorical reference above in Letter No. 10, 7 Dec. 1593, where Ireland was certainly a cause of 'fowle' weather with the Queen.

as Sir Henry Wallopp be moved to procure payment of the overplus of the Quene's ordinarie Revennue ^{due} there above al ordinarye ffees for officers of the Realm payd.[272] In the first case, Norris's 'revocation' was halted in the Scillies with Burghley's approval charged on a separate account. Burghley's estimates for future Irish expenses against the rebels, under Norris or any other commander, would produce a large shortfall in the ordinary revenue. Wallop's accuracy became pivotal for the first time since the Desmond rebellion in 1583 and he was completely unaware. When news of Tyrone's rising together with the rebel Maguire hastened the desire to relocate Norris and his officers to Ireland, Burghley sent his son the journal of the Irish marshal, Sir Henry Bagenal, in 1593 for a sense of the overall situation which would coalesce into open rebellion and war soon thereafter.[273] Wallop's estimates and accounts were so parlous as to require his presence at court with a private meeting with Burghley.[274] Their conference had little effect thereafter in a worsening situation where treasure went missing and supplies disappeared.[275] Sir Robert Gardener, chief justice of the Queen's Bench in Ireland, was summoned in early 1596 to make sense of the Irish account: 'I send yow herwith ii bundells of Ireland letters and wrytyngs containing a chaos of matters to be Metamorphosed as I thynk into some perfection';[276] the Queen was too furious to receive Gardener.

The deepest fear, civil war, the entire second realm rising against the Queen, looked possible in October 1596.[277] Two thousand further men sent in October had no money for pay. Burghley's conclusion:

[272]The matter of paying the patentees of Ireland out of deteriorating Irish revenues was put to Burghley by the Irish treasurer at war Sir Henry Wallop (then at Hampton Court) on 6 Dec. 1593, when he expressed frustration that the entire revenues from Connacht went to Sir Richard Bingham, and those of Munster to Sir Thomas Norreys. *CSPI 1592–1596*, 190; TNA SP 63/172/no. 37. The expenses for these standing allowances were balanced against an extraordinary payment of five to six thousand pounds in December 1593 sent to pay the troops and garrisons. A Privy Council brief in Willis's hand, endorsed by Cecil discussed the question of proceeding with a campaign against the rebel Maguire, TNA SP 63/172/no. 43, fols. 234r–v, 235v. Cecil was waiting for the Queen's assent. But winter was not good for such a campaign as victualling and supplies were at a premium and very expensive. Money: (fol. 234v) 'of necessitie some money would be sent to Ireland, for all that was last sent is distributed the souldiers imprest'. This undated document is filed as early Dec. 1593.
[273]Letters Nos 27, 9, 8.
[274]Letters Nos 15, 33, 37, 38.
[275]Letters Nos 81, 82, 99.
[276]TNA SP 63/186/no. 79, fol. 249r, Burghley to Cecil, 22 Feb. 1596; and for Sir Robert Gardener, see Andrew Thrush and John P. Ferris (eds.), *The House of Commons, 1604–1629*, 6 vols (Cambridge, 2010), IV, 337–338.
[277]*HMCS*, vi, 356, Russell's letter to the Queen, 28 Aug. 1596.

'And thearebie the multitude of the Q[ueen s] loiall subiectes in the English pale tempted to Rebell'.[278]

In 1597 Burghley's growing exasperation was less with Essex's aggressive move to support continental war than with generally incompetent financial officers and military officers. His irritation in 1597 and 1598 was openly dismissive of English as well as Irish tactics. The extent to which Burghley's upset was rhetorical is open to question, for he was in no haste to send money to Ireland to be squandered. Burghley outlined his summary of the debacle: 'but I lament yt, to see the great wastes of people of the Inglishe, and of Armor and municion, and of the Contries charges in Leveinge to be soe great as it is'.[279] Burghley died shortly before the disastrous Battle of the Yellow Ford, the assault to provision troops at Lough Foyle within striking distance of Tyrone's troops in late summer 1598. Then followed outright barbarity by the English troops when supply arrived soon thereafter in September. Money had been inadequate for feeding and clothing his men. Munition was disappearing. The new lord deputy, Thomas 3rd Lord Burgh, had warned of this repeatedly: he wrote in desperation for more arms in early October 1597 just before his death. Burghley noted that he was stalled in responding to this need because of inadequate information, a tactic his son would use later with Essex's ill-fated army in 1599. Remarking on the 'decaie', presumably accounted for by dead pays and deaths among the soldiers with false accounting or theft: 'I knowe not howe the Capteins are excusable for their Armors and weapons which properlie do not die of anie disease'.[280] Maurice Kyffin, muster master, accused Sir Ralph Lane, muster master general, in a private letter to Cecil for 'still certifying my checks as his own' without due correction from above, 'living here in the midst of bribery and extortion', abetted by Burgh.[281] Burgh received a blistering letter from Cecil, as did Wallop who was perturbed by Burghley's 'offence' at his failures to administer the army. Robert Cecil undoubtedly echoed his father's calculations while on his French embassy, for in March 1598 he wrote (with John Herbert) of Henry IV's renewed plea to the Queen for enough resources to expunge his territories of Spanish troops:

> We finding in them this speech, did plainly let them know that her Majesty's fleets at sea and armies which have been sent to make a diversion of the enemy's forces, besides many other great charges in Ireland and elsewhere, have so much increased on her, as she would be well advised how to engage

---

[278] Letter No. 103.
[279] See Letter No. 127.
[280] See Letter No. 127.
[281] Lane to Cecil, *CSPI 1596–1597*, 391. For Kyffin (1555–1598), see *ODNB*.

herself suddenly for others, especially seeing lieu of all that she had purchased for them, she never was yet remboursed of one half penny.[282]

A briefing paper for the embassy noted that those of the 'Religion' were panicking Henry IV away from the peace he so clearly desired but would not admit to during negotiations; meanwhile the *noblesse de robe* and other officeholders were desperate to pick up on peacetime revenues. Only the pro-Spanish nobility were to be watched as they pretended to love peace, but loved Spanish power more.[283]

Wallop's account was in complete disarray; another weapon for the Cecils to use with the Queen against him. He could not send anything for the Exchequer year ending September 1597, which caused Burghley great distress as he, with others, investigated his losses. Tyrone and his confederates had taken control of Ulster entirely, with massive inroads into Connacht, this partly because of Sir Richard Bingham's sequestration. Thus, two large musters were deemed imperative in the summer of 1598. Burghley, already very weak, castigated the Queen and Privy Council for their 'preposterous connsell' in arranging victuals after the troops had been sent.[284] Of the musters, he could not fathom why Lincolnshire men were being sent to Plymouth, and from Cornwall to Bristol by land 'which maie be done with ease by sea, wheare the other must marche over all the Land'.[285] The victuals arrived after Burghley died, in September 1598.

Cecil asked Essex, as earl marshal, in June 1598 for warrants for ordnance to be sent into Ireland: 'I have thought it my part to advertise you thereof that you may please to give direction for such things as appertain to the despatch, which being only incident to your lordship's place [master of the Ordnance in succession to Sir George Carew], I am forced to trouble you with this letter, which otherwise I would have foreborne in respect that I understand of your lordship's dislike to be cumbered with anything not necessary'.[286] A radical shift at Burghley's death was already anticipated; Essex's apparent lack of interest here must be offset by the hundred horse sent from Carmarthenshire for the Irish offensive – the Welsh supply was timely and connected to the earl's own influence. But the earl had not held a major office of state until 1597 when he exercised control over military direction arguing for the high aristocratic office following Lord Nottingham's

[282] *HMCS*, viii, 110, Cecil and Herbert to the Privy Council, 27 Mar. 1598.
[283] *HMCS*, viii, 7–9.
[284] See Roger Houghton to Cecil, 25 Mar. 1598, *HMCS*, viii, 102.
[285] Letters Nos 134, 137.
[286] *HMCS*, viii, 285, Cecil to Essex. Burghley had received the warrants as lord lieutenant of Lincolnshire, Hertfordshire and Essex, 18 July 1598, ibid. 264.

recent elevation to an earldom. During early 1598 Essex continued to champion the Low Countries' causes as most significant for England, while pro tem Secretary because Cecil was in France.[287] A hint emerges of Essex's fatigue and upset over the continued Franco-Spanish peace effort as Ireland took highest priority in Burghley's and the Queen's calculations. Cecil's remark suggests Essex found the work of reforming the military hard, if not impossible, particularly as Burghley's last missives pledge commitment to the Irish wars. Burghley was consumed by the defeat of the Queen's rebels. Ireland remained firmly outside the earl's sights as Burghley died, truly 'not necessary'.[288] Essex went into a long absence from court and Council lasting until September 1598.[289]

After lengthy treatises by his innermost circle decrying Spanish peace as disastrous and ideologically abhorrent, the current moved strongly in another direction: 'it is possible to comprehend how Essex became so easily and unswervingly convinced that a Cecilian faction plotted to divert the succession of the crown to Spain, and was so quick to identify the secretary – with unparalleled access to the Queen and power on the council – as England's deadliest enemy'. Essex's concept of Cecil had begun to conflate his secretarial dominance of the Queen, a weak tyrant whose establishment rejected the Essexians, with the despotic power of the Spanish crown, thus a mere *Irish* war against Spanish-backed rebels took energy from the wider case against the growing authoritarianism of his own Queen. Essex's alliance with Dutch republican rejection of the archdukes conformed to this 'hardened' direction at the very end of Burghley's life.[290] Alexandra Gajda's reconstruction of Essex's policies at this time grounded in pro-continental war ideological tracts frame Burghley's last letters as tacitly and resolutely opposed to Essex.

---

[287] Gajda, *The Earl of Essex*, 98–99.

[288] Gajda, *The Earl of Essex*, 101 on Essex's failure in Low Countries' policy as a platform for war against Spain, which may have caused Cecil to be cautious in approaching the earl. The earl dismissed Ireland: 'a miserable, beggarly *Irish* war'. Gajda's discussion of the treatises pro-peace and pro-war, noted Essex's partisans continued strong language about the despotism of Philip II. When the Spanish king died a month after Burghley, the Irish war continued. Cecil, the Queen and others supported peace on the continent with the Archdukes Albert and Isabella. Gajda discusses these treatises, Cecil's comment on the 'coldness' of England's Dutch allies, with the eventual establishment of the archdukes in Brussels, friendly to Elizabeth, ibid. 103–107. This turn represented the final, bitter, continental policy defeat before Essex's isolation from the Council and before his taking the Irish command in Apr. 1599.

[289] Ibid. 98–99. Essex was made master of the Ordnance in 1597, a position he used to better relations with Noel de Caron, and with the Queen's principal military there, to no avail.

[290] Ibid. 107.

P.M. Handover commented on Burghley's death that 'a monolith had fallen':[291] it left the Queen and Essex, particularly, inconsolable. The earl's political career would not recover from his *lèse-majesté*. Indeed, the patronage and intellectual tone of his coterie would rail against Cecil and the Queen, bringing Essex's failure in Ireland into open rebellion, events which cannot have been adumbrated in Burghley's incessant Irish policies in the last months of his life. Nonetheless, the letters here illustrate the financial weight of his calculations and those of his son moving against further continental commitments, as championed by Essex and some of his followers. The Cecils were clearly working on the Queen's psyche over the potential loss of her second realm and the attendant chaos in her Protestant estate. The extent of their direction cannot be underestimated here.

The Queen would not hear Burghley's name spoken and was often in tears in the months after his death. But the psychological effect on Cecil himself must have been the greatest. He would have been both relieved and deeply bereft on his father's peaceful death. But there would have been an extraordinary change in the way in which he worked and negotiated the court. Cecil, of course, inherited the firm control of paper and policy his father had bequeathed. But as the 'polarization(s)' of court, Ireland, Council and personal enmities grew worse, Cecil seemed to withdraw without his father's more social and avuncular presence (despite the great infirmity of his last years). These letters illustrate the extraordinary piling up of work, policy, and influence. Together they give a glimpse of an extraordinary dynastic succession in English, indeed 'British' administration. Whether the verdict of Essex's followers rings true, that there was a strong verge to a more absolutist control of the royal prerogative, is not within the remit of this edition. What can be said in conclusion is that if there was the distance Burghley urged so often that councillors and prince must have, it was occasionally occluded for observers; indeed, at times it appeared to disappear in the years after 1598.

The Provenance of CUL MS Ee.3.56

The correspondence between Burghley and Cecil forms a single volume catalogued as Cambridge University Library Manuscript Ee.3.56. It measures 7⅞ inches by roughly 12 inches (20 cm × roughly

---

[291] Handover, *The Second Cecil*, 179.

30 cm), bound in quarter-calf, with the spine bearing metal letters, 'ORIGINAL LETTERS'. The numbering of each letter was made on the upper right of the first page of each letter, without any foliation. It came to Cambridge University Library by way of the Royal Library in 1715 through the collection of Bishop John More, one of the greatest benefactors of the University's collections. He had owned it since at least 1697 when it was first catalogued in his collection. These are the basic facts of the volume's known existence. The collection of the manuscripts as bound gives the impression that whoever found the original Burghley-to-Robert Cecil manuscripts together may have done so from a massive archive and bound the papers in a somewhat provisional, even hasty, manner. Their chronology is imprecise, suggesting that the present volume was not meant to be its final and complete form but rather a temporary container for a unique cache of papers.

The present edition is not the first printing of many of the manuscripts here. Twenty-two were published in 1732 by Francis Peck in his *Desiderata Curiosa*[292] and with forty-four by Thomas Wright in 1838.[293] Neither editor had recourse to the massive Cecilian archives elsewhere which remained uncalendared and uncatalogued until the 1850s and after. Nor were these editors really interested in or able to place the letters within these wider archival remains: their sole purpose was to present largely unadorned primary documents together with often unrelated materials. As Peck's title suggests, the pieces were, by the 1730s, a 'curiosity' among other remains: funerary monuments, Burghley's will, manuscripts then in circulation including two lives by contemporaries, probably secretaries, one of which Peck transcribed and printed. There must have been a market for Burghley materials for an edition of the so-called 'Anonymous Life' (far more accessible) was done by Arthur Collins, also in 1732.[294] Wright's glib commentaries suggest that his interest was part antiquarian and part entertainment. He may have made his transcriptions as a student at Trinity College,

---

[292] Francis Peck, *Desiderata Curiosa: or, A Collection of Divers Scarce and Curious Pieces . . . Volume the First. Containing, I. The complete Statesman, exemplified in the Life and Action of Sir William Cecil, Lord Burghley, Lord High Treasurer of England in Queen Elizabeth's Time; largely setting forth both his public and private Conduct. With many Notes from his own MS. Diary, and other Authors [together with 29 other tracts named on the title-pages and] many other Memoirs, Letters, Wills, and Epitaphs; amounting in all to above 150 curious Articles; all now published from original MSS, communicated by eminent Persons* (London, 1732).

[293] Thomas Wright, *Queen Elizabeth and Her Times: A Series of Original Letters, Selected from the Inedited Correspondence of the Lord Treasurer Burghley, the Earl of Leicester, the Secretaries Walsingham and Smith, Sir Christopher Hatton . . .* 2 vols (London, 1838), II.

[294] Smith, *The 'Anonymous Life'*; Arthur Collins, *The Life of that Great Statesman William Cecil, Lord Burghley, Secretary of State in the reign of King Edward the Sixth, and Lord High Treasurer of England in the Reign of Queen Elizabeth* (London, 1732).

Cambridge in the 1820s working in the Dome Room of the Old Schools where the volume of letters had been placed since 1756. How he located the volume or knew of it is unknown.[295]

Scholars have used the letters in CUL MS Ee.3.56 but without extended annotations of the Cecils' transfer of dynastic power with reference to the extensive official record both men left. Conyers Read's work on Burghley in the 1960s was the first work where the papers were brought to notice. Paul Hammer and Stephen Alford consulted the originals in their work on the major players in late Elizabethan political culture as evidence of the Cecils' role in the 1590s.[296] The letters have never been edited nor their content contextualized in a wider Cecilian and late Elizabethan sense of their material production. The reason is partly geographical and their relatively obscure placement away from the main Cecil archives at Hatfield, the British Library and the National Archives. By contrast, CUL Ee.3.56 is an archival outlier.

The Cambridge volume was catalogued as part of Bishop John Moore's library at Ely Place in Holborn in 1697 by Edward Bernard as number 9229.[297] Moore's collection, by instruction in his will of 1714, was not to be broken up. Hence this volume went with it to Cambridge when King George I purchased and donated the entire collection as a gift to Cambridge University, part of a truly 'national collection', at the urging of Viscount Townshend the University's chancellor.[298] CUL MS Ee.3.56 bears the original bookplate designed by John Pine in 1737 for what was called the Royal Library as the Moore collection given by the king was known. Moore's library may have been accessioned then or later when the collection was mixed into the existing Library holdings in 1756, for the volume also bears the number 43, an earlier accession mark possibly dating from Moore's ownership.[299] The clean pages of

[295] Jayne Ringrose, 'The Royal Library: John Moore and his books', in Peter Fox (ed.), *Cambridge University Library: The Great Collections* (Cambridge, 1998), 78–89.

[296] Stephen Alford, *Burghley: William Cecil at the Court of Elizabeth I* (New Haven, CT, and London, 2008), 315–331; Hammer, *Polarisation of Elizabethan Politics*.

[297] *Catalogi Librorum Angliae et Hiberniae in unum Collecti cum Indice Alphabetico*, ed. Edward Bernard (London, 1697), 375. See also CUL MS Oo.7.50 2 for Edward Tanner's additional notes for books and manuscripts after 1697 in Moore's collection.

[298] After protracted debate on its price and importance with the 2nd earl of Oxford, Edward Harley, and his librarian Humfrey Wanley, see Ringrose, 'The Royal Library', 87.

[299] There were great riches in what the king had purchased for the Royal Library. John Moore, bishop of Ely, was said to have amassed 30,755 volumes, of which 28,965 were books, and 1,709 were manuscripts. In 1702 Bishop William Nicolson of Carlisle described it as filling five rooms with additional closets in Ely Place in Holborn. Burghley's extraordinary letters cannot have occasioned particular interest in a library which included an 8th-c. MS of Bede's 'Historica Ecclesiastica'.

the volume attest to its rarely being consulted with only a small filament of dirt at the very edges of the creamy stock paper used by Burghley.

The first person to use the volume at Cambridge was probably the Revd Thomas Baker, non-juring fellow of St John's College, and indefatigable transcriber of the University's manuscript collections.[300] Baker or a friend (possibly his protégé Zachary Grey) found the volume amidst the deep chaos of the Royal Library in the 1720s probably with the aid of Bernard's *Catalogi*. No plans remain for the physical arrangement of the Moore bequest, but it was a shambles. Baker copied from the volume itself likely kept in his rooms at the indulgence of Conyers Middleton, University Librarian.[301] These transcriptions, in his idiosyncratic hand, fill eighteen consecutive pages, his marginal notes on the transcriptions refer to 'Manu. W.B' or, occasionally, 'Manu. G. B'.[302]

Baker sent one copy to John Strype (1643–1737) the ecclesiastical historian whom he greatly admired, then in his mid eighties, going blind and no longer hunting for new materials having abandoned his projected biography of William Cecil. When sending the copy to Strype on August 9, 1729, Baker wrote:

> I have lately met with a small Volume of original Letters, from 1592 to 1598, from Lord Burleigh to his Son Sir Robert Cecill, which belonged to the late Bishop of Ely, (Dr. Moore) you may probably have seen these already, however

[300]Thomas Baker, 1656–1740, non-juror in 1687, deprived 1717, but remained a fellow until his death, made 42 folios of manuscript copies, and contributed heavily to *Athenae Cantabrigiensis*. According to his nephew and executor Richard Burton writing to Philip Williams, senior fellow of St John's: 'XXIIII Folio Volumes are bequeathed to Lord Oxford [from whom these were bought by the British Museum and are catalogued in the Harleian MSS., see pp. 107–108] XV Folios and III Quartos to the University Library, to the College Library all such Books, printed or manuscript as he had, and were wanting there. From whence the College seems to claim every Book in my Uncle's Study, of which they have not the same Edition, which in my Opinion is extending the Word a little too far', Robert Masters, *Memoirs of the Life and Writings of the Late Rev. Thomas Baker, B.D. of St. John's College in Cambridge, from the papers of Dr. Zachary Grey* . . . (Cambridge, 1784) 86.

[301]David McKitterick, introduction, in Fox, *Cambridge University Library*, 9: 'In the eighteenth century, and thanks especially to Conyers Middleton, who in 1721 was appointed to care for Moore's books, increasing emphasis was placed on the care and study of the early printed books.'

[302]Collins's volume makes a complete 'Burghley-Cecil' publication, with the life, some letters, inscriptions; Peck, inexplicably, includes with the *Anonymous Life* of William Cecil ('The Complete Statesman') and his letters to Robert, other letters from Bishop Chaderton, an account of Sir Robert Cecil's death and that of Prince Henry, before moving on briskly to some letters of Thomas Hobbes, an account of a Saxon massacre of some Danes, and an exhumation of 'Some Great Person'. One writer called the entire publication badly 'mangled', *ODNB*.

I will send you a Copy of the last Letter, rather as a Curiosity than of Use. By that you will judge whether you have seen the rest.[303]

This enclosure would become CUL MS Ee.3.56, No. 138, the final letter in the volume in its present condition. Baker seemed to think Strype knew of the letters: the word 'probably' speaks to Moore's long acquaintance with Strype and the Bishop's high regard for him. David McKitterick's invaluable tracking of the Moore bequest shows the two men were very close by this stage, Moore providing manuscripts for Strype's *Cranmer* of 1693. Strype praised his patron in 1711:

And besides, You have got me the sight of other valuable Manuscripts. Whereby I must gratefully acknowledge the considerable Improvements I have made in my Searches into the Historical affairs of this Church, when it first began to reform Abuses, and to vindicate it self from *Rome*, and as it happily proceeded under our two first Protestant Princes'[304]

In effect, Baker was assuming Strype had seen the letters for he would have known of his great debt to Moore. Strype had been an occasional recipient of Baker's copies since 1709. Doubtless Strype gave some answer to Baker's question but it has not survived. The two men worked together in 1730 editing the final version of the last volume of Strype's *Annals* for publication with Baker's student, Zachary Grey, compiling the index.[305] Strype printed two letters, Nos 66 and 138, in the final volume in the 1731 *Annals*, probably from this collaboration with Baker and Grey.[306]

Strype's assiduous compilations and arrangement of manuscripts relating to Elizabeth and her church, drew him to Moore's library from 1697. The question as to what the letters and their binding looked like at this juncture may be asked, for several reasons. The present volume may not have been exactly the volume which Moore had purchased or been given some time before 1697. Baker describes the manuscript as 'small'. Edward Bernard in his *Catologi* of Moore's library in 1697 records no. 9229 as 'A large volume of original letters of the Lord Treasurer Burleigh to his son Sir Robert Cecil'. Whether the

---

[303] Printed in Masters, *Memoirs*, pt. 1, 58–59.

[304] David McKitterick, *Cambridge University Library, A History: The Eighteenth and Nineteenth Centuries* (Cambridge, 1986), 84, see also 81–86.

[305] Masters, *Memoirs*, pt. 1, 58, 66–67.

[306] Strype printed the last Burghley holograph, CUL Ee.3.56, no. 138, in his *Annals of the Reformation and Establishment of Religion, and Other Various Occurrences in the Church of England, During Queen Elizabeth's Happy Reign* (London, 1725–1731) iv, 343: 'This was transcribed from volume of Original Letters of the L. Burghley to his Son, Sir Robert Cecil, remaining among the MSS of Dr. More, late Lord Bishop of Ely, now in the Cambridge Library', which follows the original on the dorse in Henry Maynard's hand: 'My L[ord's] last letter that ever he [The Lord Burghley] wrote with his own hand'.

78 INTRODUCTION

volume was large in number of manuscripts, or small in dimensions, is subjective. Excisions and fragments of lost letters do beg the question when and how CUL MS Ee.3.56 was left in its present state. Whether the letters were numbered when Baker transcribed them (or he numbered them himself) is not known – no formal table of contents fronts the volume. Letter No. 119 is a partial clue as it was cut out after the numbering.[307] The tiny fragment of the dorse of Letter No. 119 remaining in CUL MS Ee.3.56 is dated 9 July 1597. There may well have been others cut out for which no dorse or date remains.[308]

If the numbering in this volume was done at the point of accession to the Royal Library in 1715, which there is little reason to suppose, there were further removals and oddities which Baker may have noticed in 1729. There remains a fragment of an excised letter between Nos. 34 and 35 which bears the date '24 Dec. 1594';[309] a fragment in the crease between Nos. 65 and 66 reads 'My l[ord] about Provisions' in Robert Cecil's hand where the dorse for No. 65 is intact. Thus two letters, one certainly from Burghley to Cecil, were removed after the present binding. Immediately before No. 97 a piece of paper approximately half an inch wide runs from top to bottom without writing; a similar strip between Nos. 113 and 114 runs about four inches (10cm) from the top to the middle of the crease. These last two papers may have been part of a re-bound volume. A strange note on the dorse of No. 33 reads 'I think Sath God', with a doodle – similar to those found in Volume 120 of the Lansdowne Manuscripts in Strype's hand – but this is not certain. There is a list of Scottish nobles on the dorse of No. 40 done in pencil, but when it was done or why is unknown as it does not relate to the letter's contents. Pencil marks are found on letter 124. A much later hand, not secretarial, adds the address to letter No. 115. A very tiny '53' has been written in a way unique to these letters on the upper right side of letter No. 56. The accessioning handwriting on the bookplate is the same as, for example, the Moore copy of Bede's *Historica Ecclesiastica*. A stray note on No. 1, the 1564 letter to William Phayre, looks very much like John Strype's handwriting: 'A pacquett of old matters', is a rather odd note for a man whose life was full of such packets, but doubtless written before the letters were bound.

[307] Baker's transcriptions in CUL MS Mm.1.43 have a table of contents on the first page (p. 1) of the copies given on pp. 2–19 called 'Letters [Original] to from Lord Burghley'.
[308] A tiny fragment of the dorse remains: '9 July 1597'. The Lansdowne MSS are full of references to the affair of Dr. Baro's incendiary sermon at Cambridge, including letters in Vol. 80 from John Jegon, then vice-chancellor of the University.
[309] Maynard to Cecil, 23 Dec. 1594, *HMCS*, v, 16–17, 46 notes Burghley was unable to write, but gave his opinion to the Queen on how the forthcoming embassy to the Hanse, Danzig, could be funded by the Merchant Adventurers.

Baker wrote a second letter, probably also in 1729, to the Revd Francis Peck, an antiquarian of Stamford Baron, who was then undertaking an edition whose precise purpose remains unclear; a vastly expensive and idiosyncratic magpie volume containing Cecil-related materials. *Desiderata Curiosa* would appear in 1732 with Baker's transcriptions from the present volume.[310] The letters were first published not by Strype but the obscure Peck, a project which had Strype's full endorsement. Baker's copies of twenty-two of the CUL MS Ee.3.56 letters from Burghley to Cecil would be printed in Peck's immensely grand volume, more suitable for an editor whose frontispiece announced he was 'natus' in Stamford. Peck never saw the original manuscripts, and used Baker's copies, thanking him for his role in providing the twenty-two letters and together with more sent by Baker: 'all which (as also Sir Peter Warburton's letter to the Lord Burghley and Anonymous to Bishop Jegon) the said Mr. Baker most kindly gave me leave to write out from his own manuscript copy'.[311]

The provenance of CUL MS Ee.3.56 prior to it being listed in Bishop Moore's library can only be speculated upon, as there are no specific details provided in the manuscript itself. The volume may have been put together by John Strype, who bound together correspondence associated with his publishing enterprises. For example, the correspondence for a projected 'life' of Dr Samuel Knight was bound. This was later found in a house belonging to Knights' heirs which had been bought by John Percy Baumgartner who gave it to Cambridge University Library in the 1860s and these can be seen in CUL Add. MSS 1–10 today. Further insights into how Strype arranged his papers can be seen from his will. This set out in detail for his executrix how he had organized the bundles of papers and 'dealboxes' in his possession. On one side of his study were 'all the rest of the Manuscripts loose Papers or bound in Pastboard remaining in any place of my Study in Chest or Box or elsewhere do belong to me'.[312] Perhaps Strype sold the 'pacquett' to Moore during his financial

---

[310] I am assuming Peck received the copies at the same time Baker sent no. 138 to Strype. He tended to send things in batches.

[311] Masters, *Memoirs*, pt. 1, 60: 'Mr. Baker sent Mr. Strype likewise a long Account of Dr. Peter Baro, Margaret Professor of the University of Cambridge, and of his Family, which is barely mentioned in his fourth Volume of the Annals of Queen Elizabeth . . . These letters were afterwards published by Mr. Peck in Desid. Curiosa, Lib V, and the Account of Dr. Baro shall have a place in the Appendix.' Peck's letter of Bishop Jegon, printed in *Desiderata Curiosa* is no. XXXI in Book V and dates from 1601. It appears in the middle of the Burghley transcriptions for no apparent reason. Baker's dedication is found in *Desiderata Curiosa*, Preface, p. v.

[312] TNA PCC PROB 11/686/455.

difficulties in the 1690s and to gain access to other treasures at Ely Place in the bishop's collection.

While CUL Ee.3.56 is not precisely bound in pasteboard, its calf-skin binding covers cardboard, a rather rudimentary structure, strong, with the bifolium letters unfolded, some missing dorses, Burghley's small red seals broken and removed (as the letters were unfolded by Cecil or his secretary), and arranged carefully into the book. They were handled with great care. Their slightly haphazard chronology, removals and seemingly odd inclusions suggest that whoever chose the papers perhaps created a provisional volume for copying and circulation. Indeed, they might have been bound once only before 1697 with no further re-binding. CUL MS Ee.3.56 bears little resemblance to bindings of Strype's letters, for example.[313]

Nonetheless, Strype did have access to the greatest number of Burghley's manuscripts anywhere outside the State Paper Office (and possibly Hatfield House). He was sometime vicar at St Mary's Church at Low-Leyton in Essex, where the Hickes family at Ruckholt were the local squires. They were among the descendants of Sir Michael Hickes, Lord Burghley's patronage secretary. Sir Michael either took these papers or was given them following Burghley's death, probably 1599–1600, perhaps to work on what may well have been his biography of Burghley, the manuscript published twice in 1732 as the 'Anonymous life', written in the late 1590s.[314] His descendant, Sir William, 2nd baronet, still owned these papers at Ruckholt when Strype went there in 1669 which, after a fashion, he came to 'own'.[315] A great many of the papers were never opened in Strype's lifetime, as can be seen today by their numberings in the famed Lansdowne Manuscripts, volumes 1–122, in the British Library to which their eponymous owner's executors sold them in the early 1800s. Other than jottings, doodles and long partial notes including filing in his complex cipher, Strype's organization of the papers is guesswork – probably chronologically. After Ruckholt was torn down in 1724 it is safe to assume the remaining papers came to Strype.

Richard Chiswell, sometime printer to the Royal Society was also Strype's printer, notably of the unprofitable *Cranmer* in 1694 (using the Hickes' papers) after which further joint ventures between the two

---

[313]These bindings may have been re-done later when after Baumgartner's bequest.

[314]Smith, *The 'Anonymous Life'*.

[315]Thereafter Sir James West bought them from Strype's estate and added to them, as did Sir William Petty who purchased them from West's estate, the collection having burgeoned to ten times the size of the original 121 vols of Sir Michael Hickes's – and Strype's – archive. These were sold to the British Library in 1804 where they were catalogued 1812–1819 and bound in their present form as the Lansdowne Manuscripts.

men ceased.[316] Chiswell claimed to have bought the entire collection from Sir William Hickes in 1682.[317] There followed a seriously disputed division of the ownership and use of the manuscripts set down at length in Strype's 1737 will – at some point Chiswell promised a sum of £50 to Strype in return for clean transcriptions and annotations for publication on the understanding that Chiswell remained trustee. Chiswell did not pay and Strype did not yield the papers – if he had custody of them. CUL MS Ee.3.56 may have been made up out of Sir William Hickes' manuscripts by Strype, sent thence to Chiswell for printing but retained to make good Strype's debt, and sold to Moore to realize his loss.[318] There had once been good reason for trust: Chiswell – who bought a great deal at the 1687 Ailesbury sale – together with Strype purchased a rare copy of a translation of Eusebius' *Ecclesiastical History* which Strype used when compiling materials on martyrology. Chiswell had already collaborated on a magnificent and virtuosic edition, the vast two-volume *Works* of John Lightfoot edited by Strype in 1684. Either Strype or Chiswell could have sold these manuscripts to the bishop; Chiswell out of spite having no further use for them, Strype to gain further favour with Moore and because he was resolved on pain of legal action by Chiswell to keep them out of print. But this is all speculation.

This speculation links the largest collection of Burghley's papers with Moore at a time when the Hickes' papers were going somewhat underground at least until Chiswell died in 1711 after which they appeared with frequency in the *Annals of the Reformation*. The rift with Chiswell in 1694–1696 may have prompted Strype's renewed search for papers in fear that Chiswell would go to law over the papers already in Strype's possession at Ruckholt, papers which he never yielded up, a fear reflected in his will over forty years later.

The provenance of the letters and how they came into Moore's possession may not have been connected with Strype's enterprises. Moore, or one of his agents, might have bought the volume at the Ailesbury sale in November 1687. The vast auction of the library of Robert Bruce, earl of Ailesbury was arranged by his widow, the dowager countess Anne, an heir of Burghley's through the Exeter line. Some of these books and papers were possibly part of the Burghley

---

[316]Richard Chiswell (1639–1711), an eminent London printer, was named in 1681 by the Royal Society as printer for five vols of the *Transactions*. See Charles A. Rivington, 'Early printers of the Royal Society, 1663–1708', *Notes and Records of the Royal Society*, 1984, 1–27, 12.

[317]Strype owned a copy of the Lawrence Nowell-Burghley atlas, today BL Additional MS 62540 which he bought from Hickes and sold to Chiswell in 1682. See BL Stowe, 1056 catalogue of James West's collection, bought from Strype's estate.

[318]*Tudor Church Reform: The Henrician Canons of 1535*, ed. Gerald Lewis Bray (Woodbridge, 2005), lxiii. See also Strype's will, TNA PCC PROB 11/686/455.

House library at the house in the Strand where Burghley and Sir Robert Cecil both lived in the 1590s. David McKitterick's work on Moore's collections notes that he did buy at the 'Cecil' collection auction. The Ailesbury sale catalogue announced the contents as unique in two ways:

> The first is, that it comprises the main part of the Library of that famous Secretary William Cecil, Lord Burghley: which consider'd must put it out of doubt, that these Books are excellent in their several kinds and well-chosen. The second is, That it contains a greater number of Rare Manuscripts than ever yet were offered together in this way, many of which are rendred the more valuable by being remarked upon by the hand of the said great man.[319]

'Remarked upon' does not describe original letters, of course, and Burghley made notes on nearly everything he read.

A third possibility, other than Strype and Chiswell's dispute or the Ailesbury sale, appears in Strype's correspondence received 1694 to 1696 from Robert Martin, rector of two Stamford churches. Strype was then serious about writing a life of Burghley and asked his old acquaintance about Burghley House manuscripts owned by the earl of Exeter, especially of any in Burghley's hand; the earl was the descendant of Burghley's elder son, Thomas Cecil (1542–1623), the second baron Burghley (later earl of Exeter, 1605). Martin's cagey replies survive, a dozen of them. Strype somehow knew Martin had a connection with the steward in the earl's household. Martin and Strype were friends from St Catharine's College, Cambridge in the early 1660s. Martin, with his Bertie family affiliation in Stamford, occupied a vastly different position, as he put it 'in the Shades'. By 1696 he used his replies to educate the metropolitan Strype, of Stow's *London*, to the more politically complicated local legacy of William Cecil. Strype, in turn, wanted to know of John, 5th earl of Exeter, the provenance of royal gifts out of the Dissolution to the Cecil family in the area, a topic which understandably caused umbrage.[320] Martin criticized Burghley at every turn with the vehemence of a country Tory: his livings had been seriously depleted, by that 'puritan

---

[319] *Bibliotheca illustris, sive, Catalogus variorum librorum in quâvis linguâ & facultate insignium ornatissimae bibliothecae viri cujusdam praenobilis ac honoratissimi olim defuncti [William Cecil] libris rarissimis tam typis excusis quàm manuscriptis*, [London, 1687?], 262.

[320] Clearly the provenance of the estate lands still caused sensitive feelings in the earl, for this was the only blot on the great man's memory, a suspicion which he assured Martin through his Steward lived on by reason of 'Papisticall Recriminacion', No. 143, Baumgartner MS, CUL, Add. 2. Answers came slowly from Burghley House, No. 144, of 13 Sept. 1694. In Dec. 1694 the mystery of Nassabergh hundred was finally pried from the earl: as Martin commented on the reverse of his letter, 'you may gett all the proper Satisfaction, as to every one of your Queryes from the Mr. of the ye Rolls'.

Demagog you so admire' buying up or gaining royal gifts of former monastic lands. The former glebe now provided Burghley's heir, the probably crypto-Catholic Exeter, with money for vast improvements to his ancient house, at the expense of the clergy, and forced him to be in receipt of a pension from Dr Busby's fund. Worse, Martin knew Strype and his manuscripts made him indispensable in Low-Leyton by his histories in the height of William III's early reign, patronized by Archbishop Tenison, and Moore's patrons, the Finch family – of the 2nd earl of Nottingham – pilloried by Martin for their lavish new £40,000 house at Burley-on-Hill, a former Cecil property. Martin saw Burghley as their model in all things corrupt. 'For his share in the Reformation, my little Reading tells me How great a patron he was of the puritanicall party', noting Burghley's contradiction of the archbishop of Canterbury, an example he drew from a 'Chronicle' of the neighbourhood in his possession. Their distance was theological.

While trying to erode Strype's apparent adoration of the first Lord Burghley, Martin distanced himself fastidiously from Moore who often visited the neighbourhood; Martin knew of him and his estranged family: Presbyterians; his brother had gone mad from business losses.[321] Strype was not pursuing this line of inquiry idly. Martin dutifully supplied the inscriptions on Burghley's tomb in St Martin's Church, a description of Burghley's arms on the town gate, and of Burghley House itself: 'a Fayr house (perhaps the best in England) within a quarter of a mile' then under significant renovations, the earl was in need of money.[322]

Yet this fascinating correspondence would be peripheral save that Martin reported a unique volume worthy of note: Exeter's steward 'tells me that he has severall Letters by him of that Great Man's own writing my Lord has and One book of Manuscripts, but I think of pryvat concerns', in addition to several possible local leads. Here, speculation may point in a different direction.[323] Moore was present in Stamford and, despite the bishop's strong Whig association, the earl may have overcome his hostility to William III and his regime by parting with the manuscripts at the right price. The earl showed little nostalgia for his ancestor. Strype may have alerted Moore to the volume. Martin's description of a particular volume, however vague, could describe CUL MS Ee.3.56.

If Exeter himself sold the volume (perhaps the one mentioned by Martin) to Moore, the manuscripts or bound volume may have remained in Cecil hands until 1676 with the demolition of Exeter

[321] CUL Add. MS 2, no. 147, 16 Jan. 1694/5.
[322] Ibid. no. 145.
[323] Ibid. no. 146, 27 Dec. 1694.

House (formerly Burghley House) in London. The volume or letters may have been part of 'an old pacquett' remaining there, perhaps sent to Burghley House at Stamford with Sir Thomas's possessions after late 1598 or thereafter, particularly in 1676.[324]

The original immense Cecilian archive was scattered following Robert Cecil's death. The Salisbury line of Robert Cecil and the Exeters from his brother Thomas, though distantly related, went into something of a decline during the years of the manuscript searches and purchases in the age of Strype, Chiswell, Moore, and Baker and were unyielding of access to their papers. Presumably what was left at Exeter House in the Strand in 1676 went to Burghley House. Nearly two hundred volumes of Burghley's and Cecil's papers would remain at Westminster after their respective deaths in 1598 and 1612, the origin of the State Paper Office under the titular guardian Sir Thomas Wilson. Robert, by then earl of Salisbury, took many thousands of personal papers to Hatfield where they were bound in guard-books beginning in 1615 by Captain Thomas Brett where they were inaccessible in Strype's day.[325] It is possible that the less accessed and accessible library at Burghley House in Stamford was the resting place of a stray bound volume of Burghley's letters found at Exeter House in the Strand and moved there in 1676 or before. In this way, the volume may have left the metropolis at the exact moment the great public auctions began, with that of Lazarus Seaman. In Stamford, as Martin notes, Moore was in the neighbourhood; Strype noted interest was ripe in the great lord; and Exeter may have sold him the volume sometime in 1695–1696.[326]

A final possibility is that the papers remained in the possession of the descendants of Robert Cecil. Their London home, Salisbury House, was demolished in 1694, so at about the time the Cambridge volume of letters came into Moore's possession and when Strype was searching for Cecil manuscripts. A meticulous study of the building and changes to the fabric of the 1st earl of Salisbury's great town house suggest that members of the Cecil family had not lived there for many decades before its demolition. Nonetheless, again, the descriptor of 'an old pacquett of matters' could account for their being discovered after many years. The Exeter House connection with the Salisbury line was by this juncture more tenuous despite intermarriages. Moore's agents, on the other hand, may have been searching for materials. In any case, it is nearly impossible to separate the manuscripts and their

---

[324] See above, pp. 78–79.

[325] Unpublished essay by the Hatfield House Library, Robin Harcourt Williams.

[326] Manolo Guerci (2009) 'Salisbury House in London, 1599–1694: The Strand palace of Sir Robert Cecil'. *Architectural History*, 52 (2009), 31–78.

binding from the close circle of collectors and antiquarians in the orbit of Moore and Strype who were so assiduous in seeking manuscripts from new sales or old libraries.

This is the skeleton history of how these letters by Burghley to his younger son came to the University of Cambridge. It points to two radically different uses of them: the parochial, domestic Burghley of antiquarian fame, removed from the synthetic context of other papers and actors, a 'curiosity'. Meanwhile, the 'state' papers version of a masterful policy maker and adviser sitting at the apex of patronage and officialdom, with close care of the Queen's church, would have had more appeal to Strype in his *Annals*.

Editorial Conventions

While CUL MS Ee.3.56 contains a wide variety of scripts, Lord Burghley's and Henry Maynard's hands dominate. Burghley's spiky italic hand varied according to debility and vitality. Yet he followed precise patterns in his script, adding 'm' and 'n' frequently in dashes across their place in a word, for example, 'so[m]e' or 'co[m]e', which have been expanded silently throughout for readability. Similarly, 'lres', l[ette]res, has been expanded with the use of square bracket to distinguish it from close abbreviations such as 'lo[rd]' or 'lls' to 'lords', also expanded with square brackets. Burghley's writing in haste meant a very large number of words were given abbreviations and, in general, these have been expanded throughout with square brackets for consistency, for example in Letter No. 3: 'The Fr[ench] amb[assador] req[ui]reth me to adress hym to yow, so as hir Ma[jes]ty may receave his l[ette]res and message'. The use of square brackets here shows where expansions have been significant. Original spelling has been expanded silently in words where square brackets might cause unreadability, 'poyntes' instead of 'po[y]ntes', for example; 'ye' has been silently expanded to 'the' throughout and Burghley's invariable use of 'yt'(thorn) to 'that'. On other occasions Burghley superscripted suffixes occasionally, such as 'er' in 'over': 'a nombre of Aldermen will gyve over ther clokes', where 'er' has also been silently expanded in 'Aldermen', and 'm' in 'nombre'. Similarly, the so-called 'swash e' at the end of 'clokes' has been expanded. These 'es' additions at the ends of words have all been expanded throughout the transcriptions. 'Q[ueen]' has been expanded as has 'Archb[isho]p'. 'Mr.' and 'Dr.' have been left as they are also the modern usage. Capitalization has been retained as in the original. Excessive modernization in silent expansions of Burghley's hand would present a radical change from his original texts.

Maynard wrote in a classical secretarial hand. The reader will see patterns in his texts, as amanuensis taking notes when Burghley was too tired or unable. Nonetheless, even on these hurried occasions Maynard added vowels and endings to words, whereas Burghley's notation was generally terse. In the case of both hands identical editorial standards have been used. The use of 'ff' has been retained in all cases. Their common use of the abbreviation 'Ma[jes]tie' is always expanded thus. Ampersands have been left as in the original. Original spelling has been retained in Maynard's and others' additions throughout, including the endorsements and addresses.

All dates are Old Style as in the original manuscripts. The New Year has been taken in all of the letters as March 25. Where needed, Old Style dates have been given in French correspondence. All names have been transcribed as written. Place names have been written as transcribed and expanded and modernized only where necessary, for example, 'Fr[ance]'. Greek and Latin have been translated or paraphrased. Foreign languages have not been italicized but are left as in the original. The 1560 Geneva Bible has been used throughout.

Money has been transcribed as in the original: 'l' as librae, 's' as solidae, and 'd' as denarii, with the modernized numbers added in square brackets.

The letters have been transcribed in the original order found in the volume. Chronological confusion has been noted elsewhere. As the volume is neither paginated nor foliated, where Burghley wrote on more than one side [p. 2] or [p. 3] have been used within the lineation. Almost all of the letters are bifolium with Burghley writing beginning on the front of the first side. Only one letter, No. 14, exceeds the length of four sides. The manuscripts have not been lineated. Additional punctuation has been added to, particularly in the case of full stops. There are two occasions where he used '/' in Letter No. 1 and as noted at n. 389. These additions are faithful to the originals. Where Burghley inserted a dash in the manuscript or comma, these have also been preserved. His use of colons is also as in the originals.

Paragraphing has been added on occasion for ease of reading, particularly where sentences have been added to texts (in the latter case, the paragraph is full out rather than indented). Interlineations have all been given as superscripts. For ease of reading on the occasions when interlineations were more than one line deep over corrected sentences, the superscripts and the cross-out lines have been expanded.

THE LETTERS OF LORD BURGHLEY, WILLIAM CECIL, TO HIS SON SIR ROBERT CECIL, 1593–1598

Letter No. 1

William Cecil, Lord Burghley to Mr William Phayre, 13 February 1565

⅓ p. Holograph.
Addressed, endorsed, signed.

Text

I commend me very humbly unto yow / and wher yow have begun to deale in a course of Sir Thomas Greshams ther, although I know his owne friendshipp / and thankfulness will mene as much as yow can do for hym, yet can I not forbeare but both to prayse yow and thank yow, praying you to procede by all good meanes that you come to bring his sute to a good end / and so thy[n]ky[n]g shortly to wryte now unto yowe, at this tyme for lack of Lesure / doe end.

From Grenwich the xiii[th] of Februari 1565

Your Assured,
Loovyng friend,

W. Cecyll

Dorse

[In John Strype's hand]
a paquett of old matters of all sorts

ADDRESS
To my verie loving friend,
Mr. William Phayre, the queens
Ma[jes]ties agent in the
Court of Spaine

RECEIPT
From Sir William Sicill
The 13th of februarye and hear
The 20th of marche, madrite [Madrid]

Letter No. 2

William, Lord Burghley to Sir Robert Cecil, 21 May 1593

3 pp. Dictated to Henry Maynard, with a final holograph paragraph.
Addressed, endorsed, signed.

Text

This evening after I receved your Letter[1] I had a letter brought me
dyrected from Douer, by which I only am advertised from the Maior[2]
of his receipte of the letters which were sent yesterdaye both from
my LLs [Lords][3] and from my selfe,[4] and from the Ambassador.[5] and
within a litle tyme afterwardes my l[ord] Cobham sent me certen
l[ette]rs dyrected to him from his Livetenant of Douer.[6] To make a
Comment of those letters for myne owne ease I leave it to yow and
to gather what you thincke fitt thereof to advertise her ma[jes]tie for
that they conteyn variety of intelligence, and in some part a lewde

[1] Sir Robert Cecil's letter to Burghley of the 20 or 21 May 1593 is not extant, but in
it he clearly outlined the threat to Boulogne from Charles of Luxembourg's army. Cecil's
agent, Roger Walton, reached Burghley with Robert Cecil's cover letter. Hatfield, Cecil
Papers, 170/58; *HMCS*, iv, 325. Cecil's reply was probably responding to another of his
father's letters of 21 May 1593, in which he referred his son to the most recent intelligence.
This dispatch saw the resolution of the Boulogne dilemma. Hatfield, Cecil Papers, 169/80;
HMCS, iv, 318.
[2] The mayor was Thomas, the eldest son of Sir Thomas Fane (d.1589), *ODNB*.
[3] The Privy Council.
[4] The letter from Burghley to the mayor of Dover, sent with the Privy Council letter of
19–20 May or before, regarding the Boulogne situation is not extant, although letters from
the Council, Burghley and the ambassador are referred to in the reply of Cobham's agent,
Geoffrey Fenner. Hatfield, Cecil Papers, 169/82; *HMCS*, iv, 319–320.
[5] Letter from Pregent de la Fin, lord of Beauvoir la Nocle, vidame of Chartres (d.1624).
He was from a prominent Huguenot family who were hereditary administrators for the
bishops of Chartres. As French ambassador to the English court he here advised the Queen
and Council of the necessity of military assistance to Boulogne. Burghley sent the warrant
for levies of troops to Cecil with his letter of 21 May, which was not drawn up and dated
until 24 May. Hatfield, Cecil Papers, 22/91, 169/80; *HMCS*, iv, 318, 321.
[6] Letter from Lord Cobham, lord warden of the Cinque Ports, to Burghley of 19–21 May
from his lieutenant of Dover Castle, Thomas Fane (later Sir) the younger, which Burghley
enclosed with this letter. Hatfield, Cecil Papers, 169/78; *HMCS*, iv, 317–318. Cobham was
Cecil's father-in-law, 10th Baron Cobham (1527–1597), *ODNB*.

act of him that brought the Ladyes l[etter]rs that were dyrected to
Diep out of their waye.[7] And yett it semeth that at the tyme of the
writing of her letters to the Governor of Diep she was in some feare
of the ennemye, And for that purpose dyrected hir messenger, both to
the ffr[ench] King and to Monsieur Esparnon his brother.[8] But what
was conteyned in these letters I cannot gather. By the letters of the
Mayor of Dover you may parceave, that it is likely that the Quene's
ma[jes]ties good will wilbe notified to the lady, and to the govarnor
of the towne also. And it may be they both wilbe the bolder to Crave
some provisions of munitions, and powder, whereof if the Armye be
departed they shall have no nede.[9] And yett we shall have more nede
to kepe the same. The greate hast that the LLS [Lords of the Privy
Council] made yesterday in the morning shewed a greate difference
betwixt their humors and myne

[p. 2] ffor thowghe they were quicke as Marshall men are most
commonly, and I slowe (as men in yeares are) yett I used no delaye for
the purpose to understand the cause of the perrill. And so to provide

[7] Cecil here was trusted with sifting intelligence and canvassing Council opinion. His agent
Roger Walton's letter dated 18 May 1593, reported Charles of Luxembourg was rumoured
to have left Picardy for Gertruidenberg in Brabant to assist his father, Count Mansfeld,
against Henry IV. Count Peter Ernst von Mansfeld (1517–1604) was effective governor of the
Spanish Netherlands between the duke of Parma (Alessandro Farnese, 1545–1592) and the
arrival of Archduke Ernest (1553–1595) of Austria, 1592–1594. The rumoured siege of Étaples
came as Charles crossed northern France threatening Calais with cartloads of munitions
pilfered from the Governess's fortress, as told by Cobham's agent Geoffrey Fenner on 22
May 1593. Hatfield, Cecil Papers, 22/fol. 91r; *HMCS*, iv, 321. 'The Ladye' referred to here
is Mme de Rouillac, whose deputy, Campagnol, was corresponding with Beauvoir la Nocle
and directing Rouillac's letters to Dieppe. TNA SP 78/32/fol. 409r; *L&A*, iv, Analysis no.
337; *L&A*, v, Analysis no. 90. For Campagnol, see *Histoire Universelle de Jean-Auguste de Thou,
1542–1607* (London, 1734), 515, and for governor of Boulogne (deputy), Gustav Ungerer, *A
Spaniard in Elizabethan England*, 2 vols (London, 1976), II, 15.

[8] Aymar de Chatte (d.1603) was governor of Dieppe. Cecil's 1584 treatise on the French
aristocracy made clear the connection between Mme de Rouillac, née Nogaret, and the
duke of Épernon, for her sister Anne married Charles of Luxembourg. The senior member
of the Nogaret family was the duke of Épernon, Jean Louis, and the lady governor was a
cousin of the dukes of Montpensier and Joyeuse, leading members of the Catholic League.
TNA SP 78/12/fol. 245r; Ungerer, *A Spaniard in Elizabethan England*, Vol. I, 6, 53, 62, 343,
351, 372, 415, 418, 439, 461, 465; Vol. II, 27, 69, 127, 128, 130, 152, 160. See also Letter No.
56.

[9] Letter from the mayor of Dover to the Queen of the 19–20 of May 1593, and the prospect
for military assistance to the Governess: see Thomas Fane's letter to Cobham, forwarded to
Burghley and Cecil. Hatfield, Cecil Papers, 169/fol. 78r. Burghley was not yet advised of the
considerable theft of munitions from the fortress by Charles, news which would certainly
reach Spanish spies interested in weak points in the defence of the northern French coast.
Hatfield, Cecil Papers, 170/58; *HMCS*, iv, 325. Cecil had been notified by his father of the
Queen's requests for powder (*L&A*, iv, no. 337, according Cecil's letter to Beauvoir la Nocle,
24 May 1593).

remedy this I fynd by your letter, that hir ma[jes]tie misliked not my slownes whereby I am the better confirmed in my opynion.[10]

I wrote to daye to you, that the augmentation of the shipping might staye awhile untill we might see howe the wether would blowe over. ffor if the Officers of the Admiraltie have commandment to prepare the shipping, it will cost hir Majesty one monethes charge by presting rigging and victualling without a sennight service.[11] The matter yow write of concerning the answar to be made by Locke is very picquant[12] for difficulties on both sides. Wherein the Rule of Christian Philosophie consisteth in difference betwixt Utile, and Honestum. And yett utile incertum, and yett Honestum certum. But if Honestum were reciproche it were to be preferred to with more Constancye. In private mens causes Cretisare cum Cretensi is allowable.[13] Thus yow see how I beginne to wander before I dare affirme any thinge. If my hand were free from payne I would not commytt thus muche to any other man's hand.[14] And yett yow may impart my woordes to hir Majesty, without offence.

[10]Burghley's 'slowness' as opposed to the quickness of the 'Marshall' men of the Council: see Lord Admiral Howard's assessment sent to Cecil that 'If Boulogne be not looked to it will be gone.' As for the quality of his intelligence, Howard assured Cecil, 'I pay well for it, and if it be not believed it shall cost me no more.' Essex petitioned Cecil for a captaincy in whatever troops were raised, although none were requested from the French side. Hatfield, Cecil Papers, 169/fol. 89r, 90r; *HMCS*, iv, 324. For the lord admiral, Charles Howard (1536–1624), baron of Effingham and earl of Nottingham (1597) and Essex's rival, see *ODNB*.

[11]The new shipping to Brittany was meant, in the first part of the week, to collect the Queen's ordnance, which had been left at Dieppe. There were also demands for 500 or 600 men for Pempole [Paimpol] and Briac as reinforcements for the duke of Montpensier's service against the Spanish, which the Queen rejected. Sir John Wolley, secretary of the French tongue (1596) was co-ordinating documents. TNA SP 12/245/no. 11, 19 May 1593. See also Elizabeth's letter to Henry IV, 19 May 1593, TNA SP 78/31/fol. 218r. The purpose of the shipping was changed, for Burghley had ready for Cecil a warrant for the levy of 300 men for the Queen sign before he himself received Cobham's intelligence about the relief of Boulogne, see n. 1. A sennight, or seven-night, is one week, so here 'without one week's service'. Sir John Wolley, *ODNB*.

[12]Burghley and Cecil were using the Bothwell faction as part of a Protestant aristocratic faction forcing James VI to take strong legal moves, including forfeiture, against those of his subjects acting in concert with Spain. Henry Lock was to function as a sort of secretary to Bothwell, answering to Sir Robert Bowes, the English ambassador to James's court. *CSPS 1593–1595*, 153–155; Hatfield, Cecil Papers, 133/fol. 104r. Francis Stewart, 1st earl of Bothwell (1562–1612), *ODNB*; see above, pp. 46–47.

[13]See above, pp. 48 and 50. TNA SP 52/50/no. 5; *HMCS*, iv, 296–297; *CSPS 1593–1595*, 1–2.

[14]Sir Thomas Wilson, officer of the council (d.1629), *ODNB*. Following Cecil's death in 1612, he retained his papers as the 'state paper office'. Henry Maynard (after 1547–1610), *ODNB*; see above, pp. 12–14, 18n, 20, 26, 48 and 78. Burghley wrote to Cecil the following day, 22 May 1593, that he had written his deliberations on the matters concerning Bothwell which were so delicate that he would not trust their drafting to a secretary, and insisted that

I pray yow require Mr. Woolley to send me my l[ord] Scropes l[ette]rs, and knowe of him what answer I may make to Sir Thomas Wilsone who doth only attend here to knowe hir ma[jes]ties pleasure, being verie unwilling to enter into the charge, except there were a Governour in the towne to beare the Brunte of the charge which the late Marshall did and with which charge, Sir Robert Constable was beggard.[15] ffor the sute of Mr. Nowell in my next I will gett meanes to advartise yow.[16]

[In Burghley's hand]
I have sondry offers to ease me of my torment in my head, which the offerors conceave to come of the quicksilver, and therfor to gyve me the tyncture of Gold, my nightly paynes ar so grevous as I am redy to receave any offer, and yet with feare for offendynge of hir Ma[jes]tie, if I shold therby empayre [page torn*] helth, contrary to hir carefull advise, and yet [page torn**] will not be hasty therein, but will preserve, [page torn***] the advise of hir ma[jes]tie may have sone secret [page torn] from God hir head, and my director to ser[page torn****] for hym. Yow se that my hand now parrets my hart withowt excuse.

From my house in Westminster the 21 of May 1593 though I want fete to go to the hall, yet I forbeare not to be occupyed ther, with payne to ease others.

Your lov[ing] father,

W. Burghley

*Possibly 'my'.
** Possibly 'I'.
***Possibly blank.
****Possibly completes the word 'serve'.

Cecil receive them in person before their presentation to the Queen. Hatfield, Cecil Papers, 169/fol. 81r; *HMCS*, iv, 319.

[15] Political machinations amongst the officers at the garrison at Berwick can be determined from Sir John Carey's letters to Burghley and Cecil of 24 May 1593, wherein it is clear that the Queen did not want Carey as her deputy governor to his father Henry Carey, 1st Baron Hunsdon (1526–1596), privy councillor and the Queen's cousin, *ODNB*. Letters from Carey to Burghley and Cecil show that he knew Cecil read his father's papers, probably from his own father on the Privy Council, *Cal. Border Papers*, i, 461–462, nos 838, 839.

[16] Henry Noel made suit for the monopoly of stone jar making to Cecil several times in the summer of 1593. The closest in date to Letter No. 2, CUL MS Ee 3 56, are Noel's of 26 May 1593, and Henry Maynard's letter for Burghley to Cecil of the same date, giving the opinion of the officers of the port of London on the suit. Hatfield, Cecil Papers, 169/fol. 85r, 87r; *HMCS*, iv, 323, 342, 346–347; *HPT*, iii, 134–135.

Dorse

ADDRESSED in Burghley's hand:
To my son Sir Rob[er]t Cecill, Knight at the Court

ENDORSED in the hand of Cecil's filing clerk, Simon Willis:
21 Maii 1593
The lo[rd] Thre[sure]r to my M[aste]r

Letter No. 3

William, Lord Burghley to Sir Robert Cecil, 26 May 1593

¼ p. Holograph.
Addressed, endorsed, signed.

Text

The beror hereof nameth hymself Mouett, sent from bullen with l[ette]res to hir Ma[jes]ty. The Fr[ench] amb[assador] req[ui]reth me to adress hym to yow, so as hir Ma[jes]ty may receave his l[ette]res and message.[17]

By l[ette]res to the ambass[ador] maketh only mention of powder, argent & other munitions: but without limitation.[18]

This satyrd[ay] at noon in the Court of wards.[19]

Your lo[ving] father,

W. Burghley

[17] The identity of the messengers Mouett (seagull?) and Gerenier (granary?) are not further explained in Beauvoir la Nocle's letters to Cecil.

[18] Beauvoir la Nocle (see *L&A analysis*, iv, Analysis no. 558) made the case that the Queen could not see how men could help raise a siege if the lower town was cut off, and that no specifications of materiel needed were given. Beauvoir, in his turn, fired off letters to Rouillac and Hillez – governor of the fortress in Boulogne – about supplies needed, matters addressed also in his cover letter to Burghley of 26 May and to Cecil. Burghley had asked the ambassador to make a realistic assessment of the needs of Boulogne. TNA SP 78/31/fol. 82r, 84r, 88r.

[19] For Burghley as master of the court of wards and liveries, see Joel Hurstfield, *The Queen's Wards: Wardship and Marriage under Elizabeth I* (London, 1973).

Dorse

ADDRESSED in Henry Maynard's hand:
To my Lovinge sonne, Sir Robart Cecill knight, on hir ma[jes]ties
privy Connsell

ENDORSED in Simon Willis's hand:
26 Maii 1593, the Lo[rd] Thre[sure]r to my M[aste]r

Letter No. 4

William, Lord Burghley to Sir Robert Cecil, 26 May 1593

½ p. First paragraph dictated to Henry Maynard, with a holograph paragraph added.
No address, endorsed, signed.

Text

I have receaved from my l[ord] Keper, the form of a proclamacion in
paper for the Adiournment of part of the next terme, which I have
perused,[20] and doe send yt heareinclosed to yowe to be ingrossed in
parchement by one of the Clerkes of the Signett, which when it shall
be so written I praie yowe to offer yt to hir ma[jes]tie to signe, for that
as my L[ord] Keper writeth to mee hir ma[jes]ties pleasure is to have
yt done.[21]

Ffrom my hose in the Strand this xxvi[th] of May, 1593.

[Paragraphs added by Burghley in his own hand after the section
above was dictated and signed]
It req[ui]reth spede, that knolledg may be gyven now at the end of
this tearme.
    I fynd my self so decayeng in strength as I fynd it [more] nedefull for
me to be occupyed, about my last will and other establishementes for
my chyldren.[22]

[Maynard's hand]
Your lovinge father

[20] Proclamation on paper for the adjournment of the legal term of summer 1593 to St
Albans by reason of the plague, then rampant in London and environs, sent by the lord
keeper, Sir Thomas Puckering. *TRP*, iii, 118–119.
[21] For a discussion of the seals and procuration of letters to the signet, see above, pp. 13–16.
[22] Burghley's last will and testament, TNA PCC PROB 11, Lewyn 92; see Letter No. 6.

[Signed]
W. Burghley

Dorse

NOT ADDRESSED
ENDORSED in Simon Willis's hand:
The Lo[rd] Thre[surer] to my M[aste]r

Letter No. 5

William, Lord Burghley to Sir Robert Cecil, after 28 May 1593

1 p. Holograph,
Addressed, endorsed, signed.

Text

I have receaved your l[ette]re of this 28.[23] hereupon though I am weak, and uncertyn how I shall be hable to come to the Court, yet I am in mynd to come to morrow to the Court with opinion that after on or twoo dayes hir Ma[jes]ty will licenss me to retorn, to seke my amendment, or to tak my Jornay to follow universam viam carnis,[24] and to this latter Jornay I am most disposed, with perswasion that if sowles have sence of earthly thynges, I shall be in God's sight an intercessor for the prosperite of his chyrch here, and for hir Ma[jes]ty, as his Governor thereof to his Glory. Yow must allow me to be in this humor, for I fynd no other tast of any other thyng.

If I shall be hable by Coche or lytter (for I provyde both) I will be with yow to morrow.

[Added beside the signature]
Untill this dynnar tyme I have had nother kyn, nor Inward frend to use my sete or sit with me but multitudes of sutors that only come for ther own causes.

Your loving father,

W. Burghley

[23] Burghley's reference to his son's letter of 28 May 1593 suggests that this letter was written 29–31 May, 1593.
[24] 'Universam viam carnis': the way of all flesh.

Dorse

ADDRESS in Henry Maynard's hand:
To my Lovinge sonne, Sir Robart Cecill, knight, one of hir ma[jes]ties privy Connsell

ENDORSED by Simon Willis:
Maie 1593, The Lo[rd] Thre]sure]r to my M[aste]r

A FRAGMENT OF THE ENDORSEMENT OF THE NEXT LETTER, cut out of the volume, remains:
27 Maie 1593

Letter No. 6

William, Lord Burghley to Henry Brooke, 22 September 1592

½ p. Holograph,
Addressed, endorsed, signed.

Text

Good Mr. Henry Brook[25] I knowe not howe presently to answer yow to your contentment for I fynd that Mr. Bronker[26] had made the lyk sute afor yow, to which I gave no full assent because the party was not dead. besyde this in dede I ment this for your sistar[27] who wisshed of

---

[25] Henry Brooke, 11th Baron Cobham (1564–1619), Sir Robert Cecil's brother-in-law since 1589 and later political enemy. Brooke succeeded to the title in 1597 at his father's death, inheriting also the office of the lord warden of the Cinque Ports, which might argue for his closeness to Cecil in intelligence operations there in the new secretarial administration. He was attainted for treason for his part in the Main Plot in 1603; see *ODNB*.

[26] Henry Brounker or Bronker: Irish patentee who assisted Sir Henry Wallop (1531–1599), *ODNB*, the Queen's under-treasurer in Ireland, for whom Cecil negotiated the lucrative fee-farm of the sweet-wine imposts into Ireland – in reversion from Thomas Molyneux, but undertaken actively by Bronker from Michaelmas 1594 – in Aug. 1594 perhaps to favour Wallop. Bronker forwarded the under-treasurer's certificate of the imposts and Cecil's procuration of the suit, *HMCS*, iv, 624; TNA SP SO3/1/fol. 513r. Sir John Fortescue (1533–1607), *ODNB*, was chancellor of the Exchequer, and here joined with the lord deputy, Sir William Russell, and the countess of Warwick in favouring a senior servant of the London Customs House, George Margitts, for the place, but the suit was frustrated possibly by Cecil's criticism of Margitts' attempt to monopolize the Venetian gold and silver imports. *HMCS*, iv, 616. Thomas Molyneux (1531–1597), Irish land grantee and suspected Catholic, *ODNB*.

[27] Lady Elizabeth Cecil (1562–1597), née Brooke died of a miscarriage Jan. 1597. Burghley made changes to his will on the marriage of his grandson William (Lord Ros) by his elder son Sir Thomas Cecil, later earl of Exeter (1542–1624) in 1589; and on the birth of William's

on granted to hir which within these x dayes I promised here the next which is this. And I do not use to makes Grantes of any whylest the ancestor lyveth.

From Wadstoc, the 22 of 7bre.

Your assured loving frend,

W. Burghley

Dorse

ADDRESSED in Henry Maynard's hand:
To my vearie lovinge frend, Mr. Henry Brook, Esq.

ENDORSED by Simon Willis:
27 Sept[ember] 1592
The Lo[rd] Threasurer's l[ette]re
to Mr. hy: Brooke

Letter No. 7

William, Lord Burghley to Sir Robert Cecil, 1 December 1595

1 p., with an additional paragraph on the right margin. Holograph.
Addressed, endorsed, signed.

Text

I can not but contynew my care for Irland, and therfor though orders ar sent for procedyng with the 2 rebells Tyron and odonnell,[28] yet ther is no order for answer to the demandes of monny to pay the army ther,

---

son in 1591 and on the birth of Robert Cecil's son in the same year. See Gemma Allen, *The Cooke Sisters: Education, Piety and Politics in Early Modern England* (Oxford, 2016), 72–74, 106–108.
[28] See also Letters Nos 70, 73. Sir John Norris, *ODNB* (1547 × 1550–1597).
The earl of Tyrone, Aodh Mór Ó Néill styled Hugh O'Neill (c.1540–1616), *ODNB*, was the 2nd earl from 1587 and Baron Dungannon in succession to his brother, 1562. He had been educated in England and was a member of the household of the earl of Leicester (1588). He had co-operated extensively with the English crown. Elizabeth used Tyrone, or so she thought, as a counterpoise to his kinsman Turlough Luineach, his principal rival in the lordship of Tyrone. On succeeding Turlough he began actively working against the Crown, particularly the president of Ulster, Sir Henry Bagenal with whose sister Mabel he eloped. Sir Henry Bagenal (c.1556–1598), marshal of the army in Ireland, reported frequently to the government, *ODNB*.
Tyrone and his chief lieutenant O'Donnell created an extensive, well-supplied and well-trained military force based in the lordship of Tyrone, communicating through Irish pirates extensively with the king of Spain. Tyrone's resources were immense, estimated in his

which is very chargeable, and if the submissions of the rebells shall be perfected, it war reason to deminish the army, which can not be doone, without a paye to be made, and monny also to contynew them which shall remayn.[29] I pray yow inform hir Ma[jes]ty hereof, for my discharg, for that the Depute and the Tresorer wryte hereof, to me only, and not to the rest of the Connsell, and so they expect answer from me, as by 2 l[ette]res which I send yow may appear on from the Depute and the Tresorer dated the 8 of last month which I have underlyned.[30] the other from the Tresorer of the same date, which yow may besech hir Ma[jes]ty to heare redd because he concludeth with a demand of a larg some wherof hir Ma[jes]ty may please to have consideration, for the sonar the monny maybe sent the sonar may hir chardg deminish, which the Tresorer reporteth to be viii M l [£8,000] the month and yet ther is but half Novemb[er] payd and yet i M ii C l [£1,200] borrowed and i M ix C [£1,900] dew for Bowes so as to make a paye for November and to pay the dett, is required vii M i C

---

lordship at £80,000 per annum. O'Donnell was Tyrone/O'Neill's major confederate against the English, 1593–1600, went to the English in Tyrconnell under Sir Henry Docwra in 1600, knighted 1601, lord of Tyrconnell from 1592, Bruce Lenman, *England's Colonial Wars 1550 1688: Conflicts, Empire and National Identity.* (New York, 2001), 113. Hiram Morgan, *Tyrone's Rebellion: The Outbreak of the Nine Year's War in Tudor Ireland* (Woodbridge, 1993); O'Donnell [Ó Domhnaill], Sir Niall Garbh (1568/9–1626?), *ODNB.*

The proceedings with the rebel earl of Tyrone in Nov. 1595 followed Cecil's explicit instructions to Sir John Norris. He was to begin negotiations on behalf of the Crown with the recently allied rebels Tyrone and O'Donnell. TNA SP 63/183/no. 114, fol. 354r–v. Drafts of the fuller instructions were drawn by both Burghley and Cecil. Burghley's notes were altered in his hand on a corrected draft in Maynard's hand of TNA SP 63/183/no. 110, fols. 346r–347v, 348r–349v. A memorandum enumerating Tyrone's offences against the Queen was drafted by Maynard with corrections in a later version made in Cecil's hand, TNA SP 63/183/ no. 112, fols. 350r–351v; no. 113, fols. 352r–353v. Norris and Sir William Russell (see n. 30), the lord deputy, clashed. They extended their personal enmity to present disputes over the powers granted to Norris in these letters despite Russell's clear insistence to Cecil that the matter was far too delicate for the Irish Council to deal with alone, TNA SP 63/184/ no. 8, fol. 20r, no. 14, fols. 57r–58r; *CSPI 1592–1596*, 427. Copies of a patent for Tyrone's submission were also drawn at that time, in 'project' by Burghley and corrected by both Cecils in another draft, TNA SP 63/184, no. 42, fols. 143r–144v, no. 43, fols. 145r–146v.

[29] Expenses for the troops may have been calculated from Sir Ralph Lane's 46-page book of the Queen's charges for her Irish troops from 1 Apr. to 30 Sept. 1595, TNA SP 63/184/no. 21, fols. 68r–95v), *ODNB.*

[30] Burghley inquired of Sir William Russell (1553–1613), *ODNB*, and Sir Henry Wallop in mid Nov. 1595 regarding expenditure and the loss of treasure, particularly the inadequate provisioning by government commissaries George Beverly in Chester and Robert Newcomen in Dublin. *CSPI 1592–1596*, 428–429. Russell had complained about the same losses and shortfalls to Burghley in his letter of the 9 Nov. packet. TNA SP 63/184/no. 14, fol. 53r–v, no. 15, fols. 57r–58r. Wallop's reply of 12 Dec. to this letter of Burghley's letter to Cecil of 1 Dec. noted that the £20,000 sent would last a month once the outstanding debts were paid. This came with Ralph Lane's answers about the musters as requested by Burghley, TNA SP 63/184/ fol. 96r–97.

[£7,100] and now also monny must be sent, for December which will be at an end before the monny can come thyther.[31]

I do send yow a note of all the monnyes sent in the yer 1594 and of monnyes sent in 2 months of this present yere non beying sent in Sept[ember], Octob[er] nor November which hir Ma[jes]ty may also se, and therby be moved to resolv hir plesur.[32]

[In the margin on the right side of the page]
I pray yow gyve my most humble thanks to hir Ma[jes]ty for hir offer sendyng to know of my head and neck which on Satyrday, semed to be made of lead and yesterday soemwhat lighter as of Iron. I hope to have then only in weight boan and flesh.

[Added in a paragraph to the right of above addition in the margin]
I have not without some payne written this therfor, yt is not legible for hir Majesty.

p[rim]o Dec[ember 1595,

Your loving father,

---

[31] Two large payments in rapid succession went into Ireland in Dec. 1595 and Jan. 1596: £12,000 and £20,000 respectively, TNA SP 63/191/fol. 201r. The £32,000 pounds matched Burghley's worst fears for the projected costs of Ulster alone for the next seven months, as estimated in Sept. 1595, TNA SP 63/183/no. 68, fol. 218r. Payments were due to Sir Robert Bowes (d.1597), *ODNB*, the Queen's ambassador to the Scottish court. These were 'tokens' for John Auchinross and MacLean of Duart, adherents of the earl of Argyll who committed men and ships for a projected invasion of Loch Foyle. TNA SP 52/57/no. 59, SP 52/58/no. 6. In Aug. 1595 1,000 marks had been promised. A naval skirmish off the Ulster coast managed by these intelligence contacts and by Captain George Thornton was also paid out of the Irish Exchequer. TNA SP 63/191/fol. 122v; Letter No. 73. Sir Lachlan Mor Maclean of Duart (1558–1598), *ODNB*, and Archibald Campbell, 7th earl of Argyll (1575/6–1638), *ODNB*, were James VI's leading force against the northern earls, particularly the earl of Huntly in 1594–1596. Both Maclean and Argyll corresponded with Robert Cecil, see above, p. 50. George Gordon, 1st marquess of Huntly (1561/2–1636), *ODNB*, was the sworn enemy of the earl of Moray who was married to Argyll's sister. He was exonerated by the king in 1594 for dealings with Spain together with the earls of Angus and Erroll despite condemnation by the Kirk. The Cecils' 'labyrinth', was to create a party around Bothwell, Moray, and others who would frustrate the pro-Spanish earls in the highlands and islands. James Stewart, 2nd earl of Moray (1565/6–1592), *ODNB*, had been murdered by Huntly's men, thus exacerbating the crisis among the king's family and their opponents. William Douglas, 10th earl of Angus (c.1554–1611), *ODNB*, shifted alliances, befriending Bothwell, for example while being named in the Spanish Blanks and incurring unsuccessful royal military responses in early 1593 and Nov. 1594. The last earl of Erroll, James Hay (1564–1631), *ODNB*, was a convert to Catholicism, and with the other two was implicated directly against the Kirk, and crown, from 1589. In 1593–1596 he, too, was under prohibition but not forfeiture of the crown. Some of his lands were given to the king's lieutenant the duke of Lennox, but he returned secretly in 1596, to the consternation of Burghley and others.

[32] Burghley wrote memorials of expenditure on a nearly monthly or bi-monthly basis. This exact estimate is not extant.

W. Burghley

Dorse

ADDRESSED by Burghley:
To my loving sonn Sir Robart Cecill

ENDORSED by Sir Robert Cecil:
~~Last~~ first of December 1593
my l[ord] to me

Letter No. 8

William, Lord Burghley to Sir Robert Cecil, 3 December 1593

⅔ p. Holograph.
Addressed, endorsed, signed.

Text

I do send herewith letters directed to the Counsell from the L[ord] depute and Connsell of Irland, which I was bold to oppen and read as yow may se by my apostills in the margynes.[33] twoo or 3 matters therin ar to be answered by my LLs [Lords] uppon ther reportes to hir Ma[jes]ty wherunto I do forebeare to shew my opinion, because the matters may require debat and oppositions, so as my opinion may varye at the fyrst and yet may alter uppon a second advise.

It had bene well doone that the Depute, had caused the [Marshall] uppon his Journal of his procedynges and Marchynges to have sent a small tryck by description in paper.[34]

I send also a letter from the Erle of Northum[berland] in answer of ours to hym. he hath not bene sick at all, but troobled with a cold and is now retourned to petworth.[35]

3 December 1593

Your lov[ing] father,

W. Burghley

[33] Sir William Fitzwilliam, lord deputy of Ireland, 1590–1594, and Lady Burghley's kinsman (1526–1599), *ODNB*, was soon to be recalled.
[34] Bagenal's reports regarding the rebel Maguire's escape from his custody, *CSPI 1592–1596*, 168; TNA SP 63/172/no. 8, fol. 64r.
[35] Henry Percy, 9th earl of Northumberland (1564–1632), *ODNB*.

Dorse

ADDRESSED in Henry Maynard's hand:
To my lovinge sonne, Robert Cecill, knight

ENDORSED in Simon Willis's hand:
The Lo[rd] Thre[sure]r to my M[aste]r

Letter No. 9

William, Lord Burghley to Sir Robert Cecil, 3 December 1593

⅔ p. Dictated to Henry Maynard, with a final paragraph and some interlineations in Burghley's hand.
Addressed, endorsed, signed.

Text

I have received letters this daie from Mr. Yonge,[36] that havinge emploied an Irishman into the Lowe Contries for the doinge of summ service uppon Sir William Stanleie, whoe failing of his purpose thearein, delt with certaine Irishmen of his Regiment,[37] to warne him, and to retorne hither into the Realme: whearein he prevailed so farre with them that at this present theare are commen over from thence to the number of xi. And for that I thowght the sending of them over into theire contrie might rather doe hurt than good, in

---

[36]Richard Yonge or Young, Council servant and Middlesex JP, was used by the Cecils frequently in intelligence matters. For example, the questioning of a double agent, Thomas D'Arques, in Cecil's employ, was left to Young in late 1592 (*HMCS*, iv, 245, 246, 248, 249, 250), as was the examination of Anthony Tyrell, a Catholic with continental connections (*HMCS*, iv, 380–381, 392, 392–394, 419, 428, 432). On 30 Mar. 1593, Young was named in the commission of Council advisers who were to refer seditious persons, foreign seminarians, and other dangerous spies, to a Council committee of three, including Cecil (*APC 1592*, 7), so Burghley's referral of Young's letter was probably routine, but it involved expenditure and passed the Lord Treasurer first for comment. During the Parliament of 1593, Cecil had been placed into the commission examining Richard Hesketh's plots against the earl of Derby. For the commission's letters patent, see *CPR 35 Eliz. I*, nos 569–570.
[37]Richard Hesketh (1553–1593), *ODNB*. Sir William Stanley (1548–1630), *ODNB*, was a member of the earl of Derby's family whose career in Ireland had been furthered by Burghley in the early 1580s, but his later treasonous act of giving Deventer to the Spanish in 1587 had posed an intelligence problem, as he had significant Irish contacts. These, Burghley held here, would have to be discovered, because the link to the rebels might prove direct Spanish involvement with Tyrone and O'Donnell. See also Rory Rapple, *Martial Power and Elizabethan Political Culture: Military Men in England and Ireland, 1558–1594* (New York, 2009), 118–125. See Letter No. 122.

that I conceived that theie weare but Base persons, I wroate to Mr. Yonge to examin them as to the places of theire birthe, and of the meanes theie had to live being in theire contrye: which examinacions with his letter I send heareinclosed to yowe to be imparted to my lls [Lords] of the Connsell that theire lls [Lords] maie (if so it shall please them,) grawnt them pasportes to retorne with their letters to the L[ord] deputy in their favour: and if hir ma[jes]tie would be pleased to geve them somethinge to carry themm home, being as yt semeth in pooreCase it might [a long sentence crossed out, illegible] ᵇᵉ ᵏᵉᵖᵉ ᵗʰᵉᵐ ᶠʳᵒᵐ ᵈⁱˢᵒʳᵈᵉʳ.

So farre you well, ffrom the Strand this third of December 1593.

[Burghley's postscript]
I wish no men to retorn, without certen knolledg, how they can lyve at home, wher ther ar allredy to manny lose men as yow may se in on part of the letters from Irland [page ripped].³⁸

[In Maynard's hand, meaning that the paragraph above was added after signing]
your lov[ing] father,

[Signed]
W. Burghley

Dorse

ADDRESSED in Henry Maynard's hand:
To my Lovinge Sonne
Sir Robart Cecill knight, one of hir ma[jes]ties privie Connsell

ENDORSED by Sir Robert Cecil:
Two that came ʷⁱᵗʰ Le Grenier who bro:

ENDORSED in Simon Willis's hand:
3 decemb[er] 1593
The L[ord] Thre[asure]r to my M[aste]r

---

³⁸The substance of the rest of this letter refers to intelligence from Ireland in Dec. 1593: see Letter No. 8. Cecil was well informed of the Irish-Spanish intelligence links. See TNA SP 63/172/no. 19, fol. 127r–v, a notice of Spanish news endorsed 'Simple's report'. This may have been a Scottish agent named 'Semple', 'Semphill', most likely a close servant of the king, Sir James Semphill or Semple (1566?–1626), *ODNB*. News of the king's support or connection to Jesuits in Ireland may have been monitored by the Cecils through him.

Letter No. 10

William, Lord Burghley to Sir Robert Cecil, 7 December 1593

1 p. Holograph.
Addressed, endorsed, signed.

Text

I dare not wrtye to yow of my wowyng mentioned ^{sent for} untill I here how hir Ma[jes]ty, alloweth of my absence to follow it. Butt in the meane tyme yow may assure hir Ma[jes]ty, that I fynd no great hope of any spedy success. I fynd the lady some what strange to gyve care to my request, for that she useth not to gyve audience, in clowdy and fowle wether, and herof is here to great plenty, and yet betwixt showres I do attend and follow hir trayne.

Thus much metaphorically I trust without offence to hir Ma[jes]ty. Now literally I do send yow the l[ette]res from Mr. bowes, which I have red, and of ye decre of ye Convention, as yow may se by my notes whereunto if hir Ma[jes]ty will have me make answer I shall so do.[39]

I send yow also herwth a l[ette]re from Mr. warburton whom hir Ma[jes]ty allowed by hir warrant to exercise the office of vicechamberlain in Chester / by it yow shall se how necessary it is for execution of Justyce to all that have sutes from any superior Courtes in yt [that] Conte Palatyn, that there be a chamberlain, and therfor as hir Ma[jes]ty shall allow the now Erle to occupy yt [that] office, so may hir Ma[jes]ty do well to pass it to hym of hir meare gratuite, wthout any appearance of this necessite. If hir Ma[jes]ty assent therto may yow well to procure a bill from Mr. attorney.[40]

I look befor I slepe to heare from yow, how far hir Ma[jes]ty do allow of my simple opinion for ye Irland cawses.

7 10bre at Theb[alds]

Your lovyng father, W. Burghley.

---

[39] The Scottish convention had voted to excommunicate the northern earls, see Letters Nos 2 and 7, for their plot and Bowes's reporting of their movements.

[40] Sir Peter Warburton of Arley (*c.*1540–1621), *ODNB*, recently appointed vice-chamberlain of Chester, also recently received the call of serjeant. The Cecils had shown him favour in 1593, A.G.R. Smith, *Servant of the Cecils: The Life of Sir Michael Hickes, 1543–1612* (London, 1977), 65–66; see Letter No. 136A.

Dorse

ADDRESS
To my verie loving sonne, Sir Robert Cecill, knight, of hir Ma[jes[ty's
Privy Consell

ENDORSED in Sir Robert Cecil's hand:
from my l[ord] to me

Letter No. 11

Peter Warburton to William, Lord Burghley, 5 December 1593

1 p. Holograph.
Addressed, endorsed, signed.

Text

Right honorable my very good L[ord]. Your L[ordshi]p's speciall furtherance of me in the call of serjeantes besides other honorable favours which your L[ord] hath done me,[41] doth bynd me to carye in most thankfull remembrance your L[ordshi]p's great goodnes towardes me most humblie desiring yur good L[ord] to accomt me to be one that do beare most thankfull goodwill & love and will be ever desirous to do you the best dutie and service I can to you and yours.

I wold have attended your L[ord] for this purpose according to my dutie but percyying it is your L[ord]ship's desire not to be troubled at this tyme with London sub[jects] in respect whereof I beseech your l[ord] to allow my boldness to write.

And wher upon the death of the late Erle of derbye,[42] chamberlain of the Countie Palatyne of Chester, it pleased her ma[jes]tie (chiefly by your L[ordshi]p's favourable commendaconn) to direct her ma[jes]tie's warrant to me under the privye signett to exercise the place as vicechamberlen[43] till further order were taken which I do

---

[41] See Letter No. 10.
[42] Henry, 4th earl of Derby had died 25 Sept. 1593, *ODNB*.
[43] BL Lansdowne MS. 74 no. 78, the attorney general, Sir Thomas Egerton, forwarded the bill for the appointment of Ferdinando, 5th earl of Derby (*c*.1559–1594) as chamberlain, 30 Sept. 1593, of the County of Chester, *ODNB*. Egerton succeeded to the office on Derby's death in 1594 much to the chagrin of William, 6th earl.

accordingly, may yt please your L[ord] to be advertised that all <u>writts</u> which are awarded from these superior courtes in that cuntry are directed <u>Camararis</u>[44] and he doth make a writte under that Seale to the sheriff and the sheriff maketh his returne to him and the Chamberlen doth returne them into these courtes in his owne name so that unles there be a chamberlen no persons with causes out of these courtes can be duly returned, for ther can not be a deputie chamberlen unless ther be a chamberlen. therfor it is a matter of <u>necessity</u> that her Ma[jes]ty appoint a <u>chamberlen</u> before the next terme at which tyme they are to be returned into these courtes in the chamberlen's name, and ther is no direccionn of any writtes vicecameransis nor no precedent in that sort. In the meane tyme I may award them to the sheriff but can not returne them in my name. as for hearing & ordering of causes in equity (as ther are divers severall matters ther) this warrant is sufficient but not for things that are to be done in ordinary course of law.

I thought it my dutie to notifie your L[ord] of the state of this cause desiring your L[ord's] honorable considaracion. Thus having troubled your L[ord] I pray god preserve your L[ord] in good health with much honour. ffrom lycolns Inn vth of december 1593. (Your L[ordshi]p's most bounden,

Peter Warburton.

Dorse

ADDRESSED in Peter Warburton's hand:
To the Right honorable my very good L[ord], Wm. L[ord] Burly, L[ord] Tresorer of England

ENDORSED in another of the Cecil's secretaries' hands, possibly Richard Percival:[45]
v[th] December 1593
Mr. Warburton, Counsellor at Lawe to my L[ord]
Reasons why it is necessary that a Chamberlane of Chester should be made before the next terme

---

[44] Presumably Warburton was outlining the letters patent and fees of the office for Burghley's benefit.
[45] Richard Percival, see above, pp. 21–22, whose hand is ubiquitous in Cecil's administrative activity. Alan G.R. Smith, 'The secretariats of the Cecils, circa 1580–1612', *The English Historical Review*, 83 (1968), 482, n. 2.

Letter No. 12

William, Lord Burghley to Sir Robert Cecil, 7 December 1593

½ p. Dictated to a clerk, Michael Hickes.[46]
Addressed, endorsed.

Text

I send to yow hereinclosed a letter written unto me by the ffr[ench] Ambassador, and Brought to me by one Belott[47] who hath made his residence at Caen, for some good tyme where he hath served verie faithfullie and painfully in hir ma[jes]ty's service. This letter as yow shall parceave is written in favour of one Monsieur de St. Marie, a gentleman verie well affected to the Cause of relligion, and devoted to hir Ma[jes]tie That he may have lycence to buy and transport a pece of Ordanaunce, called a Culvaryn of 4000 waight.[48] I understand that my L[ord] of Essex should be acquainted with the request, and that the Vidam[49] hath written in his favour. I pray yow therfore speak with my L[ord] of Essex herein and geve the request your best furtherance with hir Ma[jes]tie at your best opportunitie wherein Bellott will atend your answer at Theobalds. the 7 of December 1593.

Your loving father,

W. Burghley

Dorse

ADDRESSED Michael Hickes:
To my Verie Lovinge Soone Sir Robert Cecill knight of hir Ma[jes]ties privy Consell

[46]Michael Hickes, 1543–1612, see above, p. 12; *ODNB*; Smith, *Servant of the Cecils*.
[47]Thomas Bellott was resident at Caen, as part of the Brittany intelligence connection. Cecil made notes on Bellott's suit for the shipping of ordnance and beer, 17 Aug. 1593. See Maynard's endorsement, TNA SP 78/32/fol. 46r. Cecil was similarly occupied with Sir Noel de Caron (b. before 1530–d.1624), *ODNB*, a Dieppe merchant: see *HMCS*, iv, 167, 216, 224, 245, 246, 468, 602; TNA SP 84/47/fol. 168r. Horatio Palavicino (1540–1600), merchant and money-lender, noted that Cecil read foreign matters routinely by this time, *HMCS*, iv, 351. Cecil was also assisting Sir John Norris's forces with 'Provisions of Beare, Meale and Money'. TNA SP 84/47/fol. 99r. Palavicino was a very close to Cecil in intelligence: see Lawrence Stone, *An Elizabethan: Sir Horatio Palavicino* (Oxford, 1956); *ODNB*.
[48]St Marie's suit procured to the signet seal by Sir Robert Cecil, TNA SO3/1/fol. 438v; Hatfield, Cecil Papers, 24/60. The weight of the culverin exceeded the upper limit set by statute, as drafted by both Cecils. *TRP* iii, 107–108. Burghley procured ordnance on occasion by direct warrant to the officers of the Ordnance, and for shipping to the port officers in the Customs House, e.g. TNA SP 12/243/no. 34.
[49]See Letter No. 2.

ENDORSED in Simon Willis's hand:
The Lo[rd] Thre[sure]r to my M[aste]r
In the behalf of one Mr. Bellott
Resident in Caen.

Letter No. 13

William, Lord Burghley to Sir Robert Cecil, 9 December 1593

¾ p. Nine lines in Henry Maynard's hand, one short paragraph in Burghley's hand, and a holograph postscript.
Addressed, endorsed, signed.

Text

The Bearer hereof hath browght letters to my LLs [Lords] of the Connsell, the like whereof have been directed tto my self fromm Sir John Wogan owt of Wales, with the Examinacionns of two lewde persons fugitives,[50] whoe might have been delt withall in the Contie, withowt the trowble of my lls [Lords] of the Connsell, but seeing the messenger is cumm upp, yowe maie receave the letters ^or having acquainted my lls [Lords] hearewith^ and to retaine him with such awnsweare as yt shall please my lls [Lords] to geve. Soe farre yowe well ffrom my howse at Theobaldes this ~~eight~~ ix of Deember 1593.

[Burghley]
I send also a warrant for his charges being a long foote Jornay and if he sent awey spedely yow may put in the blank of the warrant, or otherwise ı iii s iiii d.

Hytherto beyng v of the clock towrd even, I have not hard from you, concerning ethr Irland or brytan causes.

For the boglish, I think if uppon the last direction Sir Jhon norrice shall be come awey, yet my opinion Contynueth for retyring the forces to the Isles, for which lyk comission wuld be gyven to Sir Jhon Norryce electu-[51]

[In Maynard's hand]

Your lovinge father

[50] Sir John Wogan was a member of the Pembrokeshire commission of the peace. *CPR, 36 Eliz. I*, no. 1019.
[51] For the threat to Sir John Norris's forces at this juncture, see R.B. Wernham, *After the Armada: Elizabethan England and the Struggle for Western Europe, 1588–1595* (Oxford, 1984), 511.

[signed]

W. Burghley

Dorse

ADDRESSED in Henry Maynard's hand:
To my lovinge sonne Sir Robert Cecill knyght one of hir Ma[jes]ties privy Connsell

ENDORSED in Simon Willis's hand:
9 decemb[er] 1593
The L[ord] Treas[urer] to my Master

Letter No. 14

William, Lord Burghley to Sir Robert Cecil, 7 December 1593

5 pp. Dictated to Michael Hickes.
Addressed [holograph], endorsed.

Text

I have receved your letter written this daye late at nyght and because with it and other writinges which yow sent me, there are many poyntes to be answered. ffor ease of my hand I doe use my Secretarie. And do answere the partes of your letter as they lye inorder. I like well of the Conference yow had with Swynnerton[52]

---

[52]John Swinnerton (1564–1616), *ODNB*, was farmer of the Imposts for Wines and worked closely with Carmarthen and Billingsley of the Customs, a crucial source of revenue affected by war. *CSPD 1591–1594*, 511–512. The agreement alluded to Swinnerton's farming of the wine imposts as sole purveyor to the court, according to this agreement, which lasted 1593–1597 and from which he made great profit. BL Lansdowne MS 81, no. 25. Over the first year his profit through London was £4,024, with £1,454 10s through outports. His cost was £4,640, yielding a profit of £839. A 1591 agreement was made between Swinnerton with Carmarthen as the Queen's agent thus obviating the previous role of guarantor held by Thomas Fanshawe, Queen's Remembrancer in the Exchequer, for the bonds. Alderman Billingsley was to have had, by the earlier agreement, the bonds on the Queen's behalf during the first half year. The division of payment was to have followed on the half year. Burghley had noted then that he doubted Billingsley would be happy with the arrangement, because there was some question as to how Swinnerton would repay debt; the new covenant removed Billingsley and Swinnerton became sole patentee until 1597 when the Crown decided to farm the wines directly. *CSPD 1591–1594*, 140. See Allegra Woodworth, *Purveyance for the Royal Household, Transactions of the American Philosophical Society*, NS 35 (1946), 56 and n. 24. Cecil adjudicated in a dispute between Carmarthen and another customs house servant, George Margitts, in obtaining the impost of Irish sweet wines. *CSPI 1592–1594*, 424.

and Carmarthen[53] and have perused the articles of agrement, which seeing they both do Allowe, I am gladd therof and in that yow have acquainted hir ma[jes]tie therewith ʸᵒʷ have donne well. But yett as you may fynd by my note in the margent to the 2 article. I dowbt of Billingslies[54] [Alderman] consent therto or that otherwise hir ma[jes]tie may be a loser. for the explanation of one poynt in Swynnerton's patent I like well yow send for Mr. Sollicitor[55] and informe him of the Clause to be changed by the Quene's warrant, but for the perfetting thereof I thinke it mete that he speake both with Carmarthen and Swynnerton. The 2 poynt of your letter concerneth my former allegorical letter written to yow ⁱⁿ which I perceive her ma[jes]tie discouered the literall sence thereof befoer the mydst of it seene. I must confesse that my Cunninge therein was not sufficient to the hide sence from her ma[jes]tie, although I thinke never a ladye ᵇᵉˢⁱᵈᵉˢ ʰᵉʳ nor Decipherer in the Courte would ha[v]e dissolved the figure to have found the sence as hir ma[jes]tie hath done. And where hir ma[jes]tie alloweth of me, that I made my self merrye in verie truth I did it rather to make hir some sport (my self therein not altered no otherwise then hir ma[jes]tie's lute is in hir own hand, that maketh others merry, and contynueth it self as was.) ffor the matters of Ireland I parceave hir ma[jes]tie yesternight ment to heare them this day. And for the questions what somme of money might be reasonablie required I think 5 or 6000 l varie nedefull so as Sir Henry Wallopp be moved to procure payment of the overplus of the Quene's ordinarie Revennue ᵈᵘᵉ there above al ordinarye ffees for officers of the Realm payd.[56]

[Margin, in Cecil's hand]

[53] Richard Carmarthen, an officer of the London Customs and merchant, was a valuable intelligence link and investigated suspicious persons on behalf of the Privy Council; see, for example, *HMCS*, v, 15, 6 Sept. 1595. H.A. Lloyd, 'Camden, Carmarthen and the Customs', *English Historical Review* 85 (1970), 776–787.

[54] Sir Henry Billingsley (d.1606), *ODNB*, was part of the Customs House intelligence network for the Privy Council, merchant of London, and lord mayor 1596. His son married the daughter of John Quarles, merchant of London and sometime victualler of the navy. One account claimed Billingsley was far more efficient as Customs farmer in the port of London than his predecessor Sir Thomas Smith. Sir Robert Cecil had worked closely with him and Carmarthen in gathering and selling the prizes from the carrick *Madre di Dios* in 1591. *CSPD 1591–1594*, 64, 140.

[55] Sir Edward Coke (1552–1634), then solicitor general, *ODNB*.

[56] The matter of paying the patentees of Ireland out of deteriorating Irish revenues was put to Burghley by Wallop (then at Hampton Court) on 6 Dec. 1593, in which he expressed frustration that the entire revenues from Connacht went to Sir Richard Bingham, and those of Munster to Sir Thomas Norreys. *CSPI 1592–1596*, 190; TNA SP 63/172/no. 37. These

Brittany

[Text continued]
Now to the greatest matter of all theise, concerning the letters from Sir John Norreis written the last of October[57] which I retorne unto yow dated at Pontrieux and so do I also

[p. 2] now send yow another of his dated the next daye ffollowing at Pempole[58] [Burghley] which cam to me wih yours, And for the matter conteyned in his former letter and the disposition in hir ma[jes]tie for the safetie of hir Troupes uppon hir opynion of the reach of the Truce.[59] I am in doubt what to advise to give unto hir Majesty by reason of the diversitie of the dyrections which have bene sent to John Norreis. The last whereof as yow may remember was wherewith hir ma[jes]tie was acquainted.[60] That considering hir ma[jes]tie was advertised both

standing allowances were balanced against an extraordinary payment of £5,000–£6,000 in Dec. 1593 sent for pay of the garrison. A Privy Council brief in Willis's hand, endorsed by Cecil, discussed the question of proceeding with a campaign against Maguire, awaiting the Queen's assent. That winter was not good for such a campaign, because victualling and supplies were very costly. Money was sent: 'of necessitie some money would be sent to Ireland, for all that was last sent is distributed to the souldiers imprest', TNA SP 63/172/no. 43, fols. 234r–v, 235v. Sir Thomas Norris [Norreys] (1556–1599), *ODNB*, deputy to his brother in Munster (see n. 58), long-standing Irish military governor. Sir Richard Bingham (1527/8–1599), governor of Connacht, sequestrated by the government in 1596 but relieved under Essex's patronage; a Crown servant of long standing, Bingham's position in Connacht was complex and he had to deal with the lingering opposition of Burghley and Fitzwilliam, Rapple, *Martial Power*, 250–300.
   [57]Sir John Norris's letters to Burghley dated 31 Oct. 1593 from Pontrieux, TNA SP 78/32/fols. 273r–274v; *L&A*, v, Analysis: nos 270, 271, 275, 276, 277, 283, 397.
   [58]Sir John Norris to the Queen and Privy Council of 1 Nov. 1593 is not extant, but Burghley might have been mistaken about the date of Norris's second letter. Norris's dated 1 Dec. set forth French dealings which had the effect of turning the Queen's cautious support for the relief of Pempole [Paimpol] to outright revocation of her Brittany troops, TNA SP 78/32/fols. 372r–373v; *L&A*, v, Analysis: nos 282, 284. Sir John Norris, Burghley's favoured military commander, was governor of Munster. The warning of Henry IV's intentions informed Cecil's work in furnishing Norris with points to consider. Particularly suspect were the king's intentions, given (as deciphered from Norris to Cecil) 'yf he may be received into the church he wyll not only make war agaynst the protestantes of France but al Christendom', TNA SP 78/32/fols. 42r–3v, 44r–45v, 277r–8or.
   [59]Norris's opinion on the breach of the truce in Oct. 1593, in his letter of 1 Nov. 1593, is given in the previous note. Jean VI d'Aumont (1522–1595) and the duke of Mercoeur had negotiated the prolongation of the truce. Mercoeur, Philippe-Emanuel de Lorraine (1558–1602), was a commander of the Catholic League, later married to Henry IV's illegitimate daughter to secure Brittany for the French crown, and pressed his claims to the duchy of Brittany through his wife Marie of Luxembourg.
   [60]TNA SP 78/32/fol. 298r; *L&A*, v, Analysis no. 282. Burghley's careful noting of the Queen's involvement suggests that advice, rather than royal commands, had been supplied to Norris through privy councillors and their agents.

from the king and from the States of Brittanie,[61] the Duke's Deputie should come from the States to treate with hir ma[jes]tie for the Contynuacion of hir fforces and Satisfaction for hir charges paste and to come. and that Sir John Norreis desyred privately to come over he was lycenced by hir ma[jes]tie to informe him selfe well of the legations of the deputies and so to come over to give hir ma[jes]tie better information [Burghley] and to leave the troops in Juersy And this was the last dyrection made unto hym to my knowledge. Which might be allowed to contynewe, if there were not nowe matter advertised by Sir John Norreis by this his last letter, wherein he declareth his opynion that notwithstanding the Truce accepted by the Duke Mercury by letters written from the Mareschall[62] unto him he is advised to stand uppon his gard, arguing thereby a doubt whither the Truce would be performed or not. he also writing some reasons which move him to doubt of the performance of the truce for that the Spaniardes have lately dislodged from place to place to come to St. Bryene ['ryene' is added above the line in Burghley's hand] and there to Joyn with both the Lorraynners and the Ffrench[63] which place is but a good dayes march from Pempole. Besides this, he writeth that the Ffrench, which he had procured to lye nere unto him, for his assistance, ar by the Mareschall revoked and disparsed to their garrisons so as it semeth playnlie that whither the truce hold or breake he shalbe in danger by the enemye, in so muche also as I note that he doubteth that when shipping shall come to revoke him and his Troupes whither he shalbe albe to embarke the enemye comminge[so] [in Burghley's hand] nere unto him

[p. 3] and yet if shipping shall come he offreth to adventure though it cost him deare. and therefore requireth to be no longer delayed with irresolutions, wherewith I am sure he will come with a mynd to charge me with the lack of resolutions and varietie of dyrections, whereof I am sure hir ma[jes]tie will discourage me, and the various accidentes that have happened by the ffr[ench] Kinge's breach of his promises, and reiterations of better observations though not hitherto performed, will iustifye hir ma[jes]ties actions to satisfye Sir John Norries or any other reasonable man. Theise doubtful poyntes hav I

[61] Letter from the *parlement* of the States of Brittany to Queen Elizabeth informing her of their desire to send a legation to negotiate terms of the truce and her commitment, 15 Oct. 1593, TNA SP 78/32/fol. 227r–v; *L&A*, v, Analysis no. 279.

[62] Henry de la Tour d'Auvergne, marshal of France from 1592, titular duke of Bouillon (1555–1623), converted to Protestantism in 1572, Huguenot leader.

[63] The troops under Charles of Lorraine, duke of Aumale (1573–1595), prominent Leaguer who was deprived of his title by Henry IV in 1595.

gathered out of the letter which yow sent me which make me doubtfull what advise to give, for bringing awaye the Troupes as yow do write to me of hir ma[jes]tie's disposition. And to encrease theies doubtes of myne moving me to enclyne to hir majestie's disposition by his latter letter, which hir Majesty hath not yett seene, I see the intention of the sending of the deputies hither from the States, is as I at the first did coniecture to borrowe money of hir ma[jes]tie which in a paraphrasis, is to Carrye aware money and to leave writinges under seales whereof hir Majesty hath greate plentye, so as the comminge of theise Deputies may be better looked for then wellcome.[64] And therefore fynding the care which hir Majesty hath for hir people (which is varie princely) and knowing as I thinke my L[ord] Admyrall will confesse how desparate a matter it is to provide a number of hoyes in this wynter tyme, and how longe it wilbe, being too be provided in the Threasurie and how unable they shalbe this wynter tyme to brooke the seas in so long a voiage and yett to shew my disposition how to have the people saved I thinke wilth my Lord Admyrall's[65] advise to allowe the same, if 3 or 4 Barkes might be had from South[hamp]ton and Poole for the Coast and be sent to the Yles of Jersey and Gurnsey, which with the help of some smale vesselles belonging to those Ylandes, might safely bring and spede conveniently

[p. 4] all the Quene's people from Pempole to the Ylandes or to some of them the way being short, and so the people might be there in safetie, and at no greater charge to hir ma[jes]tie then they be in Brittanie. And this for the tyme ~~which~~ [Burghley] may serve to two endes. The one to have the people brought away with more safetie [Burghley] hereafter as shipping may be provided ~~hearafter~~, and so also Sir John Norreis maye with more safetie repaire to hir ma[jes]tie. [In Burghley's hand in the margin] ther ar ii or iii at Southampton that lately and fortunately took the kinge of Spayne's ship of warre. The other may well serve hir ma[jes]tie in honor in not revoking her fforces into England, untill the Deputies might com hither and to be hard what they can saye for the contynuing of hir ma[jes]ties fforces thereof.

---

[64]The Queen's expenditure in France is outlined in Wernham, *After the Armada*, 415–416. There was a massive French debt owing to England in money sent under seals out of the Exchequer. The sum for 1594 included £14,173 for eight ships off Brest; a further £36,719 for the 4,000 troops required in Brittany during the balance of the year. TNA SP 78/38/fols. 256r, 257v, 259v.

[65]The lord admiral co-ordinated this effort: 'On December 10, John Troughton was instructed upon receiving warrants and commission from the Lord Admiral, to take up twelve ships, manned and victualled at Southampton, Poole, Plymouth, Lyme and their members', *L&A*, v, Analysis nos 285, 266–267.

And for the Contentations of them of Brittanie, Sir John Norries may be dyrected and ^{that} at the time when he shalbe ready to come awaye to the Ilandes ^{[Burghley] he may have} advertise both the Mareschall and others of the States there, that the cause why he removeth his Troupes from thence to the Ylandes is for that the place where his Troupes are, is not fortified, and that he understandeth [Burghley] yt [clerk] both the Spaniard, Lorayne and French are approaching to St. Briece and that the Mareschall hath Revoked the ffrench, which laye nere unto hym to their garrisons, so that he fyndeth him selfe in smale danger, for him self and the Quene's peoples ^{[Burghley] for which purpose} he hath thought ^{[Burghley] now} to retyre him self, in some of hir ma[jes]tie's Yles, lying nere to the coast of Brittanie, there to be in some more suertie, untill hir ma[jes]tie may have hard what the deputies of the States have to treat with hir for mayntenance of hir charges, if she shall agree to Contynew hir former promise of greater forces there. By this hir ma[jes]tie may maintayne honour in hir late offer ^{[Burghley] to} to suffer ^{[Burghley] revok} them untill the coming of the deputies, ffor hereby hir generall doth but retyre them for their suretie where they may be readye hereafter to serve without Cashing of them by sending then home into England. Thus you see I am somewhat long in delivering of my doubtfull opynions, wherein none of the Counsel

[p. 5] can better iudge for their bringing away then my L[ord] Admyrall. And if his L[ordshi]p will make choice of some discrete man by the help of his vice Admyrall in Hampshire and to gett such 3 or 4 nymble Barkes there and ^{[Burghley] that may be} the Samsone I am sure if they may be sufred by hir ma[jes]tie's assent to carye each of them but xxtie tonne of beare to be solde at Pempole or in the Ylandes to which places they do use many tymes to steale some smale quantitie without lycence.

In the 2 letter which I send to yow from Sir John Norreis there is a clause in Ciphre, which I cannot deciphire here readely for lack of my Alphabete which is with my bookes at the Courte which I ghesse be to ^{[Burghley] no} other purpose, but to have the Duke Mounpensier the Governor there in favour of the Protestantes of that countrie.[66] But if my stuff be come from Windsore, yow shall fynd a <u>bigg paper Booke in folio entituled Mattars of France, in</u> which by looking into

[66] The duke of Montpensier (1573–1608) and the Brittany Protestants: see *L&A*, v, Analysis no. 284, for discussion of the factions between adherents of Jean d'Aumont and the king's lieutenants. These lengthy instructions here set forth by Burghley were incorporated into the Privy Council's directions on shipping for John Troughton, TNA SP 78/32.fol. 366r–v. Cecil was organizing much of the correspondence with the Brittany Protestants: see, for example, TNA SO3/fols. 436r–v, SP 78/32/fols. 403r–404r. Essex drew up the military plans, TNA SP 78/33/fols. 189r–v, 217r–v.

the table yow shall fynd the Alphabet of Sir John Norreis.[67] Thus have I at lenght [*sic*] enough as I thinke answered your whole letter, and the rest of the thinges sent with it.

[Burghley]
I perceave hir Ma[jes]ty looketh for me by the end of the next weke whereuppon yow may saye merely to hir Ma[jes]ty, that am so disposed if God permit me whyther I spede in my vowyng or no for if I do spede, then I may not fayle, but if I spede not by all that wekes pursute, I will trooble my self no more at follwyng here in the conntrey, but will lyve in hope to fynd hir at the Court where I know she will come[,] to serve hir Majesty all the Christmas hollydayes.

God gyve yow grace. From my howss at Theobalds the 7 of Decembre 1593.

Your loving father,

W. Burghley

[Postscript]
If hir Majesty mislyk my opinion for the ease of hir Ma[jes]ty, I am no opinionaster but an opyner.

Dorse

ADDRESSED in Burghley's hand:
for my son Sir Robert Cecill

ENDORSED in Simon Willis's hand:
The L[ord] Thre[asure]r to my M[aste]r

---

[67] Sir Robert Sidney (1564–1636), *ODNB*, governor of Flushing (Vlissingen), was on an embassy to Henry IV in 1593 undertaken partly to assure Henry IV's protection of the Huguenots after his conversion. The book of intelligence codes is secondary to the 'Matters of France' which can be identified in the SP Various 45/vol. 20, no. 45 (list) of volumes of papers Burghley left at his death at the court. Queen Elizabeth changed her mind over the best course of action concerning the relief of Pempole: on reading Norris's first dispatch she was prepared to entertain support for Henry's troops, but when the hard conditions of her offer were set forth in his second letter, she informed Norris that she would revoke his troops, *L&A*, v, Analysis no. 285; TNA SP 78/32/fols. 372r–373v, draft corrected by Burghley. Here Henry Maynard and Cecil had open access to the alphabet or cipher codes, retained in Burghley's custody. For Cecil's drafts of letter containing Sidney's instructions and orders for the end of his embassy, see TNA SP 78/32/fols. 258r–61v, SP 78/33/fols. 19r–20r, 38r–39r, 46r, SO3/1/fol. 439r.

Letter No. 15:

William, Lord Burghley to Sir Robert Cecil, 23 January 1593

1 p. Dictated to Henry Maynard, with a holograph paragraph added.
Addressed, endorsed, signed.

Text

I doe send yowe Mr. Guilpin's[68] letter and thearewith certaine letters
that he maketh mention of to be intercepted: whereof one is written
by Holt the Jesuit[69] to Cardinall Allen,[70] which doth spetially conveie
summ his privatt busines, and in sum part his Advertisements of the
execucion of Richard Hesketh.[71] An other longe letter is written from
Rich[ard] Hopkins to the Cardinall, conteininge a longe colloquie

---

[68] George Gilpin (1514–1602), *ODNB*, English accredited councillor to the Council of State of the United Provinces of the Low Countries from 1593–1602.

[69] William Holt, SJ (1553–1593), *ODNB*, rector of the English College in Rome from 1586 and polemicist, was intimate with Father Joseph Creswell, strong in his position for an English prelate in Rome. Holt's work is discussed in Anthony G. Petti (ed.), *The Letters and Despatches of Richard Verstegan (c.1550–1640)*, Publications of the Catholic Record Society, 52 (London, 1959), 77, 87, 91, 103, 222, 234. Richard Verstegan (*c.*1548–1640), *ODNB*, the Brussels publisher, was a clearing-house for Catholic intelligence emanating from Rome, especially. Holt was one of his two main suppliers of information; the other was Hugh Owen, vice-prefect of Cardinal Allen's English mission in the Low Countries until 1598, where he administered funds provided by Philip II. Holt corresponded frequently with Robert Persons, an old sparring partner of Burghley's. Holt was no. 108 in Verstegan's code used with Roland Baines. The exact matter to which this letter refers remains, as so much of this sort of material, mysterious. John Strype, *Annals of the Reformation and Establishment of Religion, and Other Various Occurrences in the Church of England, During Queen Elizabeth's Happy Reign* (Oxford, 1725), iv, 208. The letter of 6 Jan. 1594 from Holt to Allen suggests that a highly clandestine incident, possibly the move to convert Ferdinando, earl of Derby or perhaps the recently discovered implication of the Queen's physician Rodrigo Lopez in a regicidal plot. Those of 'religion' meant the papal missioners responsible for English conversion.

[70] William, Cardinal Allen, Principal of the English College at Rome (1532–1595), *ODNB*. Together with the Jesuit Robert Persons (or Parsons), he established seminaries at Douai, Rheims, and Rome, and was a leading force in providing missionary priests into England.

[71] Richard Hesketh (1553–1593), *ODNB*, convicted of the murder of Ferdinando, 5th earl of Derby who was descended from Henry VIII's sister, Dowager Queen Mary of France through his mother Lady Margaret Clifford. Wernham, *After the Armada*, 455–456; *CSPD 1591–1594*, 162, 208–209, 222, 227–228, 246, 259–263, 267, 269–277. A complex investigation of persons close to Hesketh led to Sir John Savage delivering Hesketh to the Privy Council under warrant. *HCMS*, iv, 403, 408–409, 418, 421–424, 461–463. Cecil took a leading role, together with Sir John Puckering, in the arraignment, subsequent trial, and execution of Hesketh. *HMCS*, iv, 381, 390. Willis's hand appears on Hesketh's answers to interrogations by William Waad, clerk of the council. *HMCS*, iv, 407–408.

betwene him and Moodye,[72] concerninge the letters that weare
writtenn hither into Ingland by the said Hopkins to move a tolleracion
in Religion by the meanes of the Cardinall: And for that it appeareth
their former letter tooke noe effect, which weare sent to Mr. Heneage
and so browght to mee. Modye predenteth that he hath an other
corse in hand, and looketh to heare owt of Ingland, howe to renewe
the former treatie: but what meanes Moody meaneth, or shall use I
knowe not, nor by whome, but it semeth he busieth himself muche,
and heareby the States have entred into suspicion, that his treatie
showld be done with her ma[jes]ties provitie heare, which Guilpin
hath vearie honestlie disavowed.[73] The third l[ette]re is to one Baines[74]

---

[72]Richard Hopkins (1553–before 1596), *ODNB*, was a papal agent and prominent spy in
the Low Countries. He had close ties to the English Catholic community in Rome whose
designs were at odds with the regicidal plots out of Spain in accordance with the Donative
Bull of 1588, and the Bull *Regnans in Excelsis*, 1570, anathematizing Elizabeth I, particularly
following Cardinal Allen's idea of a loyal English Catholic. The 'Colloquy' here mentioned
was with Father John Cecil or John Snowden's accomplice Michael Moody, both of whom
had presented themselves, to little avail, in 1591 to both Cecils. Snowden/Cecil (the agent)
figured prominently in Cecil's later service. A manuscript copy of this 'colloquy' in the
BL, Cottonian MS Titus B ii, fol. 225 was published in *The Letters and Despatches of Richard
Verstegan, c.1550–1640*, edited by Anthony G. Petti (London, 1959), 201, n. 11. The original
was intercepted possibly by Anthony Standen, an agent in Essex's employ who had been
discovered, necessitating his return to England. TNA SP 77/5/fol. 102r. Holt observed the
Cecils' investigation of Richard Hesketh was now underway. Hesketh was remotely linked
to John Dee, as was Derby, and a trained astrologer and alchemist. See C. Devlin, 'The
earl and the alchemist', *The Month*, NS 9, 1–3 (Jan.–Mar. 1953). This letter from Moody
appears to have been lost. For Standen and the radical shift in Essex's intelligence, see Paul
E.J. Hammer, 'An Elizabethan Spy Who Came in from the Cold: The return of Anthony
Standen to England in 1593', *Bulletin of the Institute of Historical Research*, 65 (1992), 277–295. It
discusses the Cecils' distrust and coldness once Standen had been recruited by Essex, ibid.
292–295.
[73]This disavowal was typical of Burghley's refusal to take on Walsingham's intelligence
remnant while Essex did so and underlines Gilpin's role as intelligence assistant in the Low
Countries. Cecil's notes in 1598 show these connections were still 'live': 'In such States as are
freindes to us, as Scotlande Hollande Zelande Italye Germanye Denmarke and Swedlande'
included 'Lawerence Bright in Sussex near Hastings brings news of Normandy "divers
Traitors"—this year alone discovered two seminaries and corresponds with Owen, also
friends with a priest who was with Jacques; from Brussels an unnamed who works through
Gilpin'. 'Mr. Gilpin gets letters from Balt. Peterson in Lisbon'. Stone, *Palavicino*, 238–239,
citing TNA SP 12/265/133.
[74]Roland Baines fled to the continent 1579 and was educated at Rheims: 'The
most important of [Verstegan's correspondents] at Rome for whom Verstegan acted as
intelligencer and agent was William, Cardinal Allen, who resided there from 1585 until
his death in Oct. 1594.' *Letters and Despatches of Richard Verstegan*, xx. Baines also circulated
Verstegan's correspondence to prominent Catholics in Rome. Baines was the Cardinal's
secretary and major-domo. He corresponded with Verstegan for many years, well into
the next century. Most of what is known of Baines was provided by Anthony Copley's
'declaration' before the Privy Council in 1596 (printed in Strype, *Annals of the Reformation*, iv,

that serveth the Cardinall, conteining noe matter of weight otherwise than commonn Advertisements.

Hir ma[jes]tie willed I showld consider whoe weare fitt deputies under the erle of Derbie in Lancashire, and wheare Sir Rich[ard] Sherbourne and Mr. Holland weare his deputies before, I thinke goode to forbeare Sir Rich[ard] Sherbourne, and in his place to appoint Mr. Richard Ashton of Midleton that was sherif the last yeare, a vearye sufficient gentleman and well disposed in Religion and soe is Mr. Holland.[75] In Cheshire I think theie that before weare named to be the fittest, being Sir John Savadge, and Sir Hugh Cholmeleie:[76] If her ma[jes]tie like heareof, yowe maie doe well to write to my L[ord] Keper to cawse the commision to be made accordinglye.

[Cecil notes beside the final sentence of the last paragraph in the right margin, but concerning the following paragraph]
For my l[ord] Chamberlayn[77] to reade.

Wheareas my L[ord] Chamberlaine hath of late written unto mee to further Mr. Crane[78] to the office of the Comptroller and MusterM[aste]r at Barwick I have thowght good to require yow to knowe my llords opinionn whither he cowld not allowe that Crane might have the office of the clerke of the checke and musters, with the usuall fee which [is] by the yeare and a clarke at 13 7s 8d,1 and 2

386), which notes that he was also attached to Cardinal Báthory in Poland, for whom, see Letter No. 55, and for Copley (1567–1609), *ODNB*.
[75] Sir Richard Sherbourne, Richard Ashton or Assheton of Midleton (later Sir Richard), and Richard Holland of Upholland. Burghley here suggested a continuity of county power drawing old-line families into their usual role in royal and legal administration perhaps tempering rumours of Sherbournes as papists with more Protestant lieutenants. Christopher Haigh, *Reformation and Resistance in Tudor Lancashire* (Cambridge, 1975), 318.
[76] Sir Hugh Cholmondeley (c.1513–1597), *ODNB*. Deputy lieutenants for Cheshire: Sir Hugh Cholmeley [Chalmondeley] and Sir John Savage. Of the latter it may be noted his role in sending Hesketh up for examination. See *CSPD 1591–1594*, 408–409, 418, 421–424, 461–463.
[77] Henry Carey, Lord Hunsdon (1st baron, 1526–1596), *ODNB*, the Queen's cousin through his mother Mary Boleyn. His influence in Borders affairs surpassed others on the Privy Council.
[78] John Crane's angling for office in the fortress at Berwick had support from the Careys and Cecils, and his letter of 29 Feb. 1594 makes clear his suit was successful as clerk of checks and muster master, but the office of comptroller was given to Robert Bowyer—a fact which exercised Crane somewhat, as he cited precedent including that of his predecessor Nicholas Erington, *Cal. Border Papers*, i, 521, 522. A 46-page inventory of all ordnance in the eastern Border fortresses by Crane was endorsed by Burghley in June 1594, which attests to his work. *Cal. Border Papers*, i, 535–537.

servantes at 43s 3d. which in the whole cometh to lxiiii[l] and yet one Bowier,[79] whoe is a skilful man in worke ther as his L[ord] knoweth, might be the Comptroller of the Workes, to the which theare belongeth no profitt, but accordinge to the quantitie and charge of the workes, and so to have allowance as the charges of the workes doth amownt: If his L[ordship] showlde allowe of this then theare might be a cople preferred that is Crane, whoe doth well deserve, and so might Bowier also have somme intertainment, whoe is more skilfull in workes that Crane is thowght to be:

But if his l[ord] shall not like of this devision, than yowe maie tell my L[ord] that I would have yowe to move the Q[ueen] to make the grawnt to Crane of the whole office. And so I praie yowe lett hir ma[jes]tie understand howe necessarie it is to have the office supplied forthwith by reason of the monethlie paiments, and howe fitt the man is havinge alwaies been browght up in the office under Mr. Errington,[80] & others that have gonn before him. I doe send yowe a paper conteininge the allowance to both thes offices, the better to informe yowe howe to speake thereof with my L[ord] Chamberlaine.

[Burghley's holograph paragraph]
I am not in Tune to wryt my self beyng forced with very Iaynturs to kepe my couch, 23 Jan[uary] 1593.

In ***** folly I se no poynt of treson intede to the Q[ueen] but a redynes to mak some gayn to the hurt of
[two words carefully scratched out, but two words, probably a proper name, and starting with an "R". As for whose folly: the name ***** begins with "l" and has a p halfway through—possibly "lopez"?]

W. Burghley

Dorse

ADDRESSED in Henry Maynard's hand:
To my lovinge sonne Sir Robert Cecill knight one of hir ma[jes]ties privie connsell

[79] Sir Robert Bowyer (*c.*1560–1621), *ODNB*. Bowyer, too, resorted to the Cecils with his letters. *Cal. Border Papers,* i, 520.
[80] Captain Nicholas Errington's death in 1593 left the office vacant; he was also an officer in Flushing who had served with Sir Philip Sidney, and held the constable's place in Ramekins Castle as a long-standing captain of horse. He received £64 for his place as comptroller, muster master and clerk of the check at Berwick, which he deputed to his nephew and heir Cuthbert who did not replace him. TNA SP 84/33/f. 135r.

ENDORSED by Simon Willis:
23 Jan[uary] 1593
The lo[rd] Thre[asure]r to my M[aste]r
[Cecil also wrote on the dorse]
Crane

Letter No. 16:

William, Lord Burghley to Sir Robert Cecil, 28 January 1593

½ p. Dictated to Henry Maynard, with a holograph paragraph added.
Addressed, endorsed, signed.

Text

I have receaved your letter, wheareby it semeth that hir ma[jes]tie would knowe mine opinionn towching Mr. Danyell[81] to be made sarient, whose staie at the prickinge of the rest grewe uppon an informacionn to hir ma[jes]tie that a letter showld be written to him, by tht lewde fellow Hackett:[82] whearewith I have charged Mr. Daniell, and he pretesteth deepelie that he never knewe, sawe, or ever hard from him: and so farre condemning his wickedness, as that he was one of his Judges uppon his triall and arraienement: which his speache I doe varelie beleve, for that I understand and knowe him to be, a vearie honest learned and discreate man, and mine opinion of him. I praie yowe to lett hir ma[jes]tie understand, of whose gratious favour to be hearin shewed to him, I doe not dowbt but he will be worthie

---

[81] William Danyell had been deputy recorder of the City of London, 1584–1599, and since 1589 undersheriff. *Chamber Accounts of the Sixteenth Century*, edited by Betty R Masters, London Record Society (1984), xx–xxi. He was subsequently mentioned as a member of the commission to try Rodrigo Lopez during the illness of the lord chief justice of the Queen's Bench, Lord (John) Anderson. *CSPD 1591–1594*, 449, 459–460; TNA SP 12/248/no. 26 enclosure I. He was named in the letters patent for both Privy Council commissions in Feb. and Mar. 1593 for the examination of church non-attenders, conventicles, and others of suspicion in and around London to the extent of 10 miles, see Letter No. 9.

[82] William Hacket's prophetic and public proclamation against the Queen was made in the claim that he was Jesus Christ. For an analysis of how his case was used to discredit Presbyterianism through a variety of contemporary diagnoses, rather than as merely 'lewd', see Alexandra Walsham, 'Frantick Hacket: Prophecy, sorcery, insanity, and the Elizabethan Puritan movement', *The Historical Journal*, 41 (1998), 27–66.

of. Soe fare yowe well. ffrom my house in the Strand thiss xxviii^th of January 1593.

[Burghley]
I am greatly comforted to perceave hir Majesty'y graciouss allowance of myn opinion in the Scottish case, which I do themore firmly hold, because it is warrantid by hir former.[83]

[Maynard's hand]
Your Loving Father

[Burghley]
W. Burghley

Dorse

ADDRESSED in Henry Maynard's hand:
To my loving sonne Sir Robert Cecill knight, one of her Majesty's Privye Counsell

ENDORSED in Simon Willis's hand:
28 Jan.[uary] 1593
L[ord] Treasurere to my M[aste]r his opinion of Mr. Danyell to be Serjeant
[Cecil has also entered vertical list in his own hand in the dorse, which is, characteristically, in abbreviations]
Erscot
Coop. M.S.w[ith] ye q[ueen]
fling
Daniell

---

[83] See above, pp. 46–48. Burghley's holograph postscript might reflect the secrecy of the Scottish work. He and Cecil wrote the instructions to the agents surrounding Bothwell, and the complicated embassy of Lord Zouche. In his letter of instruction to Zouche of 23 Jan. 1594, Cecil noted in the margin beside Zouche's role in the Queen's covert support of the group surrounding the earl of Bothwell, 'This argueth that the Queen would have her ministers doe what she will not avowe.' TNA SP 52/52/ fols. 25–29, 30–31; *CSPS 1593–1595*, 268–270. The ambassador was to deny any official English involvement with the earl or other disaffected Scottish Borderers. The matter to which Burghley referred to in this present letter may have been formulated in Cecil's further letter to Zouche on 1 Feb. 1594 in which he instructed the ambassador to answer the king's mention of money with the observation that he is daily surrounded by the adherents of the Catholic earls, and that the earls themselves wander freely, TNA SP 52/52/ fols. 31–35; *CSPS 1593–1595*, 274–276; Letter No. 2.

Letter No. 17

William, Lord Burghley to Sir Robert Cecil, 10 February 1593

2 pp. Dictated to Henry Maynard with a paragraph added in Burghley's hand.
Addressed, endorsed, signed.

Text

I am not in so good healthe as to write with mine owne hande, yet I cannot forbeare to impart unto divers thinges as follweth. Ffirst I praie yowe move hir Majestie from mee to grawnt hir warraunt for sum portion of monie to be sent into Ireland, wheare theare was want at Christmas last, as Sir Henry Wallop can well report, and doth nowe presse mee ernestlie to remember hir ma[jes]tie to send somm treasure thither wehare hir Armie hath had noe monie of longe time, for that the last portion of monie that was sent was at mich[ael]mas, which was £7000 wherof a great part had been borrowed there at Dublin, before it came thither and yowe maie informe hir ma[jes]tie that wheare hir yearelie charges by hir Armie cometh neare hand to £28 or £29,000 sent, so as theare is continuallie a past £20,000 sent, so as theare is continuallie a debt remaining in that land. the sooner hir ma[jes]tie shall grawnt this warrant whiche cannot be lesse than sevenn of eight thowsand pound the better it shall be for hir service there.[84]

[84] A privy seal of 19 Feb. 1593/4, issued £8,000, received 28 May 1594, *CSPI 1592–1596*, 253, with Wallop's reckoning of the discharge and remain, 248. Enniskillen was then under siege. Connor Roe Maguire, having raised a force, had secret meetings with Tyrone in November. Here was the outset of the 'Nine Years War'. Assistance was required because 'noe monie of longe time' would jeopardize the forces. Desertions and moves to the rebels were inevitable. Intelligence noted strong Spanish assistance with large numbers of troops, and covert work by Irish priests in the Low Countries and Spain could be expected. For the news leading to Burghley's conclusion, see *CSPI 1592–1596*, 181–209. Sir William Fitzwilliam was then being replaced as lord deputy by Sir William Russell amidst widespread and accurate suspicions of corruption. Fitzwilliam had to answer for his knighting so many men and provide an account of revenues which suggests Burghley knew perfectly well that the army was in peril from more than rebels. *CSPI 1592–1596*, 200, 221. See also Letter No. 14 for the Dec. payment out of the Exchequer into Ireland. Sir George Carew asked Sir Robert Cecil on 15 Feb. 1593/4 for the £1,600 owed him 'to aforder your honorable ayde to my Lord your father that I may receve some favour in this privie seal now to be granted for Ireland', offering his service only, TNA SP 63/173/no. 27, fol. 89r. Carew petitioned Burghley on 23 Feb. for speed in sending money, TNA, SP 63/173/no. 55, fol. 147r, SO3/1/fol. 445r.

I would have yowe informe my l[ord] Admirall that Mr. Quarles[85] did demaund a prest of monie for victuells to serve upponn the seas for 8000 men, which came to £16,800 wheare as at the first an Estimat was made for 12000 men, which his L[ord] knoweth was with his likinge reduced to 8000 and after this, yt was thowght good by advise of the officers to make a preparacion to serve for a lesse nomber, which being rated by the officers onelie in fowre thinges, in wheate, malt, oxenn and caske theie thowght it meete to have imprested to him, £4666, which yf his L[ord] shall finde neadefull to be taken in hand I desire his L[ord] would move hir ma[jes]tie to grawnte warrant for that, or somuch as shall please hir.[86] I doe find that the grawnt of this small quantitie for the Venetians being nozed in the Contries hath raised the price of wheate greatlie.[87] I doe hearewith send to his L[ord] a letter from Sir Thomas Leighton[88], which I thinke concerneth the same matter that yowe tolde me Trowghton[89] had written unto him,

[85]James Quarles, surveyor of the navy victuals (1582–1595), wrote to Burghley on 31 Jan. 1594 with an account of victuals required for 8000 men for three months, at a total value of £16,800, *CSPD 1591–1594*, 420. Quarles noted that the prices were good, and requested imprest of part of the money and letter of assistance. Sir William Becher (bap. 1580, d.1651), *ODNB*, was his business partner, see also Letters Nos 111–114. Quarles was clerk of the kitchen, the board of Greencloth (a Household department and committee of the lower household), in addition to navy victualler. *ODNB sub.* Sir Francis Quarles.

[86]Sir John Hawkins (1532–1595), *ODNB*, navy treasurer, and three others, appended a note to Quarles dated 6 Feb. 1594, allowing that the present service was to go ahead, but the amounts to be provided were so large that time would be saved with a smaller order: recommending 1,000 quarters (12½ tons) of wheat, 1,000 cwt of malt, 1,000 tons of cask, and 5,000 oxen, with letters of assistance as demanded, totalling £4,666, 13s, 4d. from Portsmouth and Dover. This document is referred to in the text of Letter No. 17.

[87]Giovanni Bassadona was the Venetian agent and friend of the earl of Essex's who was given the warrant of 30 Jan. 1593/4 for the transportation of 4,000 quarters (50 tons) of wheat, rye or beans, 'from those parts of the realm where, for cheapness it may well be spared, there being a great dearth of corn in Venice', Letter No. 74; *CSPD 1591–1594*, 419; TNA SP 12/247/no. 26.

[88]Sir Thomas Leighton, governor of Jersey (*c*.1530–1610), *ODNB*; Wernham, *After the Armada*, 369–370, 372. Burghley's detailed instructions had Cecil move the administrative instruments for the supply of shipping and troops then removed from Brittany to the Channel Islands. Letter No. 17 is typical of a letter to Cecil which contained numerous enclosed letters for evaluation by Cecil, the Queen, and the Privy Council. Sir Robert Cecil's closer acquaintance with the facts of this matter is telling: a messenger had been sent from Leighton to Norris at Pontrieux informing him that the ships were ready to go to Paimpol to embark the troops, but two other letters sent from Leighton to Norris note that contrary winds had delayed the messenger at Paimpol. *L&A*, v, Analysis, no. 296. The messenger returned, late, to Leighton, with the message that Norris was unable to victual his troops and make provision for the shipping. Troughton and the other shipmaster departed for England for fresh supplies. These supplies were apparently the subject of James Quarles's original petition to Burghley for imprest on 31 Jan.

[89]Capt. John Troughton, who transported English supply into Brittany and the French coast for the English government, Wernham, *After the Armada*, 511, 522, 553–554. Troughton

of which cawse I knowe not. What maie prove to be the event, but for the monie and the Apparell, ^{both} which Sir John Norris did expect before he would cumm from Pempole. I am certainlie advartized that the Apparell is alreadie come to him to Pempolle. and for the monie it was readie in the Charles the 18 of Januarye and whether by contrary winde or by negligence of him that had the charge, it came to Portesmouthe of late time, from wheare as I understand by Sir Thomas Sherley,[90] the Capteine named Franklin[91] refused to depart, thowgh

[p. 2] he had goode winde untill as he said he would have further awnsweare from my L[ord] Admirall, as I thinke Sir Thomas Sherley made it knowen to his L[ord] and I was bold in his L[ord's] absence to command the captaine by my letters to depart withowt anie further delaie.

Besides this, becawse I understand that Trowghton's victuells would shortlie be spent, I gave order to Sir John Hawkins to send him one monethes victuells more, which I knowe Sir John Hawkins hath alreadye directed to be done, and yet it maie be dowbted that Trowghton finding Sir John Norris to use delaie for his comming awaie, will be also himself come to the coast of England befor the victuells cann cumm unto him which I knowe not howe to remedie.

Theare is also a further proporcion of victuells sent to the Islandes for maintenance of the soldieurs when theie shall come thither, but when all is done that can be, I dowbt it will be founde that Sir John Norris hath noe disposition to cumm owt of Bretaigne. Of all these thinges I praie yowe make my L[ord] Admirall acquainted, and returne me awnsweare from him

[Burghley's hand]
Even now I receaved your l[ette]re wherin yow report hir Ma[jes]ties care for my helth for the which I most humbly thank hir, hopyng that her good wishyngs shall help to retorn me to strength for hir service

was to have led the shipping for supply of Norris's troops, according to a plan hatched by Burghley (Letter No. 14), and set in motion by 14 Jan. 1594, *L&A*, v, Analysis no. 271, 272, 293. The expense and delays prompted the Queen's decision to 'revoke' (re-deploy) Norris's troops on 11 Dec. 1593. Norris took his troops to Paimpol with no money for nine weeks until supply was sent in January. Captain Franklin's obstinacy was, in part, because he was on a separate mission directly to Paimpol, or Trequier which Norris had approved as more suitable points of embarkation.

[90] Sir Thomas Sherley (1542–1612), *ODNB*, treasurer at war in the Low Countries with responsibilities for French expeditions from 1586–1597 when his enormous embezzlement was proved, here to take the charge of extra shipping and provisions. *L&A*, v, Analysis nos 271, 293, 317.

[91] The Captain of the Charles, Franklin is unidentified.

which I esteme the service of God, whose place she holdeth in erth. that was spoken of my answer that befor dynnar I was no man, and after dynnar half a man was thus far misreported for I sayd befor dynnar I was but on quarter of a man and after dynar half a man and now for some incress to better, by drynkyng of a draught of redd wyne and sugar sence your goyng from me, I make accompt to be iii quarters of a man hole and one quarter syck. thus I am pleased in a phansy to express me estat, wherewith yow may acquaint hir Ma[jes]ty, whan she hath no other matter to hasten to.

I thank hir Ma[jes]ty for hir offer to me of my L[ord] Admyrall's lodgyng but I never had audacite to require other lodgyng than was allowed me. and yet I presume my L[ord] Admyrall, will withowt offence yeld therto.

God send her Ma[jes]ty a well disposed carnyvall,[92] or a Carerate to be rid of all cares.

Your loving father,

W. Burghley

Dorso

ADDRESSED in Henry Maynard's hand:
To my lovinge sonne
Sir Robart Cecill knight
one of hir ma[jes]ties privie
Consell

ENDORSED in Sir Robert Cecil's hand:
x Feb. 1593
my lord to me
[Fragment of a seal attached]

Letter No. 18

William, Lord Burghley to Sir Robert Cecil, 12 March 1593

½ p. Dictated to his secretary Maynard, with a final sentence added in Burghley's hand. Addressed, endorsed, signed.

---

[92] Here 'carnyvall': an interesting reference to the carnival of Mardi Gras preceding Lent.

Text

I made yowe acquainted this afternoon with a forme of somme letters to be directed for a privie serche,[93] as my L[ord] Admirall and yowe hath informed me to be the Quene's minde: otherwise I know nothinge of the purpose, but like yt well to have it done. I have thearefore cawsed fowre letters to be written to fowre severall places and have my self subscribed the same, which I would have yowe to impart to my L[ord] of Essex, my L[ord] Admirall, and others theare in secrett sort, and have left in everye letter towardes the ends a blanke for the daie which would be in mine opinion, either Saturdaie, or sondaie next, as my lls [Lords] shall like yt: and then the daie would be putt in a small Billet included in the letter, not to be known to the Serchers, but to the principall Commanders, beyen the time of the Execucionn. And so I remitt the matter to be ordered as my lls [Lords] shall thinke fitt. Ffrom Hampton Cort this xiii^th of March 1593.

With my blessyng to Will Cecill[94]
Your loving father,

W. Burghley

Dorse

ADDRESSED in the clerk's hand:
To my lovinge sonne Sir Robart Cecill knight
one of hir ma[jes]ties privye Connsell

---

[93] Sir Thomas Windebanke (*c*.1550–1607), owed his obtaining of the clerkship of the signet to Burghley, and he was guardian of Thomas Cecil on his continental tour. *CSPD 1547–1580*, 177–220. Burghley's direction for a privy search for evidence in the arraignments against Rodrigo Lopez's co-conspirators, and the method used gives an illuminating example of the Privy Council intelligence apparatus in the domestic arena, W.D. Acres, 'The early political career of Sir Robert Cecil, *c*.1582–1597: Some aspects of late Elizabethan secretarial administration', PhD thesis, University of Cambridge, 1992, 129. See also, Thomas Windebanke to Sir Robert Cecil, referring to the search warrant, *HMCS*, iv, 485–486; *CSPD 1591–1594*, 466–469, 432–433. An undated draft warrant for such a search in London and Westminster, confining foreigners and Irish in their beds at midnight to be incarcerated until the following day when interrogations would begin, is found in Burghley's hand, BL Lansdowne MS 75/ no. 89, fol. 199r. The Queen did not believe Lopez's conspiracy and stalled until June over his execution. The Cecils and their secretaries drafted the official version for the Crown of the investigation and proof of Lopez's treason. See Dominic Green, *The Double Life of Doctor Lopez: Spies, Shakespeare and the Plot to Poison Elizabeth I* (London, 2003), chs 13–16.

[94] William, Lord Roos (1590–1618), *ODNB*, the son of William Cecil, later 2nd earl of Exeter (1566–1640), is probably implied here: Cecil's great-nephew and grandson of Sir Thomas Cecil, later 1st earl of Exeter.

ENDORSED in Simon Willis's hand:
13 Mar[ch] 1593
Lo[rd] Thre[ausre]r to my M[aste]r
[Also on the dorse]
hast hast hast

Letter No. 19

William, Lord Burghley to Sir Robert Cecil, 25 April 1594

1 p. Holograph.
Addressed, endorsed, signed.

Text

I marvell that I heare not from yow concerning the letters to be sent into Irland, whyther also I have in redynes some from myself.[95]

Now will [yow] thynk also long to heare of my forspoken pilgrimage to the bath, but I am yet in deliberation non in Judicially. my continuance in payne withowt remission moveth me to harken to all meanes of remedy or ease. I have been occupied both with litigious cawses in the chequer and the wardes all this daye, and have found meanes to ease the just greves of Complaynants. I have had also now this evening by report, the sondry opinions of phisicions concerning the bathes, but therin are reasons of dissuasion then of provocations, and that which is worst than none any direct advise, for my care. Only exercise of body and Idlenes of mynd is prescribed. for these ii I have non to furder me but hir Ma[jes]ty.[96] if I might have a receipt thereof from hir Ma[jes]ty's Cabynett I would mak poost, to be hable to be hir

---

[95] Burghley received letters going to Ireland, Cheshire and Lancashire by Cecil after a four-day delay on 29 Apr. 1594. *CSPD 1591–1594*, 493; TNA SP 12/248/no. 84. The ailing lord deputy of Ireland, Sir William Fitzwilliam begged for recall. On 7 Feb. Fitzwilliam wrote to Cecil urging the appointment of Sir William Russell as the new lord deputy, TNA SP 63/173/no. 20, fol. 69r, no. 35, fols. 95r–98v; LPL MS 612/fol. 25r. Burghley had despaired of the 'misgovernment' of 'this Martial broken state' of Ireland in a letter to his son of 22 Feb. 1594, as the rebels increased in strength, TNA SP 63/173/no. 51, fol. 140r. Expert opinions were sounded for the new dispensation and on 13 Apr. 1594, Sir George Carew filed a treatise on Irish policy with Cecil: 'I have sent your honnour the poorest treatyse of Ireland that you have seene', TNA SP 63/174/fols. 26r, 28r–32v. Letters for Cheshire and Lancashire may have concerned the administration, or Carew's advice for the fortification of Milford Haven, SP 63/174/ fol. 28v.

[96] Burghley may have been making an oblique reference to Essex's frenetic intelligence efforts against Dr Lopez at this juncture, and he refers also to his gout and removal to the baths.

Majesty's portar at Thebaldes, uppon hir second Jornay. Thus much yow may blab to hir Ma[jes]ty if she ask of me. I wryt almost in the dark.

25 April 1594

Your loving father,

W. Burghley

Dorse

ADDRESSED Holograph:
To my son Sr Robart Cecill at [the] Court

ENDORSED in Simon Willis's hand:
25 Apr[il] 1594
L[ord] Thre[asure]r to my M[aste]r

Letter No. 20

William, Lord Burghley to Sir Robert Cecil, 5 May 1594

1 p.
Addressed, endorsed, signed.

Text

As I was comming in my Coche from Grenewych, certen letters war brought to me directed from Mr. Bowes,[97] the readyng wherof occupyed me until I cam to Lambeth feldes neare paris Garden,[98] which I folded up into a pece of paper lackyng wax sufficient which

---

[97] Burghley received the urgent dispatch from Sir Robert Bowes the Queen's ambassador to James VI, dated 30 Apr. and sent from Montrose in Scotland, TNA SP 52/53/no. 45. Bowes reported that he had followed Burghley's and Cecil's instructions on how best to answer the king's secretary (Sir Robert Cockburn) on the five articles of negotiations which concerned the conduct of the Queen's ambassador extraordinary, especially in view of the recent rising on Borough Muir outside Edinburgh Castle. Bowes responded on 20 Apr. 1594, to the Cecils' articles of instruction as to how to proceed with these articles, which were drafted in Maynard's hand and copied into Sir Robert Cecil's letter book by Willis. TNA SP 52/52/pp. 68–72; SP 52/53/no. 37; *CSPS 1593–1595*, 315–317. Cecil's private letter to Bowes of 20 Apr. and Burghley's private letter of that date were also copied by Willis into Cecil's letter book, TNA SP 52/52/pp. 68, 73–74. Two more of the Cecils' drafts of these fair copies remain, TNA SP 52/53/nos. 39, 40.

[98] Burghley may have been at his son's house at Wimbledon returning by the horse ferry at Lambeth.

I thynk also will occupy yow redyng as they did me. but how hir Ma[jes]ty will Judg therof, and how she will procede, I know not. certenly I see that without some monny the kyng will contynew his delayes.[99] I am not hable to warrant any Connsell, and yet some what must be aventured ether with monny or without monny.

I send yow a bill to be signed for ~~retorning~~ reduction of the xi^C [1,100] men from flushyng, for that I see ther is no sufficient warrant, as ther is for them that shall come from pempole.[100]

If the Scottish causes shall not hynder me, I mynd only to se Thebaldes on Wednesday at night and retorn on Thursday at night to the Court to London.

[In the margin]
I pray yow cause the bill to be ready wrytten becawse ther was left out iii^{xx} pr. [£60] to Sir Thomas Baskerville[101] for his charges in conduction. v Maie 1594.

Your lov[ing] father,

W. Burghley

[99] Bowes had had audience with King James on 29 Apr., after a postponement on 27 Apr., giving him the Queen's answers to the five articles. On the annuity, specifically, James addressed the fourth article, and here he professed himself mystified by Queen Elizabeth's tardiness in the matter of receiving Scots across the border. Elizabeth made the speedy prosecution of the Catholic earls, a condition of the royal annuity to the king; he claimed the annuity was necessary to proceed against them. The earls were to be put under forfeiture, which meant that they might never have to appear before parliament. James knew that Elizabeth, her ministers (the Cecils), and their spies had organized his cousin the earl of Bothwell as head of a 'vagabond' Protestant aristocratic faction, Bowes to Burghley, 29 Apr. 1594, TNA SP 52/53/no. 45; *CSPS 1593–1595*, 321–325. Bowes enclosed intelligence of Spanish money sent north to the Catholic earls, which might increase their strength against the king, TNA SP 52/53/no. 43, as copied by Bowes clerk, dated 29 Apr. 1594. There was also news of a Flemish barque arriving at Montrose on 29 Apr., allegedly carried priests bound for the three Catholic earls. TNA SP 52/53/no. 48; *CSPS 1593–1595*, 329–330.

[100] See Wernham, *After the Armada*, 527–529. The Spanish moved toward Brest, so threatening Henry IV's position, the English troops employed there and England's entire western shipping. A levy of 1,100 men was raised in the English counties at that time (ibid. 529). Troops under Sir Thomas Baskerville (d.1597), *ODNB*, were taken from English garrisons in the cautionary towns as her forces under Sir Francis Vere (1560/1–1609), *ODNB*, and paid by the States. But troops sent for the relief of Groningen had not yet returned to their garrisons in the towns necessitating the fresh levy. Baskerville was to have taken 1,500 men to Brest and so the 1,500 troops which returned from Groningen under Sir Francis Vere were paid by the States General. Reimbursement of the Queen's charges was outstanding at the end of 1594. See Letters Nos 34 and 36.

[101] Burghley here wished Cecil to correct a deficiency in Baskerville's warrant to conduct the Groningen troops to Portsmouth, Wernham, *After the Armada*, 529–530.

Dorse

ADDRESSED in Henry Maynard's hand:
To my loving sonne Sir Robert Cecil knight
one of her Majesty's Privy Counsell

ENDORSED in Simon Willis's hand:
5 May 1594
Lo[rd] Threasurer to my M[aste]r
[Seal: partial, cracked]

Letter No. 21

William, Lord Burghley to Sir Robert Cecil, 14 May 1594

½ p. Holograph.
Addressed, endorsed, signed.

Text

I do retorn to yow the draught of your letter to Mr. bowes havyng no
lesur nor yet cawse to alter the sence but in the report of the wordes
of the Q[ueen's] letter, by them remembred.[102] I have taken order with
Sir Thomas Shyrley to stay all expeditors savyng to have monny and

---

[102] Cecil wrote two letters to Bowes dated 17 May, final versions of the one sent to his
father on the 14th, and possibly requiring his father's attendance in conference with the
Queen. The first was the official account of the Queen's receipt of James VI's letter where
he promised to prosecute the Catholic earls, despite his having lost most of his friends by
following Elizabeth's demands. Cecil recounted the Queen's summoning of her council
in the presence of James's ambassadors: Buckhurst, Burghley, Lord Admiral Howard and
himself. Burghley put the case to the king's ambassadors (see Letter No. 19), Colville of
Easter Wemyss and Edward Bruce, that the Queen had never sponsored Bothwell in his
designs nor authorized him to go to the king's person. She had made a proclamation to
her three Borders wardens instructing them to refuse Bothwell. The Queen demanded
the king's actions against the Catholic earls before she could derive any comfort from his
words. TNA SP 52/53/no. 53, copied into Cecil's letter book, SP 52/52/, 75–79; *CSPS
1593–1595*, 332–335. Cecil's second letter of that day was more private: 'various' in detail,
but not contrary to the meaning of the first. The Queen had formulated a secret channel
to the king through Cecil as insurance against the ambassadors colouring her denials of
their requests on the five articles: Cecil asked Bowes to go straight to the king to request
his urgent prosecution of the earls, at which time she would send his annuity immediately,
without naming the sum. Cecil to Bowes, TNA SP 52/53/no. 54, SP 52/52/p. 80; *CSPS
1593–1595*, 335. Bowes received these 23 May, TNA SP 52/53/no. 58; see Letter No. 20.
John Colville (1542–1605), *ODNB*, had been a conspirator with Bothwell, but had been
pardoned. James distrusted Colville's closeness with the English Queen and court. Edward
Bruce (1548/9–1611), later 1st Baron Bruce of Kinloss, *ODNB*. See above, pp. 46–47.

apparel redy to depart to pempol, wherof they shal have nede, whyther they shall go to brest or retorn.[103]

Yow may do well to wryt to Sir Tho[mas] baskervile not to still the men, otherwise than to have them in redynes specially they of ostend, until he shall be further advertised.[104]

I meane to come thyther to morrow at night

Your loving father,

W. Burghley

Dorse

ADDRESSED in Henry Maynard's hand:
To my lovinge sonne
Sir Robart Cecill knight
one of hir ma[jes]ties privy connsell

ENDORSED in Simon Willis's hand:
14 Maii 1594
Lo[rd] Thre[asure]r to my M[aste]r
[Faint mark of seal]

Letter No. 22

William, Lord Burghley to Sir Robert Cecil, May 1594

⅛ p. Holograph.
Addressed, endorsed, signed.

[103] Burghley notified Sir Thomas Sherley of the stopping of all war expenditure on about 14 May. The victuals and apparel were for the 1,100 men set for Brest to relieve Henry IV's forces, under the conduct of Sir Martin Frobisher, sailing in the *Merehonour*, *Vanguard*, *Rainbow*, *Hope*, *Dreadnought*, and *Mercury*, with two pinnaces, Wernham, *After the Armada*, 529; Letter No. 20.

[104] Sir Thomas Baskerville replied to Cecil's letter of 23 May 1594, from Rammekens [Ramekins], TNA SP 84/48/fol. 216r; *L&A*, v, Analysis no. 117. It discussed the troops for Brittany: 'on receiving on May 22 a letter from Sir R Cecil Baskerville ordered the Ostend companies to stay there until Her Majesty's pleasure were further known'. Baskerville asked for three hoys not sent to Portsmouth to go to Ostend to carry troops to Brittany. In the event, he returned without incident, taking 1,080 troops, 500 of whom were from Ostend. The troops under Baskerville were the only English troops from the Low Countries to go to Brittany in 1594. Wernham, *After the Armada*, 530–531.

Text

If hir Ma[jes]ty shall ask of my mynd for mr. fletewood,[105] I thynk hym so Sir Christopher Edmundes[106] may have satisfaction, to be very mete for the office.[107]

Your lov[ing] father,

W. Burghley

Dorse

ADDRESSED Maynard:
To my lovinge sonne Sir Robart Cecill knight one of her ma[jes]ties privye Connsell

ENDORSED Willis:
Maii 1594
L[ord] Threas[urer] to my M[aste]r
Mr. Ffleetwood, Sir Christopher Edmundes
[Seal fragment, some wax remaining]

Letter No. 23

William, Lord Burghley to Sir Robert Cecil, March 1593

⅔ p. Holograph.
Addressed, endorsed, signed.

Text

Yow shall understand that Mr. vichamb[erlain] cam to me yesterday and did declare hir Ma[jes]ty's disposition, to have one named to be

---

[105]Sir Thomas Heneage (1532–1595), *ODNB*, vice-chamberlain of the chamber, chancellor of the duchy of Lancaster and significant pluralist, he worked very closely with the Cecils in intelligence. See above, p. 24. Sir William Fleetwood of Missenden (d.1593), recorder of London and the serjeant-at-law's eldest son, is referred to here.

[106]Sir Christopher Edmondes (1524–1596), MP for Wallingford 1584, was appointed to the commission of the peace in letters patent of 15 May 1594, *CPR 36 Eliz I*, no. 996. See Letter No. 46, where Fleetwood is referred to in documents as the receiver-general of the wards.

[107]The countess of Warwick (Anne Dudley, 1548/9–1604), *ODNB*, petitioned Cecil on behalf of Mr. Fleetwood ('the eldest brother of that name'), of Ealing in a matter (unspecified) with Sir Christopher Edmondes, Hatfield, Cecil Papers, 21 Apr. 1594; *HMCS*, iv, 514. Edmondes was appointed Receiver of the Court of Wards and Liveries, 31 May 1594, *CSPD 1591–1594*, 513.

an asistant to the lyeutenant of the tower, namyng Sir Dru. Drury,[108] whom I thought fitt for his trustynes, but I thought he would require interteynment for hym self and a nombre of servaunts, besyde that he is often syck. but in my opinion I sayd Sir G[eorge] Care[w],[109] the Lieut[enant] of the ordonnance might be meter, becawse he hath an office and an ordinary lodgyng in the towr. Whereon Mr. vichamberlayn, (as allowyng the same), prayed me to signefy thus much to yow, to be shewed to hir Ma[jes]ty, submittyng my self to hir Ma[jes]ty's Judgement.

Your loving father,

W. Burghley

[Postscript]
He Inswared of hir Ma[jes]ty's care in moovyng to hym that I might have his lodgyng for which I humbly thank hir Majesty

Dorse

ADDRESSED in Henry Maynard's hand:
To m lovinge sonne
Sor Robart Cecill
knight, one of the Q[ueen's]
ma[jes]tie's privie connsell

ENDORSED in one of Cecil's clerk's hands:
March 1593
[In another Clerk's hand]
my l[ord] Thre[asure]r to my M[aste]r
[Seals cut out]

---

[108] Sir Dru Drury (1531/2–1617), *ODNB*, became lieutenant of the Tower in 1595–1596. The current lieutenant, Sir Michael Blount, was removed under suspicion of treason, R.B. Manning, 'The prosecution of Sir Michael Blount, lieutenant of the Tower of London, 1595', *Bulletin of the Institute of Historical Research*, 57 (1984), 216–224.
[109] Sir George Carew (1555–1629), *ODNB*, lieutenant-general of the Ordnance office, and staunch Cecil ally with significant Irish experience. See Letter No. 19 for Carew's Irish treatise. Carew was then attempting reforms of the Ordnance office, Richard W. Stewart, *The English Ordnance Office, 1585–1625: A Case Study in Bureaucracy* (Woodbridge, 1996), 16, 46.

Letter No. 24

William, Lord Burghley to Sir Robert Cecil, 29 March 1594

½ p. Holograph.
Addressed, endorsed, signed.

Text

By your letter and by the Messadg of mr. Loveless, I perceave hir Ma[jes]ty wold have me com to the Court to morrow beyng Satyrday but the tide serveth me at night, for I am not in good helth, on the fornoons and therfor I will prevent the Comanndment, makyng it meritam, and with God's leve I will even thyther at this evening tide, yow may tell Symons so, but not provyde me any thyng but a new layd egg, for I have vowed to fast this day, without superstition.[110]

I send yow such 2 l[ette]res as I receaved from Sir rob[ert] Sydne.[111] the latter of the 16 by which I see that as, than he had not receaved, the letters sent from hence. I send yow also, Otwell Smyth's[112] assuryng the rendition of Roan whichi must nedes bryng on St. Mallos.[113]

---

[110] A reference to the Catholic religious practice of fasting during Lent, while Burghley was abstaining he sought to make the distinction. Mr. Symons maybe James Symons, for whom see Letter No. 47. Mr. Lovelace, messenger of the Chamber, BL Lansdowne MS 44/nos 14, 15.

[111] Burghley referred to Sidney's letters of 15 and 16 of Mar. 1594, TNA SP 78/33/fol. 138r, 141r; *L&A*, v, Analysis nos 229, 366, 410, 141, 414, 416, 484, 487, 620, 639–640, 653. Sidney was on embassy in France having been given the letters of instruction and credence on 21 Nov. 1593, audience of Henry IV on 21 Jan. 1594, and recall in early Apr. 1594. See Gary M. Bell, *A Handlist of British Diplomatic Representatives, 1509–1688* (London, 1990), 99.

[112] Otywell Smyth, merchant and intelligence source for the Privy Council received news of the cautionary towns and elsewhere in the Low Countries in Dieppe, as he had been driven from Rouen by the League in 1589, R.B. Wernham, *The Making of Elizabethan Foreign Policy, 1558–1603* (London, 1980), 77. The letter referred to here is Smyth to Burghley, 23 Mar. 1593/4 from Dieppe, where he notes that Villar, who had been virtual ruler of the city, surrendered Rouen on 20 Mar. after which he was named the duke of Montpensier's lieutenant in Normandy, TNA SP 78/33/fol. 160r. Smyth and Aymer de Chatte (governor of Dieppe) were to meet with Villar to discuss liberty of conscience in religion and privileges for English traders. *L&A*, v, Analysis no. 229. Wernham refers to this group around Smyth as the pro-Henry IV 'Dieppe' party. For Montpensier, prince of Dombes and duke of Montpensier, Henry de Bourbon-Vendome, see Wernham, *After the Armada*, 501, 518, 532–533, 543–547; Letter No. 26.

[113] The town officers of St Malo acknowledged Henry IV on 11 Aug. 1594, as Burghley here predicted. TNA SP 78/33/fol. 303r–v, 147r; *L&A*, v, Analysis, no. 340.

29 Ma[rch] 1594

Your Lo[ving] Father,

W. Burghley

Dorse

ADDRESSED in Henry Maynard's hand:
To my lovinge sonne
Sir Robart Cecill
knight, onc of the Q[ueen's] ma[jes]ties privie Connsell
At the Cort

ENDORSED in Simon Willis's hand:
29 Martii 1594
Lo[rd] Thre[asure]r to my M[aste]r

Letter No. 25

William, Lord Burghley to Sir Robert Cecil, 31 May 1594

½ p. Dictated to his clerk Hickes.
Addressed, endorsed, signed.

Text

I send you hereinclosed two billes wich I receaved from my L[ord]
Keeper to be signed by hir Ma[jes]tie, the contentes whereof yow shall
perceave by the dockets there underwritten. I praie yowe procure them
to be signed assoone as yow shall have convenient tume. And so fare
yow well.[114] Ffrom my howse in West[minste]r, the last of May 1594

Your loving father,

W. Burghley

Dorse

ADDRESSED in the hand of the clerk to whom the letter was dictated:
To my lovinge sonne Sir

---

[114] Typical example of Cecil's *de facto* secretarial work, see above, p. 20. For a description of
the seals and their uses, see also *Guide to the Contents of the Public Record Office*, 3 vols (London,
1963–1968), II, 258–259.

Robert Cecill knight of her ma[jes]ties most honrable privy Connsell
[with a small sign in the margin]

ENDORSED in Simon Willis's hand:
ul[ti]mo Maii 1594
lo[rd] Thres[ure]r to mu M[aste]r
[Seal missing]

Letter No. 26

William, Lord Burghley to Sir Robert Cecil, 4 September 1594

1 p. Holograph.
Addressed, endorsed, signed.

Text

I do send herinclosed, l[ette]res sent from Mr. Edmundes[115] of the
21 of August conteaning sondry thynges, wherof I thynk will hav hir
Ma[jes]ty will have much mislyking as that dowtfullnes of the D[uke]
of Mon[t]pensiers Jornay to brittann with new forces, wherof the kyng
by his letter made so firm a promiss, as in truth I made accompt that
we would have hard out of britanne, of his arryvall ther. herewith I
thynk hir Ma[jes]ty shuld doo well to cause the fr[ench ambassador
to be charged for as I thynk he did inform hir Ma[jes]ty, upon letters
from the kyng, of the D[uke] Monpensier's purpose.[116]

The other matter to be mislyked is the messadge under hand from
the k[ing] of Spayn to have on sent to bayon to conferr of a peace.
Wherto, though the kyng pretendth a mislyk, yet suerly the Catholique
Connsellors[117] with the disposition also of the pope will work some

[115]Thomas Edmondes (d.1639), *ODNB*, the Queen's agent to the French king, in the
capacity as *chargé d'affaires* and secretary of the French tongue in May 1596. See Bell,
Handlist, 99. Edmondes was sent 1 June 1592–14 Apr. 1596 and again in 1597 and again later
that year until 1599. Sir Thomas Wilkes was also on diplomatic mission to the French king
at the same time, but with Edmondes as his second: 8 Mar. 1592–15 Apr. 1592 and 18 July
1593–2 Sept. 1593, and finally to Henry IV with Cecil and John Herbert, Wilkes dying on
the way to the king 1 Mar. 1598.
[116]Cecil's communications with the ambassador, Beauvoir la Nocle, at this time, asking for
relief and munitions, were all balanced against Sir John Norris's letters relaying his version
of events. See TNA SP 78/34/fols. 57r, 63r, 68r, 69r, 84r, 94r, 96r, 98r, as examples. Cecil and
Beauvoir la Nocle were also having private meetings during this time. TNA SP 78/34/fols.
11r, 19r, 22r.
[117]Nicholas de Neufville, lord of Villeroy (1543–1617), was certainly one of the leading
'Catholique Councellors', Ungerer, *A Spaniard in Elizabethan England*, Vol. I, 178–183, 343,

furder operation therin. and so both England and all the protestantes in France, shall fele the smart therof.[118] but I am bold to hope of the favor of the kyng of kynges, that [blob of wax] can abridg the k[ing] of Spaynes liff, and shew some notable avendg upon the fr[ench] kyng for his perfydye towards God and Man.

My hand is so weak as I am unhable to wryt any more. 4 7[bre] 1594

Your lov[ing] father

W. Burghley

Dorse

ADDRESSED in Burghley's hand:
To my loving sone Sir Robart Cecil knight at the Court. W. Burghley

ENDORSED in Simon Willis's hand:
4 Sept[ember] 1594
L[ord] Threas[urer] to my M[aste]r
[Seal missing]

Letter No. 27

William, Lord Burghley to Sir Robert Cecil, 28 September 1594

½ p. Holograph.
Addressed, endorsed, signed.

Text

I send to yow such letters as ar directed to hir Ma[jes]ty's Connsell from Irland whch I have not opened,[119] because it is mete thath they

---

348, 434–438; Vol. II, 86–89, 95, 96, 241–244. Villeroy had been secretary of state successively to the three Valois kings before Henry IV and was a principal enemy of Épernon. Note also Henry IV's dealing with Aldobrandini the papal nephew: see N.M. Sutherland, *Henry IV of France and the Politics of Religion*, Vol. II (Bristol, 2002), ch. 15. Sutherland discusses the intricate path to the king's absolution begun once the League was reduced in earnest in mid 1594.

[118] Henry IV's use of Huguenot envoys exploited the connection between Brittany Protestants and the English crown: see a letter of 25 Sept. 1595 to Burghley, TNA SP 78/36/fol. 19r.

[119] Russell and the Irish Council to the Privy Council, 12 Sept. 1594, TNA SP 63/176/no. 12, fol. 39r. This principally concerns the lord deputy's agent Thomas Lee. See Letter No. 231.

be opened by hir Ma[jes]ty, as upon a Caveat gyven uppon the last sent from thence,[120] I perceaved was best lyking to hir Ma[jes]ty.

by a nombre of Copyes now sent not sealed, I see the uncertan accompt to be made of the Erle of Tyron.[121] Ther is both monny and munition gon,[122] whyther the Depute send for men I know not.[123]

I am rather worss than better, but better for heaven than for the world. this Satyrday
Your loving father,

W. Burghley

Dorse

ADDRESSED
To my Lovinge Sonne Sir Robert Cecill knyght of her ma[jes]ties honrable privy Connsell

ENDORSED in Simon Willis's hand:
28 Sept[ember] 1594
Thre[asure]r to my M[aste]r

Letter No. 28

William, Lord Burghley to Sir Robert Cecil, 5 October 1594

½ p. Holograph.
Addressed, endorsed, signed.

---

[120] The 'Caveat' on the last letter requesting that the Irish letters be unsealed and opened by the Queen alone may have come with Russell's dispatch of 19 Aug. 1594, TNA SP 63/175/no. 62; *CSPI 1592–1596*, 264.

[121] Russell had been out-manoeuvred by Tyrone, and he reported to Burghley on 12 Sept. that he could make only an uncertain account of the earl's dealings, and viewed future negotiations with him pessimistically. TNA SP 63/176/no. 13, fol. 41r–v. Tyrone's ambitions were documented by Carew in his treatise for Cecil in Apr. 1594, TNA SP 63/174/no. 13, fols. 26r, 28r–32v; see Letter No. 19.

[122] Russell petitioned Cecil for the swift sending of money into Ireland in the packet of 12 Sept. 1594, in which he also asked for the Queen's further instructions on how to deal with the rebels. TNA SP 63/176/no. 16, fol. 47r. Six hundred men were sent in August, and Russell asked that no new captains be appointed, as so many other petitioners begged places. TNA SP 63/175/no. 62; *CSPI 1592–1596*, 264.

[123] The situation with Tyrone deteriorated as Russell's perspective of his strength and alliances became clearer, causing his petition for a large-scale military commitment in Nov. 1594 in response to the earl's well-financed troops. TNA SP 63/177/no. 5; *CSPI 1592–1596*, 281–282.

Text

Although I know hir Majesty hath Care of all hir chyrch offices, to have them bestowed, uppon persons worthy the vocations, both as well for vertew and Godly liff, as for lernyng, yet I pray yow shew to hir Ma[jes]ty what my L[ord] of Huntyngdon wryteth for the supply of the Archb[ishopric] of york,[124] wherof the last incumbent was a person of gret sufficiency, & as well approved in the chardg, as any prelat in England. It is lykly many will gape after it, and I wish the choiss war rather in hir Ma[jes]ty's own Judgment, then in the ambitioss desyre of them which seke que sua sunt non que Dei et ecclesie.[125]

5 8^{bre v} [5 October] 1594

Your loving Father

W. Burghley

Dorse

ADDRESSED
To my Lovinge Sonne Sir Robert
Cecill knight of her ma[jes]ties honorable
privy Connsell

ENDORSED in Simon Willis's hand:
28 Sept[ember] 1594
Thre[asure]r to my M[aste]r

---

[124] The demise of Dr John Piers, archbishop of York, on 28 Sept. 1594 marked the seventh bishopric vacated by the death of the incumbent in that year, Acres, 'The early political career of Sir Robert Cecil', 162, n. 2. Neither the earl of Huntingdon's petition nor Howland's own asking was enough for his suit, and the appointments to both York and Durham, on the elevation of Matthew Hutton to the archbishopric, occasioned much clandestine manoeuvring, ibid. 164–174; Smith, *Servant of the Cecils*, 75. BL Lansdowne MS vol. 76, no. 78: 'The Earl of Huntingdon to Lord Burghley; that a worthy successor may soon be place in the room of that good Prelate deceased, Dr. John Piers.' 2 Oct. 1594. BL Lansdowne MS 76/No. 87: petition of Dr Richard Howland, bishop of Peterborough, to Burghley for the place. 20 Oct. 1594. BL Lansdowne MS 76/No. 90: 'Dr. Matthew Hutton, Bishop of Durham, to Lord Burghley, of his removal to York; he sues for a pardon for Lady Margaret Nevil, taken in company with Boast, a seminary priest, 11 December 1594'.
[125] Translation: 'Those who seek for themselves rather than God or the Church'.

Letter No. 29

William, Lord Burghley to Sir Robert Cecil, 5 October 1594

¼ p. Dictated to Henry Maynard.
Addressed, endorsed, signed.

Text

Wheare the B. Willowghbies l[ette]res sent to the lls [Lords] of the Consell with the Examinacions oof the complaints against the Erle of Lincolne by his tenantes of Tattersall theare war a writing entituled a Premonition, which writinge I have sum occasion to see.[126] And there-fore I praie yowe, to speake to the Clarke of the Connsell that attendeth theare to seke for yt, and with your next letters to send yt to mee.

Ffrom my howse in the Strand this fift of October 1594

Your lovinge father,

W. Burghley

[On the left side of the foot of this letter Maynard has written]
Sir Robart Cecill

Dorse

ADDRESSED in Henry Maynard's hand:
To my lovinge Sonne
Sir Robart Cecill knight
one of the Quenes Ma[jes]ties
privie Connsell

ENDORSED in Simon Willis's hand:
5 October 1594
l[ord] Thre[asure]r to my M[aste]r
[Seal missing]

---

[126]Edward Fiennes de Clinton, 1st earl of Lincoln (1512–1585), *ODNB*. The 'premonition' regarding the tenants of the principal residence of Edward Clinton, 2nd earl of Lincoln at Tattersall in Lincolnshire was investigated by the Privy Council by Lord Willoughby d'Eresby (1555–1601), *ODNB*. Both men sat on the commission of oyer and terminer as well as the commission of the peace the following year. *CPR 37 Eliz. I*, no. 714, 756. Burghley referred to a long-standing conflict with the earl of Lincoln and cousins in his mother's family, the Dymokes, Ayscoughs and others, 'my ancient adversaries', who had persuaded various tenants to complain about Lincoln. *HMCS*, vi, 366.

Letter No. 30

William, Lord Burghley to Sir Robert Cecil, 13 October 1594

¼ p. Dictated to Henry Maynard.
Addressed, endorsed, signed.

Text

I recevid this morninge this letter and writinges inclosed from my L[ord] Scroope,[127] whearewith I praie yowe at your soonest commodite to acquaint hir Ma[jes]tie, and Theareuppon to understand hir pleasure for the awnsweare to be made theareto, which assone as I shall understand what hir Ma[jes]tie's will shall be, I will accordinglie retorne awnsweare by post to my L[ord] Scroope.[128] Soe fare yow well. ffrom my howse in the Strand this xiii[th] v of October 1594.

Your Lovinge father,

W. Burghley

[127] Henry, 10th Lord Scrope of Bolton (1567–1609), warden of the West March and keeper of Carlisle Castle, whose letter to the Cecils received on 13 Oct. is not extant. This packet might have included a private communication over James VI's intention to progress south to the Borders to discover more concerning the ill-fated English attempt to manoeuvre Bothwell into position as a counter-poise to the three earls. Scrope himself warned 'changeable truth breeds strongest poison', *Cal. Border Papers*, i, 546–547, 547. Despite blaming his deputies for his mistakes, he alleged to those of the Privy Council that he had control of his march. However, strong management was needed in the diocese of Durham, for which it seems likely that Tobie Matthew was at this time nominated to the see instead of William Day. Day appears to have been promised the place: see Acres, 'The early political career of Sir Robert Cecil', 168–169. He was not slighted, but rather superseded by Matthew's evident political strengths in secret policy, for he was intimately linked to the Bothwell plot, particularly to Colville. *Cal. Border Papers*, i, 528. Willis endorsed Matthew's letter to Cecil: 'Mr. Deane of Duresme to my Master, a letter of Mr. Colville's [Bothwell's secretary] herewithall'. For Colville, see Letter No. 44. In Apr. 1594 Matthew reported to Cecil, 'It maie be, that it wilbe reported, thErle Bothuell and I have lately mette at Hexham . . . neither did I see his Lordship or heare from him . . . the Kinges ministers care not what reportes they geve out of me.' *Cal. Border Papers*, i, 532. Matthew had sent intelligence to Sir Francis Walsingham in these matters since 1583, when he was named dean *in commendum* with the deanery of Christ Church, Oxford. See also Letters Nos 2, 16, 20, 41; William Day, bishop of Winchester (1529–1596), *ODNB*.
[128] Burghley's flight to court (see Letter No. 31) may well have been occasioned by the receipt of letters enclosed with Scrope's which Sir Robert Cecil mentioned in his reply to the warden: 'The Queen having been informed of the King of Scots' intention to march against "the rebellious erles" to the good of both realms, commands that good order may be kept in Scrope's march, so as not to weaken the King's forces. Sir John Forster has been notified in the same terms.' Draft letters remain of those sent to Scrope and Sir John Forster by Cecil, *Cal. Border Papers, 1560–1594*, i, 548, no. 983.

Dorse

ADDRESSED in Henry Maynard's hand:
To my Lovinge sonne Sir
Robart Cecill knight
One of hir Ma[jes]ties Privy Concill

ENDORSED
L[ord] Thre[asure]r to my M[aste]r
[Seal cut out]

Letter No. 31

William, Lord Burghley to Sir Robert Cecil, 13 October 1594

¼ p. Holograph.
Addressed, endorsed, signed.

Text

I se by your l[ette]re how desyrous hir Ma[jes]ty is to have me ther. now I have a mynd to even thyther to Morrow, but yow shall not be known thereof untill I shall come. cause my chamber to be made redy. Herein I shall venture parcass [perchance] my liff, but I remitt all to God, fiat voluntas sua.

13 October 1594

Your lov[ing] father,

W. Burghley

Dorse

ADDRESSED Holograph:
To my lov. Sonn Sir Robert Cecill Kt. at the Court

ENDORSED Holograph:
13 October 1594
L[ord] Thre[asure]r to my M[aste]r
[Seal missing]

Letter No. 32

William, Lord Burghley to Sir Robert Cecil, 19 October 1594

1 p. Holograph.
Addressed, endorsed, signed.

Text

Though I did require yow to inform hir Ma[jes]ty, of my great weaknes increased uppon me sence I cam from the Court, so as I found ^{my self} unhable to perform my resolut intention to retorn as this daye, with a mynd if hir Ma[jes]ty shold remove shortly to Rychmond, to aventur to come thyther, yet because Mr. Chancelor now at xi of the clock telleth me that hir Ma[jes]ty sayd she looked for me this night which he sayd he thought I was unhable to do.

   I have thought good in this my perplexity, beyng cheffly carryed afor all other releve the Erle[129] with some grant of parkes in such sort, as may be no deminution to hir Ma[jes]ty's revennew, and yet releve hym, in a sort very resonable. I move not these thyngs for the Erle, pro merito in, but pro condeyno for hir Majesty.

[On the lower right of the text]
This Satyrd[ay] 18 or 19.

Your loving father,

W. Burghley

Dorse

ADDRESSED in Burghley's hand:
To my lovyng son Sir
Robert Cecil knight
at the Court

ENDORSED in Simon Willis's hand:
19 October 1594
L[ord] Threas[urer] to my M[aste]r

---

[129] The earl of Essex was perhaps seeking grants for himself or his retinue, although there is no specific mention of such a gift at this juncture. On 27 Sept. 1594, he and his wife Frances (née Walsingham) gained a wardship by 'bill of the Court of Wards', *CPR 36 Eliz. I*, no. 748. A few weeks later they may have begun to sue for livery: 'For the Queen rather than the earl's own merit'.

Letter No. 33

William, Lord Burghley to Sir Robert Cecil, 2 December 1594

½ p. Holograph.
Addressed, endorsed, signed.

Text

I thank yow for sendyng to me the Copy of hir Ma[jes]ty's letters to the fr[ench] kyng, assuryng my self, that ther cold no such marye come owt of any knuckles but of hirs; that in all graces by natur, by callyng, by long experience, is of such perfection, as none can attayn unto. In this letter, thowgh I knolledg my weaknes of Judg therof, yet I see every sentence full of matter of great vallew a princely kyndnes to a kyng very acceptable, in Congratualyng his escape very comfortable, in advising hym how to preserve his person more carefull than she is for hir self, otherwise than she beareth all to the care of God, in advise further to remove the nursery of his coniured ennemyes, without relenting to contrary Connsells so wisely and religiously, as of all these thoughts I am suer no secretary nor orator cold so lyvely express hir princely mynd.

For hir hope to have me dance, I must have a longer tyme to lern to goo. but I will be redy in mynd to dance with my hart, when I shall behold hyr favorable disposition to do such honor to hyr Mayd, for the old mans sake.[130]

I wish hir Majesty wold send som tresur into Irland and that hir Tresuror might se to the orderly expence therof better than his clerkes have doon these 6 yeres.[131]

The argument of my letter hath tempted my hand to wryt thus much.

Your loving father,

W. Burghley

Dorse

ADDRESSED in Henry Maynard's hand:
To my Lovinge sonne
Sir Robart Cecill knight

---

[130]This may refer to the Derby marriage or forthcoming festivities at the court over Christmas.
[131]See Letter No. 27.

one of the Quene's Ma[jes]ties
privie Connsell

ENDORSED in Simon Willis's hand:
2 Dec[ember] 1594
l[ord] Thre[asure]r to my M[aste]r
[Seal cut out]

Letter No. 34

William, Lord Burghley to Sir Robert Cecil, 23 December 1594

⅓ p. Dictated to Henry Maynard, with postscript also in Maynard's hand.
Addressed, endorsed, signed.

Text

I doe send unto yowe a letter which I have receved from Mr. Guilpin
owt of the Lowe Contries, with the contentes wherof, yowe maie
acquaint her ma[jes]tie.[132] There is also browght to mee this eveninge
a letter with thes other writinges of the B[ishop] of Limerick,[133] which
should have been sooner delivered unto mee: & althowgh it semeth by
his letter that he hath written of the same matters to her ma[jes]tie, yet

---

[132] TNA SP 84/49/fols. 255r–256r; *L&A*, v, Analysis nos 589, 544. No. 589: the letter makes
an implicit link between Gilpin's work in the Low Countries and the letter received from
Thornborough (see n. 133) concerning Irish intelligence. Of the Irish soldiers in Stanley's
regiment, 'They seemed anxious to abandon the Spanish side altogether and to serve the
States. They were very good soldiers, so they were likely to be accepted . . . As there was
long a practice to break Stanley's regiment, with Burghley's knowledge, Gilpin had agreed
upon seeking to draw them from the enemy and from returning to their own home.' It was
rumoured also that the Archduke Albert was in straits paying his Italian soldiers, and that
Spanish 'Entretenidos' (payments) were late.

[133] John Thornborough (1551–1641), *ODNB*, sometime bishop of Limerick, was a leading
player in Cecil's Irish intelligence connections, disagreeing over these matters with his dean,
Dioness Campbell. He was a kinsman of the earl of Argyll, Archibald Campbell, who was,
for a time, a powerful influence in the creation of a Scottish force against the Irish rebels'
troops in Ulster. Thornborough owed Burghley his promotion from the mastership of the
Savoy to the bishopric of Limerick. In late 1594 Thornborough examined the spy Thomas
Gravenor, who was supplying Tyrone with information, and carrying messages into Scotland
for him, together with an accomplice, John Hales. (Limerick's examination is so mentioned,
HMCS, vi, 427–428; Hatfield, Cecil Papers, 45/fol. 61r). For Gravenor's probable suicide,
see Letter No. 38. The lord deputy, Russell, appears to have been somewhat threatened by
Thornborough's extensive intelligence connections, desiring to score political points in this
area himself to gain the Queen's approval. Thornborough to Cecil, TNA SP 63/183/no.
106, fols. 331–332r; *CSPI 1592–1596*, 425. See Acres, 'The early political career of Sir Robert
Cecil', 246–248.

shall yowe doe well to acquaint hir with this as yowe find commoditie. ffrom my howse in the Strand the xxiiird v of December 1594.

[Postscript]
I received even nowe your letter sygnifienge the Q[ueen's] determinacion to send Mr. Bodeleie into the lowe Contries,[134] and D[r.] Parkins into Poland,[135] both which I doe allowe of.

W. Burghley

Dorse

ADDRESSED in Henry Maynard's hand:
To my Lovinge Sonne Sir

[134] Sir Thomas Bodley (1545–1613), *ODNB*, then on embassy to the States General of the Low Countries was given draft contractual negotiations, made in Willis's hand, which formed the substance of Bodley's instructions, TNA SP 84/49/fols. 277r–282v, 285r–288r; Bell, *Handlist*, 193. The return of English troops under the treaty is the only section of Bodley's instructions in Cecil's hand, TNA SP 84/49/fol. 289r, SP 84/50/fols. 3r–8r. These included letters of credence, endorsed 2 Jan. 1594/5, to the States General, fol. 9r; and letters to the Council of State, and to Maurice of Nassau. The negotiating points, corrected by Cecil, included the Queen's demand for reimbursement for the pay of the 1,500 men levied under Sir Francis Vere who had not been returned to their garrison, *L&A*, vi, Analysis, no. 70. Some of these men were alleged to be too ill to return to service, even though they had been used by the States in continual and dangerous employment. See Letters Nos 21, 36, 37, 43, 47. Cecil had drafted Bodley's original instructions in May 1594, TNA SP 84/48/fols. 185r–88r. This was a pattern sustained through Bodley's work with the States. See also n. 135 for eastern and central Europe.
    One way of discerning custody of papers between Cecil and Burghley is to read the procurations of the SO3, signet seal: for minutes are noticed as remaining with Cecil. For merely a few of these dozens of records indicating his own archival formation, see, e.g. instructions from the Queen to the States General covering Bodley's mission at TNA SO3/1/fol. 454r, with numerous correspondence noted and commented on by Burghley, but endorsed as noted or drafted by Willis, now bound in SP 84. The same pattern emerges in SP78. For Christopher Parkins (1542/3–1622, later Sir), see *ODNB*, a former Jesuit with extensive knowledge of Rome and diplomatic systems in post-Tridentine central Europe who came into Burghley's service in the 1590s.
[135] Christopher Parkins's embassy to Poland: see *L&A*, v, Analysis no. 680; *L&A*, vi, Analysis nos 42–43, 390. The instructions for Christopher Parkins were dated 6 Jan. 1595. Parkins was to arrive in Poland before the end of the session of the Parliament there. TNA SP 88 /I/fols. 215r–216r. 'The principal purpose of his mission was to seek to conserve the quiet trade and residence of the English merchants at Elbing.' Parkins was to speak to the king and then the chancellor. See *L&A*, vi, Analysis no. 391. Rudolf II had tried to persuade the Polish king to declare war on the Turks, but the chancellor opposed the move as potentially catastrophic before the kingdom was brought to one religion—there were Lutherans and Orthodox, of course, as the Union of Brest was signed in 1596. Ambassadors from Wallachia, Moldavia, the Emperor, Hungary and Transylvania could not prevail on the Polish unwillingness to break with the Grand Signor; while the Papal nuncio was content to let diplomatic matters rest as the chancellor pressed for the Catholic religion. Bell, *Handlist*, 59, 138. See Letter No. 55.

Robart Cecill knight, one of hir ma[jes]ties privie Connsell

ENDORSED by Simon Willis:
23 dec[ember] 1594
Lo[rd] Thre[asure]r to my M[aste]r

Letter No. 35

William, Lord Burghley to Sir Robert Cecil, 13 December 1594

Page ripped. ⅓ p. Eight lines. Dictated to Henry Maynard.
Addressed, endorsed.

Text

I doe meane tomorrowe in the morninge to give order that all such monie as shall be aunswered of her ma[jes]ties Customs outwards in the office that Mr. Yonge had, shall be paid in the Customhouse [and] & theare savelie locked upp: and to be paid at the ende of everie weeke into hir Ma[jes]tie's receipt at Westminster.[136] Owt of my bed beinge not hable to signe anie letter this xiiii[th] of december at night.

Dorse

ADDRESSED in Henry Maynard's hand:
To my lovinge sonne
Sir Robart Cecil knight
one of the Q[ueen's] ma[jes]ties
privie Connsell

ENDORSED in Simon Willis's hand:
[Date obscured in the margin]
Lo[rd] Thre[asure]r to my M[aste]r

---

[136] Richard Carmarthen was in receipt of Cecil's directions concerning the customs money on 19 Dec. 1594, presumably immediately following Burghley's order on the 14th. Richard Young's debt and abuse of his office as customer in the port of London saw Burghley order Alderman Billingsley's interim oversight. Hatfield, Cecil Papers, 29/35; *HMCS*, v. 40. Carmarthen noted that Burghley's health was impaired by the shock of Young's £10,000 debt. See Letter No. 36. Carmarthen to Burghley of 1 Feb. 1595, covered a full list of all customs received, incoming and outgoing, in the port of London from each collector, from 30 Dec. 1594 to 1 Feb., proposing monthly reckonings, Hatfield, Cecil Papers, 25/9; *HMCS*, v. 100–101.

Letter No. 36

William, Lord Burghley to Sir Robert Cecil, 14 December 1594

½ p. Dictated to Henry Maynard.
Addressed, endorsed.

Text

I doe send hearewith unto yowe an Addition to that former declaracion which yowe have of som further cawses movinge hir Ma[jes]ties dislike that the 1500 men levied for their service, have not been returned whereof hir ma[jes]tie hath often spoken and I thinke will be agreable to hir minde thearein, which yowe maye acquaint hir majestie withall as yowe shall finde commoditie: meaninge in like manner (as I maie have anie ease of my paine to sett downe sum like reasons to awnsweare the obiections that maie be made by the States that theie are not to make paiment of this monie, untill the ende of the warres),[137] but my paine is such as I cannot further travell thearein at this time. I praie yowe also to acquainte hir ma[jes]tie with the letter inclosed which I received this Eveninge from Mr. Edmondes.[138]

I am not hable by reason of the weaknes & paine of my hand to signe this letter.

ffrom my howse in the Strand this xiii[th] of December, 1594

[137] Bodley later assured Burghley that he acted under orders sent by Cecil presumably delivered verbally (Hatfield, Cecil Papers, 171/81; *HMCS*, v, 111; Thomas Birch, *Memoirs of the Reign of Queen Elizabeth from the Year 1581 until her Death . . . and the conduct of her favourite, Robert Earl of Essex . . .* 2 vols (London 1754), I, 207–208). Burghley's preparatory notes of instruction and on the terms of the treaty were made for his son's benefit. Cecil was, thus, seen to be the Queen's and Privy Council's hand controlling Bodley's embassy although he wrote equally to Essex. *L&A*, vi, Analysis nos 70, 71. The States General wanted assurance of English troops. TNA SP 84/50/fols. 29r–30r; *HMCS*, v, 102–103. Burghley's civil law interpretation of the terms of the 1585 treaty covered mutual defence between the States General and England, stipulating exact reciprocal financial and naval obligations. Burghley's treatise dated probably from early Jan. 1595, Hatfield, Cecil Papers, 25/91; *HMCS*, v, 99–100.
[138] Letter from Thomas Edmondes to Burghley dated 8 Dec. 1594, from Abbeville included Henry IV's declaration of war on Spain, TNA SP 78/34/fol. 285r enclosing fol. 283r-v. The French wanted assurance of English assistance for the duke of Bouillon, and noting the king's insistence on the boundaries of his kingdom. This was a last-ditch effort by the French to persuade Elizabeth to retain her forces in Brittany, Wernham, *After the Armada*, 553. Henry IV had been stabbed by a Jesuit, thus the order was banned outright from France. See Edmondes to Burghley, 22 Dec. 1594, *HMCS*, v, 43–44.

Dorse

ADDRESSED in Henry Maynard's hand:
To my Lovinge sonne
Sir Rob[er]t Cecill knight
one of the Q[ueen's] ma[jes]ties
privie Connsell

ENDORSED
14 dec[ember] 1594
Lo[rd] Thre[asure]r to my M[aste]r
[Seal cut out]

Letter No. 37

**William, Lord Burghley to Sir Robert Cecil,
27 December 1595**

⅔ p. Dictated to Henry Maynard, with a one sentence postscript by Burghley.
Addressed, endorsed, signed.

Text

I send hearewith unto two packettes[139] of letters browght owt of Ireland:
The greater is of elder date, and the lesse of a later. I minde not to
write unto yow the perticulers herof, for that theie be vearie manie &
therefore to be nowe diligentlie perused. My healthe serveth mee not
to enter into anie final consideracion herof, but onelie two thinges are
necessarye: Increase of the forces, which I am sorie to see longe delaied
from comminge owt of Bretaigne, althowghe I knowe not whome to
blame.[140] The second is to send monie thither for maintenance of
the Garrisons already in that Realme, consideringe it doth appear
by the Certificat of the Thres[urer's] Deputie that of treasure sent

[139] Russell warned of a swiftly deteriorating situation in Ulster on 15 Nov. 1594. He urged
that either the Queen dispose of Tyrone or lose her realm of Ireland. TNA SP 63/177/no. 10;
CSPI 1592–1596, 282. Russell sent intelligence that Tyrone was ruled by Jesuits and seminary
priests. TNA SP 63/177/no. 9; *CSPI 1592–1596*, 282. In addition, the earl's answers to the
Queen were deemed evasive. TNA SP 63/177/enclosure 3 with no. 9. Rumours held that
some rebels were ready to leave Tyrone's tyrannous rule, ibid. On 28 Dec. Burghley referred
to Russell's letter to Cecil of 8 Dec, TNA SP 63/177/no. 37; *CSPI 1592–1596*, 286. Here he
answered the Queen's criticism of several months' stalling with Tyrone.
[140] The Brittany troops under Norris were directed into Ireland. There was diplomatic
consternation caused in Anglo-French relations when this secret movement became known.
The official protest of the French ambassador, Beauvoir la Nocle, TNA SP 78/34/fol. 274,
320r; Wernham, *After the Armada*, 553–554; Letter No. 45.

over last, theare is nothinge remaininge, as by the Accompt of the Thres[urer's] deputie maie appeare.[141] But <u>thearein noe mention is made of a great some of mony that remained in the handes of the Thres[urer's] deputie this last yeare, for which the thres[urer] had good assurance for repaiment.</u> Ffrom my howse in the Strand this xxvii[th] of December 1594

[Maynard]
Your loving father

[Burghley]
W. Burghley

[Burghley's postscript]
I have no hope to amend towardes the world.

Dorse

ADDRESSED in Henry Maynard's hand:
To my lovinge sonne
Sir Robert Cecill
one of hir ma[jes]ties privie Connsell

ENDORSED in Sir Rober Cecil's hand:
28 Decemb[er] 1594
my l[ord] my Fathre to me
[Seal cut out]

Letter No. 38

William, Lord Burghley to Sir Robert Cecil, 13 January 1594

⅓ p. Dictated to Henry Maynard, with a one sentence postscript added in Burghley's hand.
Addressed, endorsed, signed.

Text

I doe send this bearer, the Quene's pusuivant at Yorke[142] with the letter from my L[ord] of Huntingdon for the Sendinge upp hither

---

[141] See Letter No. 38 for the charge on Wallop's war account.
[142] The Queen's pursuivant at York: Richard Outlawe. *HMCS*, v, 83. For a full list of the pursuivants of 1594, BL Lansdowne MS vol. 77, no. 85.

of Gravener, but as yt semeth both by the pursuivant, and by the testimonie of the Maior of Northampton, and a Phisitian theare, which I doe send unto yowe, the said Gravener is fallen soe sicke, as he is unhable to be browght from theare, and yet as the pursuivant saithe he hath left his mann with him to keape him as a close prisoner.[143] Of this yowe maie informe hir ma[jes]tie, for hir further pleasure to be done theare in.

If yowe see Sir Henry Walloppe, I praie yowe will him to comm to mee towchinge monie to be sent into Ireland.[144] ffrom my howse in the strand the xiiii[th] of Jan[uary] 1594.

Your loving father

[Signed]
W. Burghley

[Burghley's postscript]
My flux in myn eie begynneth to fall to an ebb

Dorse

ADDRESSED in Henry Maynard's hand:
To my lovinge sonne
Sir Robart Cecill knight
one of hir ma[jes]ties privy Connsell

---

[143] The Irish examinations of Thomas Gravenor, Tyrone's agent, were taken by the bishop of Limerick, John Thornborough, which reached the Privy Council at approximately this time (see Letter No. 34). Lord Huntingdon sent Gravenor south without further examination at the council of the north. Hatfield, Cecil Papers, 24/90; *HMCS*, v, 81. Cecil received most of the papers concerning Gravenor. (Edward Mercer to Cecil dated 13 Jan. 1594/5, Hatfield, Cecil Papers, 24/100; *HMCS*, v, 83.) The lord president sent in the same post Anthony Atkinson's cover letter to Cecil giving further examinations of David Ingleby, Hatfield, Cecil Papers, 27/6; *HMCS*, v, 83. Richard Topcliffe (1531–1604), *ODNB*, chief interrogator and torturer of the Privy Council (whose influence was waning under Burghley in the 1590s) was sent north to investigate Gravenor's death. He argued to Cecil for the exhumation of the corpse to determine what business of Tyrone's they were pursuing. Hatfield, Cecil Papers, 24/102; *HMCS*, v, 91. Henry Hastings, 3rd earl of Huntingdon (1536?–1595), *ODNB*.
[144] The list of privy seal payments authorized by the Queen for Ireland is found at TNA SP 63/191/fol. 201r. Burghley's chief concern here was the related contract he had made with George Beverly of Chester for the victualling of Irish troops, TNA SP 63/178/no. 34, fol. 69r; *CSPI 1592–1596*, 295. Burghley's conference with Wallop he described to his son, planning details for subsequent warrants for the Queen's and Privy Council's information, but remaining indifferent to Wallop's separate suit for Irish monies. Wallop urged Cecil separately to have the Queen sign the warrant for the repayment of his personal debt out of the monies set for Ireland. TNA SP 63/178/no. 40, fol. 92r; *CSPI 1592–1596*, 296. Wallop first spoke with Maynard about the matter and was told that Cecil was charged with moving the warrant to the Queen for signing following Burghley's draft.

ENDORSED in Simon Willis's hand:
14 January 1594 l[ord] thre[asure]r to my M[aste]r
[Seal cut away]

Letter No. 39

William, Lord Burghley to Sir Robert Cecil, 25 January 1594

½ p. Holograph.
Addressed, endorsed, signed.

Text

Though my hand be unhable to fight and my right eie unhable to take a levell, yet thay beth do stoop to return my humble thanks for contynuance of hir favor at this tyme whan I am more fitter for an hospitall, than to be a party for a marriadg.[145]

I will be a precise kepar of myself from all cold untill fryday on which daye I will ventur to come thyther.

If yow shall here that this nyght I have playd at post and pare, yowe will ghess that I shall recover, for I have lost all I playd for.

Your lov[ing] fath[er],

W. Burghley

Dorse

ADDRESSED in Henry Maynard's hand:
To my Lovinge Sonne
Sir Robert Cecill
one of hir ma[jes]ties privye Connsell

ENDORSED in Simon Willis's hand:
25 January 1594
Lo[rd] Thre[asure]r to my [Maste]r
[Seal cut away]

[145] See Letter No. 44 for Burghley's advice to the Derbys, the 6th earl, William, and his grand-daughter Elizabeth Vere, on the will of the 5th earl, whereby the heirs general rather were named as recipients of the peerage lands. Barry Coward, *The Stanleys, Lords Stanley and Earls of Derby 1385–1672: The Origins, Wealth and Power of a Landowning Family* (Manchester, 1983), 46, 53. See also Helen Payne, 'The Cecil women at court', in Pauline Croft (ed.), *Patronage, Culture and Power: The Early Cecils* (Yale, 2002), 265–281. See esp. 266–270 for discussion of the importance of the Cecil women in court office but also the unhappy beginnings to the Derby marriage in 1595.

Letter No. 40

William, Lord Burghley to Sir Robert Cecil, 12 February 1594

⅓ p. Eight lines. Holograph.
Addressed and endorsed, with a list of secret Scottish intelligence codenames in silverpoint or crayon on the dorse in Henry Maynard's hand.

Text

I know not what resolution hir Ma[jes]ty hath made with Sir Jhon Norrycc, for the service in Irland,[146] nor for the manner of dischardge of the rest of the nombres beside the ii^M [2,000] to be sent into Irland.

I understand ther ar noo Capt. in bogland than ar to serve with the ii^M [2,000] wherof regard wold be had what shall become of them.

12 febr[uary] 1594

Your lov[ing] father,

W. Burghley

Dorse

ADDRESSED in Henry Maynard's hand:
To my lovinge sonne Sir Robart Cecill knight
one of hir ma[jes]ties privie Connsell
At the Cort

---

[146] Sir John Norris's revocation to Ireland from Brittany caused difficulties with the French and a lengthy protest from the ambassador, Beauvoir la Nocle, TNA SP 78/34/fol. 320–321v, 29 Dec. 1594; Letter No. 37; Wernham, *After the Armada*, 553–554. The 2,000 troops out of Brittany and 100 horse were to be sent into Ireland for which thanks were given on 26 Feb. by the council in Dublin Castle. TNA SP 63/178/no. 54, fols. 126r–127v; *CSPI 1592–1596*, 299. Cecil had procured supply for Norris prior to his removal and charges of corruption in ordnance: see TNA SP 78/34/54r, 84r–5r, 94r, 96r, SO3/1/fol. 477r (Sir George Carew for ordnance), fol. 484r (Jean d'Aumont's letters), fol. 484v for the warrant for all manner of provisions for supply of the Queen's forces in France. The work parcelled out to Cecil begins to make sense of the terse notes sent by his father. Extant letters to Caron follow a similar pattern: nearly constant letters with notations, draft replies—commented on by Burghley— endorsed as filed by Willis, e.g. TNA SP 84/48/fols. 189r–v, 195r, 249r, 266r, 278r, 283r, 286r; 49/48r, 71r, 114r, 122r, 261r. The procuration to the signet of official royal documents was done at this time by Cecil, e.g. SO3/1/495v where two letters, on the privileges of Flushing and a royal directive to Gilpin, were procured with the minutes remaining with Cecil. Burghley's extensive notes in Letter No. 14 give a general sense of direction for how this awkward diplomatic transfer of troops would take place. Norris seemed reluctant to leave Brittany for Ireland.

ENDORSED in Simon Willis's hand:

12 ffeb[ruary] 1594

[List in Henry Maynard's hand, added in crayon, pencil or silverpoint]

6 The Duke [of Lennox][147]

2 Ch[ancellor] of Scot[land]

35 [Maitland of Thirlestane,[148] Lennox's adversary at the Convention]

B The Kyng [James VI]

[In pencil on the dorse]

80

[Seal cut out]

Letter No. 41

William, Lord Burghley to Sir Robert Cecil, 14 February 1594

1 p. Nineteen lines dictated to a clerk, ten lines in Burghley's hand.
Addressed, endorsed, signed.

Text

I would wishe yow to be carefull towching the proceding to be had for the ᴺᵒᵐⁱⁿᵃᵗᵉᵈ Bishopps of Winchester[149] and

---

[147]The 2nd duke of Lennox, Ludovick Stuart (1574–1624) – see *ODNB* – loyal to his cousin James VI, also a strong supporter of their cousin Bothwell, chamberlain and first gentleman of the king's chamber, was granted the lieutenancy of the north in 1594 to reduce the northern earls, and fought with the king at the battle of Glenlivet in Nov. 1594 when the royal forces were routed. Lennox enjoyed great favour after Maitland of Thirlestane's fall from favour in 1592 (see n. 148) and succeeded where Colville of Easter Wemyss did not. He may also have helped the English cause: when Cecil's agent (and later Essex's) Henry Lok (or Lock) fell, he was rescued by adherents of Lennox. TNA SP 52/53/no. 35. The list of names may have nothing to do with the other MSS in the volume, and refer solely to matters in a Scottish MS noted by Cecil on the dorse of his father's letter. James certainly suspected Cecil's evil will. *CSPS 1593–1595*, 485, 492, 497. In early Feb. 1595 James Colville, commends himself to Cecil, ibid. 537, 548, 550, 552. Burghley did not correspond with Colville or Lock.

[148]The chancellor of Scotland, Maitland of Thirlestane (1543–1595), *ODNB*, was an adversary of Lennox whose conflict spilled into the English intelligence network managed by Bowes at the court. He was blamed for leniency against those who attacked the king in 1589 at the 'Brig O' Dee' incident, principally Huntly who he was wrongly suspected of protecting.

[149]William Wickham (1539–1595), *ODNB*, bishop of Lincoln 1584–1594, had just been appointed when he died, after being granted restitution to temporalities following a rather sharp correspondence with Cecil who made demands of royal grants pending. After Bishop Thomas Cooper's death in 1594, Cecil had forwarded the *congé d'élire* to the signet in Dec. By Feb. 1595 arrears owing the Crown were still at issue, because the massive first fruits and tenths were unpaid. Cecil was here instructed to get the matter in motion. Warrants had to be perfected and the attorney general, Coke, had only one serjeant to assist him before

THE LETTERS OF LORD BURGHLEY, WILLIAM CECIL

Durham,[150] that before they be perfectted there be sufficient provision made, and assurance to hir ma[jes]tie of such rentes and ameties as aught to be assured by them. As namely from the B[ishop] of Winchester of a Rent Charge of CCCC^li [£400] p[er]annum graunted by the late Bishopp deceased out of the manor of Taunton and other mannors. As also, of viii^C and iiii^xx li [£880] yearlie rent essing out of the lordshipp of Allerton and other lordshipps within the Bishoprick of Durham, which the ~~late~~ now Bishop of Durham payd to hir ma[jes]tie. And further of a Cxl li [£140] yearlie rent for the Castle of Norrham, and a ffyshing uppon the ryvar of Twede, which my L[ord] Chamberlaine holdes with Rent was likewise answered to hir ma[jes]tie by his l[ordshi]p.[151] I pray yow theaifore have a Care too, theise thinges towching hir Ma[jes]tie before any further proceding be had therein. ffrom my house at Westm[inste]r the 14 of febr[uary] 1594.

[Burghley's addition]
I sent for Mr. attorney[152] to have care hereof, who is herin wary how to procede, but I have directed to speak with the L[ord] ch[ief] Justyce[153] and Mr of the rooles[154] who war attorneys, and so he will, but he complayneth of want of others, seyng ther is but on sergeant and no sollicitor, alledgyng that ther ar manny weighty cawses of hir Majesty to be ordered.

he conferred with the lord chief justice of the Queen's Bench (1592–1607), John Popham (1531–1607), *ODNB*, former attorney general, and with the master of the rolls, Sir Thomas Egerton. Wickham was now responsible for these payments but he had inherited some long and unprofitable leases made by Cooper soon before his death. Hatfield, Cecil Papers, 29/fol. 60r; *HMCS*, v, 55. Cecil warned Wickham not to expect restitution to temporalities without payment of the Crown rents. *HMCS*, v, 128. Wickham also petitioned Burghley for restitution to temporalities on 21 Mar. 1595, BL Lansdowne MS 79/no. 38, fol. 102.

[150] The newly nominated bishop of Durham, Tobie Matthew (1544–1628), *ODNB*, was elevated from the deanery of Durham. Matthew thanked Cecil for his long-delayed promotion on 16 Feb. 1594/5 (Hatfield, Cecil Papers, 171/fol. 125r; *HMCS*, v, 174), which argues for the speedy transmission of business there after the long stalling of Matthew Hutton in taking up the archdiocese of York. See, inter alia, Hutton's debate with Cecil, beginning, 13 Oct. 1594: *The Correspondence of Matthew Hutton, Archbishop of York, etc.*, ed. J. Raine, Surtees Society (1843), 86, Letter no. XXXII; Acres 'The early political career of Sir Robert Cecil', 166–175.

[151] The fight over lands in the diocese of Durham between Cecil and Hutton in Dec. 1594 involved royal and Privy Council suitors. Lord Hunsdon was angling for the suit of Sir Edward Denny for lands out of the diocese of Worcester vacated by the translation of Richard Fletcher to the bishopric of London, *HMCS*, v, 31–32, 32, 130. For Matthew Hutton (1529?–1606), see *ODNB*.

[152] The attorney general, Sir Edward Coke (1552–1634), *ODNB*.

[153] Sir John Popham (*c*.1531–1607), *ODNB*.

[154] The master of the rolls, Sir Thomas Egerton. He was also lord keeper (after Puckering's death) from 1596.

yow may inform hir Ma[jes]ty hereof, and for a serieant I know non fitter than Mr. yelverton,[155] as for any sollicitors I will not presume to name any for some respectes.

Your lov[ing] Father

W. Burghley

Dorse

ADDRESSED in Maynard's hand:
To my varie lovinge sonne Sir Robart Cecill knight of hir ma[jes]ties honorable privy counsel.

ENDORSED in Simon Willis's hand:
14 ffeb[ruary] 1594
L[ord] Threas[urer] to my M[aste]r
[Cecil's additional note on the dorse]
con. Sir J. Hawkyns sergeant
h. myll[156]

Letter No. 42

William, Lord Burghley to Sir Robert Cecil, 26 February 1594

1 p. Holograph.
Addressed, endorsed, signed.

Text

I see that I am so yoked with others, as my fortun is to be allweis thrust in to the furrow.

---

[155] [Sir] Christopher Yelverton (1536/7–1612), sergeant-at-law from 1589, *ODNB*.

[156] Henry Mill was probably an Exchequer servant; his name on the dorse of Letter No. 41 may possibly refer to the contents of Letter No. 42, where Burghley was more probably noting examinations in Henry Long's murder by the Da[n]vers brothers, to whose examination Sir Herbert Croft – [Crofts, Craftes] (*c*.1565–1629), *ODNB* – referred when he petitioned Cecil to join Mill, Mr. Osborne, and Mr. Fanshawe, the latter two also Exchequer servants. Hatfield, Cecil Papers, 173/77; *HMCS*, vi, 188. Cecil used Charles Danvers in intelligence: 'Sir Charles Danvers doth very discreetlye advertise me of all Italian occurents', Stone, *Palavicino*, 238–239; TNA SP 12/265/133, an example is found in SP 78/30/fol. 221r for Austrian, Hungarian and Turkish news in 1593. The Danvers brothers were later relieved of the charge of murder. They were cousins of Sir Thomas Cecil's wife Dorothy Nevill. Henry Danvers, earl of Danby (1573–1644), *ODNB*; Sir Charles Danvers (*c*.1568–1601), *ODNB*.

I perceave by yow that hir Ma[jes]ty is informed that I did committ on Roger Mill to prison, uppon pretence that he did inform soemthyng as a wytness ageynst Parkynson in the Cause of Davers whereto I answer that I did not of my self committ hym, but he was befor the Connsell at Sommersett houss long before the deth of Long by Daverss and by them all committed for informing of Mr. lane of some evill words to have bene spoken by parkynson at a dynnar abowt xii monthes before, whereof he cold produce no proff, but sayd that he had hard such a report, by on that had served parkynson as a soldior and was putt owt of service uppon displeasure. And parkynson beyng charged herwith utterly denyed the same, so as this Mill was committed for concealyng such speches so long tym, and cold not prove the same.[57]

This happened long befor the deth of Long by Davers at what tyme parkynson was Generally well lyked of. And yet I did move 1 month past spek to on of the clerkes of the Connsell to move the Connsell to delyver hym as sufficiently punished and so untill now I thouwght he had bene delyvered, as it may be that he remayneth only for fees of the prison.

I pray yow inform hir Ma[jes]ty, that she may see how I am wronged herein as in manny other lyk.

I thynk on of the clerkes can inform yow of the tyme and manner of his Concell, by testymony of the Connsell letter

[To the lower left side]
Your lov[ing] fath[er]

W. Burghley

Dorse

[57] Henry Long's murder continued to be investigated with Danvers family forfeitures a consequence. On 15 July 1596 Elizabeth, Lady Danvers, mother of Sir Charles and Sir Henry Danvers wrote to Cecil for their protection. *HMCS*, vi, 267–8; BL Lansdowne MS 827, no. 6, duplicated at no. 13: 'A lamentable discourse taken out of sundrie examinations concerning the wilful escape of Sir Charles and Sir Henry Danvers, knights and their followers after the murder committed in Wiltshir uppon Henrie Longe, gent.' which contains Henry Parkinson's evidence against the Danvers. On 23 July 1595, John Calley, a servant, wrote to Sir Robert Cecil on behalf of the senior Lady Danvers. *HMCS*, v, 288. During the first week of Jan. 1595 a series of examinations concerning their conduct were held by the Privy Council at Calshot Castle, and a commission of the Exchequer, John Osborne (the Lord Treasurer's remembrancer) and Thomas Fanshawe (the Queen's remembrancer) were under coroner's inquisition (which found Sir Henry, the younger guilty) to 'receive monies due on the queen's behalf' from various indentures held by Sir John Danvers, senior. *HMCS*, v, 84–90; *CPR 37 Eliz. I*, no. 1369.

ADDRESSED
To my lovynge son Sir Robart Cecill at the Court

ENDORSED in Simon Willis's hand:
26 ffeb[ruary] 1594
L[ord] Threas[urer] to my M[aste]r
[Seal cut out]

Letter No. 43

William, Lord Burghley to Sir Robert Cecil, 17 February 1594

1 p. Holograph.
Addressed, endorsed. Additions [2] in the left margin. Signed.

Text

I send to yow herewith Mr. bodeleys letter beyng the first receaved sence he departed. by it only appeareth his entrance into the matter of his chardg[158] By his next will appear uppon the States answer, what may be expected.[159] so as untill then I se no cause of his further instruction.

[Opposite the opening of the preceding paragraph in the margin]
I perceave that Mr. bodeley hath in his proposition well followed his Instruction

[Main text continues]
As for Colonells Stuartes negociation, I way it not much, if he can get for the kyng a pece of monny. I thynk it will Gage hym that waye from harkening to papaticall confederacy, or from other harmfull leage with France, from whence he may have shews of frendshipp without substance.[160]

---

[158] See Letter No. 36 for Bodley's embassy and Burghley's compilation of civil law arguments for the engaging of the Low Countries' naval support. TNA SP 84/50/fols. 29r–30r; Hatfield, Cecil Papers, 25/fol. 18r–19r; *HMCS*, v, 102–103. Bodley had appeared before the States to make the English case for repayment of debt.

[159] Note also Bodley's letter on 14 Feb. 1594. Hatfield, Cecil Papers, 171/81; *HMCS*, vi, 111. See n. 160.

[160] James Stewart, 2nd earl of Moray (1565/6–1592), *ODNB*. Colonel James Stuart of Houston had been sent by James VI of Scotland as special envoy to the States General, where he made the charge that the Scottish king was forced by English parsimony to court other sources of income, exacerbating a dangerous situation. He was also corresponding with Essex and another agent, James Hudson, LPL MS 651/fols. 21–23. Bodley replied to Burghley that several instructions from Sir Robert Cecil had kept him appraised of Stuart's

I am glad that hir Ma[jes]ty is satifyed with myn answer for Mill's imprisonment.[161]

Yow forgett the matter for the Q[ueen's] assurance of Certen rentes from the 2 BB [Bishops] of wy[nchester] and durham and therewith, the attorney's request to be furder asisted with another serieant and sollicitor.[162]

[Opposite the opening of the preceding paragraph in the left margin] I send yow also a letter from Sir Edm[und] uvedall with a confession of G. Sommersett, a person that hath long strayed.[163]

[Main text continues]

How hir Ma[jes]ty will have the L[ord] depute of Irland answered uppon your report of our Conference which because yow wryt, that yow have reported with her Ma[jes]ty's allowance, I have privatly, havyng oportunite to send to hym, by my present letter advertised hym a good part of our opinions without prescribyng to hym any direction untill hir Ma[jes]ty shall direct the same and so inform yow

ploy, providing answers to the King's alleged miseries. Hatfield, Cecil Papers, 171/81; *HMCS*, v, 111; Birch, *Memoirs*, I, 207–208. Bodley referred to Scottish affairs set forth by Cecil in his first letter of 5 Feb., where he said this was the second such advice given him by Cecil. Bodley also sent a copy of Houston's instructions, in French, to Cecil and a copy to Essex, Hatfield, Cecil Papers, 30/64; *HMCS*, v, 108–109. James VI played on his desire to defeat their common Spanish enemy, now so entrenched in the highest ranks of his nobility. References to Elizabeth were duly reverent.

Cecil had been fully informed of Stuart's embassy by his agent James Colville of Easter Wemyss, whom the king had sent on embassy into England. TNA SP 52/55/no. 24. Wemyss also sent a copy of Stuart's instructions, SP 52/55/no. 23, dated 14 Feb. 1595. Bodley sent a further copy, Hatfield, Cecil Papers, 30/fol. 64r–65r; *HMCS*, vi, 108–109. Wemyss argued to Cecil that James did not intend hostility towards Elizabeth, but because of the terms of his annuity acted out of financial desperation.

[161] See Letters Nos 42, 73 for Long's murder in which Burghley led the indictment against Mill.

[162] The orderly course of the dean and chapter of Durham returned the *conge d'elire* with Tobie Matthew's name as of 14 Feb. 1595, Hatfield, Cecil Papers, 171/125; *HMCS*, v, 174. The conference on the payment to the Crown of lands and rents was required for the drawing of books for lands, manors, and tenements where the Queen was, by statute, remainder in reversion.

[163] Letter from Sir Edmund Uvedall to Burghley of 12 Feb. 1595 enclosed the confession of George Somerset, TNA SP 84/50/fol. 39r, 41r–v. Somerset claimed to be a cousin of the present earl of Worcester, as son of a prominent Montgomeryshire gentleman (the earl's surname was Somerset also). Uvedale detained Somerset as he returned to England through Flushing, having been sent to Bruges to learn 'the language' 16 years before. Somerset was acquainted with Michael Moody, Sir William Stanley, and Stanley's lieutenant-colonel Jacques, as well as Francis Owen, pensioner to the king of Spain. Sir William Uvdall or Uvedale (d.1606), *ODNB*.

how I have remembered the same.[164] I send yow a Copy of my privat letter, which may be affirmed or controlled by a more Generall letter from the Connsell.

Your lov[ing] fath[er],

W. Burghley

Dorse

ADDRESSED in Maynard's hand:
To my lovinge sonne Sir Rob[er]t Cecill knight one of hir ma[jes]ties privy connsell.

ENDORSED in Simon Willis's hand:
7 ffeb[ruary] 1594
L[ord] Threas[urer] to my M[aste]r
[No seal]

Letter No. 44

William, Lord Burghley to Sir Robert Cecil, February 1594/5

1 p. Holograph. Main text with two additions in the margins; as the text is continuous, the shifts to the additions are marked [*1] to the lower left margin, and [*2] to the continuation in the upper left.
There is an additional sentence overleaf.

Text

I perceave by your letters, that my L[ord] chamberlain hath made an honorable report to his Ma[jes]ty of my upright and favorable dealyng in the hearyng of the cause, betwixt my L[ord] of derby and the Conntess his sistar,[165] wherin he hath done me right as he promised me that he wold and so deserveth my thankes which I pray yow gyve

---

[164]The reply of the lord deputy, Russell, to Burghley's letter of 17 Feb. was dated 12 Mar. of that year; it noted that his forces arrayed against the Irish rebels held their ground. Money was needed, a point he made at length to Cecil in a letter of 11 Mar. 1595, as Norris was delayed in getting his Brittany forces across into Ireland. TNA SP 63/178/no. 82, fol. 192r–v, 194r–195r. See the totals of payments for forces sent into Ireland and Russell's desperate further requests for money, *HMCS*, v, 165; *CSPI 1592–1596*, 308.

[165]See *CSPD 1595–1597*, 73; TNA SP 12/253/no. 15 of 15 July 1595 for the abstract of the claims of Alice, dowager countess of Derby, against William, 6th earl (1561–1642). Ferdinando 5th earl (1559–1594) had left everything in his will to his widow rather than by primogeniture, and the 6th earl bought back the estate which took until 1610, *ODNB*.

his Lord[ship]. but wher hir Ma[jes]ty hath pronounced hir graciowss
sentence of me, as of hir spryt and hath commanded yow, as yow wryt
to gyve me a million of thankes, I am most glad of hir favorable censur
for which also I most humbly thank hir Ma[jes]ty, as not merityng so
much, but for hir Millions of thankes yow may as merrely saye from
me, that she may be noted soemwhat over liberall, for to gyve a million
of thankes wher she oweth none, but may challendg all that I can do
to be as a dett not hable to fre me from bondage to hir, both by
God's ordinance, and by hir regalle and princely favors. and to wryt
seriously I have doone ^{no} thyng in this cause but that my conscience
did prescribe me. and if the Erle shall thynk otherwise of me, as I dowt
he may be thereto ledd yet he shall understand that I gave my child to
hym, but not my conscience nor my honor which no blood shall ever
gayn of me. and yet I pray yow tell hir Ma[jes]ty, if the Conntess had
not such great

[the page ends and the sentence continues as the lower of two marginal
comments]
cause of compleynt as was pretended, nother shall have if I may direct
the cause, but fyndyng some wondryng of both sydes, I only shewed
them ther errors, and directed them to the Q[ueen's] Ma[jes]ty's high
wayes, wher law and equite used to walk hand in hand, which I trust
they will follow.

[the upper of two marginal comments]
I warned both partyes, that nether his entayle nor the Conntess Dower,
shuld draw me from myn office, to se to the right of the wardes.

W. Burghley

[At the right foot]
turn this
[Overleaf]
I fynd no ease of paynes, nor increass of strength and yet I assure yow
I expedite more poore sutors, than I thynk any Judg or master of law
doth in this term.

For the duration and intense acrimony of the case, see Coward, *The Stanleys*, 56–82. The
legal squabbles came to the fore in the summer of 1595, see Burghley to Sir Robert Cecil,
TNA SP 12/253/no. 14; *CSPD 1595–1597*, 72–73: 'I am sorry my lady of Derby or friends
complain of my doings concerning her causes, without advertising me thereof. I have only
done, in the ratings of her fine to the Queen, what by law I am bound to do, as her case is, to
demand dower because she has no jointure' referring to the betrothal of his grand-daughter
Elizabeth Vere to the 6th earl.

Dorse

ADDRESSED in Burghley's hand:
To my wellbeloved sonn Sir Robart Cecill knight at the Court

ENDORSED in Simon Willis's hand:
Ffeb[ruary] 1594
L[ord] Thre[asure]r to my M[aste]r

Letter No. 45

William, Lord Burghley to Sir Robert Cecil, 29 April 1595

½ p end. Dictated to Maynard.
Addressed, endorsed.

Text

I thank yow for your letter, which I cannot answere with myn owne hand in any sort. I allowe your discretion in concealing from the Q[ueen] my last nights paines. And though I had yesterdaie a painfull iorney with my hand, & have had this night a continuance therof with some new paine in my foote, whereby I am force to kepe my bed this forenoone, yet yowe shall do well not to be knowne herof to any. If I had come well hither and the wether fayre, I might have tarryed here but two daies. But now I know not how long I shalbe forced to tarry here by this ill Accident, which seeing it was to fall out at this time I am glad I am here without Company to troble me. and so god bless yow with his grace. From my howse at Theobaldes the xxix^th of April 1595.

[To the lower left of the page]
I praie yow speake to Mr. Edward Darcy[166] to remember the Q[ueen] for the sealing of certane letters of the wardes and if he not there,

---

[166] Edward Darcy (1543/4–1612), *HPT*, ii, 16–17, privy chamber official and patentee (controversially, for sealing leather), allied with the Killigrew family politically. See Letter No. 94.

require Mr. Killigrew[167] or Mr. Stannhoppe[168] to gett them signed, for there are twise as many to do when they ar done.

I send you a letter of Mr. Caryes[169] with a ticket of a progresse intended by the k[ing] of Scottes to come to the sight of Barwick for which purpose he is desirous to know, how he shall behave himself at that time.[170] Whereof I praie yow make my L[ord] Chamberlayn privie to the intent he may understand the Q[ueen]s mind, & as for the workes to be done there, I will give order by my next letter to have the same performed.[171]

[Not signed]

[167] Sir William Killigrew (d.1622), *ODNB*, Burghley's nephew, the son of Sir Henry Killigrew (1525/8–1603) who was Burghley's brother-in-law through his wife Mary (née Cooke). See Letter No. 94, of which Killigrew was the recipient. Richard Carmarthen recalled to Cecil on 29 May 1595 that the Queen had sent Killigrew to Cecil for the drafting of a letter to Sir Francis Godolphin. Hatfield, Cecil Papers, 32/fol. 70r; *HMCS*, v, 222–223. Cecil also procured Killigrew's suit, as one of the 'Gromes of her Majesty's privie chamber' for the manors and parks of Hamworth and Colkemington in Middlesex, to the signet Seal in consequence of his expenditures while 'building and repaying there'. The bill had to be amended to relieve Killigrew of certain burdensome incidental payments due the Crown, TNA SO3/1/fols. 485r. 494v.

[168] Together with Killigrew and Darcy, Michael Stanhope was looking for grants of diocesan lands during the Crown's custodianship while the sees were vacant. See Letter No. 94. He petitioned for duchy of Lancaster lands, though his connections to the vice-chamberlain of the chamber, Sir Thomas Heneage. Hatfield, Cecil Papers, 25/fol. 21r, Petitions, 416, 422; *HMCS*, v, 104–105. Cecil procured to the signet Michael Stanhope's suit for the right of sole import of Spanish wool for twenty years, the letter having been subscribed by Burghley and the attorney general, Coke (TNA SO3/1/fol. 491r). The most influential of the sons of Sir Thomas Stanhope, cousins through Mary Cheke, was Sir John Stanhope, of the privy chamber, who was relaying political news of high secrecy and importance to Cecil at that time, e.g. *HMCS*, v, 128, 178, 219, 347, 370, 413, 431, 508, some of which included land transactions, 214. John Stanhope appeared to have some weight in seeking vacant positions after the death of Nicaseus Yetswiert, including the secretary of the French tongue. Hatfield, Cecil Papers, 32/fol. 2r; *HMCS*, v, 189. He would become treasurer of the Chamber in 1596 having been named master of the posts in 1590. See John Stanhope, 1st Baron Stanhope (*c.*1540–1621), *ODNB*.

[169] John Carey also wrote of the king's intentions to visit the borders on 25 Apr. 1595, *Cal. Border Papers*, ii, 30.

[170] Hunsdon provided the answer for Cecil the following day. The precedent for a royal Scottish visit was Mary, Queen of Scots, when Sir John Forster was the deputy to the earl of Bedford. All honour was to be done, and all the available ordnance was to be fired in their Majesties' honour, with the implication that Carey would also be his father's deputy in this case.

[171] Hunsdon wrote to Cecil the following day, 30 Apr. 1595, telling Cecil of John Carey's letter to him received at the same time as Burghley's, Hatfield, Cecil Papers, 32/fol. 7r; *HMCS*, v, 192.

Dorse

ADDRESSED in Maynard's hand:
To my loving sonne Sir Robert Cecill
Knight, of her Ma[jes]ties privy Counsell

ENDORSED
29 April 1595:
L[ord] Thre[asure]r to my M[aste]r

Letter No. 46

William, Lord Burghley to Sir Robert Cecil, 20 May 1595

½ p. Holograph.
Addressed, endorsed, signed.

Text

I am willingar than hable to come on Monday, and yet Mr. chan[cellor] and I have apoynted a special metyng here that afternoone with the office of the Custom houss, and so must my L[ord] Keper and I with other Judges mete to morrow about diffikult busynes.[172] so as I am not Idle in my afternoons, though farr unhable to beare such burdens.

I can not saye that I will come on Monday, but I must saye, I must be carryed there very paynfully, and unmete to be sene to hir Majesty's presence.

I have bene thurghly occupyed this day.

Your lo[ving] father,

W. Burghley

[172]The Court of Wards was saddled with a huge debt owed to the Crown on the death of the receiver-general, Sir George Goring; his heir, also George, wrote to Cecil, *HMCS*, v, 205. Sir George died owing £19,777 2s. 3½d., *ODNB*. Richard Carmarthen of the Customs House administration had the elder Goring's patronage and wished to protect the honour of the son, George Goring, who had failed to secure his father's receivership, *HMCS*, v, 222. Carmarthen there referred to Burghley's position as protector of the Crown's interest requiring of him to 'deal very severely' with the younger Goring for the recovery of the debt. The new receiver-general, William Fleetwood wrote to Burghley out of concern for the payment of his emolument, *HMCS*, v, 222, but the case had not been heard by 23 June 1595. *HMCS*, v, 256. The Gorings, as many families, had total 'dependence on the rewards of court connection, its extravagant outlays, and its complicated and fragile network of financial credit' *ODNB*.

Dorse

ADDRESSED
To my lovinge sonne Sir Rob[er]t Cecill knight one of hir ma[jes]ties
privy Connsell

ENDORSED
20 May 1595
Lo[rd] Thre[asurer] to my M[aste]r
'1595' and 'Mr'
[Seal cut out]

Letter No. 47

William, Lord Burghley to Sir Robert Cecil, 12 May 1595

1 p. Holograph.
Addressed, endorsed, signed.

Text

I am not yett gott owt of my bedd. what I shall be liable to do
tomorrow, I know not. for the manner of retorning of Mr. bodeley,
with hir Ma[jes]ties answer of mislykyng both of the States answer and
of his coming back uppon ther advise, I can not but very well allow
thereof, and I thynk he ~~shall~~ ought to ply them with so manny reasons,
as the tyme serveth for hir Ma[jes]ty, after x yers chardg without ether
mony or any suratye of Gratitud from them by waye of presenta[tion]
of ther thankfulness,[173] addyng that hir Ma[jes]ty is now also provoked
in Irland to enter into a charg not estimable, wherto she hath no hop
of any help, but of hyndrance by Spayne and otherwise.

If they shall be content to pay hir Ma[jes]ty's people and grant
a good yerly some, towardes the discharg of the dett, hir Ma[jes]ty

---

[173] Bodley was returning to England and George Gilpin wrote to Essex that he hoped the
ambassador would press for increased expenditure in the Queen's cautionary towns; which
might argue for the Essex's interest in supply of the Queen's troops there. Bell, *Handlist*, 194;
Hatfield, Cecil Papers, 171/fol. 136r; *HMCS*, v, 196. Sir Horatio Palavicino (*c.*1540–1600),
ODNB, had sought re-payment of bonds for raising money for the Low Countries but was
not satisfied and urged a new embassy or Bodley's swift return. Hatfield, Cecil Papers,
171/fol. 139r; *HMCS*, v, 202. Cecil was extending secret overtures into the Low Countries, as
is evidenced in a reply by James Symons, *HMCS*, v, 202. Henry Maynard's letter of 12 May to Cecil noted
Bodley was unable to draw full co-operation from the States in the matter of re-payment
of their debts. Hatfield, Cecil Papers, 32/fol. 30r; *HMCS*, v, 203. Maynard also hinted at
letters to Buckhurst arriving with intelligence through Thomas Fane at Dover.

remayning ther protector and they Contynuyng ther defence agenst the k[ing] of Spayne, I cold be content to se hir Majesty so eased of this growing chardg.[174]

This I can scrible not without payn.[175]

Your lov[ing] father,

W. Burghley.

Dorse

ADDRESSED in the same hand as Letter No. 45:
To my loving sonne Sir Robert Cecyll knight, one of her ma[jes]ties privie Connsell

ENDORSED in Simon Willis's hand:
12 May 1595
L[ord] Thre[asure]r to my M[aste]r

Letter No. 48

William, Lord Burghley to Sir Robert Cecil, 6 May 1595

¼ p. Holograph.
Addressed, endorsed, signed.

Text

I can not wryt at any length, but do send these included from Sir Ed[ward] Norryce which I pray yow shew to hir Ma[jes]ty and to know hir plesur, for his answer.[176] The matter purporteth more dannger

---

[174]See Letter No. 43. Wernham, *After the Armada*, 557: 'But already by 1595 in the Netherlands Elizabeth was not only limiting, and indeed a little reducing her present military aid, she was also beginning to send in her bill for past succors.'

[175]Burghley's instruction to Henry Maynard in the morning of this day, 12 May, noted his great pain and inability to go to court, Hatfield, Cecil Papers, 32/fol. 30r; *HMCS*, v, 203. The supply of these several paragraphs for his son's meeting with Sir Thomas Bodley attests to the importance of these lines on the Low Countries' debts. John Clapham, another of Burghley's secretaries, assured Cecil on 29 Apr. that Burghley's pain might not increase in fair and dry weather, Hatfield, Cecil Papers, 32/fol. 6r; *HMCS*, v, 191–192.

[176]Sir Edward Norris (*c.*1550–1603), *ODNB*. Sir Edward Norris's letter to Burghley, 3 May 1595, from Ostend suggested there was local secret support for Spain and stockpiling of weapons in Bruges and Antwerp for forces upon the arrival of the Archduke Ernest's body for burial. TNA SP 84/50/fols. 146r–147r; *L&A*, vi, Analysis no. 56. Norris was sceptical, but the rumours made sense of Gilpin's desire for more aid, for which he appealed also

than is mete for me to pass over without hir Majesty's Judgment. I thynk Monss. de Caron wold be acquaynted herwith.[77]

Maii 1595,

Your lov[ing] father,

W. Burghley

Dorse

ADDRESSED in Henry Maynard's hand:
To my loving sonne Sir Robert Cecill knight, one of hir ma[jes]tie's privie Connsell
At the Cort

ENDORSED in Simon Willis's hand:
6 May 1595
L[ord] Thre[asure]r to my M[aste]r
[Seal missing]

Letter No. 49

William, Lord Burghley to Sir Robert Cecil, 23 June 1595

¾ p. Holograph.
Addressed, endorsed, signed.

to Essex, *HMCS*, v, 196; Letter No. 47. Burghley had Norris's letter sent to the Queen by Cecil, as he was unable 'by some infirmity', *L&A*, vi, Analysis no. 56. The Queen did not panic over the rumours of arms. She instructed Bodley to tell the States of the condition of Ostend, requesting of them men, munitions and victual as needed. TNA SP 84/51/fol. 151r.
[77] Cecil may have replied to Noel de Caron in a conversation. Burghley replied to Sir Edward Norris on 7 May from his house in the Strand, agreeing that a siege by Count Fuentes was unlikely. Burghley, as ever, argued that the States answer these needs unless there was imminent danger, TNA SP 84/51/fol. 151r; *L&A*, vi, Analysis 56. Caron was used as an intermediary in public causes concerning the debt including repayment of Sir Horatio Palavicino's bonds. Hatfield, Cecil Papers, 171/fol. 147r; *HMCS*, v, 234. Cecil's agent Thomas D'Arques reported all of this to Cecil, as well as on Palavicino's suit for repayment, noting Caron's work on his behalf was not successful, *HMCS*, v, 220, 221, 224; Letter No. 47. Fuentes would prove a formidable enemy during the summer of 1595, taking several towns and turning toward the siege of Cambrai. But while these cost Henry IV strategic places, the Dutch negotiations were not directly affected, as they might have been at Ostend.

Text

I thynk Mr. Wyndebank will delyver yow a bill to be signed for W[illia]m Spicer and for H[enry] fade, so as H. fade shall receave no fe nor proffitt duryng Spycers estat.[178] Yow may doe well for furderance hereof to inform hir Ma[jes]ty that Spycer can not allweise personally attend, for that he is Surveyor of the workes at barwyk, and hath also cause to se to the workes at woodstock. but if notwithstandyng these reasons hir Ma[jes]ty will not have H. fades Joyned nor yet to have a Grant in revertion, I must content my self at hir Ma[jes]ty's plesure, not meaning to be a sutor to hir Ma[jes]ty for any thyng but for her favor, and allowance of my poore service.[179]

I pray yow procure the dispatch of the warrant for barwyk for the Garrison who have great nede to be helped this deare yere.[180]

Mr. wyndeb[ank] hath in redynes the letters for 1^m [1000] soldiers to be in redynes.[181] I send a letter for the matter of plymmouth for

---

[178]The bill was for a grant in survivorship from the death of Thomas Fowler to William Spicer and Henry Fadis, comptroller of works within the realm of England dated 3 and 4 Philip and Mary (1556): Burghley fulfilled the letters patent, as Spicer was to receive income during his life, and Fadis only in reversion. This was confirmed 16 July 1595, *CPR 38 Eliz. I*, no. 33.

[179]Stewart, *English Ordnance Office*, 112–113: 'There seems to have been little or no armaments or ancillary industries in the north. Almost all military supplies seem to have been sent from the central office in London.' Burghley's notice of scarcity may refer to the great cost of such shipments, Letter No. 113.

[180]Robert Vernon, surveyor of victuals reported great scarcity to Burghley in late May 1595; a conflict between Vernon and the captains had broken out over stores, *Cal. Border Papers*, ii, 30–33. There were regular suits for office at Berwick: Bishop Tobie Matthew's suit for Henry Sanderson, searcher of the port of Newcastle, possibly for the surveyorship at Berwick in preference to Vernon, Hatfield, Cecil Papers, 33/10; *HMCS*, v, 256; Ralph Gray sent his petition for one Ashton of Lancashire to replace Mr. Robert Bowes in his position as treasurer of Berwick, *HMCS*, v, 261. In any case, Burghley was not about to meddle in the letters patent for comptroller of the works.

[181]On Sir John Norris's arrival in Ireland he made harsh criticisms of Russell's military policy, disputing most of his decisions, including the lord deputy's petition for sole nomination of captains for 1,000 foot and 100 horse and their officers, a requirement apparently answered with this warrant held by Windebanke. TNA SP 63/180/no. 9, fol. 43v for Norris's criticisms of 4 June 1595; *HMCS*, v, 262 for Burghley's warranting as lord lieutenant of Hertfordshire and Essex to supply footmen for Ireland, dated 30 June 1595. Some Privy Council discussion with the Queen may have stalled the sending of the men in that week, considering Norris's opinion that the troops were unnecessary. This followed Russell's disbanding of 12 of 19 companies of English soldiers with Irish experience in early Apr. See Norris to Cecil, 14 Apr. 1595, TNA SP 63/179/no. 31, fol. 68r. These numbers connect directly with Burghley's fear in Letter No. 40, that there were no captains to serve as commanders of the 2,000 troops then in readiness.

which to be signed by the Connsellors ther, I pray yow send to me.[182]
23 Ju[ne] 1595.

Your lov[ing] father,

W. Burghley

Dorse

ADDRESSED in Henry Maynard's hand:
To my lovinge sonne Sir Robt. Cecill knight, one of her ma[jes]ties
privy Connsell, At the Cort

ENDORSED in Simon Willis's hand:
23 Junii 1595
L[ord] Thre[asure]r to my M[aste]r

Letter No. 50

William, Lord Burghley to Sir Robert Cecil, 24 June 1595

⅓ p. Holograph.
Addressed, endorsed, signed.

Text

I have red your letter reportyng the Q[ueen's] Ma[jes]ty's favorable
compassion for releff of Sir Thomas Wylkes and that hir Ma[jes]ty
wold receave knolledg from me of his sutes, which I do send in a paper
herincluded, which I pray yow to shew to hir Ma[jes]ty whose favor
my request cannot increass.[183] but suerly I thynk if he be not releved

---

[182]These warrants may have been for the provisioning of the expedition planned that
summer by Sir Francis Drake and Sir John Hawkins, as indicated by Burghley's reply to
Sir Robert Cecil, *CSPD 1595–1597*, 95–96). One Marwood was then named customer of
Plymouth on the suit of Serjeant John Hele at that time. *CSPD 1595–1597*, 71.

[183]The grant of lands was meant to defray Sir Thomas Wilkes's expenses on his embassy
for the Queen to Brussels, which did not take place, *HMCS*, v, 11, 12, 19, 20, 34, 252. Wilkes's
petitioned for lands out of the duchy of Lancaster while the chancellorship was vacant
following Sir Thomas Heneage's death, Letter No. 72. In the event he received rents of
Crown leases but not land. See 14 Feb. 1596, *CPR Eliz I*, no. 762, for the lengthy list of
Crown leases out of which Wilkes was awarded income. For Wilkes (1545–1598), see *ODNB*.
Extensive preparatory documents had been drawn for his embassy to the Archduke Ernest,
brother of the Emperor Rudolf II. Wilkes would have pressed the archduke on the Lopez
conspiracy and the implication of regicide by Philip II at the same time suggesting England
would work for peace in the troubled Danubian regions, mediating with the Turks, the Poles
and the eastern imperial armies in Hungary. As the Queen was offended by the archduke's

by some of these or some equivalent he shall not be hable to serve hir
Ma[jes]ty as he ~~very~~ is as hable to do as any of his degre in England.
24 Junii 1595.

Your lovyng father,

W. Burghley

Dorse

ADDRESSED in Simon Willis's hand:
To my lovinge Sonne Sir Robert Cecill knight,
one of hir Majesty's Privy Counsell

ENDORSED
24 Junii 1595
l[ord]. thre[sure]r to my Mr. Concerning Sir Thomas Wilkes
[In pencil on the dorse]
100
[Seal cut out]

Letter No. 51

William, Lord Burghley to Sir Robert Cecil, June 1595

1 p. Holograph.
Addressed, endorsed, signed.

Text

Yow may by the begynning of this included letter of Sir Jhon
Norrice['s] forwardnes, which yow may shew to hir Ma[jes]ty with
an Intention how it is met to tak the Erles cheff howss, which they
cannot doe, withowt passyng the blackwater, how so ever a contrary
opinion afor hir Ma[jes]ty.[184]

cover letter in reply, Wilkes was never sent. He was very close to secretarial operations.
His treatise on the office and duties of a councillor suggests he hoped to be appointed as a
second to Cecil in the office of Secretary, BL MS Stowe 296, fols. 7–20.
[184] The Blackwater fort, which stood on the river of the same name, was the earl of Tyrone's
chief house. Sir John Norris wrote to both Cecils on 13 June 1595 noting Russell's perfidy
in sending the 1,000 foot lately levied into O'Donnell's country – presumably to assist Sir
Richard Bingham in Connacht – even as Norris awaited his instructions on dealing with
Tyrone. TNA SP 63/180/fols. 110r–111r, 112r–113r. The task of proclaiming Tyrone traitor
had fallen to Norris. TNA SP 63/179/no. 41, fol. 90r–v; Bruce Lenman, *England's Colonial
Wars 1550–1688: Conflicts, Empire and National Identity* (Harlow, 2001), 116.

Yow may also se the reasons Iterated, for acceptyng of few Mc Hugh. but his offers have not been secrett, nether will his person, nor his other Companion be easely taken and delyvered.[185] I have sent for Sir H[enry] Killygrew and the rest to be with me to morrow at 7 of clock wher I wish Sir Tho[mas] Wilkes might be present & so tell hym.[186]

I thynk to speak with Sir Francis Drake this night for plymmouth.[187]

And so I thank yow your to much Care of me in sendyng to know how I do, which I thank God is well, but tyred with london sutors.

Your lov[ing] father,

W. Burghley

[Holograph postscript]
I miss 2 of my brood, a male and a female, but I thynk they are forthcomming redy to return whan they shall be called for.

Dorse

ADDRESSED in Burghley's hand:
To my loving son Sir Robart Cecill

ENDORSED in Simon Willis's hand:
June 1595, Lo[rd] Thre[asure]r to my M[aste]r

[185] Fiach Mac Aodh Ui Broin or Fiach MacHugh O'Byrne (1544–1597) was the chief of the O'Byrnes who had supplanted the O'Tooles in the vast lordship of the Wicklow mountains. He was to be dealt with by Norris with troops assigned to this campaign. Norris wrote to Cecil on 13 June 1595, reporting that Feagh McHugh's offers to the Irish Council were 'impugned' by them. Russell wrote to Cecil on 23 May 1595 that he had been occupied for five weeks in the prosecution of Feagh McHugh, TNA SP 63/179/no. 90, fols. 226r–227r. McHugh's confederate may have been his son, Turlough McFeagh O'Byrne, whom Russell planned to have put to death by extraordinary means. TNA SP 63/180/no. 41, fol. 125r–v. See also Letter No. 61. McHugh's wife had been taken, Hatfield, Cecil papers, 32/30; *HMCS*, v, 20.

[186] The projected meeting of Wilkes, Killigrew and Burghley may have been to discuss draft instructions for his proposed French embassy. For the confession of Nicholas Williamson to the lord keeper, Puckering, of 21 June 1595, where the intelligence implications of Wilkes's proposed embassy to the Low Countries was discussed, see Letter No. 50; *HMCS*, v, 252.

[187] Sir Ferdinando Gorges (1567–1648) was then in charge of the town but he was dealing with chaos, as he was contravened by the mayor in public. *HMCS*, vi, 207–208. Gorges would have the office of captain or keeper of the new fort then being built in Plymouth, and a patent of 12 June 1596 responded to these disorders giving him the power to 'remove, expel and replace foot-soldiers, gunners, porters, watchmen and others serving' at the fort and on St Nicholas Isle at the entrance to the port. *CPR 38 Eliz. I*, no. 2582. Gorges played a pivotal role in Channel defences, prevailing over local and regional interests in support of the national government. With minor breaks Gorges held this post until 1629, *ODNB*.

Letter No. 52

William, Lord Burghley to Sir Robert Cecil, 8 July 1595

½ p. Dictated to Henry Maynard.
Addressed, endorsed, signed.

Text

I hae received your letter by this bearer at xii of the clock, whearebie yowe require to understand of mee whither yowe shall move the Quene about the Bill of the Provost Marshall. ffor awnsweare, besides that I wroate unto yowe this daie by Coppin[188] concerning that matter I did move hir ma[jes]tie thearein yesterdaie, whome I fownde veary willing to have a provost Marshall[189] but very unwilling to make anie allowance to him, without which I told hir the Gentleman would not nor could not well serve, for that the service would be chargeable unto him, becawse of his continuall attendance, and that with summ good Companie to resist the violence of anie disordred person. and hearof yowe maie doe well to acquaint summ of my lls [Lords] to assist yowe in anie newe motion to be made to hir ma[jes]tie.[190]

Ffrom my howse in the strand this viii[th] of Julye 1595

[Burghley]
Your loving Father,

W. Burghley

---

[188] Burghley's secretary George Coppin's patent for clerk of the Crown in Chancery and clerk for the writing of pardons, *CPR 39 Eliz. I*, no. 269. See also Letter No. 80; *CSPD 1595–1597*, 353.
[189] See Ian W. Archer, *The Pursuit of Stability: Social Relations in Elizabethan London* (Cambridge, 1981), 1–2, for a discussion of the tensions between the lord mayor, the governance of the city and anti-alien riots. The great apprentice riot of 29 June 1595, is discussed in Manning, 'The prosecution of Sir Michael Blount', 218–219. The City and government officials left few records of questioning or procedure in Star Chamber, one reason for this was that Wilford's patent abrogated the normal course of justice, see note 190.
[190] Sir Thomas Wilford was to be named provost marshal under a commission dated 18 July 1595 'for the execution of rebellious and incorrigible offenders by martial law'. Previous Star Chamber orders to the lord mayor for imprisonment and corporal punishment had failed. This was also the case with the proclamation of 4 July 1595 to commit vagrants to prison, which had not stopped the unrest. Public execution under Wilford was deemed to the only method remaining. *CPR 37 Eliz. I*, no. 1364. See also Letter No. 80; *ODNB*.

Dorse

ADDRESSED in Henry Maynard's hand:
To my Lovinge Sonne Sir Rob[er]t Cecill, knight,
one of hir Ma[jes]ties Privy Counsell

ENDORSED in Simon Willis's hand:
8 July 1595,
L[ord] Thre[asure]r to my M[aste]r
Provost Marshall

Letter No. 53

William, Lord Burghley to Sir Robert Cecil, 11 July 1595

¼ p. Holograph except for address.
Addressed, endorsed, signed.

Text

I send herewith the last letter I had from Mr. Gylpyn[191] and also certen
letters from Mr. Edmundes[192] all which yow may impart to hir Majesty.
    I propose with God's will to be ther to night or in the morning to
impart to hir Ma[jes]ty Mr. Bodeley's last answer.[193]

11 Jul[y] 1595.

Your lov[ing] father,

W. Burghley

Dorse

ADDRESSED in Henry Maynard's hand:
To my lovinge sonne Sir Rob[er]t Cecill, knight, one of hir ma[jes]ties
privy Counsell

---

[191] Letters to Burghley and Cecil from George Gilpin of 8 July 1595, TNA SP 84/51/fol.
9r, 11r–12r; *L&A*, vi, Analysis no. 72.
[192] Thomas Edmondes to Burghley of 22 June 1595, TNA SP 78/35/fol. 178r. Burghley
used the word 'last', by way of distinguishing its contents from another letter of 14 June,
TNA SP 78/35/fol. 171r.
[193] Bodley's answers to the Cecils' and the Queen's questions were made on 11 July 1595.
As Bodley was in England, the letter arrived the same day. Hatfield, Cecil Papers, 33/30;
HMCS, v, 275.

ENDORSED in Simon Willis's hand:
11 July 1595
L[ord] Thre[asure]r to my M[aste]r

Letter No. 54

William, Lord Burghley to Sir Robert Cecil, 13 July 1595

1 p. The first section, 9 lines, dictated to Henry Maynard; the remaining section, 20 lines, holograph.
Addressed, endorsed, signed.

Text

[Maynard's hand]
Since my comminge home I have spoken with l[ord] derbey towchinge the writinge that concerneth the C[ap]teine Wainemen, whoe telleth me that he delivered the same to yowe, and therefore it semeth yowe did not remember yt this daie when the same was spoken of [in Burghley's hand] this day uppon the deliverie of Sir Edward Norris['] letter to the lls [Lords].[194] I praie yowe cawse your man to seek yt owt, and if yowe shall misse yt emongest your papers, yowe maie looke for yt emongest mine of the Lowe Contries, least peradventure yowe might leave them with mee [Burghley] which I do not remembre, but yet I remembre yow told me that Mr. bodly brought such an information ageynst weynman.[195]

[194]Sir Edward Norris to the Cecils of 8 July 1595, TNA SP 84/51/fols. 13r–v, 15r; *L&A*, vi, Analysis no. 174. This includes discussion of Wainman, a captain in Brittany presumably under Sir John Norris who had been sending intelligence of members of Sir William Stanley's Irish regiment in the Low Countries. He had been implicated in the confession of one Thomas Hull as being a connection between Stanley's lieutenant-colonel, Jacques Fransisco, and Maurice of Nassau. Wainman was now in Ireland, which underscores again the interrelatedness of intelligence in Ireland, Brittany and the Low Countries. Wainman was alleged to have conspired to blow up Maurice's store of weapons when Count Fuentes made his way into the Low Countries. Hatfield, Cecil Papers, 24/82, and copy 83; *HMCS*, v, 78; Letter No. 48. How William, 6th earl of Derby knew of this information is uncertain. Hull confessed that he was persuaded to commit treason, as had Babington and Salisbury. The circumstances of the 1593 plot to implicate Ferdinando, 5th earl of Derby, in a regicidal plot emanating from Spain were apparently known to the 6th earl despite his not being a privy councillor. Derby shared intelligence with Cecil about the Scottish ambassador, Cockburn, who was at court to collect James VI's annuity 22 July 1595, *HMCS*, v, 286.
[195]This volume reposes with much of the Cecil's official papers, but is noted as an administrative entity in 1598 as among Burghley's papers at TNA SP 45 (Various) /20. Henry Brooke was sent to find Bouillon's cipher in Burghley's papers on 1 Oct. 1595 telling of his closeness with the Cecils' and his father's intelligence work. Hatfield, Cecil Papers, 173/fol. 137r; *HMCS*, v, 1.

I send to yow herwith a bill for a warrant for monny for Sir Thomas layton, which as my L[ord] admyrall can tell yow is required to be iii^C [£300] and for Jersay ii^C [£200] with monny for iiii tons of lead. I pray yow procure these to be signed, and pass to the signet and prive seal.[196]

Yow may tell my L[ord] of Essex, that wher hir Ma[jes]ty hath apoynted certen men for Silley only for the sommar tyme I fynd the cap. bevon unwillyng to serve ther except he might have a contynuance for which I have no warrant, but express order to contynew this new chardg, but for the sommar tyme.[197]

13 Jul[y] 1595

Your lov[ing] father,

W. Burghley

[Added after signing in Burghley's hand]
I had almost lost my tyde to come under the Bridg hytherward.

the letter also for my L[ord] of Pembroke for 100 men willsh[ire] and 200 in Som[erset] wold be remembered.[198]

Dorse

ADDRESSED in Henry Maynard's hand:
To my lovinge sonne Sir Robert Cecill, knight, one of hir Majesty's Privy Counsell

ENDORSED in Simon Willis's hand:
13 Julii 1595
L[ord] Thre[asure]r to my M[aste]r
[Seal remaining]

---

[196]Despite these temporary expenditures for the Channel Islands, military expenditure would now lean towards Ireland. See the intelligence from Sir Nicholas Clifford to Essex of the landing of Spanish troops in Cornwall. Hatfield, Cecil Papers, 172/35; *HMCS*, v, 290; Wernham, *After the Armada*, 536.

[197]The note regarding the government of the fortress at Scilly may have arisen on Sir Francis Godolphin's visit to the court from his command there with news containing Irish, Breton, Spanish and Scottish intelligence. Essex presumably sponsored Captain Bevan for a captaincy, but whether this was for intelligence reasons is unclear. Hatfield, Cecil Papers, 33/29; *HMCS*, v, 274.

[198]Warrants to Burghley for levies in Essex and Hertfordshire on 30 June 1595 for troops to Chester were part of the Irish levies accompanying Sir John Norris as he took the command of the Queen's troops there. Hatfield, Cecil Papers, 33/13; *HMCS*, v, 262. See also an account of payments under privy seal warranted for Ireland in Mar. and Apr. 1594/5, dated 21 July 1595. Hatfield, Cecil Papers, 139/49; *HMCS*, v, 286.

Letter No. 55

William, Lord Burghley to Sir Robert Cecil, 23 July 1595

⅓ p. Dictated to Henry Maynard.
Addressed, endorsed, signed.

Text

I doe retorne unto yowe, three writinges of D[octor] Parkins conceipt. The one to the k[ing] of Pole, the other to the Brethren Battores of Transilvania, the third to the Chancellor of Poland.[199] The first two to be written by hir ma[jes]tie, the third by him self: the which I have perused seriouslie, and cannot in mine opinion ad or deminishe anie thinge, but thinke the same written very well cum drewro.[200]

[199]Letters were then drafted by Christopher Parkins, suspected of being Catholic, having been foreign-educated and trained as a civil lawyer. He protested that the papal legate to the emperor, Speciano (Letter No. 58) had offered £2,000 on his life. Here he was to draft letters to the king of Poland (Sigismund III Vasa, 1566–1632) married to the Archduchess Anna of Austria, who had evaded the Queen's direct questions about the provisioning of ships bound for Spain. Sigismund argued that Poland was neutral. The dwindling revenues for his nobility and his own treasury, owing to the reduced price of corn, had to be augmented; crops on the Vistula were nothing to do with Spanish trade, save that it was loaded at Danzig or Elbing, and would form part of the growing dispute and eventual Imperial embargo against the Merchant Adventurers in 1597. TNA SP 88 [Poland]/1/ fol. 230r–v; *L&A*, vi, Analysis no. 408. The Queen could not ignore a neutral power who abetted her enemies, yet this was the year before the Union of Brest which created the Uniate churches, thereby establishing Poland as a 'Catholic' power following Sigismund's own faith. Parkins also drafted letters to the Báthory brothers of Transylvania then in conflict with the Poles, which made room for manoeuvring with their affections. Alliances between the Báthorys and the Poles shifted, because the former had designs on the Polish throne. Furthermore, while Transylvania supported a war with the Turks, this was opposed by Poland. *L&A*, vi, Analysis no. 409. Parkins drafted correspondence for the chancellor of Poland, John Sarius Zamoyski (1542–1605), with a report on his embassy, TNA SP 88/I/fols. 234r–237r. Congratulations for Sigismund III were sent, as he had fathered an heir, Vladyslaus IV Vasa (d.1648), future king of Poland, by his wife Anna of Austria. Hatfield, Cecil Papers, 172/19; *HMCS*, v, 268–269. The Báthorys: Cardinal Andrew (1563–1599) and Balthasar (1560–1594) had staunchly opposed the support of their cousin Sigismund (1573–1613, Voivode of Transylvania, 1581–1594 when Rudolf II took regency) for Clement VIII's Holy League against the Turks and the resulting return of Jesuits to Poland mandated by the king. For earlier drafts of correspondence with Rudolf II, see TNA SP 80/1/fols. 179r, 185r, 186r, 187r. Parkins would also draft letters to Moulay Ahmed IV of Barbary, the chancellor of the margrave of Brandenburg, the earl of Friesland and the duke of Brunswick-Luneburg, TNA SO3/1/600v.
[200]The words may mean 'as drawn'.

And therefore, I think if theie weare redie written fitt to be signed by hir ma[jes]tie, the sooner theie be doone, and sent awaye the better.[201] but hearewith must be remembered that theare be our letter written to Mr. Barton, which would be written with somm good Caution, least it might be miscarried and so cumm to the handes of suche as ar readie to detract anie thinge, thowghe never soe well ment by hir Majestie.[202] soe fare yowe well.

Ffrom my howse at Theobaldes this xxii[th] of Julye 1595.

[Burghley]
Your loving father,

W. Burghley

Dorse

ADDRESSED in Henry Maynard's hand:
To my lovinge sonne Sir Rob[er]t Cecill knight
one of the Q[ueen's] ma[jes]ties
privie Connsell.

---

[201] The Queen's letter was sent following Parkins's draft, see n. 202; TNA SP 88/1/fol. 230r–v. There is no record of Cecil retaining Parkins's draft of the letter, or of his having procured the final version to the signet.

[202] Edward Barton (1562/3–98), *ODNB*, was agent in Constantinople, principally concerned with mercantile causes, while also gathering intelligence conveyed through his agent Thomas Wilcocks. Barton corresponded with Parkins at least once, writing on 18 July 1593, TNA SP 81/7/fol. 144r. Barton was secretly encouraging the Sultan Amurath and his successor Mehmed III against the Habsburgs and followed the sultan's army into Hungary in 1596. His efforts required the utmost secrecy because if discovered, they might have provoked 'neutral' powers against England. Parkins drafted each of the letters after soundings were taken by Cecil. Parkins and Cecil were asked by the Queen to devise 'some convenient meanes to keepe thinges quiet in Polonia with her highnes' dignitie', and to encourage the Báthorys gently by noting that the Queen would continue her 'inhibition of bearing corne to Spayne'. BL Cottonian MS Nero B II, fols. 245v–246r–v. What lay behind these diplomatic efforts to encourage a Turkish anti-Habsburg policy was an attempt to secure trade which was threatened in the Empire, see Letter No. 34. The custody of Parkins' drafts is not clear but Cecil's control of such papers may be inferred from a signet docquet entry of Dec. 1593: 'A letter to Edward Barton Esq. her Majesty[s] ambassador with the Grand Seigneur in favour of the Prince of Transilvania, The m[inute] rem[aining] with Sir Robert Cecill, dated at Hampton Court, the xxii[th] of December', TNA SO3/1/fol. 437v. For the drafting of the Turkish letters, see Thomas Lake telling Cecil in Jan. 1596 that they would be given to Sir John Wolley's man 'who knoweth the style', since his clerks (at the council) would not bear the charge of the silk used in their sealing. Rayne Allinson, *A Monarchy of Letters: Royal Correspondence and English Diplomacy in the Reign of Elizabeth I* (Basingstoke, 2012), 30–31.

Letter No. 56

William, Lord Burghley to Sir Robert Cecil, 24 July 1595

⅓ p. Holograph.
Addressed, endorsed, signed.

Text

I thank for your often wrytyng. I am glad of the Erles delyvery to his own howss, wherof I do Imagyn he shall stey a good tyme.[203] Yow wryt not whyther I be looked for ther, but I meane to be at London on Satyrday, and at the Court on Sunday.

I send yow such letters as presently I receaved from Otwell Smyth, wherein I only mislyke that which he wryteth of desparnon.[204] And so bless yow. Fom my howse of Theobaldes. 24 Jul[y] 1595.

Your lov[ing] father,

W. Burghley

Dorse

ADDRESSED by Burghley:
to my sonn Sir Robart Cecill
knight at the Court

[203] Burghley may be referring to Thomas Butler, 10th earl of Ormond and 3rd earl of Ossory (1531–1614) old friend of the Queen's, rather than Tyrone. The rebels' forces were held to be growing daily in strength and discipline. Cecil's agent John Talbot's reported: 'The traytors are growen strong and bold through to long sufferance', TNA SP 63/180/no. 45, fol. 144r; *CSPI 1592–6*, 331. Russell sent the Cecils John Bellevue's confession, in which he told of a priest on board with great sealed letters, presumably from Spain to the Irish rebels. TNA SP 63/180/no. 45, fols. 125r–v, 127r–v. Burghley collated Irish intelligence for his son on 30 June 1595, noting that in the reports of allies sent for Spain and intercepted, there was named the earl of Ormond: 'whose name I thynk is rather used to incite the Spanyard than upon sure ground', SP 63/180/fol. 184r. It is possible that Ormond returned to his house as commanded by the lord deputy and council for reasons of his own safety and security. However, he preferred to stay away from his ancestral lands, taking refuge in the south, because he was then struggling with the uprising of some of his kinsmen, *ODNB*.

[204] Otywell Smyth to Burghley of 18 July 1595, TNA SP 78/35/fol. 195r; *L&A*, vi, Analysis no. 133, 135, 136, 158, 190. Smyth enclosed three letters with his own. Of these, Burghley paused at Charles de Saldaigne's (Sieur d'Incarville) to Smyth where it was implied that Épernon, now reconciled to Henry IV, was suspected of maintaining close connections to the Spanish (he was a Lorrainer), to whom he might deliver Boulogne. Hopes were now reposed in the integrity of Campagnol, the governor of the town, to prevent this action. SP 78/35/, fol. 194r; *L&A*, vi, Analysis no. 158. For an earlier example of treachery in Boulogne and the current threat against Boulogne, see Wernham, *After the Armada*, 488–489; Acres, 'The early political career of Sir Robert Cecil', 57–67.

ENDORSED in Simon Willis's hand:
24 July 1595
L[ord] Thre[asure]r to my M[aste]r

Letter No. 57

William, Lord Burghley to Sir Robert Cecil, 3 September 1595

½ p. Dictated to Henry Maynard, with one holograph sentence added before Burghley signed.
Addressed, endorsed, signed.

Text

I am vearie well contented that my dawghter your wief maie have the use of anie part of my howse either the Chamber wheare my Ladie of derbye used to lie in,[205] or anie other place to hir choise and best likinge. and so I praie yowe to lett hir understand, and that she maie remove thither when and assone as yt shall best like hir. from the Cort, this third of Sept[ember] 1595.

[Burghley adds]
If myne owne bedchamber shall lyk hir she may command it.

[Maynard]
Your loving father,

[Signed]
W. Burghley

Dorse

ADDRESSED in Henry Maynard's hand:
To my loving sonne Sir
Rob[er]t Cecill knight, one
of hir ma[jes]ties privye Connsell

ENDORSED in Simon Willis's hand:
3 Sept[ember] 1595
Lo[rd] Thre[asure]r to my M[aste]r

---

[205] Elizabeth Vere, countess of Derby, Burghley's grand-daughter, recently married to the 6th earl of Derby.

Letter No. 58

William, Lord Burghley to Sir Robert Cecil, 12 September 1595

2 pp [recto and verso in the MS]. Dictated to Henry Maynard, with one holograph paragraph.
Addressed, endorsed.

Text

At your departure yesterdaie I had noe leisure to deliver sondrie thinges unto yowe, which nowe with thes my letters in a heape I send unto yowe.

Ffirst yowe shall receive Mr. Bodelies letter dated the 27[th] of the last moneth, the contentes wheareof yowe maie at convenient time, or the letter itself showe to hir Majestie, wherein I see he moveth som scruples and dowbtes howe hir ma[jes]tye maie be satisfied.[206]

I send to yowe also a Copie of a letter written owt of Russia by John Merick Agent for the Englishe Companie there,[207] wheareby he doth advertise a matter of summ weight delivered to him by Boros Federick principall Connsellor to the Emperor of Muscovia, by which it appeareth howe readie the Popes legat[208] hath been to slawnder hir

---

[206] Bodley to the Queen of 27 Aug. 1595 was copied to Burghley and to the earl of Essex. Hatfield, Cecil Papers, 34/69; *HMCS*, v, 352–353. Burghley referred to Bodley's pessimism about the States' ability to repay their debts to the Queen, in view of their military support of Henry IV's efforts at Cambrai. The French held Cambrai and it was besieged by the Count of Fuentes in 1595. Burghley's express instructions to Bodley had been to negotiate within the terms of the 1585 agreement.

[207] Sir John Meyrick (*c*.1559–1638/9), *ODNB*. Letters were received from Meyrick, agent for the Muscovy Company. Hatfield, Cecil Papers, 37/12; *HMCS*, v, 521–522. Burghley reiterates much of the content of the extract. The Papal legate to Russia had tried to convince both Boris Godunov and the Tsar of the Queen's support for Amurath III of Turkey, against the wishes of all other Christian princes. See n. 208.

[208] The papal legate at Prague to Rudolf II sent to Poland, Cardinal Cesare Speciano (1539–1607), see Tadhg Ó hAnnracháin *Catholic Europe 1592–1648: Centre and Peripheries* (Oxford, 2015), 152–154. The legate had made explicit Habsburg claims that Elizabeth had supported the Turks in their war. This, together with the Emperor Rudolf's later interdiction on the English Merchant Adventurers, shaped a potential European-wide isolation of England, especially if the Spanish could be persuaded by Clement VIII to lead the war against the Turks together with the Austrian Habsburgs. Burghley was concerned to let these matters to rest, hence the secrecy of the Queen's letter to Edward Barton, see Letter No. 55. The papal nuncio's policy was less interventionist in Poland where the chancellor decided that declaration against the Turks was less important than establishing Catholicism. This also exposed the Transylvanian Báthorys, to whom the pope had sent Cardinal Visconti, to Turkish aggression, see n. 209; Letter No. 34. The legate was here employing more incendiary tactics to rouse anti-English, rather than specifically anti-Protestant, feeling for the question was mercantile rather than religious.

ma[jes]tie after the accustomed manner of his master the ffather of Lies. And consideringe the discreate descoverye hereof by the Muscovite, and his not accrediting of the untrwethe, It weare well done that the Agent had hir ma[jes]ties letters both to the Emperor, and to Boros Frederick[209] declarring to themm the untrewthe of this report, and hir ma[jes]ties disposition to have peace for the Emperor of Almaigne. hir ma[jes]tie dare in honor referre hirself to the Emperor of Almaigne to whome hir ma[jes]tie did send an Ambassador expreslie a yere past,[210] offeringe all the meanes in hir power to reduce the Turk to peace. And of this matter none can better make declaracion, than D[octor] Parkyns whoe in mine opinion weare veary fitt to conceive the two letters to the Emperor of Russia and to Boris Frederick.[211]

I doe also send unto yowe a letter of Archibald dowglas,[212] whoe also came himself after his letter written in person. by his letter and speeche I finde by him a disposition to doe sum good service for quietnes in Scotland, and perticularlie for the Q[ueen's] ma[jes]tie's satisfaccion. his Negotiation consisteth upponn two partes: The one

[209] Boris Fedorovitch Godunov (1551–1605), grand duke of Moscow succeeded as tsar (1598–1605) rather than Feodor I (1551–1598), heir of the Tsar Ivan 'the Terrible', who was not considered of sound mind. Godunov appears to have been the shrewd mind behind this scepticism, although see the Queen's willingness to tread a very delicate line in this matter in her relations with the Poles and the Báthorys of Transylvania, while keeping instructions to her agent at Constantinople, Edward Barton, strictly secret (see Letter No. 55). Godunov specifically requested that Merrick supply letters from the Queen to himself and to the Tsar notifying them of the Queen's neutrality with the Turks. Cecil had procured suits for the fellowship of English merchants trading in Muscovia and Russia. TNA SO3/1/fol. 448r. On 2 Oct. 1595 the year's import of Russian timber, intended largely for the construction of ships of war, came to 4,980 hundredweight, valued at £5,810. *HMCS*, v, 399.

[210] The Queen's ambassadors to the Emperor of Almaigne, i.e. to Rudolph II, Holy Roman Emperor: Parkins had been the last emissary, 1590–1591 and 1593 to the emperor and German states, also visiting Hanse towns and Poland. Bell, *Handlist*, 138. Henry Fiennes, 2nd earl of Lincoln, would be sent 30 June–Sept. 1596.

[211] Imperial, Scandanavian, Hanse, Russian, Turkish (Edward Barton), and Danubian correspondence, all in Latin, came to Parkins for translation and drafting. Burghley was in regular communication with Barton whose letters from Constantinople were compiled into a large letter-book, BL Cottonian MS Nero B xii, fols 1–361. After the 1596 ratification of a League Defensive and Offensive, the Triple Alliance, and the restoration of a Habsburg–French balance, Parkins's correspondence with the princes of the Holy Roman Empire, particularly in the somewhat chaotic Bohemia of the Emperor Rudolf II, assumed increasing importance. Parkins sought ecclesiastical preferment by Cecil valued at £50 per year so that he might finance his work. Hatfield, Cecil Papers, 34/ 49. When Cecil was made Secretary, he petitioned with eventual success to be made a master of requests. Hatfield, Cecil Papers, 42/17; *HMCS*, vi, 248. He was not successful in his bid through Cecil to be made Latin secretary in Oct. 1596 after Sir John Wolley's death. Hatfield, Cecil Papers, 45/66; *HMCS*, vi, 432.

[212] The letters of intelligence here are from James Hudson and George Nicolson, Cecil's main Scottish connection, *CSPS* 1593–1595, no. 568. Bothwell's overture to Henry IV had been rebuffed.

for the Erle of Angus: the other for the Erle Bothwell.²¹³ The grownd of his dealinge proceadeth of a letter from his Nephewe Richard dowglas, which he did shewe mee, and whearof I send yowe a Copie.²¹⁴ The purpose is, wheare the Erle reconciled to the Kinge, and to learne of his confederacie with Huntley, Arroll and others, and if hir ma[jes]tie would intercede for him to the kinge he would discover unto hir

[p. 2] ma[jes]tie sondrie thinges preiuciciall to her State. But yt semeth except he maie have the k[ing's] favor wrowght by hir Majestie, he will not discover his knowledge. The second matter concerninge Bothewell is an offer that one James Dowglas called the L[aird] of Spott, an offender which Bothwell offreth to comm into Ingland, and so to passe into France wheare the Erle Bothwell is, and not onelie to disswade Bothwell from conspiringe with the Spaniard, but to discover all his knolledg of anie attempt against the Q[ueen's] ma[jes]ty, or hir Realme.²¹⁵ And this he offreth to performe, so as his charges be provided for, for his comming and retorninge. Of thes two matters I would yow would informe hir ma[jes]tie and receive hir pleasure.

---

²¹³Huntly and Erroll were prepared to receive Bothwell into their confidences. Archibald Douglas, Bothwell's maternal uncle, was to help with this and report through Hudson to Cecil. Douglas was then leaving for Holland with Andrew Hunter, a Cecil correspondent, who reported fully to Cecil in the latter half of 1595. TNA SP 84/51/fols. 63 r–v, 298r. In Dec. 1593, both Archibald and Richard Douglas had mishandled intelligence matters with the public knowledge of the rebel Scottish earls' petition through Sir John Fortescue, Letter No. 10.

²¹⁴See above, pp. 48–49.

²¹⁵James Douglas wrote to Archibald Douglas one month later, 13 Oct. 1595, about the plots referred to here. Archibald Douglas was to have obtained the Queen's writ to advise Scrope of James Douglas's letters reporting on the very slow progress of Angus's reconciliation with the king, noting that James VI's favour to Lady Bothwell grew out of hatred towards the lairds of Buccleuch and Cessford rather than any actual regard he held for the Bothwells. *HMCS*, v, 415–416. This letter contains a full account of the pertinent changes in Scottish government after the death of Chancellor Maitland of Thirlestane including Bothwell's attempt to gain the confidence of Henry IV of France against his cousin James VI. Hatfield, Cecil Papers, 29/40; *HMCS*, v, 41–42. This letter is calendared 1594, but Burghley's letter of Spott's interest in Bothwell dates it closer to 20 Dec. 1595. Bothwell also sought Sir Hugh Carmichael's support as aide to the prospective French envoy to Scotland, the duke of Rohan. Spott was furthering his causes for the Douglases with the earl of Cassilis. These matters were discussed in James VI's letter to Robert Bowes of 3 Nov. 1594, which criticized Spott's role as intermediary between Huntly and Bothwell. The 20 Dec. letter really gave news of Bothwell's French intrigues. Bothwell consoled Essex from Paris, probably on 3 Apr. 1596, on the death of Sir Henry Unton. *HMCS*, v, 134. Unton (*c*.1558–1596) was appointed ambassador on 30 Nov. 1595, a position held until his death on 23 Mar. 1596. Bell, *Handlist*, 100; *L&A*, vi, Analysis no. 236. Spott appears to have been quarrelling with Archibald Douglas's two nephews (James and Richard) by early 1596, which led to their causes foundering. Samuel Cockburn warned of this in a letter to Douglas on 17 June 1596, *HMCS*, vi, 216. For Spott's excommunication by the Kirk, see David Calderwood *Historie of the Kirk of Scotland* (Edinburgh, 1842), Book V, 365.

I send also unto yowe A request of the Merchantes Adventurers to be recommended to Mr. Bodelie and Gilpin, or to one of them, which request consisteth uppon two partes, both vearye necessarie for to be reformed by the States, as by the readinge thereof yowe will perceive.

And therefor I praie yowe move it to my Lordes theare that theare letters might be written to Mr. Bodeleie and Mr. Gilpin, accordinge to the request of the Marchauntes.

I have since yor departure fownd A plat of Milford haven,[216] and also the opinion of my l[ord] of Pembroke,[217] which was delivered to hir ma[jes]tie uppon hir Messuage sent by yowe unto him, whearein it doth appeare directlye that he misliketh of the fortificacion. whereof I will nowe make no report unto yowe bicawse I perceived yowe had received A copie thereof from his L[ord's] Secretary Mr. Messinger: and yet uppon a second consideracion not knowinge howe the Copie maie agree with the originall I doe send that which I thinke to be the same which was sent by the Erle, for so yowe shall find yt subscribed with his name.

[Burghley adds]
If I shall not recover my helth, at this tyme, wherein the son is departyng, I shall dispayre to contynew this next wyntar a lyve, or owt of misery, for within 40 howres I shall mak my period of lxxiiii y[ear]s, and what so ever shall be more, shall be by the Judgement of King David labor and toyle.

xiii Sept[ember] 1595

Your loving father,

W. Burghley

Dorse

ADDRESSED in Henry Maynard's hand:
To my lovinge sonne Sir Rob[er]t Cecill knight
one of hir ma[jes]ties privie Counsell

---

[216]George Owen (1552–1613), *ODNB*, for his pamphlet or platt for the expansion of the fortress in Nov. 1595. A full account is in Owen, *Description of Pembrokeshire* (1602) 531–532.

[217]This is the first letter mentioning the large-scale military preparations, including the various difficulties in mustering, for the autumn of 1595. Burghley made notes on Privy Council plans and expenditures at that time (including Milford Haven), as an invasion was expected. See also Letter No. 59; *CSPD 1595–1597*, 102. Henry Herbert, 2nd earl of Pembroke (c.1538–1601), *ODNB*, an unpopular lord president of the council of the Welsh marches; Essex was a major rival.

13 Sept[ember] 1595
L[ord] Thre[asure]r to my M[aste]r
[Misdated: see text of No. 59 where Burghley allows that he was one day out in his reckoning around his birthday, 13 September. So the letter is actually 12 September 1595.]
[Seal cut out]

Letter No. 59

William, Lord Burghley to Sir Robert Cecil, 3 September 1595

1⅓ pp. Dictated to Henry Maynard with holograph additions to 2 paragraphs as noted in the text.
Addressed, endorsed, signed.

Text

I have recevid this letter inclosed from my L[ord] of Rutland whoe is vearie desirous to have his license to be signed by his ma[jes]tie that he might at his comminge upp to take his leave of hir ma[jes]tie have noe cawse of staie.[218] Yowe shall, thearefore, much content my L[ord] to gett the same to be signed: and as I remember I gave to yoww heeretofore his bill.[219] but if the same should be missinge, yowe maie cawse Mr. Lake to make an other,[220] and thearein to inset two gentlemen, the one named

---

[218] Roger Manners, future 5th earl of Rutland (1588–1612), *ODNB*. For his grand tour and profligacy, see Lawrence Stone, *Family and Fortune: Studies in Aristocratic France in the Sixteenth and Seventeenth Century* (Oxford, 1973), 148–179. Early in 1595, the Countess Elizabeth, the 5th earl's mother, died thus reducing the jointures charged on the estate from three to two and the 5th earl, though still a minor for another two years, came into his own and overspent hugely for the next five years exactly like the earl of Southampton, ibid. 179. The Cecils were, technically, embroiled in an extensive lawsuit with the Manners family over the marriage of Burghley's grandson William in 1589 to the Rutland co-heiress Elizabeth, ibid. 177. From 1597, Rutland moved in Essex's orbit. Stone notes that the travelling which Burghley here facilitated was running at between £6,000–£7,000 a year, ibid. 180.

[219] Manners also wrote to Cecil on 6 Sept. 1595 concerning this licence to travel, asking that Cecil procure the paper for signing and thanked Cecil for his trouble on the 27th of that month, having received the licence, and wishing papers for one Tristram Tyrrwhit to travel abroad to Prague and Germany. Hatfield, Cecil Papers, 30/20, 34/102; *HMCS*, v, 365, 392.

[220] As clerk of the signet, Thomas Lake (1561–1630), *ODNB*, would become embroiled in a lawsuit *c.*1618, through his daughter Ann's marriage to the grandson of Sir Thomas Cecil, Lord Exeter.

Madox who is to attend my L[ord] in his travell, the other Robart Wellbie.[221]

I must nowe acquaint yowe with an Accident that fell owt heare yesterdaie in the afternoone, least the same showld be otherwise reported to my l[ord] of Essex then the trewthe was. Abowt tenne of the clock in the morninge one Capt[ain] Trowghton came hither to Waltham whoe is to be appointed to be muster M[aste]r of Rutlandshire, and beinge offred of the Constable and post M[aste]r to have horse, he semed not to care to have anie but rather had a minde to ride in iourney as he said. and towardes the Eveninge havinge loytered in the towne all the daie, an honest man and a trumpett of hir Majestie's that dwelleth at Totnam whose name is ffissher, comminge throwgh the towne with his wief being a sicklie womann, this Trowghton would neades unhorse ffissher and have his horse to ride past, which the other refusinge, and the Constables & post m[aste]r beinge by, and offeringe other horses, which he refused, he drewe his rapier, and hath hurt ffissher in one of his handes. wheare uppon the constables apprehended him and brought him hither to mee, together with ffissher the trompeter that was hurt, which disorder being testefied by all that camme with them, I committed him to the Custodie of the Constable. But for that he said he was my l[ord] of Essex's servant, within half an hower after I released him. Wheareuppon he had a post horse for himself, and an other for his guide. but most lewdely by the waie, towardes ware, he turned of his guide and is riden awaie with the other horse, wheareof a newe Complaint is againe made to me this morninge by the post M[aste]r and Constables. I have at length acquainted yow hearewith, that the trewthe maie be knowen to my L[ord] of Essex, as yow shall see cawse, for that I dowbt not this lewde Companion careth not what he reporteth to excuse his own misdemeanor.[222]

[Burghley's hand]

---

[221]Madox may be the Gryffyn Madox, sometime clerk of munitions at Flushing. TNA E 351/240, Discharge of account, chief officers, commissaries, entertainments, 12 Apr. 1586–30 Jan. 1587.

[222]At least one list of lord lieutenants, deputies in counties without lord lieutenants and their respective muster masters contains Captain 'Throwghton' beside Rutland, where the lord lieutenant was Lord Huntingdon, *HMCS*, v, 523. Burghley was troubled by such incidents. He wrote to Cecil on 17 Sept. 1595 calling attention to the difficulties experienced by the commissioners for musters in Northampton and hoping that the usual 'Michaelmas summer' would suffice for the training of newly mustered troops. Hatfield, Cecil Papers, 35/fol. 16r; *HMCS*, v, 381–382.

I pray yow inform my Lo[rd] herof, declaryng that dyvers coming through the town, and hearyng hereof report this Trowghton to be of very lewd liff and conditions.

[Maynard's hand, on verso, p. 2 of letter]
By your letter yowe require to have the shedule of the proportion to be sent to yow that yowe might speake with Sir G[eorge] Carroe thearof, which I conceive to be the shedule for the Isle of man.[223] If yt be that, yowe shall finde thes letters and papers I had from him in my Chamber theare at Nonsuch in one of the packettes uppon the shelfe, wheare my other papers are.[224] Soe farre yowe well. ffrom my howse at Theobaldes the xiii[th] of September, 1595.

[Burghley's hand]
I mistok yesterday to have bene the xiii[th] so as this to have bene but 13 and to morrow the 14 my birth daye, the son entryng into to libra. God send yow to lyve so manny within which tyme manny accidentes shall happen reknown to all astrologers.[225]

Your loving father,

W. Burghley.

Dorse

ADDRESSED in Henry Maynard's hand:
To my Lovinge sonne Sir Robart Cecill knight one of hir ma[jes]ties privy connsell

ENDORSED in Simon Willis's hand:
3 Sept[ember] 1595
L[ord] Thre[asure]r to my M[aste]r

Letter No. 60

William, Lord Burghley to Sir Robert Cecil, 23 October 1595

⅓ p. Holograph.
Addressed, endorsed, signed.

---

[223]The Manx ordnance appears under Carew's ordnance account, TNA E351/2610, for which the accountant was Sir Simon Musgrave with Carew as deputy. Carew laboured to reform old abuses and stop new ones as they appeared in the office and accounts during this time. *HMCS*, v, 377.
[224]See above p. 18.
[225]See Letter No. 126.

Text

The 2 letters which I send yow from Holland[226] do gyve cawse for hir Ma[jes]ty to consent to that which this daye was spoken of with Caron which the sonar it shall be doone, the more comfortable will it be to our frendes.[227]

I am advertised from Depe that the D[uke] Nevers is dead but balloygne lyved and is used in service to besege la fere. Soyssons is rendred to the Kyng.[228]

23 Oct[ober] 1595.
On Saturday I hope to se hir Majesty, with a forright head.

Your lov[ing] father,

W. Burghley

Dorse

[226] Thomas Bodley alluded to these letters in a short letter of 22 Oct. to Burghley, an appendix to his much longer advertisement of 19 Oct. 1595. The two letters were from the States General of the United Provinces, who deputed Johan van Oldenbarnveldt to advise Bodley of their contents: they had been written to the Queen and Privy Council advising them of their intention of fulfilling their contract; of the necessity of taking measures should the Queen dissolve their treaty; and to ask the Queen for her patience in the event a shorter solution to their mutual difficulty might be reached. Hatfield, Cecil Papers, 35/87; *HMCS*, v, 428–429; Letter No. 58. Elizabeth reduced her Low Countries expenditures as far as possible. In 1595, 'upon the French, too, there was pressure for some repayment of debt, but the pressure was a good deal less upon them than upon the Dutch', Wernham, *After the Armada*, 557. Over the course of 1595 the Queen had relented on the Dutch repayments, partly out of fear of a Franco-Spanish peace and more significantly because Fuentes had attacked and taken Doullens, and was turning on Cambrai. Wernham, *Return of the Armadas: The Last Years of the Elizabethan War against Spain, 1595–1603* (Oxford, 1994), 34–36.

[227] George Gilpin's letter to the earl of Essex of 18 Oct. 1595 showed Caron's role: he was to return an answer as soon as he received the Queen's and Council's response to the two letters sent by the States General. Hatfield, Cecil Papers, 35/fol. 75r–v; *HMCS*, v, 420; Letter No. 48.

[228] Otywell Smyth informed Essex, 22 Oct. 1595, that he had received news from M d'Incarville at Amiens dated 18 Oct., noting that the duke of Nevers (Louis Gonzaga, 1539–1595) was dead, his arch-rival the duke of Bouillon had gone to Sedan, on his way to Henry IV's siege of La Fère; Arles, in Provence, had surrendered to the king. Hatfield, Cecil Papers, 172/82; *HMCS*, v, 429–430. Soissons, in Picardy, was ready to surrender in late 1594 having been under the duke of Mayenne's control for the League, Wernham, *After the Armada*, 520. Smyth reported to the earl of Essex on 24 July 1595 that the governor of Soissons had ejected the Spanish after Mayenne left by alerting them to 'Lutherans' within two leagues of the town, and when the Spaniards became aware of the ruse they were refused entry to the fortress without passports. *HMCS*, v, 288–289. The duke of Mayenne's accord was certain on 8 Sept., by Saldaigne's letter to Smyth of that date, but it was not yet publicly known. *HMCS*, v, 368.

ADDRESSED in Henry Maynard's hand:
To my Lovinge sonne Sir Rob[er]t
Cecill knight one of hir ma[jes]ties
prive Connsell

ENDORSED in the hand of another of Cecil's clerks:
L[ord] Tre[asure]r to my M[aste]r
[15]95 Octob[er].

Letter No. 61

William, Lord Burghley to Sir Robert Cecil, 7 October 1595

½ p. Holograph.
Addressed only.

Text

I do send to yow this included to be shewed to hir Ma[jes]ty wherof I can mak no comment the next being so barren. I praye yow remember the cawse of feagh Mc Hue who wold ether be stablished a good subjecte, or born with all, untill hir Majesty's forces may be spared to suppress hym.[229]

The attempt of Tho[mas] Lea,[230] in killng of them that brought Walter Reogh and his 3 brothers to ther end wold be sharply reformed, for els the lyk servie will not be performed.[231]

And yet I dowt of my l[ord] deputies intention to reform it, thowgh the service which the Otooles that ar slayn was doone by his L[ord s] procurement.[232]

---

[229] For this ill-conceived plan, see Letter No. 51.

[230] Thomas Lea or Lee (1551–1601), *ODNB*, was a cousin of the Queen's Champion, Sir Henry Lee, who almost certainly commissioned the portrait of Lee as a kerne in 1594 by Marcus Gheeraerts the Younger. Lee was of dubious loyalty, and at this moment had accused Feagh O'Byrne (as it was spelled by him) of interfering in efforts to treat with Tyrone. He had returned to Ireland in Sept. 1595, and killed Kedagh MacPhelim Reagh, an act of deeply questionable legality attached to the Queen, which was here questioned by Sir Henry Harrington who arrested Lee. The two captains had a rivalry. In 1596 Lee accused Harrington of supporting O'Byrne, and preferred charges of treason against him, *CSPI 1596–1597*, 48, 304. Lee was executed at Tyburn for his role in the Essex rebellion.

[231] Throughout the years 1595–1596 Sir William Russell used Captain Thomas Lee to move against the O'Byrne chieftain. The petition of the O'Byrnes and the O'Toole's, *CSPI 1592–1596*, 329.

[232] Russell had encouraged Lee's efforts in this service.

Your lov[ing] father.

W. Burghley

Dorse

ADDRESSED in the hand of another of Burghley's clerks:
To my loving sonne Sir Robert Cecill

NO ENDORSEMENT

Letter No. 62

William, Lord Burghley to Sir Robert Cecil, 15 October 1595

⅓ p. Dictated to Henry Maynard.
Addressed, endorsed, signed.

Text

This Bearer Sir Edmund Uvedall, being as I thinke unkowen to yowe, is one whoe hath longe served hir Majestie both faithfullie and carefullie in his charge at Fflushing and in other services in the Lowe Contries.[233] And because I would have yowe to take knowledge of him and to give him your good word and speche to hir ma[jes]tie, that he maie have accesse to hir presence to kisse hir handes, I have made him the messinger heareof to yowe.[234]

Ffrom my howse in the Strand this xv^th of October 1595.
     I have been more beholdinge to this gentleman for his often writinge to mee, than to anie other.

---

[233] Sir William Uvdall or Uvedale had accounts long in arrears, which he then expected confidently to have remitted, as Sir Robert Sidney's deputy as governor of Flushing. Sidney expected his deputy's return with confidential letters in mid Nov. 1595, *HMCS*, v, 450. He suggested to Essex that if Uvedale was not returning another Flushing officer, Captain William Brown (or Broune), might be a suitable replacement (he had been an officer there since 1587 and would get command in 1598).

[234] Uvedale's information might be taken as indicative of the Cecils' discontent with Sir Robert Sidney's pointed criticisms of the Queen's policies in her cautionary towns. Hatfield, Cecil Papers, 35/fol. 105r; *HMCS*, v, 440–442. Sidney was willing to share intelligence matters with Burghley as they touched the safety of the realm. Hatfield, Cecil Papers, 20/fol. 79r; *HMCS*, v, 453–454. See Letter No. 63 for the necessity of assisting the cautionary towns.

At your next writinge hither, I pray yowe send mee Sir Walter Raleigh's Journall.[235]

Your loving father,

W. Burghley

Letter No. 63

William, Lord Burghley to Sir Robert Cecil, 18 October 1595

½ p. Holograph.
Addressed, endorsed, signed.

Text

I send to yow, these included from Mr. Bodely, to be shewed to hir Ma[jes]ty.[236] herby is to be sene what harm, the french kyng[s] reconcilment with such dishonorable and servill conditions, is lyk to work in the world.[237] but I most feare, the intent of the princes of the Empyre, that ar purposed to propownd codicions of peace to a people

[235]Burghley refers to Raleigh's *The Discovery of Guiana*, and the author himself wrote to Cecil, in a state of dejection, in Nov. 1595, inquiring 'What becomes of Guiana I much desire to hear, whether it pass for a history or fable', even as he offered less comforting news of Spanish naval preparations. Hatfield, Cecil Papers, 36/fol. 4r; *HMCS*, v, 444–445. Raleigh was at great pains to convince Cecil of the truth of his writing, and of the worth of the 'image' he had sent Cecil. He stressed the need to act quickly before the Spanish and French made their way to conquer the territory. Hatfield, Cecil Papers, 36/fol. 9r; *HMCS*, v, 457–458; *The Discovery of the Large, Rich, and Beautiful Empire of Guiana, with a relation of the great and Golden Citie of Manoa (which the Spaniards call El Dorado)* . . . (London, 1596; facs. edn, Menston, 1967), sig Ir. In the event of a Spanish invasion, Raleigh's work may have appeared extremely far-fetched as a solution. See Letter No. 69. Since the capture of the carrack *Madre di Dios* (original Portuguese name *Madre de Deus*) in 1592, Raleigh had been well disposed to Cecil and would remain so, but Burghley remained suspicious of him.

[236]The enclosure may have been Sir Robert Sidney's letter to Burghley of 13 Oct. 1595, received approximately 18 Oct. outlining these shortages. TNA SP 84/51/fol. 190r–192r; Hatfield, Cecil Papers, 20/48; *HMCS*, v, 409–412. The cover letter to Essex is of interest because it specifies the States General's difficulties over their treaties with the Imperial princes, *HMCS*, v, 408–409.

[237]Sidney felt that the Queen's refusal to assist Henry IV had created a situation whereby France would have to seek peace with Spain on conditions dictated by the enemy. *HMCS*, v, 409. Anglo-French diplomatic relations were now at stalemate during Lomenie's disastrous embassy from Henry IV charging the Queen with negligence in refusing to assist in the relief of Calais, charges the Queen refuted vigorously in Oct. 1595, following the ambassador's return to France, TNA SP 78/36/fols. 52r–54r.

wearyed of war, will worke a revolt.[238] Specially the tyme being now taken, when the Ennemy doth prosper and the States with ther forces, have decayd all this yere.[239]

The Eventes hereof ar only in God's disposition. 18 8bre [October] 1595.

Your loving father,

W. Burghley

[Postscript] It is here sayd that Mr. Vicecham[er]lien is half dead. God Bless his sowle[240]

Dorse

ADDRESSED in Henry Maynard's hand:
To my Lovinge Sonne Sir Robert Cecill knight hir ma[jes]ties privy Connsell

[238] The conditions of the cautionary towns, and the scarcity of supply, led Sidney to suspect that they would succumb to revolt if any diplomatic shift moved their control out of English hands and her servants would have to look to their adversaries for succour. *HMCS*, v, 411. Bodley's letter of 19 Oct. showed that deputies of the States were aggrieved at noting that the Chamber of Imperial deputies at Speyer had appointed commissioners for discussion at Cologne and Frankfurt. This was a delaying tactic while the Archduke Albert was awaited. Hatfield, Cecil Papers, 35/77; *HMCS*, v, 421–424. The princes charged with negotiating a Franco-Spanish peace were named in Thomas Bodley's dispatch of 26 Nov.: the elector of Mainz and the archbishop of Salzburg were to be included, *HMCS*, v, 471. Giovanni Baptista Taxis had plans for the Spanish to double-cross the French, as was made clear in his letter intercepted in the Mediterranean on their way from Austria to Spain, ibid.
[239] The decay of the forces in the cautionary towns did present diplomatic difficulties. On 21 Sept. 1595 Cecil had instructed Sidney to look to the States General for supply of his munitions and powder, although the States had never made such a grant. TNA SP 84/51/fol. 159r. The situation worsened, partly because Bodley's embassy to the States had not found success in the matter of the 1585 treaty of Nonsuch's terms, obliging them to assist England in their times of need. Furthermore, by Oct. 1595 Sidney had still not received supply of victualling and other provisions (*L&A*, vi, Analysis no. 81). In Nov. 1595 the Queen informed the States General that she had withdrawn her shipping from the cautionary towns for defence of her realm, TNA SP 84/51/fol. 246r–v. Burghley's financial plans for readiness in the face of Spanish invasion, drawn up in Sept. and Oct. 1595, urged the furnishing of ships for the cautionary towns as in 1588, TNA SP 63/182/fol. 243v.
    A Cecil agent told another story: that the Spanish troops were near to mutiny, and tales of English fears told by exiled English Catholics were worthless for such fear 'is of your own shadow'. *HMCS*, v, 433, 457.
[240] Sir Thomas Heneage (1532–1595), *ODNB*, vice-chamberlain of the chamber and chancellor of the Duchy of Lancaster was gravely ill, and died. He had worked very closely with the Cecils in intelligence. A pluralist of note, his many offices came vacant, and much patronage angling ensued. The official Council record of his passing excludes the actual date of demise, *APC 1595–1596*, 4.

ENDORSED by Simon Willis:
18 Oct[ober] 1595
L[ord] Thre[asure]r to my M[aste]r

Letter No. 64

William, Lord Burghley to Sir Robert Cecil, 10 October 1595

1 p. Holograph.
Dorse missing, signed.

Text

Robert Cecill ther ar sondry matters of hir Ma[jes]ty, that have latly
^{bene} treated of ther, but I thynk not put in due exection. and of twoo
extremities I had rather to be busy, than to neglect.

The matter of Milford Haven hath had some stay uppon the opinion
of the Erl of Pemb[roke] comming to hir Ma[jes]ty, which being
uncerten may bryng dannger consideryng all comen reportes from
spayne mak mention of the Haven.²⁴¹

Secondly all the provisions for the ordonnance have ben set down,
but no special direction how to have the same provuded specially for
powder, saltpeter nor mach. all which ar to be bought beyond seas,
Wher I here the prises do arise, and yet I have bene diligent, to thynk
of good meanes, but without the allowance of the LLs [Lords] that
have to doo therin I dare not propownd my opinion. But than also hir
Ma[jes]ty is to disburss a great some of monny, wherin I cannot be so
forward as others.²⁴²

The matter for a staple of vittelles for the army and navy this next
spryng, requireth some conference lest therby prises of vittells might

---

²⁴¹The Privy Council was united on the necessity of fortifying Milford Haven, *CSPD 1595–
1597*, 103; Birch, *Memoirs*, ii, 292–294, shows the appointment of additional deputies to the
lord lieutenant, the earl of Pembroke, for the Welsh counties, as given in the schedule sent by
the Council to the lord keeper, Puckering, for enrolment at the Great Seal, *APC 1595–1596*,
14, 17–18.
²⁴²The provisions for Milford Haven were not addressed specifically in the general Council
notes on business, but a list of provisions in Henry Maynard's hand mentions prices of
saltpetre; ordnance; and naval, chamber, and household expenditures, TNA SP 12/254/nos.
63, 64; *CSPD 1595–1597*, 153. A conference on the role of Milford Haven was intended to
resolve the use of forces in south-west Wales with Pembroke's objections, ibid. 129–130.
Burghley mentioned Milford Haven in a list of general notes, a memorial, on Irish borders
and coastal defences. TNA SP 12/254/no. 49; see Letter No. 69.

increass, and monny also to be had for the same now at Hallowmas
as my L[ord] Admyrall I thynk can best consider therof.[243]

I am both sorry and sore greved that I can not indur the paynes to
come thyther, which maketh me thus bold to will yow to informe hr
Majesty hereof.

10 Octob[er] 1595

Your lov[ing] fath[er],

W. Burghley

Letter No. 65

William, Lord Burghley to Sir Robert Cecil, 6 October 1595

[Burghley has dated 3 October in the text of the letter].
1½ pp. Dictated to Henry Maynard.
Addressed, endorsed. Not signed, but sealed with Burghley's own seal,
now missing.

Text

Thowgh I am not hable to write, yet I am not nor meane not to
be careles of hir Majestie's affayres, as I hope shall appear at my
retorne, if God shall please to inhable mee thearof, from the which at
this part I am thorowgh great torment of paine and other infirmities
discowraged. And yet I strained my self to be at this date at the
Checqhuer with the l[ord] keper and Justices for nominacion of
men to be sheriffes this next yeare, findinge great lack of Martiall
men, thowgh other wise hable for wealthe and knowledge: And so
retorninge forthwith to my howse I am Laide downe with great paine
not being hable to sitt up: and for the present having receive certaine
knowledge of great quantitie of powder and other municion intended
to be shepped from Hamborowgh ^{which is to passe in 14 sortes of shippes} for
the K[ing] of Spaine, and the same to be carried by Longe seas
above Scotland and Ireland, not knowinge how to have it intercepted

---

[243]Victualling the troops for the following spring may have referred to the nascent Cadiz
plans to have 12,000 men at sea by the following spring, TNA SP 12/254/no. 53; *CSPD
1595–7*, 121. Further to these designs, estimates were made on shipbuilding, *CSPD 1595–7*,
109, 112, 119. As for victualling, this too was plagued by the high price of grain, TNA SP
12/254/no. 10; *CSPD 1595–7*, 107.

otherwise than by direccion of the K[ing] of Scottes to his llandes of Orcany, wheare the said shippinge must neades passe.[244] I have intred onto consideracion howe the k[ing] might be stirred upp ernestlye to impeache both this and other the like[245] with Municion or graine for the king of Spaine's purpose to sett a foote A title for himself and his dawghter to the present succession to the Crowne of England, which doth appear manifestlye by a seditious Booke[246] published for the said K[ing] by a Nomber of Englishe Rebells residinge in Spaine, by which booke it is maintained that kingdoms are at the disposition of the people withowt regard of right by Blood and sucession; and to be preferred to that for their greatnes are most hable to Governe Contries. And consequentlie the Awthors of thes Bookes have manifestlie improved anie title that the k[ing] of Scottse might pretend; and in like manner disprovinge all other pretended titles onelie preferring the k[ing] of Spaine wither himself or his eldest dawghter Bretaigne, which Booke hath manie other Tirannous[247]

[244] Intelligence concerning the shipment of Hamburg cargo by way of the Orkneys: see Letter No. 69.

[245] Burghley refers to James VI's reluctance to prosecute his rebellious Catholic nobility. As for stirring the King, Roger Aston reported to the English ambassador Bowes on 28 Nov. 1595 that James VI had resolved absolutely to fight the Spanish, in Scotland and in England. This might have implied sending mercenaries or others into Ireland, *CSPS 1595–1597*, xxi, 66–67.

[246] The king of Spain is here blamed for *The Conference on the Succession to the Crown of England*. It was attributed to Father Dolman, and written by Father Robert Persons in Rome, a close adviser to Cardinal William Allen (d.1595). Rumour was rife in Spain that Queen Elizabeth's health was failing and, consequently, action after her death must be swift if the king of Spain's Scottish and English subjects were to affect their own gains. See the dispatch of the Venetian ambassador in Spain, Augustino Nani, of 23 Sept. 1595, *Calendar of State Papers and Manuscripts, Existing in the Archives and Collections of Venice and other Libraries of Northern Italy*, Vol. IX, ed. Horatio F. Brown (London, 1897), 167. A letter called 'A Jesuit to—' in the State Papers gives a fictitious and detailed account of plans for the subversion of the English crown. The notorious agent John Cecil, alias Snowden, described the book to Cecil in late Dec. 1595 as 'a dialoge betwene a civilian and comen lawer towchinge the succession'. TNA SP 12/255/no. 22.

Roger Aston further informed the ambassador Bowes on 16 Dec. that an English translation had recently arrived from Antwerp. The author excludes all those in the succession save the Derbys and the infanta of Spain by right of her title to Brittany, *CSPS 1595–1597*, 93. An Italian treatise of that year discussed James's inviolate claim to England, even though he was born outside that kingdom, while urging him to establish Catholicism in Scotland, although Henry VIII's Act of Succession is not mentioned, *CSPS 1595–1597*, 104–111. John Carey sent Burghley a long report on the *Conference* noting the 'King meaneth to answer' the text with the aid of civil lawyers and other experts. Shipping had been forced into the Orkneys as of 1 Feb. 1596, *Cal. Border Papers*, ii, 102–104.

[247] Tyranny used here to describe succession by conquest, or the right of a people to determine by force their own rulers, manifestly contravenes what Burghley calls the orderly succession of crowns and owes something to French Protestant 'resistance' theory of a kind obliquely employed by the Cecils in their secret policies against James VI of Scotland

determinacions against all ordinary sucessions of Crownes, and is nowe spetiallye published

[p. 2] to prepare the corruption of mens mindes that are spetially for poperie addicted to the k[ing] of Spaine, against the time of his intnded invasion, Which owt of Spaine is generallie threatened. And uppon thes consideracions: consideringe otherwise the Book is likely to comm to the knowledge of the k[ing] of Scottes, I wishe it weare nowe afore hand, sent to him by order of hir ma[jes]ty hearbie to move him to take hart to him against the k[ing] of Spaines tirannous practizes, and particularlye at this time to require him to geve order to the hand as in the Northe part of his Realme, and namelye the iles of Orkencis to staye all shippinge that shall comm uppon ther coastes with anie municion or graine to passe from theare Northward abowt Ireland whearein the k[ing] maie eiselie offend the k[ing] of Spaine, and the lak to himself the benefitt of all such shippinge municions and victuells.[248] This my conceipt I praie yowe impart to hir ma[jes]tie with the more speed to impeache thes Navigations intended for Spaine: The consideracion whearof notwithstanding I leave to hir Majestie's ludgement.[249] And so beinge desirous more for hir ma[jes]ties service, than for my privat condicion to be restored to somm better strength and ease of my Bodye. I ende from my howse in the Strand this third of October 1595.

Subscribed with my seale for want of a right hand.
[Seal mark: missing, with impression left]

Dorse

ADDRESSED in Henry Maynard's hand:
To my Lovinge sonne Sir Robert Cecill knight one of her ma[jes]ties privy Consill

through the earl of Bothwell in 1594. See also Burghley to Cecil, 14 Oct. 1595, TNA SP 12/254/no. 26.

[248] According to his instructions of Feb. 1596, Bowes was to present James VI with a copy of *The Conference*; the first time the book appears to have been brought into diplomatic discussion. Cecil had Bowes's instructions copied by Willis into his Scottish Letter Book, TNA SP 52/52/pp. 111–114. The interrogation of one Father Thomas Wright by the Privy Council mentioned Persons in no. 14 of the questions, TNA SP 12/255/no. 22; *CSPD 1595–1597*, 156–7.

[249] Order by the Queen to impeach navigation intended for Spain touched negotiations with the Hanse cities, of which Hamburg was principal. Dr Christopher Parkins was to be informed of any innovation or interdiction on shipping, TNA SP 12/254/no. 28, 36; *CSPD 1595–1597*, 115, 117.

ENDORSED 3 November 1595
L[ord] Thre[asure]r to my M[aste]r
[A further page, seal removed following the dorse bears Sir Robert Cecil's hand]
My l. about provisions
[No date]

Letter No. 66

William, Lord Burghley to Sir Robert Cecil, 7 December 1595

1 p. Holograph.
Addressed, endorsed, signed.

Text

The berors herof, ar. ii of the Senior fellows of St. Jhons Colledg
in cambridg, who brought me the l[ette]re included syned by 23
of the company which yow may read, and therby the caws of ther
wrytyng ^{to me} as being the Chancellor of ye university may appeare
very reasonable and just, which is to suffer and help the Colledg,
according to ther statutes to have liberty to mak a free chois of a
Master, without being impeached, as the Statutes confirmed by hir
Ma[jes]ty do warrant, or any inhibition or pression by any superior
power.[250] This ther manner of Election hath bene allweiss used, and
is most convenient for concord, and to avoid factions.[251] my request is
that yf ye shall fynd any intention in hir Ma[jes]ty upon any sinister
sute, to prefer any on other than the voyces of the Company shall frely
choose,[252] to besech hir Ma[jes]ty, that at my sute being ther Chancellor,
and havyng bene wholly brought up ^{ther} from my age of xiiii yers, and
now the only person lyving of the tyme and education, the Statutes
of the Colledg to which all that ar electors ar sworn, may not be now
broken, as I hope hir Ma[jes]ty will not in hir honor and conscience
^{do}. I my self have no purposs therin beyng a poore benefactor of the
Colledg for the which I have assured landes, to increass the Comens of

---

[250]Burghley forwarded the petitions of the 23 fellows to Cecil for presentation in which
they cited precedents for *libera electio*, BL Lansdowne MS 79/no. 62, fols. 156r–v, 170r; see
above, p. 42.

[251]Factions had already formed, Peter Lake, *Moderate Puritans and the Elizabethan Church*
(Cambridge, 1982), 197.

[252]John Whitgift, archbishop of Canterbury (1530/31?–1604), *ODNB*. Cecil was only to
present the fellows' dissenting petition, should the Queen give weight to outside suitors.
Whitgift, used Sir William Cornwallis to inform Cecil that he and Roger Manners supported
Laurence Stanton. Hatfield, Cecil Papers, 36/fol. 79r, 83r; *HMCS*, v, 497, 498.

the scollars, from iid to xiid a weke, and so hath your mother also gyven a benefitt of propertie.[253] If hir Ma[jes]ty should be privatly or otherwise moved I pray yow offer hir the letter to be redd from the fellows.

[In the margin]
This fowle wether holdeth me back, from comfort of recovery ffrom my howss. 7 10 br 1595

Your loving father,

W. Burghley

Dorse

ADDRESSED
[Date obscured]
L[ord] Thre[asure]r to my M[aste]r
lls [Letters] from the ffellows of
St. Jhon's Colledg in Cambridg

ENDORSED in Simon Willis's hand:
To my Varie Lovinge Sonne Sir Robert Cecill Knyght of her Ma[jes]ties privy Counsell

Letter No. 67

William, Lord Burghley to Sir Robert Cecil, 7 December 1595

⅓ p. Holograph,
Addressed, endorsed, signed.

Text

I send yow by this bearer Peter boon, Edmondes letter which yow may receave.[254] by my titles in the Margyn I have red wishyng that hir Ma[jes]ty wold spedely send hir Ambass[ador] to the Kyng,[255] to

---

[253] Neither Lord nor Lady Burghley endowed the College with gifts of land, but maintained commons and other gifts there out of income. It appears from Burghley's will that no further provisions of rent charges for maintenance of the College was intended, TNA PCC PROB Lewyn 92, 11.

[254] Sir Edmund Uvedale's letter to the Queen of 7 Dec. 1595: not extant.

[255] Cecil drafted documents for Unton's instructions. His complete diplomatic instructions were corrected in both Cecils' hands. Unton's passport was issued on 21 Dec. 1595. TNA SP 78/36/fols. 113r–114r, 119r–126r, 144r.

stey hym from violent courses, wherein I hope the Constable may do much good, to temper other furious actors.

Your loving father,

W. Burghley

[Beside the signature on the left side Burghley added] Of Necessite Edmondes wold be releved.[256]

Dorse

ADDRESSED [Date obscured in the margin, but] 7 Dec[ember] 1595
ENDORSED
L[ord] Thre[asure]r to my M[aste]r

Letter No. 68

William, Lord Burghley to Sir Robert Cecil, 6 December 1595

1 p. Holograph.
Addressed, endorsed, signed.

Text

I bethynk with my self of so manny thynges to mete to be considered by hir Ma[jes]ty, and by hir authoritie to hir Connsell for hir affaryes in respect of the noyss from Spayn,[257] as though I can not without conference with such connsellors as hir Ma[jes]ty shall pleass to name, do or furder such thynges to execution by my self yet I am willyng to come thyther to be neare hir Majesty though I am not hable to mak access to hir person, but of force, without more amendment in strength must presume to kepe my chamber, not as a potentat[258] but as

---

[256] Edmondes continued as *chargé d affaires*. Unton was to play on his personal friendship with Henry IV in drawing some sign from the King that he did not mean to establish peace with Spain. Bell, *Handlist*, 99; *L&A*, vi, Analysis no. 236, 179–181.

[257] News of massive Spanish preparations against England, *L&A*, vi, Analysis no. 308. English propaganda was somewhat successful at this juncture in containing the seriousness of the Irish situation, by calling attention to the earl of Tyrone's truce, TNA SP 101/95/fols. 160r–161r. A general muster had taken place. The Queen had viewed some of her coastal defences in person, *L&A*, vi, Analysis no. 308. To compound anxieties came the news of massive naval and troop movements in Flanders. Hatfield, Cecil Papers, 36/fol. 52r; *HMCS*, v, 484; Letter No. 69.

[258] Burghley may have intended a secret slight at Essex who did keep to his chamber during times of political disfavour. Cecil and Essex now conferred on Scottish secret diplomacy.

an Impotant, aged man, nether yet as a bankrupt, but as a respondent to any action or demand. and if by ^{your} speche with hir Ma[jes]ty, she will not mislyke to have ^{so} a bold person to lodg in hir howss I will come as I am, in body not half a man, but in mynd passable to the master of the rest of my good Lordes hir Ma[jes[tys Counsellors and my good friends.

God gyve yowe his grace, to ask his grace faythfully to serve hir Ma[jes]ty, and to respect non but for hir and for hir Justyce.

6 10bre [December] 1595.

Your loving fath[er],

W. Burghley

[Burghley adds at the left foot of the letter]
Upon your answer, I will mak no unecesary delay, by God's permission.

Dorse

ADDRESSED Holograph:
To my loving son Sir
Robart Cecill knight
of hir Ma[jes]ty's prive Connsell

ENDORSED in Simon Willis's hand:
6 Dec[ember] 1595
L[ord] Thre[asure]r to my Maste]r

Letter No. 69

William, Lord Burghley to Sir Robert Cecil, 6 December 1595

1 p. Holograph.
Addressed, endorsed, signed.

HMCS, v, 485; Letters Nos 69 and 70. The consensus of the Privy Council was for fortification of the realm, while some of Essex's French correspondents appeared to expect his imminent arrival with large numbers of troops to help the French king raise La Fère. Hatfield, Cecil Papers, 172/ 123; *HMCS*, v, 481. One account makes clear that Essex was to relieve Calais and he had made himself champion of the Low Countries forces at this awkward time, *HMCS*, v, 483, 485–486.

Text

I am very glad to perceave of hir Ma[jes]ty's favorable permission for my absence, and I thank you for your advise for the manner of my coming. Thynk you would expect my coming this daye, but ther sight would be dymmned with the snow. I retorn Ashton's letter, wherin manny good thynges ar well advertised, and I thynk Mr. Bowes presence necessary ther.[259]

6 10bre [December] 1595

Your lov[ing] fath[er],

W. Burghley

Dorse

ADDRESSED in Henry Maynard's hand:
To my verie Loving sonne Sir Robert Cecill knight of hir ma[jes]ties privy Consell

ENDORSED in Simon Willis hand:
6 Dec[ember] 1595
L[ord] Thre[asure]r to my M[aste]r

Letter No. 70

William, Lord Burghley to Robert Devereux, Earl of Essex, 5 December 1595

1 p. Holograph.
Addressed, endorsed, signed.

Text

My very good Lord I have perused the l[ette]res which you sent me. Ye first from the Justices with an examination of the party that cam

---

[259] Roger Aston's letter was sent to Robert Cecil from Robert Bowes from Edinburgh on 26 Nov. and received in London 4 Dec., *CSPS 1595–1597*, 66–69. He sent news of a two-pronged Spanish campaign, into Scotland and to Milford Haven. James VI's musters proceeded apace. The agent Gilbert Lamb's report, as here relayed, on Philip II's designs on the English throne were related to Person's *Conference*, suggested that Philip II's designs were known rather widely in intelligence circles to be set on Scotland and Milford Haven.

from britayn.[260] the second a letter from on Mak Cadell[261] an Irishman
servyng in Britayn to Sir Jhon Norriss.[262]

And in dede I thynk the party examyned hath sayd truth for I
now that when Sir John Norrice was in Briten, this blak[263] gaven hym
Intelligences, and promised Sir Jhon Norrice at his coming thence
so to contynew and I now he hath a brother in Gallywey whom I
discovered to be trafficquar with Spanyardes, wheruppon I advertised
Sir Rich[ard] byngham.[264] and now in my opinion Blakes letter to Sir
Jhon Norryce, is to small purpose to be yelded to, for he wold have a
ship furnished, but how or by what Collur he should have a shipp or
what assurance ther is that he wold do service therat to hir Ma[jes]ty
I see not, but an Irishman's word.

but for the letter I se no cause until may be sent Sir Jhon Norreyce,
who may comment more than I can and so praying yowr L[ordship]

[260]The examination of persons out of Brittany followed the successful English capture
of Fort Crozon from the Spanish. Most of the Spanish garrison were slaughtered almost
to a man, Wernham, *After the Armada*, 551. Norris's forces were summoned from Brittany
for deployment. Intelligence connections in these troops were notable for their usefulness
in Irish matters. See the explanation of Piers O'Cullen, TNA SP 63/no 71, VIII; *CSPI
1592–1596, 409–410.*

[261]TNA SP 63/189/no. 22 fol. 48r–v were reports from the mayor of Galway Mark
Linch receiving intelligence from James Black (Caddell). Black was the spy Burghley
refers to here. These Spanish-Irish connections are also linked to Letter No. 15,
because Cecil appears to have extended his intelligence through agents used in the
depositions taken at the time of the *Madre di Dios* done with his father's approval.
HMCS, iv, 409; BL Additional MS 48029, fols. 170v, 180v; TNA SP 94/4 (i)/fol. 33r. For
further intelligence: *HMCS*, v, 274. Caddell may well have been O'Donnell's assassin in
1607.

[262]Caddell appears on a list of all Irish priests in the Low Countries by the spy Thomas
Finglas, TNA SP 63/173/no. 18. Finglas noted Breton and Norman priests sailed directly
from St Malo or Calais to Ireland if winds were favourable. Finglas also noted the
names of dangerous Irishmen in the service of the duke of Mercoeur, including one
Cadell, alias, [James] Blake [or Black], in Brittany. Blake was a Galway merchant who
had enjoyed extensive favour with Lanco de Leyva since the Armada; Leyva paid Blake
for news. Leyva was attached to the house of the Prince of Ascoli. Further, Blake was
to recruit Irish into Philip II's service. The current use of Cadell was verified by a
priest, Piers O'Cullen, see n. 261, who claimed the intelligence links with Tyrone had
collapsed.

[263]Blake's brother Robert was arrested by Mark Linch, mayor of Limerick, in May 1596
on suspicion of fomenting pro-Spanish designs, *CSPI 1592–1596*, 518, 520, 524, 527, 528, 533.
These papers chart a very shadowy course with both Blakes. Spanish agents circled around
Tyrone and O'Donnell. Apparently, Blake was outfitted with a ship, for after Robert Blake's
arrest, the mayor asked Russell for final direction for the release of the poor Frenchman and
the ship that brought James Blake over. Sir Francis Godolphin told the earl of Essex in July
1595 of his suspicion of Cadell's desire to serve the Queen. *CSPI 1592–1596*, 527; *HMCS*, v,
274.

[264]Burghley to Bingham not extant.

to extend the sight of both your eies, to redes this staggeryng letter with a weak hand. [265]

5 Dec[ember] 1595, at your L[ord]'s Commandment

W. Burghley

Dorse

ADDRESSED in Henry Maynard's hand:
To the R[ight] honorable my vearie good L[ord] the Erle
of Essex one of the lls [Lords] of his ma[jes]ties prive Connsell

ENDORSED in Simon Willis's hand:
5 Dec 1595
L. Threr to the Erle of Essex

Letter No. 71

William, Lord Burghley to Sir Robert Cecil, 2 December 1595

½ p. Dictated to Henry Maynard, with one sentence added, the date and signature by Burghley's hand.
Addressed, endorsed, signed.

Text

By your letter Emongest other thinges yowe write, that by direcions of the lls [Lords] l[ette]res wherof yowe have sent mee the Copie, theare hath bene summ iniurie done to one Mr. Machell, Capteine of the horse in Midlesex, and that the same is done by omission by the Clerkes, which yowe would have remedied by my direcion to them.[266] But perusinge the Copie of the letter written by Mr. Waad whearunto my hand is not subscribed, I finde not anie thinge in the letter, neither doe I finde, thowgh he weare a Capteine of the horsemen, whie he should be named nowe than other Justices of the

---

[265]Essex's interest in Scottish secret policy connected to the news of Spanish naval designs on Milford Haven and Scotland. Essex and Norris clashed over the nomination captains for Irish companies which reached a climax in Oct. 1595, *HMCS,* v 413–414; *CSPI 1592–1596,* 474. Russell's reduction of the companies earlier that year contrasted with the ten new companies raised out of the shires which were to be mixed with the Brittany forces returning which needed new captains.

[266]Machell's slight was noted on the dorse of the muster list by Cecil after his omission. TNA SP 12/254/no. 60; *CSPD 1595–1597,* 124–125.

peace within Middlesex, wheare theare be divers others that are not named spetiallie by the letter whoe may thinke themselves asmuch iniured as Machell.[267] and thearefore I doe not knowe what your meaninge is howe to have this remedied, otherwise than to have a newe letter from the Connsell whearein Machell maie be named, if he be thowght so fitt, to be putt in trust, for thowgh he be A Capteine of horsemenn, yet it is not a Consequence to make him as yt were a deputie to a Lieutentante.

[Burghley adds]
As to the rest of your letter I will expect the Q[ueen's] resolutions.

2 10[bre] [December] 1595

Your lov[ing] father,

W. Burghley

Dorse

ADDRESSED in Henry Maynard's hand:
To my Lovinge sonne Sir
Rob[er]t Cecill knight one
of hir ma[jes]ties privie Connsell

ENDORSED by Simon Willis:
2 Dec[ember] 1595
L[ord] Thre[asure]r to my M[aste]r Concerning Mr. Machell

Letter No. 72

Lords of the Privy Council to Sir Robert Cecil, 2 December 1595

½ p. In Henry Maynard's hand, Privy Council letter subscribed by three of the Lords of the Privy Council.
Addressed, endorsed, signed.
[Duchy of Lancaster under commission]

---

[267] The manuscript was written by Sir William Waad (1546–1623), *ODNB*, clerk of the council, and presumably the final list was corrected. Waad is scarcely mentioned in the letters in CUL MS Ee 3.56, but he was a highly experienced council servant and diplomat who aided Cecil, Parkins and Burghley when necessary. He was probably one of the persons most able to locate and summarize documents.

Text

After our hartie Commendacions. Wheareas yt pleased the Queen's ma[jes]tie to grawnt to Sir Thomas Wilkes a lease in reversion of somuch of hir mannors and Landes as shall accommt to the yearelie vallewe of one hundred markes £33. 6s. 8d., wheareof the the one moitie to be of Landes within the Surveie of hir duchie wheareuppon we have seen particulirs which have been vewed by the Attornie of the duchie,[268] which wee thowght convenient to passe to him, but inasmuch as wee have noe warrant to cawse the booke to be drawen upp, the warrant for the duchie havinge been directed to Mr. Chancellor decesseds we thearefore praye yowe to move hir ma[jes]tie hearein, that if yt be hir good plesure wee maie have hir warrant to proceade in the same book as Mr. Chancellor might have done if he had lived, otherwise the same will cawse a stoppe in the proceadinge with Sir Thomas Wilkes grawnt, whereof he hath little neade. Soe farre yowe well. ffrom Westm[inste]r this second of december 1595.
Your vearie Lovinge frendes,

[Signed]

W. Burghley
T. Buckhurst
J. Fortescue

Dorse

ADDRESSED in Henry Maynard's hand:
To our vearie Loving frend
Sir Rob[er]t Cecill knight
one of hir Majesites privie Counsell

ENDORSED in Simon Willis's hand:
2 Decem[ber] 1595
L[ord] Thre[asure]r to my M[aste]r
L[ord] Bouckhurst
Sir Jo[hn] Ffortescue
Warrant for Sir Tho[mas] Wylkes

---

[268] One of two Privy Council letters in CUL MS Ee.3.56. Wilkes asked Cecil to further his poor bill in Jan. 1596, for the parties were to leave London at the end of Hilary term. *HMCS*, vi, 41.

Letter No. 73

William, Lord Burghley to Sir Robert Cecil, 2 December 1595

1 p. Holograph.
Addressed, endorsed, signed.

Text

I have red your letter, wherby I perceave yow have red and shewed my letter of my hand wrytyng to hir Ma[jes]ty who sayeth that she will have a battell with my fyngars and than afor hand I know who ^{shall} have the victory by the battel, for I have no warrant for my fyngars. but hir Ma[jes]ty is allowed to saye as kyng David sayth in the i C xliiii psalme, as the same was repeated the 30 of the last month: Benedictus Dominus Deus meus, qui docet manus meas ad prœlium et digitos meos ad bellum.²⁶⁹ and in his next vers [verse] he addeth that which properly belongeth to hir Ma[jes]ty: refugium meum, susceptor meas, et libertator meus, protector meus, et in ipso speravi, qui subdit populum meum sub me.²⁷⁰ and if hir ^{Ma[jes]ty's} handes or fyngars evar to fight, I durst ~~hir~~ Match hir with king philip and overmatch hym. This yowe see that I can not spare my fyngars, wher my hart is fully contented to utter my opinion of hir estate and vallew.

I am glad that hir Ma[jes]ty is disposed to send some monny into Irland wherof suerly there is great want a matter dangerous to be known to [the] rebells is [whose] yeldyng hath grown only, by sight of hir Ma[jes]ty's forces. I send yow a form for a warrant wherin hir Ma[jes]ty may do well, to allow some good rownd some, or otherwise she must be must be shortly pressed for more. for the dett ther is allredy great and untill the rebells submission be perfected,²⁷¹ hir forces may not be deminished.

---

²⁶⁹Burghley used the Geneva Bible, 1560. Psalm 144, Verse One: 'Blessed be the Lord my strength, which teacheth my hands to fight and my fingers to battel.'

²⁷⁰Psalm 144:2, 'He is my goodness & my fortress, my tower and my deliverer, my shield, and in him I trust, which subdueth my people vnder me.'

²⁷¹Notes on the Cecil's drafts of the rebels' submission: see Letter No. 7. There was to be no perfection of the rebels' submission. Russell's letter to Cecil on 26 Jan. 1596 discussed new demands for religious toleration, not unlike the demands the English made with the Brittany Protestants. TNA SP 63/186/no. 24, fol. 91r; Letter No. 75. In late Dec. 1595, the Queen sent more specific additions concerning Tyrone's submission, in view of her dislike of having to replenish her dwindling Irish forces with money and supply. TNA SP 63/185/no. 38, fol. 162r.

I wish such as nevill and waynman, war ether in some other prison, or not at liberty in the towre, wher now with a spark of fyre, they may secretly disarm the Q[ueen] of all hir powdre and armor pieces.[272]

[In the lower left margin]
2 10bre [December] 1595

Your loving father,

W. Burghley

Dorse

ADDRESSED in Henry Maynard's hand:
To my Lovinge sonne
Sir Rob[er]t Cecill knight
one of hir ma[jes]ties privie
Connsell

ENDORSED in Simon Willis hand:
2 Dec[ember] 1595
L[ord] Thre[asure]r to my M[aste]r

Letter No. 74

William, Lord Burghley to Sir Robert Cecil, December 1595

¼ p. Holograph.
Addressed, endorsed, signed.

---

[272] Burghley's concern in keeping Sir Edmund Nevyl [Neville] de Latimer (1555–1636) and Captain Waynman under closer watch away from the Tower derived from the revelation that Sir Michael Blount, lieutenant of the Tower, was implicated by these men in a plot to blow up the Queen's ordnance kept there, a design it had taken months to discover. Blount's dismissal: TNA SP 12/254/no. 77; *HMCS*, v, 476. Latimer was related to Sir Thomas Cecil's wife, Dorothy, daughter and co-heiress of Lord Latimer, and opposed her claim to the estates of the 6th earl of Westmorland, attainted for treason. Lords Buckhurst and Cobham investigated Blount together with William Waad. Manning, 'The prosecution of Sir Michael Blount', 219. Both Waynman and Nevyl were allowed the liberty of the Tower, and their long-term residence there argues for their employment as Privy Council spies, BL Lansdowne MS 79/fol. 4r. Waynman apparently offered credibly received testimony against Sir Charles Danvers during his trial for murder in Feb. 1596. *HMCS*, vi, 69. On 23 Dec. he wrote to the Council that he had received word from Sir Thomas Wilkes that he was to be warranted by them to serve Henry IV or the Emperor Rudolf II, clearly in some sort of intelligence capacity. TNA SP 12/255/no. 16; Manning, 'The prosecution of Sir Michael Blount'.

Text

I send unto you my L[ord] of Essex letter and therewith a Copy of such a saveconduct as is required for octavio the venecian at the sute of Bassadonna[273] in which form of saveconduct, I have put owt certen wordes, unfitt in my opinion, and so yow may recommend it to hir Ma[jes]ty, if my L[ord] shall allow of my abridgment.

[On left side of the page Burghley has written]
p° [primo] x^{bre} [December]
ulet inceruam

[At the right foot of the letter]
Your loving father,

W. Burghley

Dorse

ADDRESSED in Henry Maynard's hand:
To my Lovinge sonne
Sir Rob[er]t Cecill knight
one of hir ma[jes]ties privie
Connsell
At the Cort

ENDORSED in Simon Willis's hand:
pr[imo] Dec[ember] 1595
Lo[rd] Thre[asure]r to my M[aste]r

---

[273]On 18 Aug. 1595 [N.S.] the Venetian Doge, Marino Grimani (89th Doge, 1532–1609, elected 1595), asked the Queen to return Octavio Negro to them for justice. Giovanni Bassadona was to supply details, which argues that Negro was involved closely in some sort of intelligence. On 13 Oct. 1595 [N.S.] the Doge warned that Negro was further implicated in the misappropriation of exports to England which defrauded the Venetian government in collusion with Michael Simanchi and Marco Cornaro. This letter gave notice of the Queen's decision to return Negro to Venice, presumably after some intercessions and explanations by Bassadona. *L&A*, vi, Analysis no. 362. Bassadona was involved in Essex's Italian intelligence, particularly developed to court allies for loyal English Catholics. For Bassadona's career and Essex's assistance giving details of bitter Venetian rivalries, in this case by one Ribera who brought the initial charge to the Doge, see Ungerer, *A Spaniard in Elizabethan England*, II, 174–182.

Letter No. 75

William, Lord Burghley to Sir Robert Cecil, 2 January 1595

½ p. Holograph.
Addressed, endorsed, signed.

Text

I am hartely sorry, that to begyn a new yere I can send yow no better news out of Irland than such as ar for them selves greatly to be mislyked, and for the sequels likely to follow, to brying great Dannger.

And so, I am grieved to Thynk that herby I am provoked to follow with the same, which I will do to morrow as soone as I can. And therfor I leave to yow the perusal and impartyng of these Irish bad letters to hir Ma[[jes]ty and the Connsell, conteaning matters of good consultation with expedition.[274]

2 Janu[ary] 1595

You lov[ing] fath[er],

W. Burghley

Dorse

ADDRESSED in Henry Maynard's hand:
To my Lovinge sonne Sir Robart Cecill
knight one of hir ma[jes]ties
privie Connsell

ENDORSED in Simon Willis's hand:
2 Jan[uary] 1595
L[ord] Thre[asure]r to ma M[aste]r

---

[274] The result of Cecil's presentation of these letters to the Queen was a scathing indictment of Russell's financial mismanagement in which Elizabeth warned her lord deputy that no amount of the recent treasure was to be squandered by Irish councillors on private patronage, a section added in Cecil's hand at the close of the letter, TNA SP 63/186/no. 6/fols. 14r–16r.

Letter No. 76

William, Lord Burghley to Sir Robert Cecil, 2 January 1595

⅓ p. Holograph.
Addressed, endorsed, signed.

Text

This fornoone I sent to yow, by the L [ord] deputes present the Irish letters conteaning no good thynges.

and so, I return to yow Sir Jhon Norrices letters wherby I see a manifest disiunction betwixt the L[ord] depute and hym. and in on part I note that Sir Jhon Norrice, was to bold to command the Companyes in the english pale for Wat[er]ford, with out assent of the deputie, for out of Monster he hath no sole authorite.[275]

I feare contynually evil desasters

post meridiem 2 Janu[ary]

Your lov[ing] fath[er],

W. Burghley

Dorse

ADDRESSED Holograph:
To my sonn Sir Robert Cecill
knight of hir Ma[jes]ty's prive
Connsell

ENDORSED in Simon Willis's hand:
2 Jan[uary] 1595
L[ord] Thre[aure]r to my M[aste]r

[275]Russell had his jurisdiction questioned by Norris in treating with the rebels. TNA SP 63/185/no 11, fol. 27r–v. Animosity between these men dated from the time of Norris's appointment. TNA SP 63/180/no. 9, fol. 43v; *CSPI 1592–1596*, 323–326. Russell had then borne the Queen's displeasure over the loss of the fort at Monaghan, on top of other charges of incompetence he was concerned to deny. TNA SP 63/185/fol. 31r, 186/no. 6, fols. 14r–16r. Essex apparently vilified Russell at every turn. *HMCD*, ii, 197–198. In Feb. 1596 Russell alluded to Sir John and Sir Thomas Norris's continued presence in Dublin, away from their respective charges in Ulster and Munster. TNA SP 63/186/fol. 196v; *CSPI 1592–1596*, 472. Russell and Sir John proceeded together in their campaign to Armagh in the summer of 1596.

Letter No. 77

William, Lord Burghley to Sir Robert Cecil, 26 January 1595

½ p. Holograph.
Addressed, endorsed, signed.

Text

I pray inform hir Ma[jes]ty, that Mr. Treasor hath bene with my L[ord] Kepar and me, and informed us of sondry misusages of the marchantes of St. Mallos, abowt the ordonnances whereof the informacion is that it was carryed unlawfuly owt of the realm, but the proves thereof he had not redy to shew us. and thowgh the wrytt ^of error^ is lawfully granted, yet to delaye the cause, my L[ord] kepar and I have accorded, that wher we both should be in the chequer chamber.[276] Both for other wrytts and for that also, on of us shall be absent, and so the wrytt shal be delayed. Whereof the Fr[ench] men will storm, exclaiming already of Iniustyce done them.

26 Janu[ary] 1595

W. Burghley

Dorse

ADDRESSED in the hand of a Cecil clerk, Vincent Skinner's hand:[277]
To my varie Loving sonne Sir RobertCecill knight of hir ma[jes]ties honorable privy
Connsell

ENDORSED in Simon Willis's hand:
26 January 1595
L[ord] Thre[asure]r to my M[aste]r

---

[276]One of the few mentions in the letters of equity causes in the Exchequer court, usually debtors.
[277]Vincent Skinner's hand, auditor of priests from 1593. See Smith, 'The secretariats of the Cecils', 484–485, 491–493.

Letter No. 78

William, Lord Burghley to Sir Robert Cecil, 26 January 1595

¾ p. Holograph.
Addressed, endorsed, signed.

Text

I do send yow Sir Henry Unton's depeche wherein I see a most dangerous course intended, by the most ingratfull k[ing] that lyveth.[278] I will not comment hereuppon, but I am sure his Majesty will depely consider of this indignetye, and intend some courss mete herwith in tyme[279]

I thynk our Amb[assador] hath, by his privat letter to hir Ma[jes]ty enlarged his furder opinion.[280]

We had nede to crave and expect the favor and protection of Almighty God, wherof I dowt not for the goodnes of our Cause, though I can not devise the meanes.

26 Januar[y] 1595

Your Lov[ing] father,

[278] Unton received a cold welcome from the French king, who charged Elizabeth with the redundancy of an embassy where no further points of negotiation and succour were offered beyond those made by her resident *chargé d'affaires*, Thomas Edmondes. Hatfield, Cecil Papers, 37/92; *HMCS*, vi, 11–12. Unton's letter of 17 Jan. 1596 to Burghley was copied and sent to Essex, who had provided the ambassador with a set of secret instructions. *HMCS*, vi, 17; Birch, *Memoirs*, I, 353, 397; *HMCD*, i, 376. Such matters appeared to have influenced little the course of the earl's own policies in France concerning Antonio Perez, but the lingering suspicion that the resident secretary Thomas Edmondes might have been meddling in with policies other than the Queen's earned him a very sharp rebuke from Cecil in May 1596. *HMCS*, vi, 193. Unton saw little hope of reconciliation with Henry over Elizabeth's refusal to offer succour to La Fère, even as the Archduke Albert was approaching Luxembourg with 8,000 men. *HMCS*, vi, 11–12, 16–17. The king's recalcitrance on this point offered the Spanish an opportunity to attack and obtain Calais in Mar.–Apr. 1596, see Letters Nos 89, 90, 92.
[279] Cecil's spy, Wyat, told also of Unton's poor reception from Henry IV as the king occupied himself with La Fère. But this account was not received in England until 7 Feb. *HMCS*, vi, 13. It was noted that the Papal nuncio was expected, and an envoy from Henry was sent to the duke of Savoy, an intermediary between France and Philip II. The Queen's intended courses are found in her letter to Henry IV carried by the Portuguese pretender Cristofero Moro. Hatfield, Cecil Papers, 133/132; *HMCS*, vi, 19. See also the Queen's letter to Henry's sister, Catherine de Bourbon. Hatfield, Cecil Papers, 133/133; *HMCS*, vi, 21.
[280] Sir Henry Unton to the Queen of 17 Jan. was copied and sent to Essex, together with his letter to Burghley and a short cover letter to the earl. TNA SP 78/37/fols. 25r–28r; Hatfield, Cecil Papers, 171/55; *HMCS*, vi, 16–17.

bitter with cold

W. Burghley

Dorse

ADDRESSED
To my loving sonne Sir Robert Cecill
knight, one of hir ma[jes]ties Privie Connsell

ENDORSED in Simon Willis's hand:
26 Jan[uary] 1595
L[ord] Thre[asure]r to my M[aste]r

Letter No. 79

**William, Lord Burghley to Sir Robert Cecil,
20 February 1596**

⅔ p. Dictated to Henry Maynard.
Addressed, endorsed, signed.

Text

Althowgh I cannot cumm to the Cort as my desire is findinge my
infirmite rather to growe uppon mee than to deminishe, yet I can
not be careles of such hir ma[jes]ties service as I dowbt is not
remembered by others. Yowe shall understand, and so I would have
yowe informe hir Ma[jes]tie, that the Commission for the Consell
in the North, whereof the late Erle of Huntingdon was president
is nowe discontinued, and thowgh hir ma[jes]tie by hir letters the
xvii[th] of December,[281] authorized the nowe Archb[ishop] of yorke and
the rest of Conncell to continue their assemblies, and to heare and

---

[281] The death of Henry Hastings, 3rd earl of Huntingdon in Dec. 1595, left vacant the lord
presidency of the Council of the North as well as the lord lieutenancies of Leicestershire,
Rutland, Yorkshire, Cumberland, Northumberland and Westmorland. Yorkshire was
assumed by Burghley; Cumberland by George Clifford, earl of Cumberland. Claire Cross,
'The third earl of Huntingdon's death-bed: A Calvinist example of the *ars moriendi*', *Northern
History*, 21 (1985), 80–107. As Burghley noted, the council's work had to continue. The
Queen's letter of late Dec. 1595 authorized a commission pro tem headed by the new
archbishop of York, Matthew Hutton. In Feb. 1596, the bishop of Durham, Tobie Matthew,
was given 'the leadership of the Commission to treate amongst others with the K[ing] of
Scottes Commissioners for mutual redresse of incursions upon the boarders'. TNA SO3/fol.
572r; *CPR 38 Eliz. I*, no. 1066. See also the letters of 13 Jan. 1596 to the archbishop of Yorke
and sheriff of the diocese of Durham to raise 80 light horse for service under the warden of
the Middle Marches, TNA SP TNA/503/1/fol. 568r.

detemine cawses of the Subjectes, as hearetofore they used to doe in the absence of the L[ord] Presedent, which theie have done as I understand vearie diligentlie: yet bicawse the late L[ord] Presedent did before his deathe appointe a generall session to be kept the first of marche, wheareof by hir ma[jes]ty's instruccions theare be onelie fowre kept in the yeare, which genearall session cannot be kept, but in the presence of a Lord president or a vicepresident to be named by the President: thearefore this generall session appointed to beginne the first of Marche cannot take place, withowt the authorite of A president or vice president, which is to be performed by hir ma[jes]ties Com[missio]n, and otherwise theie that remaine theare Councellors cannot Juditially proceade: And herof bicawse the time approcheth, And not knowinge what hir ma[jes]tie hath determined hearein, I requier yowe with speed to advertise hir ma[jes]tie accordinge to this my writinge. So as hir ma[jes]tie maie determine hir plesure in convenient time.

Ffrom my howse in the Strand, this xx[th] of February 1595.

Your Lovinge father,

[Burghley]
W. Burghley

Dorse

ADDRESSED in Henry Maynard's hand:
To my lovinge sonne Sir Robart Cecill knight one of hir ma[jes]ties privie Connsell

ENDORSED in Simon Willis's hand:
20 ffeb[ruary] 1595

Letter No. 80

William, Lord Burghley to Sir Robert Cecil, 7 February 1595

1 p. Dictated to Henry Maynard with a holograph addition
Addressed, endorsed, signed.

Text

I send unto yow hearewith two warrantes, one in paper to the office of the Ordonnance for sendinge of municion to Barwick, Carlile and

Newcastell accordinge to a Scedule in paper conteining the parcells within the same:[282] And an other Bill parchemente to be signed by hir ma[jes]tie for a privie seale for severall sommes of monie to be paied for the said townes of Barwick, Calile and Newcastell, which I praie yowe procure to be signed assone as nomination of my l[ord] of Essex.[283]

[Burghley]
I pray yow lett my Cosyn Sir Jhon Stanhop,[284] understand that whan Mr. Watson[285] of the Chancery lyved and was in helth, uppon knolledg of hir Ma[jes]ty's regard to paynfull service of my servant G[eorge] Coppyns wiff to grant this sayd office in revertion to hir husband, I did abteyn my L[ord] kepars good will therein notwithstanding that he had a determination to have preferred on of his own therto, and sence that tyme understand that my Cosyn Stanhope hath bene a sutor to hir Ma[jes]ty for hym self, which I thynk if he had known of hir Ma[jes]ty's former disposition towardes the Gentlewoman notefyed offen by sondry both ladyes and others of hir chamber he wold not have interrupted this the Gentlewoman's sute.[286] Whereof I pray yow do inform hym, assuryng hym that the office is not of that vallew, that I thynk he is informed of.

ffrom my howss in Strand 7 feb[ruary] 1595

Your lov[ing] fath[er],

W. Burghley

[Holograph postscript]
I am ashamed to have warned Sir Thomas Wilford to prepare hym self to be the provost Marshall, wherein he loketh for some fee for his

---

[282]Warrant issued on paper noted by Burghley was doubtless duplicated; for Berwick, see *Cal. Border Papers*, ii, 105.

[283]Who Essex supported is not clear, but Godolphin got the place, an extension of the Scillies command, so it is likely Essex supported Godolphin. Sir Francis Godolphin (1534–1608), *ODNB*, was already exercising the role of lieutenant in the Scilly Islands by July 1595. *HMCS*, v, 274. See Letter No. 70 for his role in intelligence.

[284]Sir John Stanhope was made treasurer of the Chamber in 1596.

[285]Roland Watson (d.1595), *HPT*, iii, 589. The deputy clerk of the Crown in Chancery from 1574, he lobbied Burghley and Sir Thomas Bromley thereby obstructing the reversion of Thomas Powle's clerkship of the Crown in 1589. Powle outlived Watson, see n. 286.

[286]George Coppin (d. 1620), *HPT*, i, 652–653, received the office. He attended Burghley in last of his illness. On 28 Jan. 1596 he received Watson's reversion, succeeding Powle in 1601 – Sir Thomas Egerton, master of the rolls and lord keeper (at this time), had the gift in his office. See above, p. 26.

mayntenance which will be chargeable, as the Connsell knoweth who gave hym comfort to put hym self in redynes. but I am more ashamed that the same hath bene publyshed by hir Ma[jes]ty's proclamation that such on shold be, and the Cite also warned thereof. if now noon shuld be I pray yowe perceave some of my Lordes to remembre hir Ma[jes]ty hereof.[287] and so I shall be discharged.

Dorse

ADDRESSED
To my Lovinge sonne Sir Rob[er]t Cecill knight, one of hir ma[jes]ties privie Connsell

ENDORSED by Sir Robert Cecil:
My l[ord] to me

Letter No. 81

William, Lord Burghley to Sir Robert Cecil, 21 February 1595

¼ p. Holograph.
Addressed, endorsed, signed.

Text

I am begynning of a lesson that is to me iii^{xx} and x [70] y(ea)res old, that is to hold my pen in order to wryte. but being as yet unhable I only retourn yow for answer the book of the Irish army as it was the last quarter.[288]

Your loving father,

W. Burghley

---

[287] Sir Thomas Wilford (*c*.1530–1610), *HPT*, iii, 618–619; Letter No. 52. He was a distinguished soldier in the Low Countries, governor of Ostend (1586–1589), deputy lieutenant of Kent 1589, and marshal of Berwick 1593. On 5 Apr. 1596, Wilford was appointed colonel of the English forces for the invasion of France. L. Boynton, 'The Tudor Provost-Marshal', *English Historical Review*, 87 (1962) 437–455.

[288] The expenditure of the Irish army in the last quarter of 1595 was noted in the book of receipts of Eliz. 36 ending in Michaelmas, which the Irish auditor Christopher Peyton sent Burghley in lieu of the current account. TNA SP 63 186/no. 69 I, fols. 223r, 226r. Other evidence suggests that the Irish packets were delayed by poor weather in the Irish Sea, and that Peyton's letter dated 17 Feb. may have arrived in London with much earlier packets, or was expected by Burghley at the time he wrote Letters Nos 81 and 82.

Dorse

ADDRESSED in Henry Maynard's hand:
To my lovinge sonne
Sir Rob[er]t Cecil knight
one of hir ma[jes]ties privie Connsell.

ENDORSED in Simon Willis's hand:
21 ffeb[ruary] 1595
L[ord] Thre[asure]r to my M[aste]r

Letter No. 82

William, Lord Burghley to Sir Robert Cecil, 22 February 1595

⅓ p. Holograph.
Addressed, endorsed, signed.

Text

I forgott to delyver to yow, these included from Mr. wallop and Just[ice] Gardener.[289]

Yow may shew ther lamentable opinion of Irland by 4 or 5 lynes in the first page of ther letter which I have underlyned.

Other partes of ther letters sheweth disorders, without advise how to reform them because the fete dare not reform the head. and so

---

[289]Wallop to Burghley, 9 Feb. 1596 telling of the extreme dangers posed by O'Donnell's confederacy with all other Irish and Ulster chieftains, TNA SP 63/186/no. 52, fol. 183r–v. This destroyed English hopes of dividing and conquering. Sir Robert Gardener (*c.*1540–1620), chief justice of the Queen's Bench in Ireland from 1586 was expected in England, exercising pro tem judicial head of the Exchequer and Chancery in Ireland. As Burghley warned Robert Cecil, 'I send yow herwith ii bundells of Ireland letters and wrytyngs containing a chaos of matters to be Metamorphosed as I thynk into some perfection by Sir Robert Gardener, but when he wil be here I know not'. TNA SP 63/186/no. 79, fol. 249r. Sir Geoffrey Fenton warned of Wallop's distress at the financial corruption in Ireland, SP 63/186/no. 83, fol. 256r. Sir John Norris saw Gardener as impartial, but he was never granted audience of the Queen, so incensed was she at the failures of her Irish administration. Sir Robert Gardener, SP 63/186 no. 63, fol. 211r–v; Thrush and Ferris, *The House of Commons, 1604–1629*, IV, 69.

maye yowe say to me, that nether have a good ~~fete~~ head nor fete, but no body is payned herewith but my poor self alon.[290]

22 feb[ruary] 1595

Your father's weak hand,

W. Burghley

Dorse

ADDRESSED in Henry Maynard's hand:
To my lovinge sonne Sir
Robart Cecill knight
one of her ma[jes]ties
privie Connsel.

ENDORSED in Simon Willis's hand:
22 February 1595
L[ord] Thre[asure]r to my M[aste]r.

Letter No. 83

William, Lord Burghley to Sir Robert Cecil, 23 February 1595

½ p. Dictated to Henry Maynard, 21 lines.
Addressed, endorsed, signed.

Text

I do send unto yowe herewith a drought of a Commission of the northe agreeable to former Commissions. Showing that there is noe presedent

[290]Grave Irish news may have arrived in plenty at this juncture following a spell of poor weather which delayed shipping and posts. Sir John Norris complained that his packet had been delayed while the lord deputy's was sent secretly, so implying that Russell wanted to control communication, TNA SP 63/186/no. 34, fol. 124r–125r. Norris saw an English ceasefire as a necessary evil given the Irish rebels' unification and the decay in English forces and supply SP 63/186, no. 34 fol. 126r–v. Russell's special letters to the Cecils berated Norris and his fellow commissioners' failure to draw Tyrone and his adherents to submission, SP 63/186, no. 22. There were 19 inclusions by Russell, most of which were handled by Cecil: 300 horse, money victuals and Scottish mercenaries were requested. Tyrone demanded of Russell a full compliance with the terms of the cessation, SP 63/186, no. 58 I, fol. 199r–200r. On the other hand, Norris's alarm at the increase of rebel forces was typical of English reports that Tyrone had no intention of fulfilling his part of the treaty, SP 63/186 no. 63, fol. 211r–v. Burghley's chagrin at lack of initiative by the lord deputy and the Irish Council appears to have been laid at Russell's feet. See above, pp. 61–62.

made for that Connsell, to which draught have put my hand, for the warranting thereof to be in good forme.[291] So as yowe maie apresentlie cause yt to be ingrossed in parchemente by somm of the Clarkes of the Signet & so to be signed by hir ma[jes]tie to serve as A warrant to the L[ord] kepar to passe the great seale;[292] executed by the first of Marche: And yet by a clawse which I have added to an instruccion hearewith also sent, it shall suffice to have the same begonne at anie time after the first of Marche. And for that theare is a clawse in this Com[missio]n ordinarie to referre them to the former Instruccions, I have not formed anie number of newe Articles for the Instruccions but have onelie formed 3 Articles to supplie the want of anie newe Instruccions to be nowe sent, which Articles I would yowe showld also cawse to be written in paper to be signed by hir Ma[jes]ty.[293] And so I committ the care hearof to your Expedition. ffrom my howse in the Strand this xxii[th] of feb[ruary] 1595.

[Burghley]
Your lov[ing] father,

W. Burghley

Dorse

ADDRESSED in Henry Maynard's hand:
To my lovinge sonne
Rob[er]t Cecill knight
one of hir ma[jes]ties privie Connsell.

ENDORSED in Simon Willis's hand:
23 Feb[ruary] 1595
Lo[rd] Thre[asure]r to my M[aste]r

[291] See Letters Nos 80 and 86.
[292] The new commission, their instructions, and a warrant to the receiver-general of Yorkshire for their pay and provision was passed at the signet, TNA SO3/1/fol. 572r; Letter No. 79.
[293] The paper version (enregistered) of the 3 additional articles supplying legal remedy for the situation, which would obtain in the Commission after 1 Mar., 1596 was addressed by Tobie Matthew, bishop of Durham, responding to Burghley's letters and articles of instructions of 23 Feb. Matthew wanted administrative matters for the renewal of the Ecclesiastical High Commission taken in hand. He argued a precedent for military musters in the vacancy of the lord presidency of the Council might be looked to in the case of a Spanish invasion, a condition which Archbishop Hutton of York wished to rectify. *HMCS*, vi, 72–74, 95; *CPR 38 Eliz. I*, no. 1065.

Letter No. 84

William, Lord Burghley to Sir Robert Cecil, 23 February 1595

¼ p. Holograph.
Addressed, endorsed, signed.

Text

I wold not have yowe come hyther to me, for by God's leave, I will venture to be ther to morrow by water in the afternoone wher I pray yow to send but 2 horsses for to accompany me with my coche from Mortlack. If this night shall mak me be unhable I will in the morning send yow word. This Monday, 23 feb[ruary] at night.

Your lov[ing] father,

W. Burghley

Dorse

ADDRESSED in Henry Maynard's hand:
To my lovinge sonne
Rob[er]t Cecill knight
one of hir ma[jes]ties privie Connsell.

ENDORSED in Simon Willis's hand:
23 Feb 1595
L[ord] Thre[asure]r to my M[aste]r
Mortlake, near Richmond Palace, on the Thames

Letter No. 85

William, Lord Burghley to Sir Robert Cecil, 13 March 1595

1 p. Holograph.
Addressed, endorsed, signed.

Text

I thank yow for your letters for which I looked untill now at 8 I received them. I am sorry to se the uncertenty for resolution consideryng the delaye doth harm, both weyss as well as for loss in contynuance of the matter ^[that?] shuld dissolve as for hyndrance to the expedition, by the staggeryng.²⁹⁴ I do hold and will allweiss this courss in such matters as I differ in opinion from hir Majesty as long as I may be allowed to gyve advise. I will not chang my opinion by affurmyng the Contrary for that war to offend God to whom I am sworn first, but as a servant I will obey hir Ma[jes]ty's commanndment, and no wise contrary the same, presuming that she be God's cheff minister hear it shall be God's will to have hir commanndmentes obeyed after that I have performed my dutye as a Counsellor, and shall in my hart wish, hir Commanndmentes to have such good successes, as I am sure she intendeth. Yow se I am in a mixture of divinite and polycye preferring in polecy, hir Majesty afor all others on the erth and in dyvynitie the Kyng of heaven above all betwixt alpha and omega.

This my cogitatons yow may use to your own good besechyng God to bless yow.

This Satyrd[ay] 13 March 1595

Your lov[ing] fath[e]r,

W. Burghley.

Dorse

ADDRESSED in another clerk's hand, Hickes or Percival:
To my Loving sonne Sir
Robert Cecyll knight
one of hir ma[jes]ties
privy Connsell.

ENDORSED in Simon Willis's hand:
13 March 1595
L[ord] Thre[asure]r to my M[aste]r.

²⁹⁴Lord Admiral Howard was principally responsible for the victualling of the fleet for Cadiz then numbering 260 men at great charge to the Crown, an expense which probably met with Burghley's objections. Hatfield, Cecil Papers, 30/106; *HMCS*, vi, 85–86. There was also the movement of troops in the Low Countries, 700 of whom were sent out of Zutphen to Flushing, which suggests the possibility of a naval force there to be joined with the main group bound for Cadiz. Hatfield, Cecil Papers, 30/111; *HMCS*, vi, 88. Protracted negotiations with the States General of the Low Countries had borne fruit in their agreement to supply men and ships for the English naval expedition, as is shown in Essex's strategic calculations for the supply and use of these forces made in Apr. 1596. Hatfield, Cecil Papers, 47/97; *HMCS*, vi, 162.

Letter No. 86

William, Lord Burghley to Sir Robert Cecil, 14 March 1595

⅓ p. Dictated to Henry Maynard
Addressed, endorsed, signed.

Text

I have bene here earnestlie moved by this Bearer ffrauncis Goston for my favor in the obtyninge from hir ma[jes]tie of the Revercion of the Receevershipp of Nottingham and derbie because I knowe him of myne own knolledge to be a varie honest man and varie sufficient for the place as also for that he hath served hir ma[jes]tie under Mr. Connyers²⁹⁵ many yares, varie dilligentlie and painfulliie. And becawse he did likewise require my letter to yowe for the preferring of hir Bill to hir ma[jes]tie for the desire I have procure it unto him, as sone as Convenientlie may be to avoid prevenccion.²⁹⁶ I pray yow, if so yow dare to make offer of it unto her, to take yor best opportunitye yow can fynd for the effecting of it. ffrom my howse at Westmin[ste]r the 14 of Marche, 1595.

[Burghley]
Your lov[ing] father,

W. Burghley

Dorse

ADDRESSED in a different clerk's hand, this one larger and rounder and more labourious:
To my vaire Lovinge sonne Sir Robert
Cecill knight one of

---

²⁹⁵ Francis Guston, an auditor of the Imprests granted the auditorship of the imprests and foreign accounts in 1597, on reversion after Charles Wednester's death. BL Lansdowne MS 83/nos 76, 78; *CSPD 1598–1601*, 382. Letters Patent were issued, see *CPR 38 Eliz. I*, no. 386, 19 July 1597: 'to determine all accounts, and views of accounts of clerks and surveyors of the Queen's works in England and Wales and the marches thereof, the treasurer or keeper of the Queen's ships, the master of her ordnances, all persons accountable for any sums of money concerning the Queen's business, the clerk or keeper of the hanaper of Chancery, the keeper of the great wardrobe and the chief butler of England', together with an auditorship of First Fruits and Tenths. Whether he received the reversion for Nottingham and Derby is not known.
²⁹⁶ John Conyers (d.1610), *HPT*, i, 643, auditor of the prests and foreign accounts, and greatly involved in military accounts. *HMCS*, ix, 82–83; xi, 141–142; xiii, 114.

hir ma[jes]ties privy Connsell

ENDORSED in the hand of Simon Willis:
[14 March 1596]
L[ord] Thre[asure]r to my M[aste]r
In favour of Ffrancis Guston

Letter No. 87

William, Lord Burghley to Sir Robert Cecil, 16 March 1595

1 p. Holograph.
Endorsed, signed.

Text

I have receaved your letter with the paper book for the Commission wherin as it semeth hir Ma[jes]ty wold have some caution to restrayn the Generalls from offendyng of such as ar not [in] hir Ma[jes]ty's ennemyes, but ar in amyty both with the k[ing] of spayn and with hir Ma[jes]ty wherin hir Ma[jes]ty's care and wise forsight is highly to be commended.[297] And therfor though these ii lordes being Connsellors[298] and knowyng what complayntes remain ar satisfyed to Denmark,[299]

---

[297]The terms of the generals' commission were revised, as a clerk of the signet, Thomas Windebanke, wrote to Cecil advising him of the inclusion of clauses by the Queen for avoiding offence to those who were neither the enemies of England nor of Spain. Hatfield, Cecil Papers, 31/fols. 20r, 21r; *HMCS*, vi, 101, 101–102. Windebanke mentioned that the Queen had informed Essex that she had signed the paper book of the commissions, a fact which caused the clerk some perturbation as his first letter of the day alludes to some covert action on Cecil's part to have the books signed without conference with the commanders. For the impossibility of avoiding the secretarial seals in the passing of this paper directly to Chancery, see *CSPD 1595–1597*, 188; Wernham, *Return of the Armadas*, 57–58. See also Burghley's letter for the document and the general's reply, *CSPD 1595–1597*, 189, 190–191. The preparations were defensive, so as not to offend neutral powers, Wernham, *Return of the Armadas*, 58. Their commission passed the Great Seal 18 Mar. 1596, authorizing 5,000 men and 5,000 mariners. For the substance of the commission, see *APC 1595–1596*, 257, 307–309, 323–324; *HMCS*, vi, 114, 117–118.
[298]The earl of Essex and Lord Admiral Howard were joint commanders of the expedition. Howard complained to Cecil on 13 Apr., 'My commission in being joined with the Earl [of Essex] is an idle thing, for I am used as but the drudge', a situation dramatically different from that which he had anticipated on his final audience of the Queen before departing. Hatfield, Cecil Papers, 40/fol. 6r; *HMCS*, vi, 144.
[299]Thomas Ferrers, agent of the Merchant Adventurers in Stade made mention of an outstanding suit of the merchant Roloff Petersson. For example, *HMCS*, vi, 98–99.

and sondry for cites in Germanny.[300] For some spoyles made, will carefully ^{have} regard ^{for} all such offences yet ad maiorum cautelum. I have by enterlyning in certen places, added such special wordes, as in my poore concept will manifestly directly ^{then} whom iustly to invade and offend, and observyng those wordes, no frende of hir Ma[jes]ty's shall have cause to compleyn, except they shall openly shew ennimyte to hir Ma[jes]ty.

But I leave this my opinion to hir Ma[jes]ty's censure and to the Lls [Lords] allowance.

I am here all this daye bedred, by reason of sorre head and stomach tormented syck night past, and yet in my head and stomack tormented, so as I wryt this with payne of head, hart and hand, and therfor I do desyre of hir Ma[jes]ty pardon, I shall not have satisfyed hir expectations which is the mark I desyre to shoot to.

Out of my bed at 3

Your Lov[ing] Fath[er],

W. Burghley

Dorse

ENDORSED in Simon Willis's hand:
26 Mar 1595
L[ord] Thre[surer] to my M[aste]r

---

[300] The embassy of the earl of Lincoln and John Wroth to the Landgrave of Hesse and others were to offer a separate negotiation, because the English merchants' position was deeply unpopular with imperial traders and the Hanse cities who felt constricted by their absolute powers under Elizabeth's mandate. Bell, *Handlist*, 138–139. For Lincoln's correspondence with the Secretary of State, Cecil, see *HMCS*, vi, 254, 255–256, 289–290. Cecil shadowed the embassy with an agent used in Spain, George Cramner (ibid. 289–290). Thomas Ferrers's letter to Burghley of 23 Mar. 1596 names Hamburg and Lubeck as specifically preparing against the Merchant Adventurers. Two spies were noting the proliferation of shipping: Joachim Showmaker and Francis Tusser the latter working for Lord Buckhurst in Scotland. *HMCS*, vi, 98–99, 112. A dispute over ordnance with the German duke of Holstein touched Hamburg shipping, as Andreas Hoffman, the duke's agent complained to Cecil, 27 Feb. 1596, *HMCS*, vi, 71–71. The English trading monopoly had a direct bearing on Anglo-Spanish conflict. Ferrers wrote that Spanish pensioners were raising trouble among the German princes. Hatfield, Cecil Papers, 40/3; *HMCS*, vi, 143–144. The king of Denmark's double toll charge on Spanish shipping to pass the waters between his kingdom and Holstein was also unpopular with the territorial rulers in the empire and east. A polemic, 'Reasons for James VI joining with the Pope', allied the king with the Hanse Cities, the Danish king and many German princes, because of the Queen of England's piratical practices on the seas. *CSPS 1595–1597*, xii, 230–233, 232, pt. 16.

Letter No. 88

William, Lord Burghley to Sir Robert Cecil, 31 March 1596

¼ p. Dictated to Henry Maynard.
Addressed, endorsed, signed.

Text

I doe send yow hearewith such letters as at this present I received from Sir Henry Unton,[301] and Mr. Edmondes bearer Capteine hart browght hither,[302] whoe can informe yowe of the weake estate whearin he left the Ambassador.[303] ffrom my howse in the Strand this last of Marche, 1596.

Your Lovinge father,
[Burghley]

W. Burghley

Dorse

ADDRESSED in Henry Maynard's hand:
To my lovinge sonne
Sir Rob[er]t Cecill knight
one of hir ma[jes]ties privie
Connsell

ENDORSED in Simon Willis's hand:
Ulm March 1596

Lo[rd] Thre[surer] to my M[aste]r

---

[301]Unton wrote to Burghley on 20 Mar. 1596, giving Henry IV's objections to the withdrawal of English troops from the Low Countries, although men from Zutphen and elsewhere were already bound for Ireland, TNA SP 78-37-fols. 112r–113r. A copy of Unton's letter to Burghley was made for Essex, *HMCS*, vi, 106.

[302]Thomas Edmondes, who replaced Unton, wrote of Unton's great illness and enclosed his last letter, TNA SP 78-37-fol. 117r. Simon Willis retained and endorsed this letter.

[303]Following a bad fall from his horse Unton had caught the plague which ravaged the forces in the camp near Coucy, as Edmondes informed Essex on 17 Mar. Unton was forced to use Edmondes as his intermediary *HMCS*, vi, 103, 106. The French *chargé d'affaires* and minister of the French church, Robert le Maçon, *dit* de la Fontaine, held secret discussions with Essex on the English relief of Cambrai, and expressed his alarm over Unton's health at that delicate juncture, ibid. 131. For the post mortem on Unton by Henry IV's doctor, see Wernham, *Return of the Armadas*, 61; TNA SP 78/37/fol. 119r.

Letter No. 89

Henry Maynard to Sir Robert Cecil, 31 March 1596

½ p. Holograph.
Addressed, endorsed, signed.

Text

Sir, My l[ord] hath willed mee to write to yowe himself not beinge
well hable withowt paine, of removinge to be sett upp, that he is
much trowbled in his minde with the Alarme of Callis, whereof my
L[ord] Admirall wrote to him, and which advertisement he sent yow
by his L[ord]'s servant:[304] And thearefore for the quiett of his minde he
praieth yowe, assone as yowe shall understand anie certaintie theareof,
to lett him knowe the same: And in case it showld fall owt to be trewe,
his opinion is that my L[ord] of Essex and L[ord] Admirall, cannot
with more honnor emploie them selves, hir Majestie's forces, then
to be the succoringe theareof even theare whole paie to be answered by hir Ma[jes]ty
but this his opinion his L[ord] would have yowe as yet to keape to
your selfe.[305]

And so, I most humble take my leave. ffrom my L[ord's] howse in the
Strand this last of March 1596.

Most humblie at your honours Co[mmandme[nt],

H[enry] Maynard

[Added to the lower right of the above text, and directly to the right of the signature, and
therefore, added after signing]

[304] Vidausin (seigneur de Widessan), the governor of Calais, raised the alarm about a
Spanish attack under Fuentes and Velasco to the lord admiral on 30 Mar. 1596, TNA SP
37/110r. Burghley was notably exercised about the need for English assistance, realizing this
was a great success for the Archduke Albert's army, Wernham, *Return of the Armadas*, 64. The
Council, but not the Queen, agreed with Burghley: 'England may not endure this town to
be Spanish'. Edmund Lodge, *Illustrations of British History, Biography and Manners in the reigns
of Henry VIII, Edward VI, Mary, Elizabeth, and James I* (London, 1838), ii, 459–66. Wernham
calls Henry's unpreparedness at Calais by committing of his forces to the siege of La Fère
'astonishing', *Return of the Armadas*, 64. The town remained under Spanish control for two
years until the Peace of Vervins.
[305] Referring to Sir Henry Palmer (*c*.1550–1611), *ODNB*, to whom the relief effort would
have been entrusted. For the logistics of provisioning Calais, see Letter No. 90. Vidausin
alerted Henry IV's ambassador to the United Provinces, Paul Choart, lord of Buzenval, to
the necessity of providing shipping near Gravelines. To Villeroy, chief negotiator for peace
with Spain, Vidausin argued that if the siege continued, the mighty English preparations
might be diverted entirely to Calais. *HMCS*, vi, 132.

Nowe towardes eveninge my l[ord]s paine beginne to hold him in his head and neck, as yt did yesterdaie, but I hope with lesse grief.

Dorse

ADDRESSED Holograph [Maynard]
To the R[ight] honorable
Sir Rob[er]t Cecill knight
one of hir ma[jes]ties right
honorable privy Connsell
At the Cort

ENDORSED in Simon Willis's hand:
Ulm March 1596
Lo[rd] Thre[surer[to my M[aste]r

Letter No. 90

William, Lord Burghley to Sir Robert Cecil, 31 March 1596

1 p. Holograph.
Addressed, endorsed, signed.

Text

This alarm of Calliss hath kept me wakyng all night, and hath styrred up in me manny cogitations. first that it war necessary to be informed from the Governor, what he wanteth of men or munition to defend the town[;] how he is hable to receave succors[;] of what nombres the army ar that doth besege it. Wher the battery is planted. How the haven remayneth fre for such succor to come with shypping. if the haven be possessed by the enemy with his shipping. Why may not ayd be sent by shippiyng to a place est from Callies toward Gravelienes or to willoby and if the town may be defended for xiiii days, in this space la fare will be yelded or taken, and ther it may be hoped that the Kyng will levy the sege.[306] Wharunto he had v or v[i]^M [5,000 or 6,000] Footemen, that may be had in this sort, ii^M [2,000] from London, i^M [1,000] from Essex, ii^M [2,000] from Kent, i^M [1,000] from Sussex or such lyke for England may not endure this town to be Spanish. and the Q[ueen] that also promised hym ayde.[307] I wish these men war

---

[306] See above, p. 185.
[307] Vidausin's requests to the English did not arrive until 4 Apr. by which time Thomas Windebanke and Palmer had been sent on a fact-finding mission. *HMCS*, vi, 133, 134.

put in order that ether some of them may spedely enter Callis to hold rule. and that powder and musketts was presently, sent to Dover.[308] but of these thynges I am sure, more will be ther forsene.[309] I confes I am trobled so herewith as I se not well what I wryt.

[Margin]
Your lo[ving] father,

W. Burghley

Dorse

ADDRESSED in Henry Maynard's hand:
To my Lovinge sonne
Sir Robert Cecill knight
one of hir ma[jes]ties
privie Connsell
with speed

ENDORSED in Simon Willis's hand:
un[ti]mo March 1596
L[ord] Thre[asure]r to my M[aste]r

Letter No. 91

William, Lord Burghley to Sir Robert Cecil, 30 March 1596

¾ p. Holograph.
Addressed, endorsed, signed.

---

[308] Howard and Essex held their places as they awaited further instructions later in the week, especially for news of the removal of troops and supply, as outlined by Burghley in the present letter. Essex and Howard were eager to relieve Calais from the forces and supply already assembled for their proposed expedition. *HMCS*, vi, 135. The English stalled for the need of better information, and their slowness came in agreement with Sir Henry Palmer's alarm of 9 Apr. that the Spanish were setting sail for the Scillies, and thence to England or Ireland, ibid. 138. Sir Francis Vere was outraged at the prevarication, yet urged the Cadiz voyage to move royally forward, ibid. 140. Burghley added his voice to those who supported the immediate aid, adding to the letters here on the need for relief, Hatfield, Cecil Papers, 39/fol. 111r; *HMCS*, vi, 141, 10 Apr. 1596. Five thousand men were needed in the Cadiz levies which could have been used for Calais, *HMSC*, vi, 126.
[309] See *CSPD 1595–1597*, 189. Burghley received an answer from the Queen that the Cadiz forces could be re-deployed to Calais. See Ian W. Archer, *Gazetteer of Military Levies from the City of London, 1509–1603* (2001) at https://ora.ox.ac.uk/objects/uuid:adb577fc-6ffb-440b-9dd9-7c5c39a4a64c, no. 085 for 6 Apr. 1596 for the relief of Calais, 1,000 troops on City charge to be sent to Dover, 11 April, Easter Day, 1596.

Text

I send yow a letter wrytten to me by Sir Geoffrey Fenton which yow
may as se cause, shew to hir Ma[jes]ty and procure such answer as
shall best please hir, and if she shall still rest uppon stryct poyntes as
I have noted she hath doone hir charges and dannger for hir whole
realm being now become insupportable, and yet I can not deny but
hir royall state moveth hir, to be so precise as she is, but non sunt
procendi rumores ante salutem.[310]

I understand that my L[ord] Depute hath gyven commandment by
his french man, that no letters shall be suffred to pass owt of Irland to
me, but by his L[ord's] own warrant. what his L[ord] meaneth herby I
know not though I can probably gess, for herein yow ar also included.
I wish my Lord had such skill or good Luck in his government as ther
neded no advertisement or advise but from hym self.[311] I heare ther
cometh over with his L[ord's] passport many soldiers out of Ireland,
more hable, than such as now ar redy to go over.[312] for so proby[313]
wryteth to me, how mych it is mislyked, to send from hence new men,
whan sufficient men come from there, but I will not [text continues
on the left margin] deale heron, for my L[ord] depute is privatly

[310]Referring here to the Queen's proposed articles of negotiation with the rebels. See also
Letter No. 81. 'Nothing good may proceed on rumour alone.'
[311]This control of the posts from Dublin Castle to the presence Chamber admits the
quarrel between Sir William Russell and Sir John Norris had affected court and Privy
Council, for Norris told Burghley on 31 Jan. 1596 that the general packets had been delayed
by poor weather, while Russell's letters were sent separately to the Queen and Privy Council
by means of special shipping, TNA SP 63/186/no. 34 fols. 124r–125r. The Cecils allied
themselves with Norris, also using Sir Geoffrey Fenton as their link with the Council during
the negotiations with Tyrone. See Fenton's receipt of specially sealed letters from Sir John
Norris's secretary in Jan. 1596, TNA SP 63/186/no. 26, fol. 99r; *CSPI 1592–1596*, 459.
[312]Evidence for the release of soldiers out of Ireland by Russell's warrant over objections
from Norris came in the packet stalled at Chester. Norris railed at Russell over the inefficiency
of returning perfectly good troops brought to Ireland with Norris, in favour of a large-scale
muster of untrained new troops to be sent to Bristol, at the expense of all Irish shipping.
TNA SP 63/187/no. 46, fol. 111r–v; *CSPI 1592–1596*, 498–499.
[313]Peter Proby, Burghley's man running the Chester posts was likely a significant part of the
Cecils' intelligence to and from Ireland and in the port of Chester and environs. Burghley
had made exhaustive notes on his letters patent and estimates for all distances to court
and back, BL Lansdowne MSS, vol. 78, nos 92–100. He had been in the employ of Sir
Thomas Heneage, *HMCS*, ii, 177, 182. Proby to Burghley, 29 Mar. 1596, noted that Russell's
Frenchman, Mons. Meroelack, had brought word that no post without the lord deputy's
warranting could proceed to Burghley, TNA SP 63/187/no. 64, fol. 149r–v. Proby then held
letters from Sir John Norris and Sir Geoffrey Fenton and advised Burghley on the 19th
that, as instructed, he had asked the lord deputy to return all shipping from Ireland for the
transport of troops. TNA SP 63/187/no. 41, fol. 96r–97r; *CSPI 1592–1596*, 493. He held a
cipher of Burghley and may have been charged with opening mails as well as passing them
on. Proby had petitioned Cecil for a pension of 100 pounds in a letter dated 1595, Hatfield,
Cecil Papers, 35/fol. 37r; *HMCS*, v, 525.

advertised that all his family ar sought out by me. I wish they did not deserve to be sought owt.[314]

Your lo[ving] father,

W. Burghley.

[Postscript]
I have this last night some ease of me head by a sleep or ii.

Dorse

ADDRESSED in Henry Maynard's hand:
To my lovinge sonne Sir
Robart Cecill knight
one of hir ma[jes]ties privie
Cownsell

ENDORSED by Sir Robert Cecil:
30 Martii, my l[ord] to me

Letter No. 92

William, Lord Burghley to Sir Robert Cecil, 4 April 1596

⅔ p. Holograph.
Addressed, endorsed, signed.

Text

I wryte with payne, and se many difficulties, which I dare not tak uppon me to resolve.

---

[314] Burghley may have meant 'family' to mean the extended Russell clan, but the countess of Bedford's loyal gesture in sending suspected Jesuits to Cecil on 16 Mar. 1596 precludes enmity between the Cecils and all the Russells. They were, in any case, close relations through Robert's aunt, Lady (Elizabeth) Russell, née Cooke. *HMCS*, vi, 100. Russell may have been convinced of faction all around him, since by Norris's letters, it appears that he was adept at creating one devoted to undercutting Norris. Norris felt that his collision with the earl of Essex over the nomination of Irish captains in Aug. 1595 was, even in Feb. 1596, insufficiently cooled: 'His Lordship will not be an indifferent interpreter of my actions.' *CSPI 1592–1596*, 474.

I send yow my L[ord] of Essex letter who semeth very diligent in this cause.[315] by Sir Co[nyers] Clyfford we shall know more certenly.[316] I marvell the Holland shippes will not attempt the boates of Gravelyng.[317] the night tydes must serve for our men to pass the town.

I have drawen a warrant for my L[ord] Cobham[318] and for monny to be delyvered to Sir Thomas flud, which can not be expressly sett down, but by Estimation consideryng the uncertenty of the shippyng, and victells wherof if ther be sufficient in Calliss, the care will be the less, so as every soldier carry with hym self, some bread and chese for a weake or ii weake. [sic].[319]

[315]The earl of Essex worked ceaselessly to relieve Calais, as reported in a letter sent by Lord Thomas Howard. See Letters Nos 2 and 90. While Burghley was writing this letter, Essex received the Queen's letter as he returned from Dover to court, Wernham, *Return of the Armadas*, 65; *HMCS*, vi, 133, 138, 141; *HMCD*, i, 335; *APC 1595–1596*, 338–342; Stow, *Annals*, 1281–1282. The letter assured him of her desire to wrest Calais from the Spanish. Sir Robert Sidney had been sent to negotiate English custody of the port in exchange for succour. Henry turned his back on the ambassador, ending the Queen's support.

[316]Sir Conyers Clifford (d.1599), *ODNB*, was integral to the Cadiz preparation. A commission in his name to one Captain Fowkes dated 31 Mar. 1596 is perhaps mistitled 'Expedition to Cadiz', for this might have been the earliest warrant for a levy to relieve Calais, as the warrant was never sent and may have been stopped by the Queen. Hatfield, Cecil Papers, 47/fol. 107r; *HMCS*, vi, 126.

[317]French sources made it clear to Essex that English relief of Calais must begin with the disembarkation of Her Majesty's troops at Boulogne. This plan was hinted at in intelligence received by 9 Apr. 1596 by Sir Thomas Leighton on Guernsey where Spanish moves on Pempole where expected, *HMCS*, vi, 136, 138. The French were never going to let the English govern Calais, even temporarily.

[318]Cobham's warrant was probably close in content to the privy seal letters directed to Burghley as lord lieutenant of Essex to raise 1,000 men to be sent into Picardy, Hatfield, Cecil Papers, 39/fol. 101r; *HMCS*, vi, 138. For these documents, see Archer, *Gazetteer of Military Levies*, at https://ora.ox.ac.uk/objects/uuid:adb577fc-6ffb-440b-9dd9-7c5c39a4a64c, no. 086. Burghley had recommended the numbers, the most convenient being 2,000 men from Kent where Cobham was lord lieutenant, Letter No. 89. The Queen decided against assistance for Calais, presumably sticking on Henry's refusal to cede her custody of Calais, a move which angered Essex and displeased Burghley. On 10 Apr. 1596, Burghley wrote to Cecil, noting that, even as the Queen reversed her warrants, the earl of Essex was to have embarked that morning: 'And surely I am of opinion that the citadel being relieved will be regained, and if for want of her Majesty's succors it shall be lost, by judgement of the world the blame shall be imputed to her'. Hatfield, Cecil Papers, 39/111; *HMCS*, vi, 141. This was one of the harshest verdicts Burghley made of the Queen. He was concerned by the imminent arrival of Henry's envoy, Nicolas de Harlay, Sieur de Sancy (1546–1629), superintendent of the king's finances 1594–1599. Sancy grossly overestimated the size of the Queen's forces assembled in the Channel for Cadiz, as he arrived to negotiate the Leagues Offensive and Defensive. Wernham, *Return of the Armadas*, 63; *HMCS*, vi, 171. Maynard's note of French bonds due since 8 Sept. 1589 included the loan of £6,000 to France for present relief (7 May 1596), ibid.

[319]Sir Thomas Flood's accounts as payments of the Castle of Dover, Walmer, Deal, Landover, Sandgate, and at Queenborough, and of Archliffe Bulwater, TNA Ao/1/2516, roll 574, 15 June 1596–1598 May 1599.

I wish the Capt[ains] had no allowance of dead payes. the nombres wold consist of pykes and shott.[320]

I can not endure to wrytt any more

Your lo[ving] father,

W. Burghley.

Dorse

ADDRESSED Holograph
Robart Cecil knight one of hir ma[jes]ties privie Connsell

ENDORSED by Sir Robert Cecil:
From my l[ord] to me

Letter No. 93

William, Lord Burghley to Sir Robert Cecil, 26 May 1596

½ p. Holograph.
Addressed, endorsed, signed.

Text

Yow filled my hart so full with your large reportes of hir Ma[jes]ty's allowance of my insufficiencyes as sufficient and of hir superabundant care and desyre of my amendment, as I cannot conteane in the flowyng of my hart, withowt sendyng to yow to be presented to hir Ma[jes]ty, some portion of the comfort of my hart by waye of most humble thankfullnes to hir Ma[jes]ty with a porcion also of my sacifice to Almighty God by my harty prayers, In the contynuance

---

[320]Sir Thomas Sherley confirmed to Burghley the landing of troops at St Valéry on 10 Apr. noting imprest for one week was to be paid to these men, for their six month's service was ended on 3 Apr., Hatfield, Cecil Papers, 40/1; *HMCS*, vi, 141. For the dead pays: Burghley was trying to save money by withdrawing the 10% allowance for men, i.e. pay for 150 men for only 135 actual soldiers. Burghley made this clear to Cecil, 10 Apr. 1596, when he criticized the Queen's changed plans several times during the previous ten days as unpopular. He chastised his son for allowing public knowledge of this vacillation, for 'These so many changes breed hard opinions of counsel.' Hatfield, Cecil Papers, 39/fol. 111r; *HMCS*, vi, 141.

of hir happynes, wherin she exceedeth, all hir equalls in body and Government.

My hart hath forced my weak hand thus farr. 26 maii.

Your lov[ing] father,

W. Burghley.

Dorse

ADDRESSED in a clerk's hand:
To my Lovinge sonne Sir
Rob[er]t Cecill knight
one of hir ma[jes]ties privy Connsell.

ENDORSED in Simon Willis's hand:
26 March 1596
L[ord] Thre[asure]r to my M[aste]r

Letter No. 94

William, Lord Burghley to William Killigrew, 26 May 1596

1 p. entire. Dictated to Henry Maynard
Addressed, endorsed, signed.

Text

Sir,
Wheare I understand that theare remaineth with yowe a Bill for hir ma[jes]ties signature for one Cornelius Cure to be joined in patent with olde Yonge the Master mason, beinge a man throwgh age and sicknes verie unhable to discharge his duetie in that place: I doe thearefore praie yowe to take summ good oportunitie to offer the said Cures bill for hir ma[jes]tie's signature, being a man both honest, and of as good understandinge and skile to discharge that place, as anie other.[321] And so I commend me vearie hartelie to yowe. ffrom my howss in the Strand xxv^{th} of Maye 1596.

---

[321] Cure was to be joined in letters patent for the reversion of master mason in the Tower of London, issued 28 June 1596 which he surrendered in 1605, *CPR 38 Eliz. I*, no. 589.

Your verie Lovinge frend,

[Signed]
W. Burghley

[Postscript dictated to the clerk]
Since the writinge of this letter, I understand the olde man is dead
and of this man I dare affirme and so hath spicer and the rest of
the officers of the workes testified that he is both honest, expert, and
full of invencion and hath seen much work in forrein places. And of
annie place this had neade to be supplied being dailie to be used in
hir ma[jes]ties workes, especially Seeinge theare is noe Surveior.

Dorse

ADDRESSED in Henry Maynard's hand:
To the R[ight] worshipful my vearie lovinge frend
Mr. William Killigrewe Esquier one of the Gromes
of hir ma[jes]ties privie
Chamber And in his absence to Mr. Darcye [322]

ENDORSED in Simon Willis's hand:
26 Maii 1596
L[ord] Thre[asure]r to Mr. Wm. Killagrewe

Letter No. 95

William, Lord Burghley to Sir Robert Cecil, 27 May 1596

½ p. Dictated to Henry Maynard.
Addressed, no receipt, signed.

Text

I have perused the warrant yowe sent unto me for plimmowthe, whch
I retorne unto yowe, and like the same well, savinge wheare by the
same it is expressed that the soldiers showld onelie have such paie as
they have in the Lowe Contries, yowe shall understand that wheare

---

[322] Darcy and Killigrew were grooms of the privy chamber assisting Cecil with procurations
of the Queen's signature, as the volume of his secretarial work increased, Letter No. 45.
They received minor rewards, for example Killigrew retained the warrant for the payment
of Maundy money in Apr. 1596, to be directed to the bishop of London as well as a suit for
his uncle Sir Francis Carew of the Queen out of Winchester diocesan lands in 1594. TNA
SO3/fol. 578r; Hatfield, Cecil Papers, 29/fol. 39r; *HMCS*, v, 41.

the wages of solder commeth to iiis viiid a weeke, theie have but iis vid theareof paid them for lendinges and the rest is aunsweared them in Cloathes and Armes, and thareof ᶠᵒʳᵉ the warrant is to be considered in that point, so as theie maie have theire full paie, and what that same commeth unto, and what offices I thinke fitt to have kept theire, will appeare unto yowe, by this Colleccion of mine heareinclosed.[323] ffrom my howse in the Strand this xxviᵗʰ of Maye 1596.

Your Lovinge father,

[Burghley]
Forced to kepe to my bed to my great payn,

W. Burghley

Dorse

ADDRESSED in Henry Maynard's hand:
To my Lovinge sonne
Sir Robt Cecill one of Her Ma[jes]tys
Privy Consell

Letter No. 96

William, Lord Burghley to Sir Robert Cecil

⅓ p. dictated to Henry Maynard
Addressed, endorsed, signed.

Text

This letter which I send yow included came hither by the comon Poste from the l[ord] Scroop to certifie the comminge of certen of the Graimes committed to come as prisoners, contrary to the advise geven to the said l[ord] Scroop bethowgh nowe by his letter thowght necessary to change. This matter would be well considered of and better then my leisure serves me to give advise in. Therfore yow may do well to impart the same both to hir Majestie and to hir Counsell for their dyrection against the comminge of theise prisoners, whose accusations do not yett appeare, but are as I perceave to follow from

[323] A warrant issued in late May 1596 for soldiers embarking at Plymouth, soldiers levied for the relief of Calais – the Cadiz expedition was now on hold–at Low Countries wages of 4s. 8d. per diem. Further levies were now going ahead – for 180 foot in Essex with a disbursement of £6,000. See Letter No. 92; *HMCS*, vi, 193.

my l[ord] Scroope after they be committed,[324] ffrom my howse at Westm[iniste]r the 30ᵗʰ of Maye 1596.

[Burghley]
Your lov[ing] father,

W. Burghley

Dorse

ADDRESSED
For the right honorable Sir
Robert Cecill one of hir ma[jes]ties Privey Counsell.

ENDORSED in Simon Willis's hand:
30 May 1596
L[ord] Thre[asure]r to my M[aste]r

Letter No. 97

William, Lord Burghley to Sir Robert Cecil, 30 May 1596

½ p. Dictated to a clerk [Henry Maynard], with 2 sentences added in Burghley's hand.
Addressed, endorsed, signed.

Text

I send unto you here included a letter directed into me for the Archbishop of Yorke, brought by a Purcevante who hath also brought upp with him the 6 Graimes and hath them here in howse taken upp for them, and because theare is nobody als here to take charge of them I pray you move the Quene to knowe hir pleisure what shalbie donne with them and send me woorde forthwith because the Messenger may

---

[324] The various branches of the Grahams, while often raiding each other, could raise 3,000 men. On this occasion, the laird, Walter Scott of Buccleuch (1566–1611) violated the marcher laws with a spectacular raid on Carlisle Castle and the rescue of William Armstrong of Kinmount (*c.*1540–1603), a noted border reiver. This was a formidable display of force which directly touched the amity of the kingdoms. The affair occupied a great deal of council time during 1596. A full account is given in John Spottiswoode, *History of the Church of Scotland* (Edinburgh, 1850) Book Six, 1–4. The warden of the East March from 1593, Scrope, governor of Carlisle Castle – the raid happened on the watch of his deputy, Richard Lowther – sent various Grahams named in a schedule to London for investigation by council their journey to proceed 'shrife' to 'shrife' (sheriff to sheriff), because they had no security of bonds, BL Lansdowne MS 82/no. 7/fol. 14r.

be retyrned and I no futher trobled with them.[325] ffrom my howse at Westm[inste]r the last of Maye 1596.

[Burghley]
I have already wrytten to my L[ord] Scroop, not to com upp, but to send some sufficient person with proves ag[ainst] these Grymes.[326]

Your lo[ving] father

W. Burghley

[Postscript]
God send me some good howres, for I have no good dayes.

Dorse

ADDRESSED in Henry Maynard's hand:
To the right honourable
Sir Robert Cecil knight
of her Ma[jes]ties privy Connsell.

ENDORSED in Simon Willis's hand:
Wmo May 1596
L[ord] Thre[asure]r to my M[aste]r

Letter No. 98

William, Lord Burghley to Sir Robert Cecil, 13 July 1596

⅔ p. Dictated to Henry Maynard, with two holograph postscripts.
Addressed, endorsed signed.

Text

I Doe send hearinclosed unto yowe A peticion of Nicholas Sanders whoe as it semeh remaineth under arrest at Plimmowthe at the suite of the Maior there, upon some bargaine passed between them for the part of his prize sugers. But inasmuch as Mr. Sanders is by order & dirrecion of the Generalls to follow them in this Action, as doth

---

[325] Burghley noted a general tightening of Border defences at that juncture to Cecil, TNA SP12/259/no. 60; *CSPD 1595–1597*, 253.

[326] The Privy Council wrote back and forth all summer about the Grahams, the place of their custody and the method of their correction. Scrope wrote to Burghley, on 30 May 1596, noting he had already sent the Grahams southwards by way of the Council of the North at York, thence to London, *Cal. Border Papers*, ii, 131–132.

appeare by theire writinge under their handes and seales, I see noe reason he showld be staied at anie privat persons sute.[327] And therefore I praie yowe to acquaint my lls [Lords] of the Connsell that are theare at the Cort with the peticion and to procure theire LLs [Lords] letters to Sir fferdinando Gorges, to treate with the Maior, so as he maie take sum such order as he can betwene them, whearebie Mr. Sanders maie be released to proceade on his voiadge, the staie wheareof I cannot but be vearie chargeable to him.[328] Soe fare yowe well. Ffrom my howse at theobaldes this xiii[th] of Julie 1596.

Your loving father,

[Signed]
W. Burghley

[Burghley]
I am forced to kep my bed all this day, havying small hope of amedment.
    I long to heare some good news of Hulst[329]

[Maynard]
I send yowe a letter signed for Mr. Sandars to ease the messinger from retorning hither for my
hande.

[In Maynard's hand at the left foot of the page]
Mr. Secretary

Dorse

ADDRESSED in Henry Maynard's hand:
To my Lovinge Sonne
Sir Robert Cecil, knight
hir ma[jes]ties principall secretarye

---

[327] The mayor of Plymouth informed Cecil of a merchant, Nicholas Sanders or Saunders, who was embroiled in a dispute over the custody of his prize sugars. Hatfield, Cecil Papers, 42/39, 40; *HMCS*, vi, 258–259, 259. Sanders had been licensed to proceed according to higher instructions – probably Howard's or Essex's – and had been detained under suspicion of theft.

[328] James Baggervas, the mayor of Dover, *HMCS*, vi, 209–210.

[329] George Gilpin warned Essex that the loss of Hulst would certainly mean the consequent loss of Bergen-op-Zoom and Auxelle. Elizabeth was pressured heavily to send troops and men, while Henry IV redeployed forces used to relieve Calais and Boulogne, *HMCS*, iv, 243–244, 258, 294–295, 276. The archduke was defeated by a combined force with English troops with the earl of Lincoln, *HMCS*, vi, 289–290.

ENDORSED in Cecil's hand:
This L[ette]re comes to me from my L[ord]. I pray yowr L[ordshi]p reade it and that Inclused to which my l[ord] wold be glad of your hand in maiorem authoritatem.

Letter No. 99

William, Lord Burghley to Sir Robert Cecil, 16 July 1596

⅔ p. Holograph.
Addressed, endorsed, signed.

Text

I am right sorry that I can send yow no better stuff out of Irland by these letters and other wrytyngs wherby I se no lykhood of peace ther and therfor Hir Ma[jes]ty must be forced for a present furder chardg, to proceede more rowndly with force than with words.[330]
I meane though I am still possessed with payne to come thyther to morrow, to attend this and other service for I se a harvest of busyness more redy, than a good harvest of corn.[331]

from my bed almost at x of the clock
16 July 1596

You lov[ing] father,

W. Burghley

[Postscript added after signing]

[330] The Queen had proclaimed Tyrone and O'Donnell rebels and traitors at this juncture, and the proclamations were read in early July, to little response. Tyrone burnt his castle of Dungannon to the ground, razing the land in his estates, preventing forage for any troops. The rebels had refused the articles for their 'submission' and were now officially outside the law. An anonymous report then attached referred to the present attainder of Feagh McHugh O'Byrne, whose tormenting of the English on the southern edge of the Pale unbalanced any future campaigns to the north. The lord deputy, Russell, had licensed Sir John Harrington (1560–1612), *ODNB*, to proceed with a savage attack on O'Byrne. *CSPI 1592–1596*, 334–337.
[331] Burghley may well have referred to the heavy administrative work ahead for raising horse and foot out of the counties for Ireland and Flushing, with the attendant needs of victualling, apparel, arms, and transportation. See his memorandum of 21 July 1596, TNA SP 12/259/no. 74; *CSPD 1595–1597*, 288; Letter No. 111.

I have severed the advertisements and wrytyngs accordyng to ther several conditions and tyed with threds.[332]

Dorse

ADDRESSED in Henry Maynard's hand:
To my Lovinge Sonne
Sir Robart Cecill
knight, hir ma[jes]ties
principall secretarie[333]

ENDORSED in Simon Willis's hand:
26 July 1596
L[ord] Thre[asure]r to my M[aste]r ffrom Theobaldes

Letter No. 100

William, Lord Burghley to Sir Robert Cecil, 15 July 1596

1 p. Dictated to Henry Maynard.
Addressed, endorsed, signed.

Text

With your letters nowe received theare is comen letters from the Archb[ishop] of Yorke and the Counsell theare directed to mee whereof the one concerneth a priest named Dawson, beinge A ronagate into and owt of Ireland, whose Examinations also I have seen:[334] And consideringe he sheweth himself obstinat in awnsweringe, it weare convenient that the Counsell would take order to cawse him to be pinched with manacle or summ such like thinge, withowt danger of anie member of his Bodie, and thereby compell

---

[332] Burghley had suffered serious infirmity during Apr. and May 1596, and from 20 Apr. to 14 May virtually all Irish letters were retained by Cecil.

[333] Here is the first mention of Cecil's appointment as the Queen's Principal Secretary of State, for which no letters patent survives on the rolls.

[334] Miles Dawson, a priest, was examined by Hutton, archbishop of York on 23 July 1596. Here Burghley refers to Hutton's letter of 10 July 1596. Direction to proceed with Dawson's examination the following day was returned by Hutton, BL Lansdowne MS 82/no. 29; Strype, *Annals of the Reformation*, iv, 305; *HMCS*, vi, 283, 431, 432. Dawson's orders were in question. He provided salient intelligence of his travels in Ireland and Scotland and knew Essex's rehabilitated Jesuit servant, Thomas Wright. He had been to Spain and met Cecil's agent, John Cecil. A further examination before Hutton in Oct. 1596 yielded more information about Wright and his 'cavilling' to 'worshipful Bacon', in fact the truth of Essex and Anthony Bacon's use of Wright in their intelligence. *HMCS*, vi, 431, 432. See Hutton's list of cases for Burghley, 15 July 1596, BL Lansdowne MS 82/31/fol. 64r.

him to answeare more directlie. And yet nevertheless to for beare proceadinge against him at ther Asisses, for that he maie afterwardes be further tried by ordinarie commission theare of oyer and terminer.[335]

The other letter concerneth one Atkinson, whoe if he doe not appeare the xvii[th] daie before the Counsell heare, as it is written, he is commaunded. but whither it be uppon bond or noe is not expresse, then is theare anie cause to ~~doubt~~ feare that he shall proceade at the Assisses the xix[th] as he pretended to doe.[336] One other letter which yowe have sent me from Mr. Attorneie, concerneth the confession of the great Cossener Williamson, which I meane to keepe with mee untill I cumm to the Cort.[337] and soe I will doe these from Yorke, And be bold to make awnsweare to that Connsell by my privat letter.[338] But a letter of most importance is that which is written to mee from Mons[ieur] Caron, expressinge the same dangers, whareof yowe mak mention in your owne letter.[339] And the same also confirmed by the letter written by the States of Zeland to the Counsell heare,[340] which I doe returne unto yowe with mine opinion.[341] that it is most necessarie

[335] Burghley wished to extract a further confession from Dawson and appears to be requesting that the Privy Council warrant the use of a minor form of bodily inhibition – the manacle – rather than full torture, which might require Dawson's removal to London.

[336] Richard Atkinson appeared before the Privy Council answering charges that he had assaulted the gaoler at Ripon, BL Lansdowne MS 82/no 31, fol. 64r; *HMCS*, vi, 252, 252–254. Hutton later sought Dawson's pardon, BL Lansdowne MS, 84/no. 78. Atkinson may have worked in some capacity for the Cecils in Scottish intelligence, *HMCS*, vi, 378.

[337] Nicholas Williamson had been accused of trying to turn the earl of Shrewsbury into an enemy of the Crown. The Talbot entourage was then engaged in a huge quarrel with the Stanhope family, ostensibly over weirs on the Trent. For the period covered by these letters, see Thomas Stanhope to Cecil cited in Wallace T. MacCaffrey, 'Talbot and Stanhope: An episode in Elizabethan politics', *Bulletin of the Institute Historical Research*, 33 (1960), 73–85. While this feud is not touched in Burghley's letters here, both sides approached the Cecils, with an extensive correspondence remaining at Hatfield in the Cecil Papers.

[338] No copy of this letter is extant.

[339] Noel de Caron's urgent message referred to the relief of the Low Countries' forces, which were protecting territory from the Archduke Albert who had attacked Hulst rather than heavily defended Ostend.

[340] Noel de Caron advised the earl of Essex on 21 July that the States were pressing the Queen for reinforcements of 500–600 men with promises of 800–1,000 more. They had all wished that Essex and his fleet had been there to help, *HMCS*, vi, 276. These matters refer to the Triple Alliance then being negotiated first between England and France before it was widened to include the Dutch, Wernham, *Return of the Armadas*, 80. The League capitulated to the king and signed 14 May 1596, TNA SP 78/37/fol. 194. In the following months, Henry IV would continue secret negotiations with both papal legates and the Archduke Albert earning blistering criticism from Burghley. The balance between continental and Irish expenses would galvanize the Cecils, as Essex was frustrated by the continental peace and the depth of anti-Spanish sentiment outside the States General.

[341] Burghley's reply is not extant.

that hir Ma[jes]tie should have speedie regard thearto be aidinge them
with somm further succourse to be sent to Flusshinge, accordinge
both to the necessitye of the cawse and for the promise made by Sir
Fr[ancis] Veare in hir ma[jes]ties name, which to my remembrance
he had warrant so.[342] And thowgh I finde my selfe nothing amended
of my greefe yet uppon this occasion I will with Gods leave, if I
shall be hable to lie in my Coache, be theare on Saturdaie night,
or Sondaie some time of the daie. From Theobaldes this xv of July
1596.

[Burghley]
Your lov[ing] lame,
paynfull father.

W. Burghley

Dorse

ADDRESSED in Henry Maynard's hand:
For the Q[ueen s] Ma[jes]ties Affayres
To my Lovinge sonne Sir Robarte Cecill
knight hir Majesties principall Secretary

[Signed, on the dorse]
W. Burghley

[Maynard]
hast
post hast
hast

ENDORSED in Burghley's hand:
at Theob[alds]
15 Julii, 1596

---

[342] Sir Francis Vere had been advised to give verbal assurances while the amount of
assistance possible was calculated. He sought assurances that his forces would not be depleted
in the relief of Calais, but a new force entirely would be raised. See Letter No. 91; *HMCS*, vi,
140, for Vere's men were used extensively as auxiliaries to the Dutch. In June 1596, Burghley
replied to Sir Robert Sidney at Flushing that ordnance was 'to be defalked again upon the
pay of the garrison' by the treasurer at war in the Low Countries, Hatfield, Cecil Papers,
41/fol. 62r; *HMCS*, vi, 212. Burghley alluded here to the royal assurances made to the States
General for provisions for Flushing given by Sir Francis Vere.

Letter No. 101

William, Lord Burghley to Sir Robert Cecil, 28 July 1596

¼ p. Holograph.
Addressed, endorsed, signed.

Text

I most humbly thank hir Majesty for impartyng to me the reportes of hir victoryes hopyng to have that knolledg so verefyed by hir own Generals, as hir Ma[jes]ty shall have iust cause to have publyck thanks gyven to that Almighty God that maketh hir so mighty ag[ainst] hir ennemyes and and most humble to acknoledg from whence she hath hir strength and wordly glory.[343]

28 July 1596

Your lov[ing] father,

W. Burghley

Dorse

ADDRESSED
To my lovinge Sonne
Sir Robart Cecill knight
Principall Secretarye
to hir ma[jes]tie.

ENDORSED in a clerk's hand [Henry Maynard?]
28 July 1596
Lo[rd] Thresorer to my M[aste]r.
[Note: This hand could be that of Richard Percival, the same clerk who took over the compilation of the Scottish Letter Book, TNA SP 52/52]

---

[343]The first news of the spectacular success of the Cadiz raid. The correspondents from Rome, Antwerp, Venice, Madrid, and Middlebury all reported the English rout and subsequent slaughter of the civilian population. *The Fugger News-Letters*, 2nd ser., ed. Victor von Klarwill (London, 1926), 276–281. The Cecils would be among those to make a very critical assessment of the voyage's true value later in 1596.

Letter No. 102

Draft of a Privy Council Letter dated 13 October 1596

¾ p. with slightly frayed left margin.
Signed by Burghley and Lord Buckhurst.[344]
Dorse: missing.

Text

After our hartie commendatcions unto yow. According to her ma[jes]ties pleasure signified by your letter, we called before us aswell suche Creditors being about vi on nomber as did impugn the sute of all the rest of the Creditors of Umfrie Abdey for her ma[jes]ties protection unto them as also certein Alderman and other[s] who came before us in name of all the rest of the Creditors being above syxteen in nomber.[345] and after we had heard both parties we concluded in the end that with the generall consent of them all her ma[jes]tie might at her good pleasure graunt the said protection which the said Alderman and the rest of the Creditors had so humbly and so ernestlie desired, as they affirmed before us that if her ma[jes]tie did not vouchsave at their humble peticens to graunt the same it wold redound to the grete losse and hindraunce of the said Crediters. We did also caus diligent enquirie to be made for such as had exhibited any petitcens to Abdey, we cold not lerne of any suche. but thus much we understand That there hath ben in several peticons exhibited to her ma[jes]tie [page frayed] by sundrie of the Crediters of on Umfrie Abdey for the not graunting of his protection by her ma[jes]tie, which likehood may be thos peticens wherof her ma[jes]tie spake with you. And thus we wishe you hartelie well this xii[th] of October 1596.
you verie loving ffrendes,

[Signed]

[344]Thomas Sackville, 1st Baron Buckhurst and 1st earl of Dorset (1536–1608), *ODNB*. He was Burghley's successor as Lord Treasurer and an ally of Cecil on the Council.
[345]Humphrey Abdey or Abdie was responsible for settling debts out of his father, Roger Abdie's, estate. Abdie had died on 20 June 1595 leaving assets totalling £23,767 6s. 3d. against debts of £20,748 15s. 5d., for which the son was bound to make good, *CSPD 1595–1597*, 113. One creditor, Tristram Conyers, petitioned Burghley's secretary Bernard Dewhurst for payment of the £205 owed him, ibid. In Feb. 1596, another creditor, Alexander Wellor, clothier, appealed to the Privy Council for them to cease their protection of Abdey, otherwise the creditors 'should be prejudiced to ther utter undoing for the benefitt of one privat man' well capable of payment. *APC 1595–1596*, 202. Cecil and others gave the council order to a committee of oversight composed of Sir Richard Martin, Sir William Webb, the recorder of London (John Croke), Alderman Houghton, Thomas Campbell, George Sutherton, and Sheriff Loe.

W. Burghley
T. Buckhurst

[No dorse, no address]

Letter No. 103

William, Lord Burghley to Sir Robert Cecil, 31 October 1596

1 p. Dictated to Henry Maynard.
Addressed, endorsed, signed.

Text

I neither can my self write, nor yet forbeare to expresse the grief to thinke of the dangerous estate of hir ma[jes]ties Armie in Ireland, wheare all the treasure sent in August is expended,[346] and the Armie consistinge of the number of abowt seaven thowsand widening [withdrawing?] paie of her ma[jes]tie, besides a great number of others havinge extraordinarie paiments by waie of pentions and such like, the monethlie charges whereof commeth to viii^M v^C ix l sterlinge [£8,509], and heareunto is to be added 1000 newe men nowe latelie transported, whose monethlye paie must cumm to MCxxii l [£1,122] the moneth, for which the treasurer hath never a pennie in Ireland & nowe to this charge doth presentlye followe the charge of 2000 newe men alreadie levied and appointed to be sent thither for whome at their arrival there, there is also noe monie to entertaine them.[347] What great danger this maie be I doe trembell to utter, consideringe theie will force the Countrie with all manner of oppressions, rather than furnishe. And thearebie the multitude of the Q[ueen s] loiall subiectes in the English pale tempted to Rebell. Thes unpleasant lines I am most sorie to be presented to hir ma[jes]tie, but I cannot endure to

---

[346] *CSPI 1596–1597*, 142–146. The lord deputy, Russell, and the Council outlined their considerable needs, 15 Oct. 1596.

[347] The earlier payment of treasure on Aug. 1596 was swamped under the arrival of 1,000 troops levied in 18 counties for Irish service *CSPI 1596–1597*, 289). Burghley issued warrant for 100 foot out of Lincolnshire, 27 Aug. 1596, *HMCS*, vi, 330. A warrant to pay Sir Henry Wallop, treasurer at war in Ireland, was sent in Nov. 1596, £20,000 of which £15,000 was for the army and £5,000 for victualling. The warrant stipulated that the lord deputy and Irish Council were to advise Wallop on expenses with ordinary pay defalcated from the monthly checks, and all new, extraordinary contracts and changes to be avoided. *CSPD 1595–1597*, 306. See above, pp. 69–70.

bethinke my self of the perill. ffrom my howse in the Strand this last of October, 1596.

[Burghley]
I am homo illiterate

W. Burghley

Dorse

ADDRESSED in Henry Maynard's hand:
To my Lovinge Sonne
Sir Rob[er]t Cecill
knight, hir ma[jes]ties
principlall secretarye
Ul[ti]mo Oct 1596
Lo[rd] Thr[esore]r to my M[aste]r

Letter No. 104

William, Lord Burghley to Sir Robert Cecil, 1 November 1596

¼ p. In Henry Maynard's hand. Two lines in Burghley's hand.

Text

For that Mr. Lake war not in the waie to engrosse the warrant for the Ile of Wight, I doe the messure herinclosed send the same to yowe to be written by such of the Clerkes of the Signett as attend theare at the Cort which is all I have at this time to write yowe.[348]

[348]The warrant for 900 men for the Isle of Wight was recalled by the Queen through Cecil of Windebanke, the clerk of the signet present, who had taken it to Richmond, TNA SP 12/260/no. 113; *CSPD 1595–1597*, 358.

Burghley was writing detailed memorials for the security of the ports and coasts of the realm in case of a Spanish armada that winter or the following spring, *CSPD 1595–1597* 303, 305. There was a general tightening of Cecil's secretarial control at this time, particularly over privy seals, with Cecil's command to Maynard to produce letters and to continue a monthly docquet for the Queen. At the same time as his father was making calculations for the proposals, he was preparing them for his son to set before Queen and Council, *CSPD 1595–1597*, 306; see above, p. 26. The alarms of Nov. 1596 contrast with a long 'memorial' Burghley wrote on 1 Oct. in which he set down the priorities: Scrope was to be licensed to court (during the parliament for which writs were sent); commission for the Borders; lawyers for the court of Requests; bishoprics of Chester and London in need of supply (levies); renewal of Sir Robert Carey's 20 horse at Berwick; need for horse by Eure and

Ffrom my house in the strand this first of November 1596.

[Burghley]
An other such tormenting night will
Shorten my dayes, wherof I desyre some end.
Your lo[ving] father,

W. Burghley

Dorse

ADDRESSED by Henry Maynard:
To my Lovinge Sonne
Sir Rob[er]t Cecill
Knight hir ma[jes]ties
Principall secretarye

ENDORSED by Simon Willis:
L[ord] Thre[asure]r to my M[aste]r

Letter No. 105

William, Lord Burghley to Sir Robert Cecil, 6 November 1596

⅓ p. Holograph.
Addressed, endorsed, signed.

Text

I send to yowe heareinclosed a letter which I received this morninge from the Maior of Dartmouthe directed to my lls [Lords]: of the Counselle with certaine Advertisementes theareinclosed.[349] I have

Scrope, as well as need in Berwick. Again, while these matters required steady order and drafting, the Council and the Cecils had to move quickly in another direction with the expected return of the Spanish armada. Cecil having obtained the seal of the office, now seemed to concentrate less on the tasks parcelled out to him in the earlier letters, delegating matters to trusted messengers (e.g. Darcy, Killigrew, the Stanhopes), concentrating instead on policy and renewed rigour in the administrative instruments of his office and their records. Due to Cecil's and the Queen's suspicions about fraudulent or suspicious privy seal accounting, he asked Windebanke on 23 Aug. for the original warrants paid by him since the death of Walsingham, *CSPD 1595–1597*, 269. This suggests that Burghley in turn had given others work not sufficiently tracked during his pro tem secretariat.

[349] Russell was similarly alarmed in Aug. 1596, calling the entire kingdom in conspiracy against the Queen, while the army was destitute of money and victuals, *HMCS*, vi, 351. The charge here entered was nearly £10,000 per month, approaching the level of expenditure

thearewith acquainted my L[ord] of Essex and yowe maie impart the same there to hir Ma[jes]tie or the Counsell as yowe shall see cawse. ffrom my howse in the Strand this vi^th of November 1596.

[Postscript]
I have received a certaine Advise from my L[ord] Willoughby which I have sent to my L[ord] of Essex.³⁵⁰

Yo[ur] Lovinge
father,

W. Burghley

Dorse

ADDRESSED in Henry Maynard's hand:
To my Lovinge Sonne Sir Robart Cecill knight, hir Ma[jes]ties principall secretarye

ENDORSED in Simon Willis's hand:
6 Nov. 1596
L[ord] Thre[asure]r to my M[aste]r

in the Low Countries, 1585–1589, which by treaty had been set at about £120,000 per annum.

³⁵⁰ Intelligence from Morlaix was taken from seven Flemings whose ships and goods were seized by the king of Spain and sent by the mayor of Dartmouth, Gilbert Staplehill, to the Council. Dartmouth, as other ports, was a rich ground for Cecil's intelligence. TNA SP 12/260/no. 87; *CSPD 1595–1597*, 301–302; Wernham, *Return of the Armadas*, 272–273. Essex and Willoughby d'Eresby were included in a commission of senior military advisers, a council of war, created in late 1596 for planning the Islands expedition. Hatfield, Cecil Papers, 46/fol. 32r; *HMCS*, vi, 469; Wernham, *Return of the Armadas*, 136–137. Willoughby's advice may have been incorporated into Burghley's general proposition which gave opinion on the Adelantado, TNA SP 12/260/nos. 92, 93, 94; *CSPD 1595–1597*, 302. Further notes by Burghley on the wider scope for defence may have been incorporated into Willoughby's papers, because he sent his ideas to him in writing on at least one occasion when he was not notified of the meeting of Council, allowing that words might be misconstrued and offering clarification as needed. TNA SP 12/260/nos. 82, 101, 102; *CSPD 1595–1597*, 298, 305; Wernham, *Return of the Armadas*, 144–145. There were, throughout, major points of disagreement for the so-called 'council of war'. Another member, Sir John Borough, proposed divergent ideas as well. TNA SP 12/260/no. 83; *CSPD 1595–1597*, 209–210; Letter No. 106.

Letter No. 106

William, Lord Burghley to Sir Robert Cecil, 7 November 1596

⅓ p. Dictated to Henry Maynard.
Addressed, endorsed, signed.

Text

I send to yowe hearewith such letters as I have this daie received. yowe maie as yowe shall see cawse acquaint hir ma[jes]tie both with Mr. Bowes letter[351] and the L[ord] Scropes, towchinge his request for the paie of the footebandes theare.[352] Yowe shall also do well to acquaint hir ma[jes]tie with that part of Sir Edward Norris letter, wheareby he advertiseth the sendinge of certaine forces to Callis, which in mine opinion hath good probabilitie in yt.[353] So farre you well. ffrom my howse in the Strand, this vii[th] of November 1596.

Your Lovinge father,

W. Burghley

Dorse

ADDRESSED in Henry Maynard's hand:
To my Lovinge Sonne Sir
Robart Cecil knight, hir ma[jes]ties principall secretary

ENDORSED in Richard Percival's hand:
7 Nov. 1596
Lo[rd] Thre[surer] to my M[aste]r

[351] Letters from Robert Bowes to the Queen or Council or the Cecils would have come with Scrope's, see n. 352.

[352] Scrope's letter was received with the Scottish post for the pay of footbands in the marches. Acknowledging his letter of the 12th received that day with the Queen's command to return the 100 footmen to Berwick, Scrope argued against the order. He explained that when he wrote for leave to go to court, he noted the march was quiet and likely to remain so only by means of these 100 men. He asked that the footbands remain and that the laird of Buccleuch not be released for he would disturb the peace. *Cal. Border Papers*, ii, 206, 208–209.

[353] Norris's advice was taken at the very height of the armada scare of Nov. 1596. It dovetailed with Lord Willoughby's dissenting view of a 1597 naval expedition against Spain directly in favour of a large army sent through Ostend. See Birch, *Memoirs*, ii 164–168. No one knew precisely if the Spanish fleet would attack, but the Council was unified in the need for an offensive manoeuvre, as no single coastal town could have withstood an invasion. Crippled by slow and untimely intelligence, the Council only knew that the Spanish fleet had already been beaten by the weather. Wernham, *Return of the Armadas*, 69–81 137–145, 156.

Letter No. 107

William, Lord Burghley to Sir Robert Cecil, 9 November 1596

⅓ p. Holograph.
Addressed, endorsed, signed.

Text

Though at your departure, you found me not disposed to mak any censur of the certificates thynkyng the borden to heavy for me alon, yet if yow Fynd hir ma[jes]ty's disposition or expectation from me, yow may shew hir this included, which I began by Candell light, but my head would not answer my desyre.[354]

I have gyven this mark in the margats, for the matters to be executed.

Your loving father,

W. Burghley

[Postscript]
I send yow my L[ord] Willoughbyes opinion much vareyng from the rest.[355]

[354]Burghley's work on the privy seal certificates in this letter are discussed above, p. 25. Burghley was not left completely alone in drafting the certificates for levies, musters, imprests, and money, all of which emanated from the preparations of new defences by the war commission prompted by the rumoured Spanish invasion. Letters Nos 103, 104, 105; TNA SP 12/ 260/nos. 120,121. A reckoning of payments was issued at Easter 1596 for the Cadiz expedition and further charges issuing from Michaelmas 1595 until 16 Nov. 1596 at which time Burghley may have completed a thorough accounting of such payments, *CSPD 1595–1597*, 313. Monies had been disbursed as follows: for Cadiz, £16,000; for the year 1595–1596: to the Admiralty, £55,685 16s. 7d.; for victualling, £63,491 3s. 6d.; for ordnance, £14,788 6s. 8d.; for powder, £16,445 15s.; for Ireland £91,579 1ls.; for the Low Countries £75,145 4s.; total, £330,135 10s. 9d. Burghley made rough notes on 14 Nov. for the victualling and arming of the forces, TNA SP 12/260/no. 105; *CSPD 1595–1597*, 306; Letter No. 105. Ireland was a growing concern directly related to the Spanish threat through the rebels. For the Exchequer year, 1 Oct.–30 Sept., Sir Henry Wallop's new privy seal was issued 11 Nov., for £20,266 13s. 4d. Sterling, or Irish £27,022 4s. 5d. ob. Irish. TNA E 351/236 mn 19b. See Letter No. 103.
[355]*CSPD 1595–1597*, 305. For Willoughby's idea of an army through Ostend thence to Calais, Birch, *Memoirs*, ii, 164–168. The Council was generally agreed on Burghley's notations, to begin preparing against a rumoured Spanish invasion. The Council list is comprehensive: heavy shipping to combat light Spanish vessels out of the Low Countries, would prevent them landing in England or crossing from an occupation of Calais, see Letter No. 106. Domestic preparations were in hand: the soldiers had to be sent to train the newly mustered men; horse and armour and new captains with troops were levied to fight a Spanish landing. A second, inland army was to protect the land and the Queen's person, with the

Dorse

ADDRESSED in Michael Hickes' hand:
To my loving sone Sir Robert Cecyll knight hir ma[jes]ties principall Secretarie.

ENDORSED in Richard Percival's hand:
9 November 1596
The Lo[rd] Thre[asure]r to my M[aste]r

Letter No. 108

William, Lord Burghley to Sir Robert Cecil, 14 November 1596

3–4 pp. Holograph.
Addressed, endorsed, signed.

Text

I was first advertised this evening by my Lo[rd] Chamberlens letter, that hir Ma[jes]ty deffered hir remove unto Wednesday which is the very daye of hir access to the Crown and now by your letter I perceave the lyk beyng right sarry for the cause.[356] and therfor I pray yow whan tyme may serve yow, lett hir Ma[jes]ty know that I do send to heare of hir Ma[jes]ty's ammendment, for by hir impediments to order hir affayres, all hir realm shall suffer detriment.[357]

Thames and estuary guarded, and new fortifications, not unlike 1588 and the renewed articles drafted by Burghley in late 1595, *HMCS*, vi, 472–473. Pinnaces for reconnaissance were also necessary. Munitions were to be sent so that all towns and counties were amply provisioned with gunpowder and ordnance. All ports under strict surveillance. The French and Dutch churches required to present the names of 'strangers' in and around London newly attending at their churches. The defence of the Isle of Wight, Plymouth, Portsmouth, and the Isle of Man were to be addressed. The levies were countermanded in late Nov. 1596 when the danger had passed.

[356]The Queen's accession day, 17 Nov. Burghley here refers to another generational replacement, that of 2nd Baron Hunsdon, George Carey (1548–1603), *ODNB*, who was named captain of the gentlemen pensioners after his father's death, 23 July 1596, lord chamberlain and privy councillor (14 Apr. 1597), and knight of the garter (23 Apr. 1597). Hunsdon's death left vacant the governor's place at Berwick to which the second baron eventually succeeded. His brother John, frequent correspondent with both Cecils, was marshal of Berwick, 1596–1598, ibid.

[357]Burghley may have alerted his son to the necessity of bringing matters of expenditure to a final account, especially in view of the £20,000 sent into Ireland three days before for victuals and pay, with deferment of unnecessary rewards, *CSPD* 1595–1597, 306. The present need also touched on the delegation from the Low Countries then in England, with

I have not bene Idle sence yow went havyng (though not prophaned this sabeth day) made it a full workyng day such is the Importunitie of sutors and now wearyed I end my scriblyng.

14 Nov. at night.

You lov[ing] father,

W. Burghley

Dorse

ADDRESSED in Henry Maynard's hand:
To my Lovinge sonne Sir Rob[er]t Cecill knight hir ma[jes]ties principall secretarye

ENDORSED Possibly in the hand of Richard Percival:
14 Nov. 1596
Lo[rd] Thr[esuro]r to my M[aste]r

Letter No. 109

William, Lord Burghley to Sir Robert Cecil, 15 November 1596

1 p. Holograph.
Addressed, endorsed, signed.

Text

I know not, what determination hir Ma[jes]ty hath for any furder proceedyng in the cause for which the deputies of the States cum hyther.[358]

But for your information I have thought good to sett down brefly the State of the cawse, as I do tak it now to rest.

---

whom terms of payment for the cautionary towns were now under negotiation. See Letter No. 109. Burghley was also here stressing the Queen's pre-eminence in affairs, ordering the working of her kingdom directly to her person.

[358] See Burghley to Cecil, 15 Oct. 1596: 'I send the answer made the States' deputies of which only a short answer was given to them; with their reply in French. I see no cause to answer further till the Queen has been acquainted therewith. I have sent for Mr. Bodley, and required him to deliver them the Queen's message.' TNA SP 12/260/no. 62; *CSPD 1595–1597*, 294. Burghley's reference is to the delegation in England, then negotiating outstanding payments due by treaty.

Beyng moved therto becawse by the suspence hereof hir Ma[jes]ty is charged with the contynuance of hir auxiliary, which at the lest is above l^M l [£1,000] yerly. and if the nombres that ar contrary to the Contract, brought into the Cautionary towns, might be paid by the States, hir Ma[jes]ty might therby be eased of a gretar some. but as those ii towns, have drawn in from the auxiliary great nombres, the chardg of the auxiliary now cometh but to xxiiii^M v^C iii^{xx} iii [£24,563] which is the some of the States pretend to discharg, and so hir Ma[jes]ty for hir cautionary shall still stand charged with xlii^M [£42,000] yerly.[359]

These matters ar not pleasyng, and yet I can not please my self, withowt disburdening my self therof, and so at tyme convenient I pray yow inform hir Ma[jes]ty hereof.

15 Nov[ember] 1596

Your lov[ing] father,

W. Burghley

Dorse

ADDRESSED in Henry Maynard's hand:
To my Lovinge sonne Sir Robart Cecill knight hir Ma[jes]ties principall secretarye

ENDORSED in Richard Percival's hand:
15 Nov 1596
My lo[rd] Thre[suro]r to my M[aste]r

---

[359]The English wanted relief from the charge of £42,000 for the cautionary towns of Brill and Flushing. Instead, the Queen wanted outstanding debts repaid, because a vast expedition was planned for the summer of 1597, *CSPD 1595–1597*, 313. Bodley's embassy in 1595, set forth by Cecil, began to move in this direction until the Triple Alliance was signed in Oct. 1596. Burghley's figures here were meant to argue that the English bore more than their share. For a summary of the expenditure for the towns, Brill and Flushing, in 1598, see TNA SP 12/268/no. 8. There was disagreement on both sides about amounts, as can be seen from the various accounts maintained by Sir Thomas Wilkes and their interpretation by Burghley, TNA SP 12/259/nos. 90, 91, 92; *CSPD 1595–1597*, 265. These figures included expenditure on Cadiz, with troops drawn from the cautionary towns for the expedition, according to a brief made by the treasurer at war, Sir Thomas Sherley, TNA SP 12/259/no. 92. Amidst the pressing matter of the Low Countries treaty and the confusion in English accounts, Cecil's desire to have sole control of the privy seal warrants at this juncture appears abundantly justified. See Letter No. 107. The armada threat during this time caused concern. Archduke Albert's aggression in France continued, although he was without funds, as the Spanish crown was about to declare bankruptcy.

Letter No. 110

William, Lord Burghley to Sir Robert Cecil, 15 November 1596

¼ p. Dictated to Henry Maynard, signed.
Addressed, endorsed, signed.

Text

I doe send hearewith unto yowe the letters that yowe left with me of the L[ord] Scroopes, which I doe returne unto yowe,[360] and thearewith the forme of a submission conceived by mee to be made by the Graimes which I think inditfernt for them to make, and for the L[ord] Scroope to receive from them.[361] ffrom my howse in the Strand this xv^th of November 1596.

Your Lovinge ffather,

W. Burghley

[Left foot of the page in Maynard's hand]
Sir Robert Cecill

Dorse

ADDRESSED in Henry Maynard's hand:
To my Lovinge Sonne Sir Robart Cecill knight, hir Ma[jes]ties principall secretarie

ENDORSED in Richard Percival's hand:
15 Nov 1596
My Lo[rd] Tresorer to my M[aste]r

Letter No. 111

William, Lord Burghley to Sir Robert Cecil, 19 December 1596

½ p. Holograph.
Addressed, endorsed, signed.

---

[360] See *Cal. Border Papers*, ii, 210. Scrope's letter to the Privy Council, 1 Nov. 1596, is endorsed: the submission which his lordship requires at the hands of the Graymes and by Cecil, 'To be shewed to the lordes. R. C.' with a further enclosure which was the manuscript.

[361] The version of Grahams' indifferent submission received by Burghley at that time with their offer to Scrope, *Cal. Border Papers*, ii, 211–212.

Text

Neither my hand nor eie sight alloweth me to wryte. I thynk it will be hard to persuade the Citizens to be at a new charge, consideryng the lavy set for Cales, is not yet discharged, althowgh they had my L[ord] of Essex and L[ord] admyrall solemn word for to be answered of the spoyles.[362]

The Cite also taketh it unkyndly that hir Ma[jes]ty priviledgeth both billingsley and rich[ard] Saltygsto [Salstonstall] to wax rych, and to be disburdened of the Corn charges of the Cite wherby a nombre of Aldermen will gyve over ther clokes.[363] I can not but wryte this though I will do my uttermost for hir Ma[jes]ty's service.
W. B.

Dorse

ADDRESSED possibly in the hand of Hickes or Clapham:
For Mr. Secretary

ENDORSED in Simon Willis's hand:
19 Dec 1596
L[ord] Thre[asure]r to my M[aste]r

Letter No. 112

William, Lord Burghley to Sir Robert Cecil, May 1597

⅓ p. Holograph.
Addressed, endorsed, signed.

---

[362] Burghley's note refers to the preparations for Calais, then underway. The correspondence concerning the tax-free imports of grain and corn, probably an investor arrangement between the commanders and City merchants, seemed inequitable to Burghley. The letter may be dated in Dec. 1596 or Jan. 1597.
[363] Grievances over taxation were growing in the City. The lord mayor, Henry Billingsley, and Sir Richard Saltonstall, *ODNB*, lord mayor in 1598, had proposed a joint stock venture of merchants to provide corn for the City and the Queen's forces as well as an import of wheat and rye exempt from ordinary customs. The syndicate included John Jolles, victualler of the Queen's forces, see Letter No. 134. Two others, William and Ralphe Freeman, were to provision 3,000 quarters (37½ tons) of wheat, also exempt from customs, *CSPD 1595–1597*, 307, 325. Here Burghley notes offending the aldermen was risky. They had already asked the lord mayor and commonalty for relief from provisioning warships for the following summer's proposed expedition. *HMCS*, vi, xv–xvi, 534–536; Archer, *Military Gazetteer*, 095; Ian Archer, 'The burden of taxation in sixteenth-century London', *Historical Journal*, 44 (2001), 599–627. Carmarthen opposed Saltonstall's interim appointment as customer of the London port after Thomas Phelippes's massive debt and imprisonment, *HMCS*, vi, 529.

Text

This lack of a resolut answer from hir Ma[jes]ty dryveth to the wall. Therfor I pray yow once ageyn move hir Ma[jes]ty for hir people suffre great extremities for want of releff of monny and clothes, as yow may se by Sir Rob[er]t Sydney's letter.[364]

I dowt how to gett Mr. Chancellor to come because he complayneth of his helth.[365]

I way not who shall have the offer.

Your lov[ing] father,

W. Burghley

Dorse

ADDRESSED in Burghley's hand:
To my son Sir Robert Cecill hir Ma[jes]ty's principall Secretary

ENDORSED in Richard Percival's hand:
Maii 1597
My lo[rd] Tresorer to my M[aste]r

Letter No. 113

William, Lord Burghley to Sir Robert Cecil, 13 May 1597

⅓ p. Dictated to Henry Maynard.
Addressed, endorsed, signed.

---

[364] English food supplies had been scarce all winter. The Queen was known to be negotiating fiercely for the reduction of expenditure in the granting of licences for her military supply, *Fugger News-Letters*, 287, 293. There were complaints from Sidney to which answer was made 21 May 1597; the Privy Council's letter to Sir Francis Vere enclosed the Queen's letter outlining resolutions taken for the relief of Flushing and Brill, *APC 1597*, 132–133. The bankruptcy of the government's contractors for the supply of apparel, as well as that of several leading merchants, created delays in the delivery of supply as well as money, with the government ordering the paymaster of the troops in the Low Countries to defalcate apparel charges immediately, *APC 1597*, 135; Letter No. 113.

[365] Sir John Fortescue had to assist in the deliberation over options then available for sending money and clothing to the troops in the Low Countries. Sir Thomas Sherley (see Letter No. 113) was then ordered to declare his Treasurer's account amidst charges of staggering peculation, thereby causing merchants' failures. On relieving Sherley of his office, the government had to find a new treasurer at war and compound with new contractors.

THE LETTERS OF LORD BURGHLEY, WILLIAM CECIL

Text

Even nowe Mr. Carmarthen and Becher came unto me, and acquainted mee with the offer of Quarles, mr. Becher's brother in Lawe, for this service which Anton should undertake, which is (as I understand) to give v^C I [£500] yearelie more then Anton offreth.[366] It is likelie that this increase will cawse hir ma[jes]tie to alter her minde: therefore I have thowght good to lett yowe understand the same, that hir ma[jes]ties pleisure thearein maie be knowen. ffrom the Strand the xiith of Maie 1597.

[To the left of Burghley's signature, added after signing]
I send yow herewith also a letter which this daie I received from Sir Robert Sidney.[367]

[To the right foot of the text]
Your Lovinge father,

W. Burghley

Dorse

ADDRESSED in Henry Maynard's hand:
To my Lovinge Sonne
Sir Robart Cecill, knight,
hir ma[jes]ties pricipall secretarie.

ENDORSED in the hand of Cecil's clerk:
13 May 1597
My lo[rd] Tresorer to my M[aste]r.

---

[366] George Anton's tender was for clothing, victuals, and armour at an amount some £500 a year less than other bidders, *CSPD 1595–1597*, 440–441. Having backers and estimates which met the standards of the Wardrobe, his letters had been drawn up by Burghley, *HMCS*, vii, 196, 311, 531. Becher and Quarles had strong City connections. Quarles was a senior Household administrator of Greencloth, at a time when tensions grew over provision for the 1597 naval expedition. Sherley had been sequestered from his office of treasurer at war and had been replaced by George Meredith, paymaster. The substance of Burghley's point here was the provision of apparel for the Low Countries, *HMCS*, vii, 200. He had already drawn up the warrants for Anton's offer when Carmarthen and William Becher submitted a competing bid on behalf of Edward Quarles, James's brother, who had bonds for the performance of his proposed contract. Burghley's comment to Cecil, 'I will do as the potter doth, in breaking of a pot already made and in forming of a new', complaining of ravaging gout and the hope to see the Queen and 'some spiritual sight of the Holy Ghost this Pentecost', *HMCS*, vii, 200.

[367] The commanders in the Low Countries had been left without a proper supply structure and paymaster.

[The filing clerk could be Percival by reason of one interesting correction: 'My' is scratched over 'the' before 'Lord Tresorer', which tells that the hand belonged to someone who was regarded as a servant of both Cecils.]

Letter No. 114

William, Lord Burghley to Sir Robert Cecil, 25 May 1597

½ p. Holograph.
Addressed, endorsed, signed.

Text

I parceave that hir Ma[jes]ty lyketh augmentations of proffitt by accepting of Quarles offers he thought hatched by Beachor. I will expedit the matter whan the partyes shall come to me.[368]

I pray yow to deliver this pacquet to my L[ord] of Essex, the labor wherof hath wearied my hand and my head but unmete for any matter of weight.[369]

If I can amend, which as yet I fynd no hope of, I will be ther before your next workyng souper but rather as a roge, than a laboror.

25 Maii 1597

Your lov[ing] father,

W. Burghley

Dorse

ADDRESSED
To my lovinge sonne Sir Robart Cecill, knight hir Ma[jes]ties principall Secretarie

ENDORSED probably in Richard Percival's hand:
15 May 1597
Lo[rd] Thre[asure]r to my M[aste]r

---

[368] For reference to Mr. Becher's brother-in-law, James Quarles, see *CSPD 1595–1597*, 398. For Becher's business partner, George Leicester and Quarles's bankruptcy, see ibid. 518. Their patent and disputes were related to payments with the treasurer at war, Sir Thomas Sherley. For his disputes, ibid. 394, 408, 516; for Quarles's transactions with Sherley, ibid. 326, 393–395, 397, 402, 408–413, 493, 494, 495, 503–505, 508, 509, 512–518, 524, 526, 537.
[369] See Letters Nos 120–122.

Letter No. 115

William, Lord Burghley to Sir Robert Cecil, 4 July 1597

1 p. Holograph.
Addressed, endorsed, signed.

Text

I have red Sir An[thony] Mildmays letter which I do retorn with a
weak hand as yow may se consideryng the charges past which I shall
accompt last on hir M[jes]ties part, and if hir ayde be not contynued,
the fr[ench] K[ing] may be reyned and pycardy possessed at hir dooer
by an unplacable ennemy beside manny other increass of his strength
and therfor the remedy being but a monny matter, and pecuniam in
Loco negligere est Lucrum.[370] I wish hir Ma[jes]ty wold without delay
whilest the fr[ench] k[ing s] Irons ar hoth supply hir nombers for 2
or 3 monethes.[371] and so for lack of a strong hand I end. Wishyng yow
God's Grace to serve hir Ma[jes]ty, and my blessyng to your Comfort.
all your offspyng ar here mery

from Theob[alds] 4 July 1597.

[370]pecuniam in loco negligere[, maximum interdum] est lucrum, Ter.*Ad*.II.2, translated
as 'All is not Won that is pvt in the purse', by William Robertson, https://archive.org/
stream/dictionaryoflatioorobeuoft/dictionaryoflatioorobeuoft_djvu.txt. Sir Anthony Mildmay (*c*.1549–1617) had been sent as a junior to Gilbert Talbot, 7th earl of Shrewsbury,
1553–1616, from 27 Aug. 1596–22 Oct. 1596, thereafter remaining as resident ambassador
until 15 Aug. 1597. For a complete reference to all correspondence, instructions and letter
of credence, see Bell, *Handlist*, 100. The exhaustion of the French crown's resources was
described by Sancy to Antonio Perez as 'this hungrie State', Ungerer, *A Spaniard in Elizabethan
England*, II, 120. As for English assistance there was scant hope, especially with the Cadiz
expedition in preparedness. Robert Naunton relayed Sancy's expectation of any assistance
at that miserable time to the earl of Essex: 'And as I wrote the other day vnto yo[u]r Lo.
that he had bene tempering with Conestable, so he entered with him likewise touching the
same pointe of seeking to her Ma. for assistance. He answered him that *ex cordis visceribus*,
as he affirmes to me, that he was vtterlie oute of hope of any good comming from thence
& that he diswaded the k. in Councell from ether demaunding or expecting any seasonable
resolucion from Englande & that it was now more likelie then before that yow would worke
& playe all vppon the aduantage ouer theis their instant calamities, yea & would happelie
stand vppon the exaction of more vnreasonable conditions now at the pinch then would
satisfie the common Enemye; & therfore in his iudgement he determined it least we should
conceiue that he had quite cast his ffianancier coate [*lupus vilis mutat non ingenium*], that the
onelie sure moyne the k[ing] kould aduance & raise to himselfe would be to leuie another
subsedie out of hand by some new deuise of impost.' Ungerer, *A Spaniard in Elizabethan
England*, II, 121–122.

[371]Money had been sent for the relief of Amiens: £1,242 for French merchants out of the
sale of Sir Thomas Sherley's confiscated goods, *CSPD 1595–1597*, 447, 453.

Your old lovyng father,

W. Burghley

Dorse

ADDRESSED in two clerk's hands:
For hir Ma[jes]ties affayres.
[In Henry Maynard's hand]
To my verie lovinge sonne, Sir Robert Cecyll knight,
hir ma[jes]ties principall secretarie, at Court.
hast
post hast
hast
[Signed by Burghley]
W. Burghley

ENDORSED by Cecil's filing clerk, possibly Percival:
4 July 1597
Lo[rd] Thre[asure]r to my M[aste]r from Theobalds

Letter No. 116

William, Lord Burghley to Sir Robert Cecil, 5 July 1597

½ p. Dictated to a clerk, possibly John Clapham, who was in attendance on Burghley in his last years.
Addressed, endorsed, signed.

Text

I doe send yow a letter herewith written to my L[ord] of Essex,[372] to whom I did not wryte since his departure, nor untyll now, that god hath shewed him favour from heaven with the new moone to send him a prosperous wind. I could not write comfortably neither for myself nor for him. And now I doe write unto him with my weak hand onely to Congratulate with him for this favour of god, I doe exhort him, as a Christian soldier to acknowledge the same beyond all mans power and witt. I have also written unto him that I am sure yow will frequently advertise him of thinges convenient, and so supply my want, remembering a true saying of Tully in these words: Omnibus peregrinantibus gratum sit, minimarum quoque rerum quae domi

---

[372] The naval expedition under Essex was then underway.

gerantur, fieri certiores.[373] I pray yowby the next safe messenger send
this my letter to his Lo[rdship] letting him know that I am here
Licensed for a while to be at my howse, where I assure yow, I continue
in such paine of my foote, as I am not able to stirre abroad but in my
Coach. from my howse at Theobaldes the v[th] of July 1597.

[Signed]
Your loving father,

W. Burghley

Dorse

ADDRESSED In same clerk's hand, perhaps Clapham:
To my verie Lovinge Sonne, Sir Robert Cecyll knight
hir ma[jes]ties principall Secretary
At Court

ENDORSED by Cecil's filing clerk, Richard Percival, whose hand completes the entries
after September 1596 in Cecil's Scottish Letter Book, TNA SP 52/52:
5 July 1597
L[ord] Thre[asure]r to my M[aste]r

Letter No. 117

William, Lord Burghley to Sir Robert Cecil, 8 July 1597

2 pp. Holograph.
Addressed, endorsed, signed.

Text

I have with your letter wrytten yesterday receaved the letters to yow
o[n] from my Lo[rd] of Essex wrytten on monday[Wednesday] 6 sence
which tyme I have gladly observed every daye a most favourable
wynd to send hym forward, so as God hath lyk a gratiouse father
after a fewe dayes frowning to mak his power known, hath changed

---

[373]The phrase 'omnibus peregrinantibus gratum sit, minimarum quoque rerum, quae
domi gerantur, fieri certiores' is a fragment from Book VIII, letter no. 1, *M. Tulli Ciceronis
Epistolarum ad familiores liber octavus, M. Caelii Epistolae ad M. Tulliam Ciceronam*, F 8:1. Here
Marcus Caelius Rufus (82–48 BCE) informs Cicero, his former teacher, now on his way to
be governor of Cilicia, of news in Rome. Burghley takes this role, using Caelius' voice to
satisfy the earl's curiosity of news at home through Cecil, without proclaiming himself the
only interpreter of events. Caelius' letter concludes with a recitation of papers, writs and
official business enclosed in a packet.

his countenance into blessyng, whereby may be sayd to the army, viriliter agile, et confortetur ~~vestrum~~ cor vestrum omnes sperantes in Domino.[374]

Your other letter from Sir Anthony Mildmay with the copy of the fr[ench] k[ing]'s letter to hym, can scantly have any good sence whereon to found any present connsell. for I see no lykhood for the fr[ench] kyng to seke peace at this part whan by all advertisement the cardynall as yet hath no monny to wage his men to come to the releff of Amyens,[375] nor his new levyes as yet come owt of Italy which advises being trew, I se no cause in necessite ether to offer or to harken to peace. But yet it may be that the pope and his legat[376] and the Cardihar [Cardinal] may tempt hym therto and the K[ing s] discontented state may move hym to forgett his honor. On the other side it may be inspected, that this chantyng of peace, is a song only to allure the Q[ueen s] Ma[jes]ty to yeld hym still aide of more men or monny or both, wherein I can yeld no other opinion, than that hir Ma[jes]ty should yeld no more than good reason may warrant with conversation of hir own estate and so haveng

[p. 2] warrant of a good conscience in that she hath or shall in hir benefittes strayne hir own State, to become unhable to preserve hir self, havyng no hope nor apparence to be ayded by any other, as she hath ayded manny and though it may be feared, that by the fr[ench] kynges peace hir ennemy the Spanyard may become more to be feared, yet in God's goodnes whose cause hir Ma[jes]tty defendeth, she may saye with David saye: Exaltabo te domine quoniam suscepisti me, nec

[374] Translation, Psalm 31:24, Geneva Bible 1560: 'All ye that trust in the Lord, be strong and he shal establish your heart.' Burghley's letter to the earl of Essex reflects a general peace at court and with the Queen. But this particular reference to hope for Essex recalls that the earl had put his faith in Cecil, having charged him with control of his affairs. Hatfield, Cecil Papers, 52/80; *HMCS*, vii, 278. Essex's servants, his secretary, Edward Reynolds, and Henry Lindley, petitioned Cecil for renewal of their master's sweet wine monopoly, noting the earl's huge private debts to merchants which Cecil took to the Queen, Hatfield, Cecil Papers, 58/212; *HMCS*, vii, 283. Burghley here expands on the text of his letter, urging him to attribute his success to God and by implication to the Queen, thereby avoiding any charge of vainglory.

[375] For the general tenor of the negotiations, see Letter No. 116. The relief of Amiens came near the bitter end of the French civil wars of religion – Henry IV's great want of money meant that he was weak in his possible peace-making with Spain – and the Archduke Albert was running out of money to continue the siege. Wernham, *Return of the Armadas*, 106, 216, 220.

[376] Clement VIII's legate Cardinal Alessandro de' Medici (1535–1605, later Pope Leo XI, 1605) had been at the court of Henry IV since the summer of 1596, but his work was frustrated by the secret Triple Alliance with the English and the States General. Even more complicated was the effect of the Spanish assault on Amiens, because Medici was to broker relations between France, Spain and the papacy.

delectasti inimicos meos sup[er] me.[377] but yowe may saye, my concepts ar spirituall and therby aught all human actions to be governed. Thus to shew my self bold, to arm, in an obscure, subiect, I will end with a very weary hand, untill I shall understand the event of Mr. Mildmaye's forces,[378] from my howss at Theobalds the rooms wherof I have not sene, more than my bedchamber, my dyning place and my chappell, so lame I am on on legg as Sir Edw[ard] Hoby[379] I think can shew yow, by whom I retorned my most humble thanks to hir Ma[jes]ty motefyeng to hir that when I spent at the Cowrt the substance of my poore wytt, I fynd no meanes here to restor it, [word obscured by margin] forced dayly to fede of an asses milk and so subiect to be dull, as my ass

from Theobalds, 8 July 1597.

Your lov[ing] father,

W. Burghley

Dorse

ADDRESSED in Holograph:
To my son Sir Robert Cecill, knight pricipall secretary to hir Ma[jes]ty

ENDORSED by Richard Percival:
8 July 1597
Lo[rd] Thre[asure]r to my M[aste]r from Theobalds

Letter No. 118

William, Lord Burghley to Sir Robert Cecil, 9 July 1597

1 p. Holograph.
Addressed, endorsed, signed.

[377] Psalm 30:1, Geneva Bible, 1560: 'I will magnifie thee O Lord, for thou hast exalted me and hast not made my foes to rejoice over me.'
[378] Mildmay had been given provisions in negotiations by the Queen and council which had passed the signet on 1 July 1597 to disburse some of the monies realized from the sale of Sherley's goods which had been confiscated to meet his very large debt to the Crown. The funds were then disbursed to French merchants. *CSPD 1595–1597*, 557.
[379] Sir Edward Hoby (1560–1617), *ODNB*, was Burghley's nephew by Elizabeth Hoby (née Cooke). Among the many offices he held was constable of Queenborough Castle.

Text

Your letter wrytten yesternight the 8, I have this 9th, after my dinner receaved ~~yours~~ conteining sondry thynges, as first hir Ma[jes]ties opinion how to mete with the fr[ench] k[ing]'s enchantyng, but untill our ambass[ador] shall advertise his negotiation with the k[ing] the resolution may be suspended.[380] Secondly you advertise the retorn of Mr. fulk Grevill with letters from the Erle and his assistant Connsellor as appeareth by the Copy yow sent methough without date of daye or place.[381] But by the Erles letter to my self I se it dated the 6 of this month, but from no place.[382] and as to ther letter, I see no speciallite of ther request for any quantitie of vittells, although by your leter to me it should seme to be for 1 monthes vitell but for what nombre, whyther for the army of land men or for them and the men of the navy, I fynd not but I do Imagyn for all – which is worthy consideration, how spedely to provyde it, and in what Contries. Whereof conference wold be had by my L[ord] admyralls with Quarles and dorrel if he be not gon.[383] you and borowgh also wold be spoken with all, but I thynk the Erle and Sir Walter Ralegh will explane ther requests in some particularetyes, but herin I troble my self to much fyndyng the uncertentyes of ther requests. Whan I shall have the prive seals for pycardy I shall know what to direct.[384]

[380]Fulke Greville, 1st Baron Brooke of Beauchamps Court (1554–1628), *ODNB*, poet and friend of Cecil and Essex. Greville was on account as one of the paymasters for the 1597 Azores expedition for £9,000, TNA E 405/441/fol. 32v. Greville was a messenger for Essex's and the council of war's letters to Lord Admirall Howard and Cecil of 7 and 10 July 1597, *CSPD 1595–1597*, 451, 457. Essex wrote to Cecil for more victualling which was granted: 'If the Queen will dispense with [my] absence, get my cousin Fulk Greville the conducting of it, but if she will not let him, then I think Sir Robert Crosse is very fit.' See Letters Nos 119–122.
[381]James Quarles and Marmaduke Darrell held accounts for navy victuals. TNA E 351/2393–2398, Jan. 1595–31 Dec. 1599. They were on account for both expeditions, 1596 and 1597. TNA E405/440/fol. 19v, 441/fol. 32v. On 10 July, Quarles and Cecil's clerk made two separate reckonings for the cost of a further 28 days victualling for 10,000 and 9,000 men, reaching identical figures of £8,681 pounds for 10,000 troops, and £8,000 for 9,000 men, with more calculations on 11 July 1597, *CSPD 1595–1597*, 457. The warrant dated 12 July under privy seal was £8,765 10s, *CSPD 1595–1597*, 458. Essex's letter to Cecil of that date included a personal note thanking Cecil for his affectionate messages, TNA SP 12/264/nos. 8, 9; *CSPD 1595–1597*, 450–451. Burghley's letter may have arrived with this packet.
[382]The Queen granted another month's victuals, *CSPD 1595–1597*, 451–452; Wernham, *Return of the Armadas*, 162.
[383]Evidence of the Raleigh, Essex, Cecil triumvirate as well as Sir John Borough included with others. Essex and Raleigh had, during the previous winter, fallen out of favour and were extremely jealous of each other, see TNA SP 12/264/no. 21; *CSPD 1595–1597*, 457. Raleigh had now been restored to the Queen's affections.
[384]The warrant for the privy seal payment for £1,772, 13s. was dated 9 July 1597, with defalcations for persons absent, dead or deficient; Captain Henry Poore as he succeeded

I assure yow, I am greatly afflicted with my payne in my foote, not able to sit upon horss back nor to stand up right, but forced to go abrod only in a litle coche.

9 Julii, 1597,

Your loving father,

W. Burghley

Dorse

ADDRESSED Holograph:
To my lovinge sonn Sir Robert Cecill, knight
principall secr[etary] to hir Ma[jes]ty

ENDORSED in Robert Percival's hand:
Lord Thre[asure]r to my M[aste]r, from Theobalds
[Letter 119 appears to have been removed from the volume, but enough remains to show the date: 9 July 1597.]

Letter No. 120

William, Lord Burghley to Sir Robert Cecil, 10 July 1597

1 p. Holograph.
Addressed, endorsed, signed.

Text

I thank yow for your letter, wherey I perceave how kyndly and frendly my L[ord] Admyrall emparted my manner of service to hir Ma[jes]ties lyking for the which his accustomed favourable opinion of me beyond my wordynes [worthyness], I must remayn a dettor to his lordship for not hable otherwise to acquit my dett but with thankfullnes, and a firm disposition, to do the lyk for hym which I may with better warranty, perform for his Lordsh[ip's] Just desert, that may be for my self.[385]

It is my comfort that hir Ma[jes]ty maketh such a comparison of my symplicite with hir pryncely wordynes [worthyness], to which in very truth, I thynk nether forayn prynce nor brytish subiect can approache.

Sir Arthur Savage as second colonel in Picardy, *CSPD* 1595–1597, 453–454. Accounts signed by the Secretary, Cecil, TNA SP 12/265/no. 102; *CSPD 1595–1597*, 562.
[385] Wernham, *Return of the Armadas*, 161.

I have redd the l[ette]re from the Erle and his assistance and do hope he and they do gyve thanks for ther particular hard accidentes.[386]

If I cold styrr, truly I wold not mislyk that hir Ma[jes]ty might see my howss, for consideryng how small tyme I have to live, I wold not spare for the [ye] cost.[387]

I pray yow require Mr. Darcy and Mr. Southwell to procure hir Ma[jes]ty, at some sundry tymes to sign the bills of the warrants.[388]

10 July 1597

Your lov[ing] father,

W. Burghley

Dorse

ADDRESSED
To my verie Lovinge
Sonn Sir Robert
Cecill knight principall
Secretary to hir Ma[jes]tie [Clapham]

ENDORSED [Percival]
10 July 159[/]
Lord Thre[asure]r to my M[aste]r from Theobald

Letter No. 121

William, Lord Burghley to Sir Robert Cecil, 12 July 1597

1 p. Dictated to Henry Maynard.
Addressed, endorsed, signed.

---

[386] See Letter No. 121.

[387] The Queen was to go on progress to Theobalds in Aug. 1597. Hatfield, Cecil Papers, 54/fol. 101r; *HMCS*, vii, 370. Henry Maynard wrote to Michael Hickes on 12 Aug. 1597, 'One manner of alteracion havinge of late over our fleete yet departed for anie thinge wee knowe/ wee greatlie fear that from haveringe the Queen will Theobaldes, but as yet it is not set downe. I wowlde be glad to be gonn hence, but this progresse much trowbleth me, for that wee knowe not what corse the Q[ueen] will take', BL Lansdowne MS, 85/no. 24, fol. 47r. Maynard was writing from the court, and he noted that Burghley had arrived somewhat revived the day before, 11 Aug., 'into his booke chamber' for more work.

[388] Edward Darcy and Mr. Southwell, grooms of the privy chamber with William Killigrew and Sir John Stanhope. See Letter No. 94. Probably [Sir] Francis Southwell (1563–1599), who was at court and married to Elizabeth (d.1646), daughter of the lord admiral, now the earl of Nottingham, and the Queen's cousin Catherine Carey (1547–1603).

Text

I have with your letters received suche memoriale as yow sent mee concerning a newe monethes victualinge of the navie and Armie whiche I doe retorne unto yowe with a draughte for a Privie seale accordinge to your request.[389] And so wishe yowe to make expedicion thereof to the intent the provicions may be begonne to be made whearein I doe note a vearie great charge to arise for the transportacions, whereof I mervaile the Erle did not remember to have left from shipping alreadie prepared that he might have spared to have eased part of that burden:[390] And as I remember yow reported from Mr. Greville's mowthe that theare was such a meaninge in him.[391] I have seen this daie a proclamacion printed for reformacion of Apparells without anie title to the same, which I doe see is agreeable in most partes to the former that hath been heeretofore published: the proclamacion itself would have been dated as well, as the last clawse of the Articles.[392] I dowbt much, that the length of all this commandments and provicions will be hardlie executed abroad, untill theare be somm

[389] The Queen granted this as in Letter No. 118, a symptom of her temporary enthusiasm for the voyage, *HMCS*, vii, 460. Warrants were issued 'to pay Jas. Quarels and Marmaduke Darrell £7,402 10s., for a month's victuals more, to supply any lack that may grow by contrary winds; also to Roger Langford, navy paymaster, £1,363 for charges of transporting the same to the army and navy, wherever it shall be', *CSPD 1595–1597*, 458. Burghley ordered 700 quarters (8¾ tons) of wheat to the surveyor, to be converted to biscuit for the victualling. Longford received a very large payment, approximately £29,000, for the troops out of the Exchequer. TNA E 405/441/fol. 32v.

[390] Essex needed extra ships to take the victualling to the fleet then left at Plymouth noted in his letter to Cecil of 12 July 1597, written 'last Sunday', TNA SP 12/264/no. 12; *CSPD 1595–1597*, 458. William Stallenge's account of 16 July saw the extra shipping costing dearly, TNA SP 12/264/no. 28; *CSPD 1595–1597*, 459. A note made in the same week concluded 'For the transporting of such victuals it will be requisite to have 12 ships of 200 tons and 35 men each, furnished and victualled for 70 days' at a cost of £2,465, 10s. TNA SP 12/264/no. 24; *CSPD 1595–1597*, 459.

[391] Greville arrived at court with Essex, for Howard's and the council of war's deliberations on 6 or 7 July. Essex wrote to Cecil, 'We have told [Dorell] our opinions that it should consist of beer, bread, butter, cheese, fish but not beef . . . ; he must bring it to us at the Islands, except we send other directions.' TNA SP 12/264/no. 21; *CSPD 1595–1597*, 457.

[392] Burghley here doubted that the terms of the first version would be executed. Larkin and Hughes print the 6 July 1597 version in *TRP*, iii, as no. 786, 'Enforcing Statutes and Proclamations of Apparell'. The original draft was done by Cecil, with the original date of the schedule for printing 29 June 1597, Hatfield, Cecil Papers, 141/fol. 84r–v. The first version was too wide-ranging to be enforceable. Cecil received several petitions on this matter from other privy councillors. The lord keeper, Egerton, and Lords North and Buckhurst brought this complexity to Cecil's attention on 11 July 1597 suggesting that the imperfections needed to be 'better digested' with Burghley's comments here added to the need for a re-drafting. Hatfield, Cecil Papers, 53/fol. 29r; *HMCS*, vii, 298.

The second proclamation draft was issued on 23 July 1597 with dispensations from the articles granted to various ranks and offices in the social hierarchy: judges, Exchequer servants, principal councillors, heads of towns, lawyers, graduates of the universities, students

good Example in the Cort and in the Citie: the one to be by the l[ord] Chamberlaine, and the whetestores and Grenecloathe:[393] the other by the Maior and Aldermen of London in their severall wardes, for which purpose if summ of the Aldermen weare sent for to the and had spetiale charge to proceade to the Execucion theareof, by inquisicion within everie warde it might serve for an Example to the Counties.[394] I doe include hearein a letter to my ladie Scroope, which I praie yowe to cause to be delivered to hir.[395] ffrom my house at Theobaldes this xii[th] of Julie 1597.

[Burghley]
Your Lovinge father,

W. Burghley

[Postscript in Maynard's hand]
I praie yowe send mee word what daie the Q[ueen] meneth to goe abroade from thence, bicause I would be loath to comm thither when she is absent.[396]

Dorse

ADDRESSED in Henry Maynard's hand:
To my Lovinge sonne Sir Robert

of the Inns of Court with further exemption for all nobles' servants, the Queen's servants and messengers, *TRP*, iii, 179–180, no. 787. Privy councillors then met but William Waad, clerk of the Privy Council, did not tell them Cecil would be absent, thus a record of their discussion on the new text survives in the form of a minute to Cecil, dated 13 July 1597, Hatfield, Cecil Papers, 53/fol. 53r; *HMCS*, vii, 306. Cecil may have left his corrections, for Egerton praised him for the two letters sent, assuring Cecil *noli altum sapere*, nothing is above wisdom. The second proclamation took effect on 24 Aug. 1597, removing the difficult clauses of the first version.

[393]Court finance was administered by the lord chamberlain, William Knollys, 1st earl of Banbury (*c.*1545–1632), *ODNB*. No accounts remain for the 1590s for the board of Greencloth, a Household department and committee of the lower household under the Lord Steward which fell to Knollys (no lord steward was named after Leicester's death in 1588 for the duration of the reign). The board was attended by the treasurer (Stanhope), comptroller (Knollys), and various other officers including navy victualler James Quarles. Accountants of the lower household such as Quarles held other lucrative (potentially) Crown accounts for supply of victuals. *Guide to the Contents of the Public Record Office*, Vol. II (London, 1963), 211–214.

[394]The aldermen and commonalty of the City would have received the Proclamation in the Queen's name, despatched by the Privy Council. This was an instance where Council clearly deliberated over several drafts between them, issuing the final product in the Queen's name.

[395]Philadelphia Carey, Lady Scrope, daughter of 1st Baron Hunsdon, and a cousin of the Queen.

[396]See Letter No. 120.

Cecill knight hir Ma[jes]ties
principall secretarye At the Cort

ENDORSED in Robert Percival's hand:
12 July 1597
Lo[rd] Thresorer to my M[aste]r from Theobalds

Letter No. 122

William, Lord Burghley to Sir Robert Cecil, 13 July 1597

1 p. Dictated to a clerk [neither Maynard nor Hickes], with a holograph sentence added at
the end of the letter above the signature.
Addressed [by Burghley], endorsed, signed.

Text

I have recyved with yow yesterdaies letter the Certificat from one
Danet, of the nomber of his shippes that caryed the Captens and the
soldiars to the number of 5000.[397] The charge wherof must next be
verie great, ffor the number of shippes are about [In Burghley's hand]
xxxiii. To which nomber in charge are to be added, so many as Caryed
the victualls whereof he makes me Cartificat: Besides the number of
all the shippes of warre Both englishe & strangers whereof I there
include them in a certificat sent unto the Quene. And for encrease
of theise nombers it semethe there are no smale number of voluntary
shippes. The knowledge of all which were worth the havinge therby
to understand the whole number of shipping at this tyme, whereof I
doubt how any knowledg can come unto from Plymouth considering
I think the Navie is nearer Spayne the [*sic*] of England.[398] I have
also receyved the letter from S[i]r R[obert] Sidney dyrected to me,
with which thear should be an Irishe woman come into England of
whom many things might be understood Concerning the nombers
of the Quene's subiectes both Irishe, and englishe that serve Stanley,

[397] Marmaduke Darrell needed victuals for the month's provisions as in Letter No. 118 on
10 July 1597: 'List of 33 fly-boats taken up and victualled for the transportation of 5,000
soldiers belonging to captains named, sent with the earl of Essex, with no. of men in each
boat.' This is not the certificate, but this enclosure would have arrived in London on 13 July
1597. TNA SP 12/264/no. 19 enclosure I; *CSPD 1595–1597*, 456.
[398] Burghley could not make a reckoning for the expenditure of the entire shipping with
the fleet nearer Spain than England (see Letter No. 118). Darrell noted, 'There are many
voluntary barks ready to follow the fleet, but the number of them or of their men, or for
what time they are victualled is not known. I have written to like effect to the Lord Admiral.'
CSPD 1595–1597, 456.

or otherwise be in the service of the Ennemye.[399] And where her Ma[jes]tie liketh to have yow to procure them to engage them selves in some exploits,[400] I pray yow in writing thease to Sir R[obert] Sidney to declare unto him: my absence from the Court, so as I could not make answar to his letter my self, which if I had bene present I would have donne.

[Burghley] I mynd to be at West[minster], on thursday at night or frydaye, and to come to the Court on Satyrday, wherof yow shall not speak there to any.

xiii Jul[y] 1597

Your lov[ing] father,

W. Burghley

Dorse

ADDRESSED Holograph:
To my Sonn
Sir Robert Cecill

ENDORSED by a clerk, probably Richard Percival:
13 July 1597
Lo[rd] Thresorer to my M[aste]r from Theobalds

Letter No. 123

William, Lord Burghley to Sir Robert Cecil, 21 August 1597

⅓ p. Dictated to Henry Maynard.
Addressed, endorsed, signed.

---

[399] Sir William Stanley's 'Irish' regiment. The informer is unidentified but the Irish-Low Countries' intelligence link continued. This might refer to the possible second visit of the 'pirate queen' Grainne O'Malley, see Rapple, *Martial Power*, 253–254, 282; Letters Nos 15, 16, 34. On 24 June 1597 Burgh and Wallop informed Cecil that their agent Burnham had news of Sir William Stanley and Sir Hugh Welsh, noting all Irish shipping remained in Spain. Burgh and Wallop concluded that the informer was a man 'of many words and little secrecy and in his estate very poor', *CSPI 1596–1597*, 324.

[400] This is Burghley's first indication in these letters that his son had taken control of official intelligence matters. See his annual account for secret service, TNA E 405/440/fol. 19v, 441/fol. 32v.

Text

I doe send hearewith unto yow a letter from my L[ord] Eures to mee together with a Testimoniale of the B[ishop] of durham, in the behalf of this bearer Mr. John Smaythwaite,[401] to be preferred to a benefice in Northumberland in hir ma[jes]ties disposicion. And althowgh I doe not use to recommend anie of myself to anie benefices: yet consideringe the testimonie given of him aswell by my L[ord] Eures, and the B[ishop] wheare he maie doe God and hir ma[jes]tie good service: I doe therefore praie yow to move hir ma[jes]tie on the said Smaithwaites behalf, that hir ma[jes]tie be pleased to bestowe the said benefice on him. Soe farre yow well. ffrom my howse at Theobaldes this xxi[th] of August 1597.

[Burghley]
Your Loving father,

W. Burghley

Dorse

ADDRESSED in Henry Maynard's hand:
To my lovinge sonne Sir Rob[er]t Cecill knight. Hir ma[jes]ties principall secretarie. At the Cort at Haveringe[402]

ENDORSED [Possibly Richard Percival]
21 August 1597
Lo[rd] Thre[asure]r to my M[aste]r in favour of Mr. Smaithwaite

Letter No. 124

William, Lord Burghley to Sir Robert Cecil, 24 August 1597

1 p. Holograph.
Addressed, endorsed, signed.

[401]Ralph, 2nd Lord Eure, 1558–1617, *HPT*, ii, 92–93, warden of the Western Marches. He wrote to Burghley on 17 Aug. 1597 proposing the successful suit for one Smaithwaite, supported by Tobie Matthew, bishop of Durham, to replace the late Mr Mason, rector of Woodholme in Northumberland, his presentation dated 22 Sept. 1597, *HMCS*, vii, 354; *CSPD 1595–1597*, 502. Matthew's support of Smaithwaite is found in a letter to Cecil of 17 Aug. 1597, *HMCS*, vii, 354.
[402]There is record of a Privy Council meeting there, *APC 1597*, 353, on 21 Aug.

Text

I do send hereinclosed 4 letters, 3 of myn own hand wherof 2 to my lady of Derby, that this marked she may have openly, the other on particularly to hir own hand.[403] The 3 letter is to the Erle of Comberland only for complement and thanks.[404] the 4 is to Sir Edward phytton of thanks both to hym and my lady his wiff.[405] These I had made redy befor your messenger cam. I thank yow for your honest report of my paynes, which in truth by the weaknes of my hand, ar more Grevass to me than the lyk war in fomer tymes.

Sir Edm[und] Cave dyning with me this day reported the accident of yesterdayes skyrmish in the Foyle.[406] I looked to have had the last

---

[403] One of Burghley's letters to his grand-daughter was to remain private, the other she could receive publicly. A court scandal had erupted according to Thomas Audley's later account to Edward Smith in Paris, *HMCS*, vii, 396. Essex was then in disgrace with the Queen, as 'he lay with my Lady of Derby before he went, as his enemies witness'. His retinue had followed him to sea, and the creditors, especially silk merchants, despaired of being paid. On 11 July 1597, Lord Thomas Howard reported to Cecil that the countess was very ill, and asked for her uncle. The author of this news appears to have been an agent Cecil placed within the Derby household, one Edward Mylar, Hatfield, Cecil Papers, 54/fol. 14r; *HMCS*, vii, 339. By 11 Aug. the earl had calmed himself and was on his way to the equanimity he showed to Cecil on 22 Aug. in a joint letter with his countess, *HMCS*, vii, 344, 362; Hatfield, Cecil Papers, 54/fol. 21r, 77r.

[404] Burghley wrote to George Clifford, earl of Cumberland and his wife, as Cumberland was intimate with the legal arrangements for the countess of Derby, standing as Derby's feoffee at Burghley's request. Edward Mylar's report to Cecil of 11 Aug. 1597 outlines Cumberland's role in the presentation of the papers conveying the lands to the countess, Cumberland having 'shewed himself a kind friend to my Lady and a good uncle to the Earl', Hatfield, Cecil Papers, 54/fol. 21r; *HMCS*, vii, 344.

[405] Sir Edward Fytton (1548–1606), *ODNB* – sometimes 'Fitton' or 'Phytton' – and his wife Alice (née Holcroft, d.1626) wrote to Cecil in late July 1597 advising him of the legal necessity of assurances for the conveyance of the countess's jointure to Burghley's grand-daughter Elizabeth Vere. The matter was to be kept secret, as Fytton had a private conference with Burghley and Cecil. Fytton also provided a very detailed account of the earl and countess's return to Lancashire from court, noting the number of men who greeted them in Cheshire and in Lancashire. Lady Derby entertained at Sir Thomas Gerrard's, who assumed the administration of the Isle of Man, formerly a Derby possession now returned to the Crown. Hatfield, Cecil Papers, 54/fol. 110r; *HMCS*, vii, 327–328. Fytton continued to provide Cecil with details of the Derby marriage during the next months. In Oct. he reported the countess's gratitude to Cecil, her decision to follow the prescribed jointure agreement, and to her imminent arrival at the Fyttons. Cecil used Edward Mylar to send information from within the intimacy of Knowsley, while Fytton was managing the legal details. *HMCS*, vii, 339–340, 344; Coward, *The Stanleys*, 50 and n. 41. Mylar and Fitton may have been the same person. See also Joanna Rickman, *Love, Lust and Licence in Early Modern England: Illicit Sex and the Nobility* (Aldershot, 2008) 64–65.

[406] Sir Edmund Cave may have been a draper of London, a Cecil cousin and relation of the Cave family of Leicester who produced several high sheriffs of the county.

letters from Irland from whence I look not for such success, as was pretended.[407]

The warrant for apparell for Irland wold be sent.[408] I thynk it shall not be nedefull to send any letters into Wales, Wher I thynk the derth groweth not by engrossers.[409]

To morrow I shall have all my kynred within v or vi myles Compass with all ther messes pr. [present?].

24 August 1597.

Your lov[ing] father,

W. Burghley

Dorse

ADDRESSED Holograph:
To my wellbeloved sonn Sir Robart Cecill knight, princ[ipal] Secretary

ENDORSED in the hand of a Cecil clerk [Munck]
24 Aug 1597
Lo[rd] Thre[asure]r to my M[aste]r

Letter No. 125

William, Lord Burghley to Sir Robert Cecil, 25 August 1597

½ p. Dictated by Burghley to a clerk [possibly Hickes].
Dorse: Addressed, endorsed.

[407]See Letter No. 125.

[408]Warrant for apparel into Ireland dated 28 Aug. 1597: payment of £12,219 3s. 4d. to merchants of London who bargained 'to furnish the footmen in Ireland, both winter and summer liveries, for their winter apparel; also on 1 Apr., or on any other time agreed on £3,147 18s. 4d. for their summer apparel and to continue the same during pleasure, the same to be charge in the accounts of the treasure at war in Ireland, so as to be defalcated from the wages of the bands' *CSPD 1595–1597*, 494. The clause 'or at any other time agreed on' prevents the dating of Letter No. 132 – wherein the summer apparel payment is discussed by Burghley and his son – with absolute certainty as 1 Apr. 1598, particularly in view of the circumstances of other Irish expenditures made at that time.

[409]Burghley notes weather and other natural disasters can drive up prices as effectively as anyone engaged in the 'engrossing' or inflation of food prices—or other commodities— which was of concern for war supply. For the notes taken for Cecil on legislation against engrossers in Parliament 1597, see Hatfield, Cecil Papers, 56/85; TNA SP 12/265/no. 29; *HMCS*, vii, 498.

Text

I have recyved from yow the l[ord] deputies letter dyrected to your
self with the other writinge therewith sent.[410] And likewise Sir Arthur
Savages letter. All which I do returne unto yow, allowing greatlie
the deputies resolut manner of writing, and especially his impacions
answer to the Rebell Tyron.[411] The some yow send me the warrant
for Irland, and the other also for Barwick, it shall muche content
me, ffor both theise hold the Quene's service in suspence untill by
these warrants I may procede.[412] And so I end. ffrom my howse at
Theobaldes the xxvth of August 1597.

[Burghley]
Where I had at dynner of old and yong 14 descended of my body.
Your loving father

W. Burghley

Dorse

ADDRESSED in the hand of the clerk to whom the letter was dictated:
To my very lovinge sonne
Sir Robert Cecill knight
Principall Secretarye
to hir Ma[jes]tie

ENDORSED in the hand of Cecil's filing clerk:
25 Aug 1597
Lo[rd] Thre[asure]r to my M[aste]r from Theobalds

---

[410]TNA SP 63/200/nos. 97, 98; *CSPI 1596–1597*, 382–387. The letter had to be forwarded
to Cecil on progress.
[411]The lord deputy's account of his answer to Tyrone's propositions: clearly the packet
went to Cecil first and not to Burghley, *CSPI 1596–1597*, 385. The earl of Tyrone had refused
to respond to the demand that he fulfil certain pledges because the Queen's forces had
broken the truce on 10 Aug. 1597. It had been hoped that the proposed truce would reduce
expenditure: 'the future dimunition of her Majesty's charge unto which you look already
pleaseth the q[ueen] in contemplation', *HMCS*, vii, 361–362. After Thomas Baskerville's
death, Sir Arthur Savage (1513–1597) was sent to the relief of Amiens in 1597. The raising of
the siege after capture by Count Mansfeld was the final Spanish/Leaguer incursion before
Henry IV's peace with Spain.
[412]Warrants issued under privy seal for payment into Berwick and Ireland for the Queen's
troops and supply at this juncture. See Letter No. 124; TNA E 403/2560/p. 119, 119b.

Letter No. 126

William, Lord Burghley to Sir Robert Cecil, 13 September 1597

1 p. Dictated to a clerk [either Hickes or Clapham].
Addressed, endorsed.

Text

Since my last writing to yow I am more unable to write then I was, and therfore am forced to use a nother mans hand: And so I pray yow lett hir Ma[jes]tie understand, for my reasonable excuse. By your letter I understand that hir ma[jes]tie would have me, with my presence, to advise how to answere this Danishe Ambassador,[413] for with purpose she would have me Come to London, wheare she hath appointed my L[ord] Keper, my L[ord] of Buckhurst, and Sir John ffarston to Joyne with me, and to consider what were ffitt to be sayd to them in aunswere, and theareof hir ma[jes]tie being first advertised and so hir ma[jes]tie to allow or disallowe as shall please hir, and thereuppon consequently to give [Burghley] them [Clerk] an answere at my howse.[414] I have considered of their demandes propounded whearof the principal matter tending to a mediation of peace, requies many Circumstances of waight beyond my habilitye to resolve thearon.[415] The other matter being a demand of ffree Traffick I and navygations uppon the Sea, I thynk can not be more reasonably answered, then was answered to the Polishe Ambassador. Although I see by the danishe Ambassadors they tempar ther request with a modification.[416] Thus yow see how doubtfull I am in theise 2 great matters. But yett hir

[413] The Danish ambassador and the final negotiations in the Baltic and with the Hanse. They travelled thence to Edinburgh where they were received by King James VI and Queen Anne, daughter of Christian IV of Denmark (1588–1648) where they had no better satisfaction. The embassy was lodged either at Alderman Houghton's house or Mr. Customer Smith's, *APC 1597*, 363.

[414] The Danish ambassadors were Arild Hvitfeldt (1546–1609) and Christian Barnekow (1556–1612), both experienced diplomats.

[415] The formulation of negotiating points with the Danes were being drafted by Burghley, *HMCS*, vii, 390. In response to the mandate the English were concerned about the rights of shipping through the Sound. TNA SP 12/265/ nos. 71, 145.

[416] The Polish ambassador was Paul Dzialynski (sometimes referred to as 'Pauli de Jaline') accompanied by the English agent in Danzig, Georg Lisman. Documents had been assembled as early as July in anticipation of his embassy, *HMCS*, vii, 320. At issue were the removal of Merchant Adventurers and the stoppage of English goods through Stade, Wernham, *Return of the Armadas*, 199. The embassy was a famous disaster. TNA SP 75 2/fols. 193–240. Sir John Stanhope reported to Cecil on 27 July 1597: 'Her Majesty sent for me about 10 o'clock in great haste commanding me presently to write to you, that as she lived my lord your father's speech which he had drawn in answer of th'ambassador's of Powlacke

ma[jes]tie Joyninge me with other great counsellorrs, It may be by
their advise I may have some clearer understanding: Though my
body be this very daye at the period of iii^{xx} xvii [77] yeares, and
therfor farre unable to travayle either with my bodye, or with lively
spirittes, yete I fynd my self so bound with the superabundant kyndnes
of hir ma[jes]tie in dispensing with my dishabilities, as god permitt me
I wilbe at Westminster to morrowe in the afternoone readye to attend
the LLs [Lords] 13 7^{b} [September] sol in libra.[417]

Your old lovyng father,

W. Burghley

Dorse

ADDRESSED in the hand of the clerk to whom the letter was dictated:
To my varie Loving Sonne Sir Robert Cecill, knighte, Principall
Secretary to hir ma[jes]tie

ENDORSED in Simon Willis's hand:
13 Sept 1597
Lo[rd] Thre[asure]r to my M[aste]r

Letter No. 127

William, Lord Burghley to Sir Robert Cecil, 2 October 1597

1⅔ pp. Dictated to Henry Maynard.
Addressed, endorsed, signed.

above anything she had ever heard in that nature, and she said I would have left admiring
that little she had spoken to have wondered at the great learning expressed in his Lordship's
speech, with the elegancy of words and deepness of judgement, so, rather to serve for a
remembrancer than otherwise, she thought fitt to commend to his lordship's memory the
manner of the beginning of his speech to be in this form: Cum potentissima serenissima et
excellentissima Regina nostra, or in such like, but with the fulness of that style which both
due and requisite in such beginnings. A second thing is that, because he is now called to
answer than to negotiate at first, her Majesty thinketh it more proper for an answerer to
stand awhile at first, than to have a seat offered him; though, when he hath satisfied the first
proposition, she would have him offered a seat, and all other compliments of courtesy, but
yet not to be sat as one of yourselves jointly, but with a distance and a regard of the person
he represents.' Hatfield, Cecil Papers, 53/fol. 71r; *HMCS*, vii, 320.

[417] *Sol in libra*: Burghley's natal chart. Burghley consulted astrologers and was a patron of
several including the eminent polymath John Dee. Various treatises addressed the question
of shipping and international law with regard to the Merchants Adventurers' diplomatic
difficulties, William Howard Sherman, *John Dee: The Politics of Reading and Writing in the English
Renaissance* (Amherst, 1997), 198–200.

Text

I have perused, not withowt offence of mine Eies, all the letters and writinges which yowe sent mee, which I doe retorne unto yowe, and thearewith also a letter from Sir fferdinando Gorges with a Shedule conteining the quantitie of Armor and Municions left with him by the Erle of Essex, whereof he noteth a great decaie, but in whose defawlt I knowe not,[418] althowgh it is a generall disorder of all the Capteins.

He maketh also mention of a charge for provicion of victuell for the shippes, whearin Sir John Gilbert shewed: but he sendeth noe perticuler declaracion theareof, nor anie generall estimacion: but yet presseth paiment very urgently wheareunto for want of awnswerare: It maie be he hath written to my L[ord] admirall or to yowe theareof wheareunto I doe referre him for more certain awnswere.[419]

By the l[ord] deputies letters in Ireland, I see noe towaardlines of anie good ende theare, but a perpetuall charge heare to the Realm in levienge still more men withowt accompt what is becomm of the fomer nombers.[420] And thowghe yt seameth theire decaie is growen by deaths, yet I knowe not howe the Capteines are excusable for their Armors and weapons which properlie do not die of anie disease, but ought to remaine to the furnishinge of the supplies. And I mervaile my L[ord] deputie requireth so great nombers of men, withowt showinge howe the Quene is discharged of hir paie, for so manie as he desireth to supplie, whereof he maketh noe mention, nether yet what is becomm of theire Armor and weapon: But this my obiections will not I thinke suffice his demandes: but I lament yt, to see the great wastes of people of the Inglishe, and of Armor and municion, and of the Contries charges in Levienge to be soe great as it is.[421] nonetheless

---

[418] Sir Ferdinando Gorges' memorandum concerning munitions is dated 27 Sept. 1597 noting Essex's armaments which had been left were 'unserviceable' but not irreparable. Hatfield, Cecil Papers, 175/112; *HMCS*, vii, 403.

[419] There was confusion about where responsibility for the victuals rested. Gorges thought Sir John Gilbert was to put the charge on Essex's Azores account but the expedition was seriously delayed and Gilbert was deeply in arrears. Cecil asked James Quarles, victualler of the navy to begin a new account onto which Gilbert's charge could be added and administered by Cecil's ally at Plymouth, William Stallenge. *HMCS*, vii, 398, 400.

[420] Burgh requested 1,500 new troops for his service dated 10 Sept., making this exchange of letters extraordinarily rapid with Cecil's reply on the 17th. Burgh complained all the troops which had been sent with him into his new charge as lord deputy of Ireland were gone, having been 'transported, vanished, or died', before he went into the field. *CSPI 1596–1597*, 394–395, 398.

[421] Burgh looked for supply for the campaign to Loch Foyle, the garrison positioned within striking distance of the Ulster territories dominated by the rebels. Burgh was in a quandary over the disappearing funds, having not enough to feed, clothe, and arm his men. The muster master Maurice Kyffin remonstrated over abuses in the muster rolls and administration generally with the muster master general, Sir Ralph Lane. Lane had profited from his

it is very convenient that hir ma[jes]tie be acquainted with the request & due consideracion had by hir ma[jes]tie, with advise of hir connsell.[422]

In Sir Arthur Savage's letters, I see noe disposicion in him for the companies to be discharged:[423] but doth rather assent to have the ffrenche kinge to send hitherto hir ma[jes]tie for theire continuacion.[424]

[p. 2] I have perused my L[ord] Scroope's Instruccions,[425] which are vearie well conceived, so as theie had been committed to a man of reputacion, fitt to have executed them, the partie being not sufficient for Creditt and reputacion in the Contrie, as I feare dishonnor will followe to the theare, and spetiallie nowe when the k[ing] himself shall comm to Dumfries the frontier, when he shall finde noe warden in the Contrie, nor anie man of worthe deputed theareto: but as I feare the k[ing] will take it for a storme to have noe better man to awnsweare him. but howe theis cann be remedied I knowe not, except upponn my

labours but wrote to Cecil unhappy at his unhappy work in an administration tolerated by Burgh. *CSPI 1596–1597*, 391. See above, p. 71.

[422] Cecil's angry letter to Burgh was meant as a private letter and not a dispatch in which he reprimanded Burgh for writing only private letters to him with no general deliberations of the council there, *CSPI 1596–1597*, 398.

[423] Sir Arthur Savage was sent into France under Sir Thomas Baskerville (d.1597), as was noted in the latter's commission as colonel general of 2,000 foot sent into Picardy at Henry IV's request under direction from the Privy Council. Savage was to be Baskerville's lieutenant. TNA SP 12/260/no. 54; *CSPD 1595–1597*, 292.

[424] The extent of Henry IV's peace initiatives with Spain took on new depth following his papal absolution on 6 Oct. 1597. Robert Naunton had been employed by Essex to accompany the Spanish traitor Antonio Perez into France. Naunton reported to Essex on 8 Dec. 1597 – when the peace initiatives by the French and Spanish were well in train – after the second Cadiz expedition, that the earl's efforts to secure for Henry a stronger hand with Spanish had failed. This was because of the designs of the Cecils and their adherents: the French now preferred to use for their 'Protestant' alliance Robert le Maçon *dit* de la Fontaine, the minister of the French church in London and agent of Henry IV. Essex was now removed from any special French favour: 'This mixture of mungrell divinitie, poll[icie] seemes to be ingendred of the late congresses and alliances betwene the daughters of M[*achiauel*] & the sonnes of God, I meane La Fontaine, their grand politice [politician] and prophet. It is a stiring age likely to follow when our prophetes & the sonnes of Prophetes become Masters of policie to quite Moses for Machiauel and turne their zeales into practises of state. We heare that the new L. Warden of the 5 [Cinque] Ports is one of the greatest archangels that inspire him with the most of those reuelations.' This was Henry, Lord Cobham, Cecil's brother-in-law. Ungerer, *A Spaniard in Elizabethan England*, II, 140.

[425] Letters of Instruction to Lord Scrope for his conduct in attempting to impose order on the reiver families of 2 Oct. 1597, *Cal. Border Papers*, ii, 399–400. Burghley saw difficulties in having Henry Leigh left as Scrope's deputy because he had no title or rank. Nor did another deputy, Richard Lowther, Scrope's lieutenant, who was deputy constable of Carlisle Castle at the taking of 'Kinmount Willie'.

Lord Chamberlain's letters, the L[ord] Scroope will either retorne, or make a better choice of a deputie.[426]

I have perused the matters of Wryght and Alabaster, whoe both would be streightlie examined of many things necessarie to be understood, for theire combinations and Companions.[427] And so beinge wearie with perusing thes writinges, I leave them to be further considered by hir Ma[jes]tie and hir Connsell theare, as the causes doe require. ffrom my howse in the Strand this second of October.

[On the lower left beside the signature]
Your letters beinge written yesternight came not to mee untill after xii of the clock this daie.

[Burghley]
Your Lovinge ffather,

W. Burghley

Dorse

ADDRESSED in Henry Maynard's hand:
To my lovinge sonne Sir Robert Cecill knight:
hir Ma[jes]ties principall Secretarye
At the Cort

ENDORSED by Cecil's filing clerk, probably Percival:
2 October 1597
Lo[rd] Thr[easurer] to my M[aste]r

[426] Scrope had received the writ for Parliament and was on his way to London having criticized Leigh to the Queen after a private berating. Richard Lowther was commissioned to take the Scottish pledges. He, too, quarrelled terribly with Scrope and was replaced by Leigh. *Cal. Border Papers*, ii, 442, 464, 475, 485, 500. Hunsdon died in London while warden of the East March (22 or 23 July 1596) and his son Sir Robert Carey, then his deputy, was continued by Elizabeth as locum tenens, without the full authority of warden, his elder brother John holding the government of Berwick on the like footing. These arrangements gave great dissatisfaction to both brothers, who made many complaints to the Lord Treasurer and Sir Robert Cecil.
[427] See Alexandra Gajda, *The Earl of Essex and Late Elizabethan Political Culture* (Oxford, 2012), 109–110, 120–122, 127–140. On the use of the Jesuit and his associates in Privy Council business, see Paul E.J. Hammer, *The Polarisation of Elizabethan Politics: The Political Career of Robert Devereux, 2nd Earl of Essex, 1585–1597* (Cambridge, 1999), 269–315; Thomas Wright (*c.*1561–1623), and William Alabaster (1568–1640), *ODNB*.

Letter No. 128

William, Lord Burghley to Sir Robert Cecil, 1 October 1597 [?]

[There is no date in the letter or on the dorse, but the contents of the letter suggest the year].
⅓ p. Dictated to Henry Maynard (or Hickes, or Clapham).
Addressed, endorsed, signed.

Text

Immediatley after your departure hence I revyved a letter from my L[ord] Scrope[428] with a nother enclosed therein to my La[dy] his wife,[429] which I pray yow see delivered. And I do send unto yow myne answar to his L[ordshi]p, in a letter unsealed, which when yow have reade and knowe no cause to the contrarye yow may seale and send awaye by Poste.[430]

[Burghley]
p° [Primo] Oct[ober] horr 4° [4 o'clock]

Your lov[ing] father,

W. Burghley

Dorse

ADDRESSED in Henry Maynard's hand:
To my verie Lovinge Sonne Sir Robert Cecill knighte Principall Secretarye to hir Ma[jes]tie

ENDORSED in Simon Willis's hand:
1 Oct[ober] 1597
L[ord] Thre[asure]r to my M[aste]r

---

[428]Scrope wrote to both Cecils stating his return to London as per his writ for the forthcoming Parliament, 22 Sept. 1597, *Cal. Border Papers*, ii, 399.

[429]Philadelphia Carey.

[430]Burghley to Cecil, makes clear his wish to have all in readiness for the king of Scots' proposed viewing of pledges, matters (in Scrope's absence) entrusted to Sir William Bowes. Burghley concludes with his pre-occupation with the City's request, *Cal. Border Papers*, ii, 423–424; see n. 431.

Letter No. 129

William, Lord Burghley to Sir Thomas Egerton [Lord Keeper of the Great Seal], 15 October 1597

½ p. Dictated to a clerk [Clapham].
Addressed, endorsed, signed.

Text

My good L[ord]. When your servant came to me with the 2 writinges exhibited for provision of Corne for the Cittie,[431] I was beginninge to write my Conceit thereof, agreable to my message sent yow yesternight by my servant Maynard.[432] and though now by your servant I understood yow allowed of my opinion and wished to drawe some forme of letters for execucion thereof: I have thought good in writinge at some length to send yow my opinion; but doe forbear to endite any letters thereupon Untyll the rest of the connsell shall determine hereupon. Considering this later opinion is contrary to the resolucion of them all & of my self also before time. But now by newe necessitie I doe alter my former resolucion; And so submit this my opinion sent to your L[ord] to the Censure of the rest of the connsell.[433] ffrom my howse in Westm[inste]r the xv[th] of October 1597.

[Burghley]
Your l[ord's] most assuredly,

W. Burghley

Dorse

ADDRESSED in the hand of the clerk above:
To the Right honorable my verie
good L[ord] Sir Thomas Egerton knight,
L]ord] Keeper of the great seale of England

ENDORSED by a Cecil clerk:
My lo[rd] Thre[asure]r Lo[rd] Keeper

---

[431]The Privy Council issued a letter of 16 Oct. 1597 requiring warrants be directed to all deputy lieutenants of the counties and commissioners of musters for the relief of wheat for London, indicating a better harvest, and the parliament there straining resources within the City markets. *APC 1597–1598*, 41–44.

[432]Not extant.

[433]Burghley may be referring here to letters received from Ireland, or reckoned the final tally of the ruined stores from the Irish shipment of Sept. 1597. For example, James Quarles to Burghley, *CSPI 1596–1597*, 401–402.

Letter No. 130

William, Lord Burghley to Sir Robert Cecil, 12 October 1597

½ p. Dictated to Henry Maynard.
Addressed, endorsed, signed.

Text

Untill this afternoone I could not reade the Mandat for that it could not be soone translated, beinge at very great length, and verie terriblie and sharplie written forbidding our marchantes all manner of trade, in anie the partes of the Empire, either with Cloathe wooll, or other Commodities and to be executed by the ende of this moneth which in mine opinion requireth verie good consideracion and thearefore yowe shall doe well to acquaint hir ma[jes]tie thearewith, that she maie be pleased to committ the conservation theareof to som such as best are acquainted and understand ther causes:[434] and that the sooner for that when nowe in december next the diet is to be held in Germanie, wheare it were very fitt that somm weare sent fom hir ma[jes]tie.[435] Soe farre yowe well. ffrom the Strand this xii[th] of October 1597.

[Burghley]
I am worss sence my physick being now Μονοπους & Μονοχειξ, but not Monoculus.[436]

[434] A proclamation 'Ordering Deportation of Hanse Merchants' of 9 Jan. 1598 answered the Imperial proclamation of 22 July 1597 forbidding cloth trade. The Imperial proclamation removing English merchants from the Hanse and Empire came on 12 Oct. 1597. *TRP*, iii, 186–188; *CSPD 1595–1597*, 515.

[435] There was some hope of reconciliation with the Hanse and with the Imperial Diet. Sir Henry Wotton was charged with an embassy. He was accompanied by John Wroth who had been junior to the earl of Lincoln on his embassy to the Landgrave of Hesse. In Dec. 1597 Wotton asked Cecil to clarify the course of what was to be a wide-ranging embassy for he did not want to be put in the position of competing with his junior, *CSPD 1595–1597*, 449, 553. Wroth was to visit Rudolf II in Prague; the dukes of Saxony (Upper: Elector Frederick William; Lower: Christian II), Pomerania (John Frederick), Brunswick (Henry Julius; and Brunswick-Luneburg, Henry), and others in the Eastern Empire. Wotton was to see the Catholic electors, the Elector Palatine; the Landgrave of Hesse (strictly speaking, Hesse-Cassel) and other western princes. Christopher Parkins wrote a clause for Cecil to insert into letters of credence for princes close to the Merchant Adventurers at Stade-Holstein, Bremen, Hamburg, Luneburg and Brunswick – noting Count Schaumberg's arrest of four English merchants, a matter to be negotiated with them. Ibid. 548. In the event, Wotton did not serve.

[436] One-footed or one-handed but not Monoculos—one-eyed or a Cyclops.

Your Lovinge father,

W. Burghley

Dorse

ADDRESSED in Henry Maynard's hand:
To my lovinge Sonne
Sir Robart Cecill knight
hir ma[jes]ties principal
Secretarie
At the Cort

ENDORSED in the hand of a clerk:
12th October 1597
Lo[rd] Thresorer to my M[aste]r

Letter No. 131

William, Lord Burghley to Sir Robert Cecil, 7 June 1598

½ p. Dictated to Henry Maynard.
Cover letter to No. 132, and the dorse follows that letter.

Text

I send to yow hearewith three writinges. The one being the Copie of
the Polish Ambassador's oration to hir ma[jes]tie,[437] with an awnsweare

---

[437] Draft of the Polish ambassador, Paul Dzialynski's, oration (see Letter No. 126) to the
Queen was itself an embarrassment given the Queen's allegedly extemporaneous and
scathing reply to his statement that she was inhibiting the Polish trade against ancient Hanse
privileges bestowed between the English and the kings of Poland at Danzig (Gdansk). In
effect, he accused her in the language of the Imperial *mandat* so appearing to serve double
interests. See Wernham, *Return of the Armadas*, 199–200; BL Lansdowne MS 85/no. 19,
94/no. 50. The reply circulated under the title 'Responsio reprehensoria Reginae Eliz.
ad orationem Pauli de Jaline, Sigismundi Ill(ustrissim)i Poloniae Regis Legati, extemp.
locuta'. On this occasion, Burghley may have been recalling points in the answer, as he
composed the instructions for the embassy of Lord Zouche and Dr Christopher Parkins
to King Christian IV of Denmark and others – in the event, the bulk of the diplomatic
burden with the German princes was taken up by Wroth and Stephen Lesieur. After
their foray, Sir George Carew went into Denmark, Sweden, Hanse cities and Poland on
an embassy to Sigismund III, principally, and to assess the complicated manoeuvres of
Baltic shipping and the political conditions in Poland. See Bell, *Handlist*, 139, 154, 155,
214.
     Zouche's (later Wroth's and Lesieur's) embassy was handled by Parkins and Beale, assisted
by Dr Julius Caesar a prominent civilian of the Court of Requests, judge of the Admiralty,

da[ted] theareunto.[438] and the third beinge a Copie of the awnsweare made to Lisman; with all which it weare good that Mr. Carewe weare made acquainted and that he had Copies thearof,[439] with when theie shall be written owt, I praie yowe to retorne unto mee my Copies againe. ffrom my howse in the Strand this viith of June 1598.

[Burghley]
Your loving father,

W. Burghley

[Added beside the signature in Henry Maynard's hand]
I have made awnsweare to my L[ord] Northe and Mr. Comptroller, which I do send by this bearer.[440]

HMCS, vii, 320, 404, 405. The strongest English diplomatic connection appears to have been with George Lisman or Liseman of Danzig. His correspondence listing of the names – Parkins, Caesar and Beale – occasioned hurt feelings and quibbles over precedence among the doctors especially in view of Parkins's embassies in 1590–1591 and 1593. Bell, *Handlist*, 154.

[438] Another version of the Queen's answer was kept with Cecil's papers. A Latin copy with Italian translation found its way to either Cecil's or Essex's hands; the translation appends an additional paragraph, so propaganda may have been the intention of this version, *HMCS*, vii, 315–316. Relations with Poland cleared somewhat, as Polish merchants were dispensed from the terms of English proclamation against Hanse trade, which might have been a result of Lisman's correspondence and negotiation on behalf of Danzig, see n. 439.

[439] Lisman, of Danzig, was a fixture in English-Hanse and Polish diplomacy and trade particularly with the London Steelyard. In Oct. 1597 he solicited Burghley for peace with the merchants of Poland, against the disastrous Dzialynski embassy on behalf of the Polish king. BL Lansdowne MS, 84/no. 51; *HMCS*, vii, 319, 404, 405. According to Robert Beale's account of 27 July 1597, Lisman outraged the Queen without compromising the Polish ambassador's own message on behalf of the Danzigers. The ambassador was meant to have addressed the rights and privileges of the Hanse, and then to have moved to the prickly question of Spanish peace. He appears to have blundered: unlike Henry IV and other monarchs, Elizabeth had few unemployed soldiers liberated from service with the prospect of European peace, for the escalation of the Irish rebellion created further need of men and money to outfit the army. A Hanse trade embargo deprived the Crown of necessary revenue, hence the high temperature of the talks. For the recall of Carew's embassy in May–Dec. 1598 and negotiations with Lisman, which contributed to establishing better relations with Poland and the Hanses, see 'A relation of the state of Polonia and the United Provinces of the Crown, anno 1598', in G. Mews, *Deutschland und Osten* (Leipzig, 1936).

[440] Roger, Lord North and Sir Thomas Knollys: Burghley replied to North's and Knollys's letter to Burghley on 6 June 1598. Hatfield, Cecil Papers, 204/74; *HMCS*, viii, 199; BL Lansdowne MS, 86/no. 77, fol. 193r; Letter No. 134.

I showld thinke my self well discharged: for by that letter I required to be awnsweared nowe my dowbtes weare to be accepted: and upponn awnsweare theareunto, I would assent to anie resolucion theare to be taken. But to this my letter, I never received awnsweare.[449] And in cumming with Jollis before Mr. Chancellor he confessed, considering he must provide the shipping in London. he did not thinke the victuell could be in Ireland with anie suretie under three monethes space.[450] And if now victuell could be shipped thither sooner, the sendinge of menn before it weare theare landed, weare rather to furnishe themm than to containe them. I praie yow deale with my l[ord] North from mee in frendlie manner to have the sight of my letter [page rip] and procure a warrant to be made from hir ma[jes]tie to make such points to Jolles the merchant, as hath been agreed upponn by the Articles: and to lett mee have with the warrant a Copie of the Articles,[451] and I shall be readie to cause the monie to be delivered: which is asmuche as I can doe in furtherence of this service.

I praie yowe as yowe find the Quene not satisfied with mee so to praie hir to heare this my letter.

I thinke hull a sure place for the pledges: but as I have had Sir William Bowes sine,[452] It was conditional that they showld not cumm

[449] Three months was a conservative estimate if Francis Ware's note on Jolles is an accurate indication, for 50 quarters (12½ cwt) of wheat under the June contract arrived in Ireland on 11 Sept. 1598 from the July 16 privy seal of £2,000 pounds out of the Exchequer to the merchants. The delay, then, was two to three months. *CSPD 1598–1601*, 94.

[450] The payment to Jolles and other merchants was carried out in stages, as required presumably to ensure checks on expenses. The warrant of 14 June under privy seal was made against their bonds exhibited in the Exchequer for £6,000 for due performance of the contract. A further entry of June 29 1598 records a Council letter to Burghley asking for a privy seal letter for £2,000 pounds on their £6,000 bond. A final £2,000 pounds was authorized by Council letter of 16 July 1598, earmarked for forces sent the year before for the invasion of Lough Foyle in Aug. 1597. Burghley's fear that adequate victualling would not precede the troops then sent was justified. *APC 1598–1599*, 520, 553, 591.

[451] The articles referred to here were incorporated in the 14 June warrant. The previous articles mentioned were those prepared by North and Knollys after conference with Jolles and Wood, which they sent with their letter of 6 June 1598, BL, Lansdowne MS 86/no. 77, fol. 193r. Robert Cecil followed the substance of his father's instructions, see Letter No. 135, when Burghley's presence at Theobalds may have delayed matters slightly.

[452] Sir William Bowes was named a commissioner for the Middle March, commissioner for Borders affairs 1596–1597 and treasurer of Berwick-upon-Tweed from 20 Apr. 1598. He was joint ambassador to Scotland with his uncle Robert Bowes in Jan.–Feb. 1598 and again May–July 1599. Bowes was rigorously adhered to his instructions and was a formidable negotiator in Border matters for the Crown, 'unshakeably insistent upon the niceties of protocol', *HPT*, i, 467–469. The exchange of pledges here referred to was begun in 1597 after the lairds of Buccleuch and Cessford, two of the Scottish wardens, behaved in a manner which 'infringed [Bowes's] mistress's sovereignty', a matter which touched directly on the amity of the crowns. Bowes helped to negotiate the Treaty of Carlisle (1597). He followed others in finding the office of treasurer of Berwick – that 'costly postern' of the kingdom

further into England than to York. but if fowlt shall be fownd thearein, theie maie soone be retorned, and kept either at York, or at the Castell at Sherifhutton.[453] And so I did with as ill a stomack to write of thes matters, as I have to my meate, which is hitherto fitter for fasting than for feasting. And the weather so cold as I am fitter for the fire [than] for a garden. ffrom my howse at Theobaldes this x^th of June 1598.

[Burghley]
Your loving father,

W. Burghley

Dorse

ADDRESSED in Henry Maynard's hand:
To my Lovinge sonne
Sir Robert Cecill knight
hir ma[jes]ties principall
secretary
At the Cort

ENDORSED in Simon Willis's hand:
x^mo [Decimo] Junll
L[rord] Thre[asure]r to my M[aste]r

Letter No. 135

William, Lord Burghley to Sir Robert Cecil, 11 June 1598

1 p. Dictated to Henry Maynard with a holograph paragraph, postscript. Signed.
Dorse: Addressed, endorsed.

Text

I am in sum part certefied by your letter received this morninge, what corse the Quene will have taken for the victualinge, whearein I would be glad to understand what resolucion shall be taken with Jolles and

- onerous and fractious, besieged as he was by endless criticism and rivalry within the crumbling administration there, thus steering away from the Carey family politics following Hunsdon's death. Scrope's difficult relationship with his deputies Lowther and Leigh was mitigated by Bowes's consistent presence and ability throughout 1597 and 1598. *Cal. Border Papers*, ii, *passim*.

[453] Burghley suggested York or Sheriff Hutton, while the Council letter of 11 June 1598 stipulated York *APC 1597–1598*, 510–513.

Beverlie for proceding thearein.[454] As for that which was obiected that Beverleie was trusted with monie: he never had monie before hand, but was before hand himself, by sending victuell fromm Chester in Ireland, which commonlie was expedited within xx^{tly[tie?]} daies, by the shortnes of the passadge betwixt Chester and dublin; wheareas now Jolles provisions must goe from london. but as I shall have warrant to deliver the monie so I will doe: as farre forthe as Mr. Chancellor cann helpe mee to provide so much, wheareof I have written to him in vearie perticuler manner, which I wishe yowe would require to be seen.[455]

I like vearie well, that Beverleie would provide butter and cheese at Chester, so as it be at such price, as may serve the soldier after the rate of iiis iid in proporcion accordinge to Jolles offer; for I have calculated the severall prices of the quantitie of butter and cheese, as the same monie be provided as Jolles hath sett it downe. And so expectinge the resolucion that shall be made, and the warrant for the monie, I forebeare to trowble either my self or yowe anie more, beinge heare still oppressed with my former infirmities: and withowt hope of amendment ffrom my howse at Theobaldes this xi^{th} of June 1598.

[Burghley's postscript, as it is added beside his signature]
I pray yow present my humble thanks for hir Ma[jes]ties frequent messages, for thow I knoledge my dett gretar than I am hable to accompt, but yet I will gage my hart to be thankfull with prayer.

Your lovyng seke father,

W. Burghley

---

[454] *APC 1598–1599*, 14. George Beverly was named in the Council letter confirming the payments to Jolles and Wood for Irish victualling, ibid. 520. Beverly had encountered some difficulty with his accounts for Irish provisions being declared in Dublin rather than London in Mar. 1598, *CSPI 1598–1599*, 75. In Dec. of that year he asked Cecil to clarify matters after the Irish Council's appointment of Robert Newcommen as provisioner of grains and victuals, a matter he noted which reversed his appointment under the late Lord Burghley, ibid. 404. The reason for Beverly's displeasure is not clear, as Newcommen had formerly held the position as Victualler for Ireland.

[455] Burghley to the chancellor on this occasion. Burghley's explicit instructions to Cecil for warranting George Beverley in Feb. 1595 make plain that granting him sole control of victualling (at 6d. per diem entire) was intended to cut down on the enormous expenses incurred by the surveyors of the victuals and the purveyors alike in administrative and transportation costs which had run to 20 shillings per day. TNA SP 63/178/no. 34, fol. 69r–70v. Unless Burghley was mistaken, Beverley had been entrusted with a privy seal payment of £1,648, 12s., directed to him by Wallop's petition to Cecil in Feb. 1595 for payment of supply, TNA SP 63/178/no. 40, fol. 92r.

Dorse

ADDRESSED in Henry Maynard's hand:
To my lovinge sonne
Sir Robart Cecill knight
hir ma[jes]ties principall secretarye
At the Cort

ENDORSED in Simon Willis's hand:
xi^{mo} Junii 1598
L[ord] Thre[asure]r to my M[aste]r

Letter No. 136A

Number 136 consists of two parts: the first (136A) is a list of 19 names, probably compiled to assist in the nomination to the office of serjeant-at-law; the second (136B) is a cover letter to the list from Burghley to Sir Robert Cecil.

136A

[Clerk's hand]
Yelverton
Harrys
Glanvyle
Danyell
Kyngsmyll
Lewkenor
Warburton
Hele
Savyle
Sparling
Wylliams
Heron
Flemynge, Solicitor.[456].

Mr. Coventree
Mr. Gybbes

[456] Persons who had been or were currently serjeants-at-law. See *ODNB*: Sir Christopher Yelverton (1536/7–1612); John Glanville (1542–1600); William Kingsmill (*c.*1557–1618); Sir John Hele (1541/2–1608); Sir John Savile (1546–1607); Sir Thomas Fleming (1544–1613); Sir Thomas Coventry (1547–1606).

Mr. Shyrley
Mr. Tansable
_____
Mr. Hesketh Alternat Warbu [rton]
Mr. Houghton

Letter No. 136B

William, Lord Burghley to Sir Robert Cecil, 21 June 1598

1 p. Dictated to a clerk [possibly Clapham or another of the secretaries in attendance on Burghley] with a holograph paragraph added.
Addressed, endorsed.

Text

I have perused the paper contayning the names of 13 serieants and 6 other practisers and counsellors of the Lawe out of which hir Ma[jes]ty is to make choice onely of two persons, the one to be a second Justice in the Comon place,[457] & the other to be the third Baron in the Eschequer, both which must be also Justices of Assise in some Circuite. For choise whereof it is most Convenient, & agreable with order that they be chosen out of the seriauntes whereof there are 13, and amongst these both for Learninge and Anncientry I think Seriant Yelverton most eligible and yet I think it as necessary for him to contunie the Q[ueen's] Serieant,[458] as to be a Justice, where there shall he doe the Q[ueen] more service, as hir Seriant, then to be a Second Justice in the Common place. Thus if hir Ma[jes]ty shall so please: she may be well served of a Justice, by Mr. Kingesmyll, who already is a Justice of Assise & well able to knowe the burden of service, being a man unmarryed. As for choice of a Baron I think Seriant Heale able both for Learninge, wealth, & strength of body to continue, being also a personable man, which I wish to be regarded in choice of such officers of publicje calling. But if theare be cause to mislike of this choise, I

---

[457] The offices: baron of the Exchequer and second justice of the Common Pleas.

[458] Serjeant John Glanville became the second justice of the Common Pleas. In the Exchequer, the place of second baron came vacant in May 1598, following the death of Matthew Ewens (c.1548–1598). *HPT*, ii, 94–95. Ewens had been named baron in 1594 as second to lord chief baron Sir William Periam. Ewens was named serjeant also in 1594, and had never been elevated to Queen's serjeant. Strong service as serjeant removed Yelverton from the running.

think Savyl or Williams may supply the place of a Baron, though they bee men of small living.

[Burghley]
I pray yow shew this paper to hir Ma[jes]ty, addyng that if hir Ma[jes]ty should not hir self, mak better choiss, of these 2 officers, than in leaning to my choiss, she may perchance miss the mark she shooteth at.

I can no[t] bost of amendment though hir Ma[jes]ties comfortable wishyngs, fede me with hope.

Dorse

ADDRESSED in Henry Maynard's hand:
To my lovinge sonne Sir Robart Cecill knight hir ma[jes]ties principall secretary.

ENDORSED in the hand of a Cecil clerk, possibly Munck:
21 June 1598
Lo[rd] Thre[asure]r to my M[aste]r

Letter No. 137

William, Lord Burghley to Sir Robert Cecil, 21 July 1598

½ p. Dictated to Henry Maynard.
Addressed, endorsed, signed.

Text

I have receive your letter, which doth nothinge satisfie mee for the sending of the Lincolnshire menn to Plimmouwthe to be theare embarqued, being the remotest part of the Realme from that Conntie: neither is it alike for them of Cornewall to come to Bristell, which maie be donne with ease by sea, wheare the other must marche over all the Land.[459] And thearefore if my lls [Lords] shall not like to alter this corse, theie may then write theire letters into Lincolnshire to send thes men to Plimmowthe, for I am unwillinge in my time, and by my

---

[459]Warrants for levies of troops to be moved in this arrangement directed to Burghley as lord lieutenant of Essex and Hertfordshire were dated 18 July 1598, issued under sign manual. *HMCS*, viii, 264; see above, p. 72.

direcions to committ such an Error.[460] ffrom my howse in the Strand
this xxi^th of Julie 1598.

Your Lovinge father,

[Signed]
W. Burghley

Dorse

ADDRESSED in Henry Maynard's hand:
To my lovinge sonne, Sir Robart Cecill, knight
hir ma[jes]ties principall secretarye

ENDORSED
21 July 1598
Lo[rd] Thre[asure]r to my M[aste]r

Letter No. 138:

William, Lord Burghley to Sir Robert Cecil, 10 July 1598

¾ p. Holograph.[461]
Addressed, endorsed, signed.

Text

Thoughe I knowe yow connt it yowr duty, in nature so contynually,
to shew yow carefull of my state of helth, Yet war also unnatural, if I
showed not tak comfort therby, and to besek almyghty God to bless
yow with supply of such blessynges, as I can not in this infirmyte yeld
yow.
Only I pray yow diligently and effectually, let hir Ma[jes]ty understand
how hir syngular kyndnes doth overcom my power to accept it. Who

---

[460]The arrival of the last levy in Ireland was noted by Fenton to Cecil on 24 July, when
1,600 of the 2,000 troops called for were at Dublin, the remaining 400 at Chester. *CSPI
1598–1599*, 211–212. Of these, 1,000 were dispatched north to 'frustrate' Tyrone's incursions.
Fenton advised that the Pale should be reduced, then the defence of Leinster organized,
only then should Lough Foyle be attempted. As he wrote, Samuel Bagenal, the marshal,
rode north for the execution of the Lough Foyle project. Meanwhile, Burghley's alterations
were put into practice. Complete changes were made to this earlier plan, many of them
executed after Burghley's death in Aug. 1598. The Privy Council instructions for changing
the course of troop movements, and many other aspects of the Irish levies and supplies are
dated 3 Aug. 1598. *APC 1598–1599*, 12–23, 26–38, 39–42, 43–46, 48–62, 70–1.
[461]See above, p. 15.

though she will not be a mother, yet she sheweth hirself by fedyng me with hir own princely hand, as a ^{carefull} Nurss and if I may be wayned to fede my self, I shall be more redy to serve hir on the erth. if not I hope to be in heaven, a servitor for hir and Gods church and so I thank yow for yowr partriches.

Serve God by servyng of the Quene for all other service is in dede bondage to the Devil.

10 July 1598

Your languishyng father,

W. Burghley

Dorse

ADDRESSED in Henry Maynard's hand:
To my vearie Lovinge
Sonne Sir Robert Cecill
knight principall Secretary
to hir Ma[jes]tie

ENDORSED
1598 x^{mo [Decimo]} July
Lo[rd] Thre[asure]r to my M[aste]r
[In another hand]
My lords last letter that he wrote with his own hande

BIBLIOGRAPHY

Unpublished Primary Sources

British Library

ADDITIONAL MANUSCRIPTS

MS 48029	Materials relating to the 1592 carrack *Madre di Dios*.
MS 62540	Lawrence Nowell-Burghley Atlas.

COTTONIAN MANUSCRIPTS

MS Caligual D ii	Transcriptions of State Papers Scotland (TNA SP 52).
MS Nero B II	Dr Christopher Parkins's correspondence.
MS Nero B xii	Edward Barton's Turkish Letter-Book.

HARLEIAN MANUSCRIPTS

MS 36.	
MS 4648	Transcriptions of State Papers Scotland (TNA SP 52).

LANSDOWNE MANUSCRIPTS

44, 74–86, 121	Burghley Papers.
827	Discourse on the murder of Henry Long.

STOWE MANUSCRIPTS

MS Stowe 296, fols 7–20	Sir Thomas Wilkes' treatise on the Office of Secretary.
MS 1056	Catalogue of James West's collection.

Cambridge University Library

MS Add.1–10   John Strype: Correspondence, MS Add.2 (John
                    Percy Baumgartner MSS).
MS Ee.2.32 fol. 349r   'The Oath of a Secretarie of State'.
MS Ee.3.56   Letters of Lord Burghley to Sir Robert Cecil,
                    1593–1598.
MS Mm.1.43   Papers of Thomas Baker.
MS Oo.7.50.2   Edward Tanner's Catalogue of John Moore's
                    Library after 1697.

Hatfield House, Hertfordshire

CECIL PAPERS   19, 20–24, 26–29, 31–36, 38, 40–43, 45–48, 98–99,
                    133, 136–138, 140, 142–143, 147, 169, 170–173,
                    204, 242–243.
FAMILY PAPERS   Inventory of 1611, Box A/I; Petitions; 416, 422, 881,
                    1311, 1656, 2422, 2467.

UNCALENDARED DEEDS
219/20   Sir Robert Cecil's Letters Patent as Principal
                    Secretary.
117/4   Burghley's Will.

Kew: The National Archives

C66   Chancery: Patent Rolls.
E 403   Privy Seal Books for warrants out of the Exchequer,
                    Tellers' Views.
E 351   Declared Accounts on the Pipe Rolls including War
                    Accounts of Treasurers-at-War and Paymasters.
PROB PCC   Probate Prerogative Court of Canterbury.
SO 3/1   Docquet Book, Vol. 1, Signet Office.
SP 12   Domestic, Eliz. I.
SP 45   Various, Eliz. I.
SP 52   Scotland, Eliz. I.
SP 63   Ireland, Eliz. I.
SP 75   Denmark, Eliz I.
SP 77   Flanders, Eliz. I.
SP 78   France, Eliz. I.
SP 80   Imperial Germany and Hungary, Eliz. I.

SP 81   Germany, States, Eliz. I.
SP 82   Hamburg and Hanse Towns, Eliz. I.
SP 84   Low Countries, Eliz. I.
SP 85   Italian States, Eliz. I.
SP 88   Poland, Eliz. I.
SP 94   Spain, Eliz. I.
SP 99   Venetian, Eliz. I.
SP 101   Treaties, Eliz. I.

Printed Primary Sources

Acts of the Privy Council of England, NS, ed. J.R. Dasent, 46 vols (London, 1890–1964).

Archer, Ian W., *Gazetteer of Military Levies from the City of London, 1509–1603* (2001) at https://ora.ox.ac.uk/objects/uuid:adb577fc-6ffb-440b-9dd9-7c5c39a4a64c.

Robert Beale, *Instructions for a Principall Secretarie, Observed by R.B. for Sir Edwarde Wotton, Anno Domini, 1592*, ed. Conyers Read, in Conyers Read, *Mr. Secretary Walsingham and the Policy of Queen Elizabeth*, 3 vols (Oxford, 1925), I, 423–443.

Bernard, Edward (ed.), *Catalogi Librorum Angliae et Hiberniae in unum Collecti cum Indice Alphabetico* (London, 1697).

Bibliotheca illustris, sive, Catalogus variorum librorum in quâvis linguâ & facultate insignium ornatissimae bibliothecae viri cujusdam praenobilis . . . [William Cecil]: libris rarissimis tam typis excusis quàm manuscriptis [1687].

Birch, Thomas, *Memoirs of the Reign of Queen Elizabeth from the Year 1581 until Her Death . . . and the Conduct of Her Favourite, Robert Earl of Essex . . .* 2 vols (London, 1754).

The Border Papers: Calendar of Letters and Papers relating to the Affairs of the Borders of England and Scotland Preserved in Her Majesty's Public Record Office, London, ed. Joseph Bain, 2 vols (Edinburgh, 1894–1896).

Bruce, John (ed.), *Correspondence of King James VI of Scotland with Sir Robert Cecil and Others in England, during the Reign of Queen Elizabeth*, Camden Society, old ser., 78 (1861).

Calderwood, David, *The History of the Kirk of Scotland*, ed. T. Thomson, 8 vols (Edinburgh, 1842–1849).

Calendar of Letters and State Papers, relating to English Affairs, Preserved Principally in the Archives of Simancas, ed. M.A.S. Hume, 4 vols (London, 1892–1899).

Calendar of Patent Rolls, 35 Elizabeth I (C66/1395–1404), ed. Christine Leighton, List and Index Society, 282 (2000).

Calendar of Patent Rolls, 36 Elizabeth I, 1593–94 (C 66/1405–1424), ed. Simon R. Neal, List and Index Society, 309 (2005).

Calendar of Patent Rolls, 37 Elizabeth I, 1594–95 (C 66/1425–1442), ed. Simon R. Neal and Christine Leighton, List and Index Society, 310 (2006).

Calendar of Patent Rolls, 38 Elizabeth I, 1595–96 (C 66/1443–1457), ed. Simon Neal and Christine Leighton, List and Index Society, 317 (2007).

Calendar of Patent Rolls, 39 Elizabeth I, 1596–97 (C 66/1458–1476), ed. Simon R. Neal, List and Index Society, 322–323 (2008).

Calendar of Patent Rolls, 40 Elizabeth I, 1597–98 (C 66/1477–1492), ed. Carrie Smith, Helen Watt, Simon R. Neal, and Christine Leighton, List and Index Society, 326–327 (2009).

Calendar of State Papers and Muniments, relating to English Affairs, Existing in the Archives and Collections of Venice, and in Other Libraries of Northern Italy, IX, ed. Horatio F. Brown (London, 1897).

Calendar of State Papers, Domestic Series, of the Reigns of Edward VI, Mary, Elizabeth [and James I], 1547–1625: Preserved in Her Majesty's Public Record Office, ed. R. Lemon and M.A.E Green, 12 vols (London, 1856–1872).

Calendar of the State Papers relating to Ireland, of the Reigns of Henry VIII, Edward VI, Mary, and Elizabeth: Preserved in the State Paper Department of Her Majesty's Public Record Office, ed. Hans Claude Hamilton, 11 vols (London, 1860–1912).

Calendar of State Papers relating to Scotland and Mary Queen of Scots, 1547–1603, Preserved in the Public Record Office, and Elsewhere in England, ed. Joseph Bain, W.K. Boyd, H.W. Meikle, A.I. Dunlop, M.S. Guiseppi, and J.D. Mackie, 13 vols (Edinburgh and Glasgow, 1898–1969).

Camden, William, *Annales Rerum Angliae et Hiberniae Regnante Elizabetha,* ed. Thomas Hearne, 3 vols (London, 1717).

Camden, William, *The History of the Most Renowned and Victorious Princess Elizabeth, Late Queen of England . . .* (4th edn, London, 1688).

Sir Robert, Cecil, *The State and Dignitie of a Secretarie of Estates Place, with the Care and Perill thereof,* (London, 1642) sig. 4r.

Cicero, M.T., *On Duties (De Officiis),* ed. M.T Griffin and E.M. Atkins, Cambridge Texts in the History of Political Thought (Cambridge, 1991).

Clapham, John, *Elizabeth of England: Certain Observations concerning the Life and Reign of Queen Elizabeth,* ed. E.P. and C. Read (Philadelphia, 1951).

Collins, Arthur, *The Life of . . . William Cecil, Lord Burghley, Secretary of State in the Reign of King Edward the Sixth, and Lord High Treasurer of England in the Reign of Queen Elizabeth* (London, 1732).

Historical Manuscripts Commission, *A Calendar of the Manuscripts of the Most Honourable the Marquis of Salisbury, KG, &c . . . Preserved at Hatfield House, Hertfordshire,* 24 vols (London, 1883–1976).

Historical Manuscripts Commission, *Report on the Manuscripts of Lord De L'Isle and Dudley Preserved at Penshurst Place,* 6 vols (London, 1925–1966).

Hammer, P.E.J., 'Letters from Sir Robert Cecil to Sir Christopher Hatton, 1590–1', in Ian W. Archer (ed.), *Religion, Politics and Society in Sixteenth-Century England,* Camden Society, 5th ser., 22 (2003), 197–267.

Holt, William, S.J., *How the Catholic Religion Was Maintained in England during Thirty-Eight Years of Persecution, and How It May Still Be Preserved There, 1596.* Printed in T.F. Knox (ed.), *The First and Second Diaries of the English College* (London, 1878).

Hughes, C. (ed.), 'Nicholas Faunt's *Discourse Touching the Office of Principal Secretary of Estate &c.,* 1592', *English Historical Review,* 20 (1905) 499–508.

Klarwill, V. von (ed.), *The Fugger Letters, Second Series . . . relating to Queen Elizabeth and Matters relating to England during the years, 1568–1605,* trans. L.S.R. Byrne (London, 1926).

List and Analysis of State Papers, Foreign Series: Elizabeth I, Preserved in the Public Record Office, ed. R.B. Wernham, 7 vols (London, 1964–2000).

Masters, Betty R. (ed.), *Chamber Accounts of the Sixteenth Century,* London Record Society, 20 (1984).

Masters, Robert, *Memoirs of the Life and Writings of the late Rev. Thomas Baker, B.D. of St. John's College in Cambridge, from the Papers of Dr. Zachary Grey* . . . (Cambridge, 1784).

Nichols, J., *The Progresses and Public Processions of Queen Elizabeth: Among which are Interspersed Other Solemnities* . . . 3 vols (London, 1823).

Peck, Francis, *Desiderata Curiosa, or, A Collection of Divers Scarce and Curious Pieces (relating Chiefly to Matters of English History) in Six Books* . . . 2 vols (London, 1732– 1735).

Percyvall, Richard, *Bibliotheca Hispanica: Containing a Grammar with a Dictionarie in Spanish, English and Latine* (London, 1591).

Petti, A.G. (ed.), *The Letters and Despatches of Richard Verstegan (c.1550–1640)*, Publications of the Catholic Record Society, 52 (1959).

Pollen, J.H., 'Tower bills, 1575–1681, with Gatehouse certificates, 1592–1604', *Catholic Record Society Miscellanea*, 4 (1907), 23–46.

Raine, J, *The Correspondence of Dr. Matthew Hutton, Archbishop of York* . . . Surtees Society, 17 (1843).

Raleigh, Sir Walter, *The Discovery of the Large, Rich, and Beautiful Empire of Guiana, with a relation of the Great and Golden Citie of Manoa (which the Spaniards call El Dorado)* . . . (London, 1596); facs. edn as Sir Walter Raleigh, *A Report of the Truth of the Fight about the Iles of the Acores (The Last Fight of the Revenge), 1591: The Discouery of the Large, Rich, and Bewtiful Empyre of Guiana, 1596* (Menston, 1967).

Smith, A.G.R., *The 'Anonymous Life' of William Cecil* (Lewiston, NY, and Lampeter, 1991).

Spottiswoode, John, *History of the Church of Scotland*, ed. M. Russell, 3 vols (Edinburgh, 1847–1851).

Stevenson, R.J. (ed.), *Correspondence of Sir Henry Unton, Knt, Ambassador from Queen Elizabeth and Henry IV King of France in the years MDXCI and MDXCII* (London, 1847).

Stow, John, *The annales of England. Faithfully Collected out of the Most Autenticall Authors, Records, and Other Monuments of Antiquitie* . . . *vntill this Present Yeare 1605* (London, 1605).

Strype, John, *Annals of the Reformation and Establishment of Religion, and Other Various Occurrences in the Church of England, during Queen Elizabeth's Happy Reign* (London, 1725–1731).

Tudor Church reform: The Henrician canons of 1535, ed. Gerald Lewis Bray (Woodbridge, 2005).

Tudor Royal Proclamations, ed. James F. Hughes and Paul Larkin, 3 vols (New Haven, CT, and London, 1964–1969).

Thou, Jacques-Auguste de, *Histoire universelle de Jacque-Auguste de Thou depuis 1543 jusqu'en 1607*, ed. A.F. Prévost d'Exiles, P.F. Guyot Desfontaines, J.B. Le Mascrier, J. Adam, C. Lebeau, N. Leduc, J.C. Fabre (London, 1734).

Ungerer, G., *A Spaniard in Elizabethan England: The Correspondence of Antonio Pérez's Exile*, 2 vols (London, 1974–1976).

Wilson, Thomas, 'The state of England, anno. dom. 1607', ed. F.J. Fisher, Camden Miscellany, XVI, Camden Society, 3rd ser., 52 (1936).

Wright, Louis B., *Advice to a Son: Precepts of Lord Burghley, Sir Walter Raleigh and Francis Osborne* (Ithaca, NY, 1961).

Wright, Thomas, *Queen Elizabeth and Her Times: A Series of Original Letters, Selected from the Inedited Correspondence of the Lord Treasurer Burghley, the Earl of Leicester, the secretaries Walsingham and Smith, Sir Christopher Hatton* . . . 2 vols (London, 1838).

Secondary Sources

Acres, W.D., 'The early political career of Sir Robert Cecil, *c.*1582–1597: Some aspects of late Elizabethan secretarial administration', PhD thesis, University of Cambridge, 1991.

Adams, Simon, 'Eliza Enthroned? The court and its politics', in C. Haigh (ed.), *The Reign of Elizabeth I* (Basingstoke, 1984), 55–77.

Alford, Stephen, *Burghley: William Cecil at the Court of Elizabeth I* (New Haven, CT, and London, 2008).

Alford, Stephen, *The Early Elizabethan Polity: William Cecil and British Succession Crisis, 1558–1569* (Cambridge, 1998).

Alford, Stephen, *The Watchers: A Secret History of the Reign of Elizabeth I* (London, 2012).

Allen, Gemma, *The Cooke Sisters: Education, Piety and Politics in Early Modern England* (Manchester, 2013).

Allinson, Rayne, *A Monarchy of Letters: Royal Correspondence and English Diplomacy in the Reign of Elizabeth I* (New York, 2012).

Archer, Ian W., 'The burden of taxation on sixteenth-century London', *Historical Journal*, 44, 3 (2001), 599–627.

Archer, Ian W., *The Pursuit of Stability: Social Relations in Elizabethan London* (Cambridge, 1991).

Barber, Peter, 'Was Elizabeth I interested in maps – and did it matter?', *Transactions of the Royal Historical Society*, 6th ser., 14 (2004), 185–198.

Barnett, Richard C., *Place, Profit, and Power: A Study of the Servants of William Cecil, Elizabethan Statesman* (Chapel Hill, NC, 1969).

Beckingsale, B.W., *Burghley: Tudor Statesman, 1520–1598* (London and New York, 1967).

Bell, Gary M., *A Handlist of British Diplomatic Representatives,1509–1688* (London, 1990).

Bindoff, S.T., J. Hurstfield, and C.H. Williams (eds), *Elizabethan Government and Society: Essays Presented to Sir John Neale* (London, 1961).

Bowden, Caroline, 'The library of Mildred Cooke Cecil, Lady Burghley', *The Library*, 7th ser., 6 (2005), 3–29.

Boynton, Lindsay, *The Elizabethan Militia, 1558–1638* (Newton Abbot, 1967).

Boynton, Lindsay, 'The Tudor provost marshall', *English Historical Review*, 87 (1962), 437–455.

Breight, Curtis C., 'Entertainments of Elizabeth at Theobalds in the early 1590s', *Records of Early English Drama*, 12, 1 (1987), 1–9.

Canning, Ruth, 'James Fitzpiers Fitzgerald, Captain Thomas Lee, and the problem of "secret traitors": Conflicted loyalties during the Nine Years War, 1594–1603', *Irish Historical Studies*, 156 (2015), 573–594.

Chambers, E.K., *The Elizabethan Stage*, 4 vols (Oxford, 1923).

Collinson, P., *The Elizabethan Puritan Movement* (London, 1967).

Collinson, P., *Richard Bancroft and Elizabethan Anti-Puritanism* (Cambridge, 2013).

Colthorpe, Marion, 'The Theobalds entertainment for Queen Elizabeth I in 1591, with a transcript of the gardener's speech', *Records of Early English Drama*, 12 (1987), 2–9.

Colvin, H.M., *The History of the King's Works*, Vol. IV: *1485–1660* (London, 1982).

Coward, B., *The Stanleys, Lords Stanley and Earls of Derby, 1385–1672: The Origins, Wealth and Power of a Landowning Family*, Chetham Society, 3rd ser., xxx (Manchester, 1983).

Croft, Pauline, 'Mildred, Lady Burghley: The matriarch', in Pauline Croft (ed.), *Patronage, Culture and Power: The Early Cecils* (New Haven, CT, 2002), 283–300.

Croft, Pauline, 'The new English Church in one family: William, Mildred and Robert Cecil', in Stephen Platten (ed.), *Anglicanism and the Western Christian Tradition: Continuity, Change and the Search for Communion* (Norwich, 2009), 65–89, 225–229.

Croft, Pauline (ed.), *Patronage, Culture and Power: The Early Cecils* (New Haven, CT, and London, 2002).

Cross, Claire, 'The third earl of Huntingdon's death-bed: A Calvinist example of the *ars moriendi*', *Northern History*, 21 (1985), 80–107.

Cruickshank, C.G., *Elizabeth's Army* (2nd edn Oxford, 1966).

Daybell, James, *The Material Letter in Early Modern England: Manuscript Letters and Culture and Practices of Writing, 1512–1635* (Basingstoke, 2012).

Doran, Susan, *Elizabeth I and Her Circle* (Oxford, 2015).

Doran, Susan, and P. Kewes (eds), *Doubtful and Dangerous. The Question of Succession in Late Elizabethan England* (Manchester, 2014).

Elton, G.R., 'The Elizabethan exchequer: War in the receipt', in Bindoff, Hurstfield, and Williams, *Elizabethan Government and Society*, 213–248. Repr. in G.R. Elton (ed.), *Studies in Tudor and Stuart Politics and Government*, 4 vols (Cambridge, 1974–1992), I, 355–388.

Elton, G.R., 'Tudor government, the points of contact, 1: Parliament', *Transactions of the Royal Historical Society*, 5th ser., 24 (1974), 183–200. Repr. in Elton, *Studies in Tudor and Stuart Politics and Government*, III, 3–20.

Elton, G.R., 'Tudor government, the points of contact, 2: The council', *Transactions of the Royal Historical Society*, 5th ser., 25 (1975), 195–211. Repr. in Elton, *Studies in Tudor and Stuart Politics and Government*, III, 21–37.

Elton, G.R., 'Tudor government, the points of contact, 3: The court', *Transactions of the Royal Historical Society*, 5th ser., 26 (1976) 211–228. Repr. in Elton, *Studies in Tudor and Stuart Politics and Government*, III, 38–57.

Evans, F.M.G., *The Principal Secretary of State: A Survey of the Office from 1558 to 1680* (Manchester, 1923).

Evans, R.J.W., *Rudolf II and His World: A Study in Intellectual History, 1576–1612* (Oxford, 1984).

Fox, Peter (ed.), *Cambridge University Library: The Great Collections* (Cambridge, 1998).

Gajda, Alexandra, *The Earl of Essex and Late Elizabethan Political Culture* (Oxford, 2012).

Graves, M.A.R., *Burghley: William Cecil, Lord Burghley* (London, 1998).

Green, Dominic, *The Double Life of Dr. Lopez: Spies, Shakespeare and the Plot to Poison Elizabeth I* (London, 2003).

Guerci, Manolo, 'Salisbury House in London, 1599–1694: The Strand palace of Sir Robert Cecil', *Architectural History*, 52 (2009), 31–78.

Guide to the Contents of the Public Record Office, 3 vols (rev. edn, London, 1963–1968).

Guy, J., *Elizabeth: The Forgotten Years* (London, 2016).

Guy, J., *Tudor England* (Oxford and New York, 1988).

Haigh, C., *Elizabeth I* (London and New York, 1988).

Hammer, P.E.J., 'An Elizabethan Spy Who Came in from the Cold: The return of Anthony Standen to England in 1593', *Historical Research*, 65 (1992), 277–295.

Hammer, P.E.J., *Elizabeth's Wars: War, Government and Society in Tudor England, 1544–1604* (Basingstoke, 2003).

Hammer, P.E.J., *Polarisation of Elizabethan Politics: The Political Career of Robert Devereux, 2nd Earl of Essex, 1585–1597* (Cambridge, 1999).

Handover, P.M., *The Second Cecil: The Rise to Power, 1563–1604, of Sir Robert Cecil, later 1st Earl of Salisbury* (London, 1959).

Hay, M.V., *The Life of Robert Sidney, Earl of Leicester (1563–1626)* (Washington DC, London and Toronto, 1984).

Hayes-McCoy, G.A., 'The completion of the Tudor conquest and the advance of the counter- reformation, 1571–1603', in T.W. Moody, F.X. Martin, F.J. Byrne (eds), *A New History of Ireland*, III: *Early Modern Ireland, 1534–1691* (Oxford, 1976), 94–141.

Hayes-McCoy, G.A., *Scots Mercenary Forces in Ireland (1565–1603)* (Dublin and London, 1937).

Hume, M.A.S., *Treason and Plot: Struggles for Catholic Supremacy in the Last Years of Queen Elizabeth* (London, 1901).

Hurstfield, J., *The Queen's Wards: Wardship and Marriage under Elizabeth I* (London, 1958).

Hurstfield, J., 'The succession struggle in late Elizabethan England', in Bindoff, Hurstfield, and Williams, *Elizabethan Government and Society*, 369–396.

Husselby, Jill, 'The politics of pleasure: William Cecil and Burghley House', in Croft, *Patronage, Culture and Power*, 21–45.

Husselby, Jill, and Paula Henderson, 'Location, location, location: Cecil House in the Strand', *Architectural History*, 45 (2002), 159–193.

James, M.E., *Family, Lineage and Civil Society: A Study of Society, Politics and Mentality in the Durham Region, 1500–1640* (Oxford, 1974).

Lee, M., *John Maitland of Thirlestane and the Foundation of the Stewart Despotism in Scotland* (Princeton, NJ, and London, 1959).

Lake, P., *Moderate Puritans and the Elizabethan Church* (Cambridge, 1982).

Lenman, Bruce, *England's Colonial Wars, 1550–1688: Conflicts, Empire and National Identity* (Harlow, 2001).

Loades, D.M., *The Tudor Court* (London, 1986).

Lloyd, H.A., 'Camden, Carmarthen and the Customs', *English Historical Review*, 85 (1970), 776–787.

Lloyd, H.A., *The Rouen Campaign, 1590–1592: Politics, Warfare and the Early Modern State* (Oxford, 1973).

Loomie, A.J., *The Spanish Elizabethans: The English Exiles at the Court of Philip II* (New York, 1963).

Macauley, Thomas Babington, 'Nares' *Memoirs of Lord Burghley*', *The Edinburgh Review*, 55 (1832), 271–296.

MacCaffrey, W., *Elizabeth I: War and Politics: 1558–1603* (Princeton, NJ, 1994).

MacCaffrey, W., 'Place and patronage in Elizabethan England', in Bindoff, Hurstfield, and Williams, *Elizabethan Government and Society*, 95–126.

MacCaffrey, W., *The Shaping of the Elizabethan Regime* (London, 1969).

MacCaffrey, W., 'Talbot and Stanhope, an episode in Elizabethan politics', *Bulletin of the Institute of Historical Research*, 33 (1960), 73–85.

McConica, J. (ed.), *The History of the University of Oxford*, III: *The Collegiate University* (Oxford, 1986).

McCoog, Thomas J., *The Society of Jesus in Ireland, Scotland and England, 1589–1597: Building the Faith of Saint Peter Upon the King of Spain's Monarchy* (Farnham, 2012).

McGurk, John J.N., *The Elizabethan Conquest of Ireland: The 1590s Crisis* (Manchester, 1997).

McKitterick, David, *Cambridge University Library, A History: The Eighteenth and Nineteenth Centuries* (Cambridge, 1986).

Manning, R.B., 'The prosecution of Sir Michael Blount, lieutenant of the Tower of London, 1595', *Bulletin of the Institute of Historical Research*, 57 (1984), 216–224.

Merritt, Julia, 'The Cecils and Westminster, 1558–1612: The development of an urban power base', in Croft, *Patronage, Culture and Power*, 231–246.

Moore, Peter R, 'The Fable of the World, Twice Told, Part II', *Shakespeare Oxford Society Newsletter*, 27, 4 (1991), 5–9.

Morgan, Hiram, *Tyrone's Rebellion: The Outbreak of the Nine Year's War in Tudor Ireland* (Woodbridge, 1993).

Nares, Edward B., *Memoirs of the Life and Administration of the Right Honorable William Cecil, Lord Burghley* (London, 1828–1831).

Neale, J., *Elizabeth I and Her Parliaments, 1584–1601* (London, 1957).

Nolan, John S., 'The militarization of the Elizabethan state', *Journal of Military History*, 58 (1994), 391–420.

Nolan, John S., *Sir John Norreys and the Elizabethan Military World* (Exeter, 1997).

Tadhg Ó hAnnracháin, *Catholic Europe, 1592–1648: Centre and Peripheries* (Oxford, 2015).

Parmelee, Lisa Ferraro, *Good Newes from Fraunce: French Anti-League Propaganda in Late Elizabethan England* (Woodbridge, 1996).

Payne, Helen, 'The Cecil women at court', in Croft, *Patronage, Culture and Power*, 265–281.

Rapple, Rory, *Martial Power and Elizabethan Political Culture: Military Men in England and Ireland, 1558–1594* (Cambridge, 2009)

Read, Conyers, *Lord Burghley and Queen Elizabeth* (London, 1960).

Read, Conyers, *Mr. Secretary Walsingham and the Policy of Queen Elizabeth*, 3 vols (Oxford, 1925).

Rickman, Johanna, *Love, Lust and License in Early Modern England: Illicit Sex and the Nobility* (Burlington, VT, and Aldershot, 2008).

Ringrose, Jayne, 'The Royal Library: John Moore and his books', in Fox, *Cambridge University Library*, 78–89.

Rivington, Charles A., 'Early printers of the Royal Society, 1663–1708', *Notes and Records of the Royal Society* 39 (1984), 1–27.

Sherman, William Howard, *John Dee: The Politics of Reading and Writing in the English Renaissance* (Amherst, MA, 1997).

Smith, A.G.R., 'The secretariats of the Cecils, c.1580–1612', *English Historical Review*, 83 (1968), 481–504.

Smith, A.G.R., *Servant of the Cecils: The Life of Sir Michael Hickes, 1543–1612* (London, 1977).

Starkey, D. (ed.), *The English Court from the Wars of the Roses to the Civil War* (London and New York, 1987).

Stewart, Alan, *Close Readers: Humanism and Sodomy in Early Modern England* (Princeton, NJ, 1997).

Stewart, Richard W., *The English Ordnance Office: A Case-Study in Bureaucracy* (Woodbridge, 1996).

Stone, Lawrence, *An Elizabethan: Sir Horatio Palavicino* (Oxford, 1956).

Stone, Lawrence, *Family and Fortune: Studies in Aristocratic Finance in the 16th and 17th Centuries* (Oxford, 1979).

Sutherland, N.M., *Henry IV of France and the Politics of Religion, 1572–1596*, 2 vols (Bristol, 2002).

Sutton, James M., *Materializing Space at an Early Modern Prodigy House: The Cecils at Theobalds, 1564–1607* (Aldershot, 2004).

Thrush, Andrew, and John P. Ferris (eds), *The House of Commons, 1604–1629*, 6 vols (Cambridge, 2010), IV.

Tytler, Patrick Fraser, *History of Scotland*, 9 vols (Edinburgh, 1828–1843).

Walsham, Alexandra, 'Frantick Hacket: Prophecy, sorcery, insanity, and the Elizabethan Puritan movement', *The Historical Journal*, 41 (1998), 27–66.

Wernham, R.B., *After the Armada: Elizabethan England and the Struggle for Western Europe, 1588–1595* (Oxford, 1984).

Wernham, R.B., *Return of the Armadas: The Last Years of the Elizabethan War against Spain, 1595–1603* (Oxford, 1994).

Woodworth, Allegra, 'Purveyance for the royal household', *Transactions of the American Philosophical Society*, 35 (1945), 1–89.

Younger, Neil, *War and Politics in the Elizabethan Counties* (Manchester, 2012).

INDEX